Legal Regulation of Private Actors in Outer Space

India's Role

Legal Regulation of Private Actors in Outer Space

India's Role

Dr. Malay Adhikari

KNOWLEDGE WORLD

KW Publishers Pvt Ltd
New Delhi

ISBN 978-93-86288-20-2 Hardback
ISBN 978-93-86288-21-9 E-PUB ebook

Published in India by Kalpana Shukla

KNOWLEDGE WORLD

KW Publishers Pvt Ltd
4676/21, First Floor, Ansari Road
Daryaganj, New Delhi 110002
Phone: +91 11 23263498/43528107
Marketing: knowledgeworld@kwpub.com
Editorial: jose@kwpub.com
Website: www.kwpub.com

2011 FPBA BEST PUBLISHERS AWARD (ENGLISH)

Printed and Bound by Bhavish Graphics.

Dedicated to

INDIAN PRIVATE ACTORS
IN OUTER SPACE

Contents

Acknowledgement

This acknowledgement is desired to so many persons and institutions for developing this small research study followed by a book. There are institutions besides Jawaharlal Nehru University (JNU) wherefrom the academic resources and other relevant supports have been provided. But first it starts with JNU.

My esteemed supervisor, Prof. (Dr.) Bharat H. Desai has helped me a lot specially how to make analysis with the data and then arrange it for writing this thesis. In spite of my lacunas in so many terms and conditions, this small work would not have been possible without his support, supervision and advices. Prof. (Dr.) B.S. Chimni, my revered teacher, has inspired me to start research with history in any topics of international law; obviously this history must be Indian one. All the historical inputs within this study are product of such inspiration. His lectures on international trade law along with WTO have attracted me to think about commercialization of Indian space activities in much elaborated way.

Prof. (Dr.) Yogesh K. Tyagi is another respected teacher who inspired me in different way.

My esteemed teacher, Prof. (Dr.) V. G. Hegde advised me all along to select the PhD topic and to prepare relevant synopsis.

There are many scientists and persons from ISRO and its various centres. It is not possible to acknowledge everybody's contribution here. Late Hon'ble ex-President Dr. APJ Kalam motivated me on mentioning this small study and its different dimensions during his speech in 1st Research Scholars' Day programme at Indian Institute of Space Science & Technology, Thiruvananthapuram in December 2011. Shri K R Sridhar Murthy, ex-MD ANTRIX Corporation; Dr. MYS Prasad, ex-Director of SDSC SHAR; and Shri V. Gopalakrishnan, Space Law & Policy Analyst in the Office of Scientific Secretary, ISRO are specially to be acknowledged here for their valuable interactions over number of years. Dr. R. Shivakumar, ex-CEO and

NDRMS Head in the Department of Science & Technology, has provided me a constant support whenever needed.

Ms. Tasleem Raheel, Manager International Affairs, SUPARCO (Pakistan) is acknowledged for her greatness to share some space law developments in Pakistan. I also acknowledge the International Institute of Space Law, France and the Centre for Law and ICT of KU Leuven, Belgium for enriching me to prepare this thesis.

Dr. Mukund Rao, ex-Adjunct faculty, National Institute of Advanced Studies, Bangaluru enlightened me over a discussion on privatisation of space activities and its future prospects in India.

I would like to acknowledge my M. Phil. supervisor Prof. (Dr.) V. Balakista Reddy, NALSAR University of Law, Hyderabad and Dr. KPR Menon from National Remote Sensing Centre, Hyderabad.

I would like to acknowledge all my predecessors like Prof. (Dr.) Saligram Bhatt, Late Prof. (Dr.) V.S. Mani who did pioneering research on space law from JNU.

I am highly indebted to my teachers Dr. G.S. Sachdeva, Prof. J. L Jain, Dr. B.G. Sidharth for their continuous and constant support that they have shown towards me throughout the research work. I am especially indebted to Dr. G.S. Sachdeva for allowing me to interact over so many informal and friendly discussions since the beginning of my research.

I specially acknowledge the role of all staffs of the libraries like JNU, Indian Council of World Affairs, Indian Society of International Law and Institute of Defence Studies & Analysis, New Delhi; National Remote Sensing Centre, Hyderabad, National Institute of Advanced Studies, Bengaluru and National Library, Kolkata for supplying me in time the necessary books and journals.

But this study would not have been possible without the friendly support from DELNET. In fact the full credit goes to them to make availability of the books from libraries outside JNU. The research study would not have been completed without their co-operation.

I also highly acknowledge the support and help of Centre for International Legal Studies' (JNU) office staffs – Smt. Savitri Bisht and Shri Hariom Patel. Both have helped me in various ways over years.

Finally, it is the speedy and sincere effort of my publisher Ms. Kalpana Shukla along with her team members like Mr. Jose Mathew, Ms. Vandana Palli who have full credit to bring this small book to its readers.

Some names are beyond acknowledgement for this research study like Shri Deepak Kr Yadav and Shri A.K. Trivedi. Therefore it is better not to write a single word for them. I would also like to apologize not to mention some names or unintentionally forgot them in writing this acknowledgement. Simply my humble acknowledgement is for all of them for cooperating me from different corners to prepare this small piece of work to contribute to develop space law in India.

New Delhi

Dr. **Malay Adhikari**

Introduction

Human beings started their journey to outer space long ago. The beginning has not been through their physical presence in outer space. The journey prima facie commenced with sky observation. It required indomitable patience as well as some assumptions based on scientific logics and findings. Along with these, some artists envisaged astronomical sketches which showed our virtual presence in cosmos. The approaches of these philosophers cum scientists cum artists were different. It varied from one space visionary to another. In a nutshell, everybody with their benign but great vision cherished a dream throughout their life to reach outer space. Several landmark events have happened between the modest beginnings and the present era of space activities known as 'space age'. The invincible human spirit has overcome all the hurdles and conquered outer space with their physical presence.

In the course of this study, it has been assumed that some historic incidents are more relevant than others that happened since the dawn of space era. All these have become landmarks in the history of humankind. These include: launching of Sputnik, the artificial satellite going beyond the gravitation force of earth by the then USSR; presence of first human being in outer space, Yuri Gagarin of former USSR; landing of human being on the Moon, Neil Armstrong of USA; and lastly sending of cargo to International Space Station (ISS) during 2012 by Space X, a private company from USA.

The moment dreams or imaginations become reality, it is likely that a large number of people from all walks of life especially science discipline view outer space from different perspectives. Hence the field of astronomy has expanded in different branches. It is fascinating that outer space is growing to be more complex strategically that human beings never imagined before. There are different reasons behind this scenario. One of which is relative absence of international legal regulation. A significant initiative has been triggered by none other than United Nations itself through its General Assembly resolutions. Its purpose was to prevent arms race including nuclear weapons in outer space in near future because the very birth of United Nations was a result of the Second World War.

It is in this context that the Treaty on Principles Governing the Activities of States in the Exploration and Use of Outer Space, including the Moon and Other Celestial Bodies (1967), popularly known as 'Outer Space Treaty' (OST), assumed significance. It governs outer space activities. This is the major treaty on outer space governance till now.

Its salient features provide basic international space law norms. These are peaceful uses of outer space; free exploitation and use by all states on the basis of equality; not subject it to national appropriation by claiming sovereignty; all the activities in outer space to be carried out as per international law including principles of the United Nations (UN) Charter to maintain international peace and security, and promoting international cooperation and understanding; sharing benefits with all countries who have no technological acumen to pursue outer space activities and lastly, outer space to be the province of mankind.

At the outset, space exploration was limited to a very few countries when the Outer Space Treaty was formulated in 1967. The United States and the then USSR were the two major states that had optimum potential to pursue space activities. Accordingly, the OST stressed on "equitable and egalitarian principles". It is to be mentioned here that the 1963 UN General Assembly resolution on *Declaration of Legal Principles Governing the Activities of States in the Exploration and Use of Outer Space*, laid the foundation for these "equitable and egalitarian principles".

The Outer Space Treaty was followed by the other space treaties subsequently under the United Nations Framework. It consisted of: (i) Agreement on the Rescue of Astronauts, the Return of Astronauts and the Return of Objects Launched into Outer Space (1968), (ii) The Convention on International Liability for Damage Caused by Space Objects (1972), (iii) The Convention on the Registration of Objects Launched into Outer Space (1976), and (iv) The Agreement Governing the Activities of States on the Moon and Other Celestial Bodies (1979).

These space treaties were concluded within a span of some 15 years keeping in view the strategic and technological developments during that period. Some of the basic international legal principles incorporated in these treaties could be summarised as: (i) to use outer space for peaceful purposes; (ii) all humanitarian assistance to rescue astronauts by any state parties in case of accident of a spacecraft even not falling in the jurisdiction of a particular state; (iii) absolute liability to pay compensation in case of damage caused by a space object of a launching state on the surface of earth or to aircraft flight but no compensation if the damage is not in conformity with international law including United Nations Charter; (iv) Moon and its natural resources to be regarded as Common Heritage of Mankind.

Along with this legal development within the UN Framework, there were slow but steady parallel developments of space activities carried out by private actors. The first significant step was conducted during 2012 by Space X of USA. The policy of USA is to commercialise outer space through its private actors since the drafting of space law treaties. Therefore, USA is the pioneer in this regard.

Later on there is an international paradigm shift towards private actor-centric space activities. This shift has different phases from least to most advance. The well-established private actors belong to most advanced stage. But very few countries achieve this stage. The state dependent private actors belong to less advanced phase. Most of the countries are in this stage. It is true that some countries have no scope for private actors. They are just developing the space programes through state actors like a national space agency.

Thus it opens a new vista for the private actors. In this regard there is a natural query in the context of this research study: whether any regulation besides the existing state-centric treaty regulation is required for these private actors? There could be multiple possibilities against this query.

First could be based on the time-frame of making all the above space treaties. The existing space law treaties, negotiated during cold war days, do not seek to address commercial activities in outer space. The fast technological developments in space all over the world enhance the potential of this commercialisation to such a height that cost-effective space technology could be affordable by the private actors besides the states'. Space is all set to be used extensively by these actors in the 21st century.

As a consequence, these actors have grown in some old space-faring states followed by the others. The difficulty arises in the process of regulating such private actors. It would be required to provide them maximum opportunity for pursuing their commercial goals at present and in the near future. The existing legal regime lacks in many of the space-faring and non-space-faring countries. However, most of the governments do not want to allot more budgets in space sector due to uncertainty as well as high risk involved. The existing international space law regime is mainly state-centric where there is no direct provision for regulating the private actors.

Secondly, the meaning of the role of private actors in outer space is not explained properly within the Outer Space Treaty itself. The problem of defining the outer space existed since the inception of space law regime designed under the United Nations. The boundary between air space and outer space is not codified legally. The area above 100 km from the sea level comes within the jurisdiction of space law. Still, the lack of clear definition brings additional problems to the private actors. The air space belongs to the sovereign states. Unlike the outer space that has been declared as *res communis* i.e. common to everybody or where no national sovereignty exists. It makes the problem more complicated by raising the debate as to who will be the owner of mineral resources extracted from the celestial bodies?

The next problem is strategic i.e. national security. Since sovereignty of a state is directly linked with national security of that state, it could better be governed above the territory e.g. outer space. Therefore, it is pertinent to examine how far states are willing to cede their sovereign legal authority in outer space. Hence the national security is at stake concerning any possible regime of private actors.

However, when the strategy for national security is focussed on the individual, it means safety of the actors. The actors mean users of space technology like persons engaged in launch of satellites. Therefore, the issue of space safety could not be ignored when the existing regime is silent about commercial or industrial safety to be maintained by private actors.

Then the problem of liability could not be left behind along with these undecided legal issues. Liability is a common legal issue to any industry dominated by private actors. Under the international space law regime, the Liability Convention, 1972, does not address liability in the event of injury or financial loss of private actors. The states are ultimately liable under this Convention. Now the time has come to share the state liability by the private actors because their number and activities are also increasing. Moreover, they could cherish more high risk activities than before like asteroid mining.

There is now a new attraction of space tourism. The space tourism initiated by private actors opens up issues like commitment of crimes by a space tourist which is not addressed in the existing space law regime. The space tourism as well as other commercial activities have effect on space environment just like on the earth. One example is that the private actors will create additional space debris with the existing one for their high-profit commercial activities in due course of time. There is no legal provision to remove these space debris caused by them, if detected. Even the liability could not be imposed directly as mentioned above. It seems the domestic legal framework of most of the space-faring states' lacks in reducing the space debris during the time of authorisation of launch.

To overcome the above mentioned problems, the idea of national space legislation has come into force. These are legislations where international space law, mentioned above, encompasses national law. The government and non-government actors are mainly regulated for their ongoing or upcoming space activities especially for commercial ventures. Very few states have enacted comprehensive space legislation till now. But many of the states have started the process of making national space legislation in different forms and under different organisational umbrellas including national space agencies. These regulations under national space legislation are not uniform. Instead these are country-specific.

In the case of India, there is no comprehensive space law or specific provision for space activities within other domestic legislations. There may be some existing supportive or related legislations that could satisfy the prescribed authority for the time being. How long and how much this will continue in practice? It is a million dollar question as well as a matter of proof. Therefore, there has been a long standing demand about the introduction of national space legislation.

The 12th Five Year Plan (FYP) of India has already proposed for 'Space Act' in consequence of industry and private sector participation in building up space industry. This is also a follow-up of international trend for private space activities.

The fallacy is that space activities were extensively monopolised by the government itself since the establishment of Indian Space Research Organisation (ISRO) during 1969. The ANTRIX Corporation being a fully government owned company was established in 1972 as a commercial wing of ISRO. But it is not so worthy till now to promote and facilitate the private actors to perform independently i.e. not as outsourcing agents of ISRO.

However, it is assumed that this monopolisation appears to be gradually diminishing in the current background of India's space foray like Chandrayaan-I or Mangalyan. Accordingly the domestic private actors from big corporate to small start-ups are industry partners in such far-reaching missions. The success of these missions within limited time period and over optimum budget prove the efficiency as well as potential of these private actors. Furthermore, the foreign telecommunication companies have already been licensed to operate in India. Thus, as a whole, it necessitates fervent demand of this research study from government side (for proposed 'Space Act') as well as private actors' side for detailed analysis to observe and understand the effectiveness or lacuna of the present legal scenario.

The basic purpose of this research study is to analyse how and to what extent the above extension of provisions of international space law would be implemented to regulate private actors along with their activities in outer space. In view of this, it remains to be seen as to how the concerned legal issues like sovereignty and proprietary rights, national security, intellectual property rights, dispute settlement etc. are addressed in the era likely to be dominated by private actors. Moreover, how the regulations of different countries justify the current need of such actors? If it is justified more, then what and how much would be the limit?

This research study has sought to specifically focus on the private actors of developing countries. Being not so much strong sound in space technology like the space-faring nations, their regulations for private actors could take time to emerge. India is the prime focus amongst these countries. There is no dedicated law or even a comprehensive national space policy in India. But how and in which way the existing general legislations of India will fulfill the need of private actors is within the scope of this research study. This study covers the feasibility of making comprehensive national space legislation in India.

This study has sought to make an attempt to address the following research questions: (i) Whether existing space treaties along with its principles adequately address the need for regulations for private actors in outer space? (ii) How far such actors would be permitted within the existing space treaties? (iii) Whether a voluntary international code of conduct for business and industry is feasible to regulate the private actors in outer space? (iv) How far framing of national space legislation or policy is crucial for regulating these actors? and (v) What kind of domestic regulations will be required in India?

Three hypotheses arose from above questions: (i) the existing space law provisions are inadequate to regulate private actors in outer space; (ii) the heterogeneity between space treaties and space legislations that exist as of now is responsible for the ineffective regulation of private actors in outer space; and (iii) Indian regulations are inadequate to regulate such actors.

Everything originates from history. So chapter I is to analyse the history of space regulations. Moreover, it tries to make an effort to find out whether Asian countries especially India has any historical contribution to develop space law. History reveals that it is the science which triggers any technological domain including space. Law only follows through post-science technological developments. Therefore, the history of regulating private actors in outer space along with the study of India's role becomes inseparable without history of space science and technology itself. Though it was United Nations at the forefront to initiate the real development of space law but the other non-governmental international organisations like International Telecommunication Union (ITU), International Law Association (ILA), International Astronautical Federation (IAF), International Institute of Space Law (IISL) etc. came up with the passage of time. These organisations made immense contributions to develop international space regulations since their inception.

There may be doubts about the meaning of private actors in outer space and their kinds, especially after analysing the historical evolution of international space law in chapter I where only the States are considered capable to ensure activities in outer space. It was beyond imagination to think about private actors in final frontier. This imagination is not misplaced because space activities till now are carried out mainly by governmental agencies like national space agency in most of the countries. Therefore, chapter II titled as 'Private Actors in Outer Space' begins with making sense of words 'private actors'. Then it describes nature of the space activities in outer space. It shows the concentration and trend of such actors in different space activities. Also, the example of these actors may show as to why states are willing to encourage these private space activities. This would probably help in justifying to make regulations for private actors only. The private actors are engaged in carrying out activities in different sectors like satellite communication and broadcasting, commercial satellite imageries, space tourism, celestial mining etc. Lastly, it provides scenario of private actors in India.

The private actors along with their activities in outer space are assumed to face problems with some legal issues. Now we have reached a stage to make legal regulation for these actors in the international domain. This is sought to be addressed in chapter III on 'Legal Issues'. These legal issues are seemed to be sovereignty, national security, intellectual property rights, liability, dispute settlement, safety, environment, ethics, corporate social responsibility, financing etc. that are critically analysed. All these issues may be either core or subsidiary depending on the particular circumstances or problems as analysed in the chapter.

According to the provisions of international space law treaties, the problems which cropped up from such legal issues have no satisfactory solutions. Some of the issues like IPR became much more significant during post-establishment period of these treaties. Therefore, the countries have initiated the process of regulating outer space activities at domestic level with the help of policies, legislations and institutions. The framing of 'national space legislation' is also included in the overall process. This is examined in chapter IV under the title 'Space Regulations outside India'. The focus is mainly on how the legal issues are settled through policies, legislations and institutions in pursuit of developing private actors in outer space. In this regard, some countries are more advanced legally; some are in transition process and the rest are yet to decide the regulations because the modern space technology is rarely available to them.

Chapter V covers issues relating India. This assumes significance in view of emergence of India as space power in 21st century. As such it makes great sense to study, and, the pattern and trend at work as regards India's role to work out international legal regulation of private actors in outer space. As a corollary, it is very much desirable to analyse Indian policies, legislations and institutions related with space activities. It would facilitate understanding the legal issues in Indian context.

Thus chapter V titled as 'Space Regulations in India' seeks to examine regulation of private actors in outer space from India. Accordingly, the chapter covers—first regulation through policy, then through legislations and lastly, through institutions to regulate the private actors in India. The regulation through policy comes first generally to make plan and structure the private space activities. It follows existing legislations required to regulate private actors. Then last are institutions where some governmental bodies, business houses and societies have participated to contribute in developing the regulation for private actors in outer space.

Chapter VI concludes this research study with some recommendations under the title 'Conclusion'.

At the end there is some caution to enjoy the reading of this research study. It relates with regulation of private actors commercially using space technology that is ever changing at different speed from country to country. Not only that, political mandate to regulate the national space programme of any country is simultaneously changing. Therefore the information used to analyse this study may be partially or totally changed with the passage of time. It may be highly possible that some new private actors, policies or legislations or some institutions concerned with space activities exist currently in a country. It may be the case that the countries not mentioned in the overall analysis have started regulating their space programmes. In this regard, there may be some developments in India also. In such scenarios, the submission is made to consider this analysis as a background of these recent developments. This is particularly applicable from chapter II onwards.

Abbreviations

A.D.	After Death
AIR	All India Radio
ALC	African Leadership Conference
ARABSAT	Arab Satellite Communication Organisation
CAG	Comptroller & Auditor General
COTS	Commercial Orbital Transportation Services
B.C.	Before Christ
BARC	Bhabha Atomic Research Centre
BIS	British Interplanetary Society
COMSAT	Commercial Satellite
COSPAR	Committee On Space Research
CSIR	Council for Scientific & Industrial Research
CSS	Commercial Space Station
CSR	Corporate Social Responsibility
CNES	National Centre for Space Studies France
DAE	Department of Atomic Energy
DOS	Department of Space
DOT	Department of Telecommunication
DRDO	Defence Research & Development Organisation
DST	Department of Science & Technology
DTH	Direct to Home
EADS	European Aeronautic Defence & Space Company
ECSL	European Centre For Space Law
EO	Earth Observation
ESA	European Space Agency
EU	European Union
EUTELSAT	European Telesatellites Communication Organisation
FDI	Foreign Direct Investment
FYP	Five Year Plan
GEO	Geosynchronous Earth Orbit

GSLV	Geosynchronous Satellite Launch Vehicle
IAA	International Academy Of Astronautics
IAC	International Astronautical Congress
IAASS	International Association for The Advancement of Space Safety
IACS	Indian Association for Cultivation of Science
IAF	International Astronautical Federation
ICAO	International Civil Aviation Organisation
ICBM	Intercontinental Ballistic Missile
ICJ	International Court of Justice
ICS	International Council for Science
ICSU	International Council for Scientific Union
IGO	Inter-Govermental Organisation
IGY	International Geophysical Year
IISL	International Institute of Space Law
ILA	International Law Association
INCOSPAR	Indian Committee on Space Research
INMARSAT	International Maritime Satellite Organisation
INSAT	Indian Satellite System
INTELSAT	International Telecommunications Satellite Organisation
ISAC	ISRO Satellite Centre
ISRO	Indian Space Research Organisation
ISS	International Space Station
ITU	International Telecommunication Union
IUCCA	Inter-University Centre for Astronomy and Astrophysics
IUGG	International Union for Geodesy & Geophysics
JAXA	Japan Aerospace Exploration Agency
KARI	Korean Aerospace Research Institute
LBS	Location Based System
LEO	Lower Earth Orbit
MOM	Mars Orbiter Mission
MOU	Memorandum of Understanding
NASA	National Aeronautic & Space Administration
NPL	National Physics Laboratory
NRSC	National Remote Sensing Centre
OST	Outer Space Treaty, 1967
PCA	Permanent Court Of Arbitration

PMO	Prime Minister's Office
PRL	Physical Research Laboratory
PSC	Philippine Space Commission
PSLV	Polar Satellite Launch Vehicle
RISAT	Radar Imaging Satellite
SAO	Smithsonian Astrophysical Observatory
SATCOM	Satellite Communication
SDSC SHAR	Satish Dhawan Space Centre, Sriharikota
SITE	Satellite Instructional Television Experiment
SPOT	Satellite for Observation of Earth
SPS	Solar Powered Satellite
SUPARCO	Space & Upper Atmospheric Research Organisation
TERLS	Thumba Equatorial Rocket Launching Station
TIFR	Tata Institute For Fundamental Research
TRAI	Telecom Regulatory Authority of India
UAV	Unmanned Aerial Vehicle
UN	United Nations
UNGA	United Nations General Assembly
UNESCO	United Nations Economic & Civil Organisation
UNCOPOUS	United Nations Committee on Peaceful Uses of Outer Space
UNIDROIT	International Institute for The Unification of Private Law
UNISPACE	United Nations Conference on The Exploration And Peaceful Uses of Outer Space
UNOOSA	United Nations Office for Outer Space Affairs
VSAT	Very Small Aperture Terminal
VSSC	Vikram Sarabhai Space Centre

I. History of Space Regulations

Introduction

The regulation of space activities have never arouse if the outer space would not have been overcrowded gradually since the launching of *Sputnik* in 1957. The human beings did not achieve this success of *Sputnik* easily to escape from the gravity of earth. It has a long standing history which has its own ancient origin with the scholarly contributions from so many visionaries all over the world. But the very beginning of this origination lies with astronomy which is the scientific study of celestial bodies like stars, planets, galaxies etc. It later on follows astronautics - the science and technology of space flight in general. Here it confines within manufacturing rockets leading to the launching of satellites in the present context.

The discourses of history would like to make an effort to trace out the requirement of law, if any, within astronautics. Now when the satellite has reached outer space overcoming the gravity of earth, the United Nations have started to think about regulation of outer space apprehending the threat to international peace and security. Gradually with the passage of time the major organisations nurturing astronautics have started to study and research on space law for satisfying their own purpose. The following paragraphs analyse this historical development briefly.

History of Astronomy

The earliest knowledge that humans exchanged with other communities was their ideas on astronomy. The cultures all over the world exchanged astronomical ideas and observations. Such type of knowledge carried forward over generations along with religions. These exchanges were taken for granted in those ancient eras. Therefore its documentation was barely required in those days.[1] The case of India was not an exception from this traditional practice. The tradition of Indian astronomy was one of the biggest traditions of astronomy in the world. There were vast literatures produced from so many sources. It formed a mine of further investigations.[2] The in-depth research of early theories of astronomy proved historically that India was a central hub in this field. Afterwards the beginning of 19th century showed the attraction of European scholars towards Vedic literature. These literatures contained indigenous Hindu astronomy. The exchange and interchange of literatures and ideas had happened between India and Western countries. Also, the same had happened with Eastern countries. Finally, India became enriched with more advanced literature when it was brought here.[3] This background divides Indian astronomy into three parts – ancient, medieval and modern.

ASTRONOMY IN ANCIENT INDIA

It is very difficult to start with the exact time period regarding the beginning of astronomy. Like the answer to the question who first realised that the earth was a spaceship had most probably no positive reply.[4] The people from different parts of the world tried to know about the mysteries of Sun, Moon and other celestial bodies. So this research study would like to confine within the significant works in ancient astronomy, especially, in India.

In our Vedic literature like Rig-Veda (composed not earlier than 1200 B.C.) had the references of the Sun, Moon, their motions through stellar constellations, solar eclipse, division of time, days, months, years etc. This was the beginning of astronomy and calendrical sciences.[5] At present there are no definite evidences to the astronomical knowledge of the Harappan people. So the oldest astronomical text in India is the *Vedanga Jyotisha* (astronomy as part of the Vedas), one part of which attributed to *Lagadha*.[6]

The Rig-Veda period had *Rig-Veda-Samhita* (1500 B.C. - 1000 B.C.) which described that Soma (moon) was stationed near naksatras (lunar mansions). It gave the names of two constellations which was most probably used to indicate the position of Moon. The literature contained creation of the universe; the zodiac, the solar system, the Moon and the Earth; the heliocentric universe; the spherical shape of Earth along with its revolution; the circumference of the Earth; day and night caused by the Sun; Sun was the star of daytime and there were many such Suns; Moon drew light from the Sun; the solar eclipse; the planets, comets and meteors.[7]

The leading astronomers were Aryabhata I (A.D. 476), Varahamihira (A.D. 505), Bhaskara I (A.D. 600), and Brahmagupta (A.D. 598). A fundamental text, *Surya-siddhanta*, was the most popular work of mathematical astronomy between 10th and 11th century A.D. It was written in Sanskrit. Here it was mentioned that a day began from midnight. But the modern tradition was changed to count a day from sunrise. Its author was not known.[8] But the concept of time was also described in Hindu Puranas. The astronomers shared lot of data which was almost similar like those used in cosmology of the Puranas. There were debates whether the astronomers took the data from Puranas or the vice-versa. But the Puranas were proved to be the original construction.[9]

Howsoever Aryabhata's work, *Aryabhatiya*, was the earliest preserved astronomical text. It consisted of the name of an individual of the scientific period of Indian astronomy. But there were other astronomers when this text was written. Since their works were lost, very little known about their contributions.[10] Aryabhata was the first amongst Indian astronomers to have mentioned the rotation of the earth. This explained the apparent daily motions of the fixed stars. He mentioned the eastward rotation of the earth.[11]

Besides Aryabhata, another famous name was Varahamihira who was the author of *Panchasiddhantika*. It appeared from this work that he was a compiler and historian of astronomy than as an astronomer of originality. The greatest exponent of Aryabhata's system of astronomy was Bhaskara I (A.D. 505). His contribution was to fully explain the method and its application to astronomy which was ruled by Aryabhata. In A.D. 598, Brahmagupta wrote *Brahmasphutasiddhanta*. Its contents were the planetary motions, problems of time, space and distance, lunar and solar eclipses, rising and setting of planets etc. Indeed, the Arabs were influenced by his works and introduced new mathematics-based astronomy.[12]

After Brahmagupta, there were several astronomers like Lalla (8th or 9th century A.D.), Sripati (11th century A.D.) but Bhaskara II or Bhaskaracharya (A.D. 1114) was frequently mentioned. The reason behind was that Indian astronomers of the pre-modern period were known only through their own works. It happened in most of the cases. But there was very little information about their life and family. In case of Bhaskara II, his grandson left an inscription about him. Another inscription showed the lineage of Bhaskara II. So his work, *Siddhanta-siromani*, was carried forward later by his grandson.[13] He discussed the mean and true motions of the planets, the three problems relating to time, direction and the place, the eclipses, risings, settings and the conjunction of the planets etc.[14]

The Kerala School of Astronomy had many innovations in the Indian astronomical tradition. Nilakantha Somayaji was perhaps the most famous scholar in this school. His *Tantrasangraha* ranked with the works of

Aryabhatiya and *Bhaskaracharya.* He introduced a major revision of the traditional Indian planetary model. According to him, the five planets Mercury, Venus, Mars, Jupiter and Saturn went in eccentric orbits around the mean Sun which in turn went around the earth. It was his contribution to provide the methods for determining the time from shadows, exact *lagna*, middle of eclipse, exact angular separation between the centres of the discs of the Sun and the Moon.[15] This is very brief of astronomy in ancient India which follows the next part—astronomy in medieval India.

ASTRONOMY IN MEDIEVAL INDIA

The medieval period of Indian history is divided into the Sultanate or pre-Mughal (A.D. 1191-1526) and Mughal (A.D. 1526-1857) periods. This part of astronomy mainly came into the category of Observational astronomy developed under the patronage of both the Indian Sultans and Mughal Emperors. Sultan Firoz Shah Tughlak (1351-1388) was known to be a maker of astrolabe himself. He ordered to write a book *Yantra-raja* on the same in Sanskrit for the first time. It was completed around 1370. His effort was to copy the Persian and Arabic Zizes (observational tables), and, made comment and sanskritised to an extent.[16] The next example was Emperor Humayun (1530-1556) who was an astronomer himself.[17] Jahangir, the Mughal Emperor of India (1605-1627), was very fond of astronomy.[18]

The last significant contribution during this phase came from Maharaja Sawai Jai Singh II (1686-1734) of Jaipur. He showed tremendous interest in astronomy. His interest was developed at a very early stage of his life. Jai Singh studied the Hindu, the Arabic and the European systems of astronomy. But his greatest contribution was to set up modern observatories for getting qualitative observational data and for producing more accurate astronomical tables. Jagannatha was his principal Hindu astronomer. According to him, Jai Singh had the skill in the use of astronomical instruments. Moreover, he was expert in exhibiting new methods with globes and instruments. The observatories established were in the places like Jaipur, Delhi, Ujjain, Varanasi and Mathura. He realised that the progress of science depended on drawing upon knowledge and know-how from wherever these were found. So, Jai Singh was one side a patronage of Hindu astronomy and the other side admirer of Arabic astronomy. Later, he became interested about astronomy of Christian Europe when he learnt their works. He sent his astronomers to foreign countries as well as invited the foreigners in India.[19]

The astronomy in medieval India signifies some positive changes. First is a sharp contrast with the ancient part. Unlike astronomy in ancient India, medieval period shows the mixture of knowledge between Hindu scholars and non-Hindu scholars mainly Islamic scholars. Second, this effect of diffusion of knowledge ultimately enriched Indian astronomy which reached the foreign countries through non-Hindu scholars. Then started the era of British colonisation more or less when the astronomy in modern India was developed which follows below.

ASTRONOMY IN MODERN INDIA

The period from Aryabhata to Bhaskaracharya II (c. 476-1150) was the golden period of astronomy in India. The western countries were little developed in astronomy during this period. The Arabs translated Indian works in Arabic. But with the arrival of Copernicus, Kepler, Galileo and Newton, astronomical thoughts and notions became revolutionary from its earlier past. Its effect brought a vibrant culture for strong beginning of astronomy in 16th and 17th centuries' Europe.[20]

Incidentally, this time was the period of colonisation of the East by the West. The scientists from these countries cooperated to again revive astronomy in India. Modern astronomy came to India with the interest of the Europeans. Their needs concerned with navigational and geographical aid. There were many British and French astronomers who initially came to India to observe the celestial events like planetary transits and solar eclipse. The geopolitical situation of India was good compared to their countries. They brought many instruments and a general awareness of astronomy to colonial India. But when the British realised that they had strong base in India, the Madras Observatory was established. Later it was shifted to Kodaikanal and made significant studies of Sun. Even it is working today also. Many observatories were established in Dehradun , Kolkata, Pune and Hyderabad.[21]

All these were effects of positional astronomy which was taking shape in Europe. Basically it was the beginning of new science of physical astronomy or astrophysics. Its impact had double-sided interest. Like the European solar physicists who wanted to get advantage from India's sunny sky were welcomed by Indian Government. Their study would anticipate the failure of the monsoons in India.[22]

Besides the above development, some scholars from different fields had contributed to make the astronomical infrastructure strong and sound.

They were mainly Indians attracted by British. The Indian Association for the Cultivation of Science (IACS) was established with the support from a missionary, Fr. Lafont, and Dr. Mahendra Lal Sircar. A telescope was presented to this Association. But after a long period of time, Sir Chandrasekhar Venkat Raman first utilised this telescope and maintained life-long interest for astronomy. Another important development was the establishment of Astronomical Society of India at Kolkata with the advent of comet Halley in 1910. Raman served this society in different ways. A significant member of the society was from legal field who was Nagendra Nath Dhar, a sub judge. But outside this society it was Radha Gobinda Chandra who was a scientific apprenticeship to a lawyer Kalinath Mukherjee. The later was editing a star atlas. Radha Gobinda observed comet Halley. He became a regular observer of variable stars and a member of the American Association of Variable Star Observers. They gifted him a telescope in 1926 as an award for his contribution.[23] It discloses the fact that Indians having legal background cultivated the knowledge of astronomy.

Though the above contributions were very significant to modernise the Indian astronomy, but it was the individual contribution from Saha who first realised in 1937 that there was a need from outside the Earth's atmosphere. At Chennai, Subramanyam Chandrasekhar, also for the first time applied the theory of special relativity to the problems of stellar structure and obtained preliminary results about white dwarf stars. It was clear that British would leave India very soon at the end of World War II. In December 1945, Meghnad Saha formed a five member committee for chalking out a plan on astronomical and astrophysical observatories in India. In 1955, a National Almanac Unit was formed in Kolkata as a follow-up of Saha's individual effort. Later, it was renamed as Positional Astronomy Centre in 1979. The purpose of this Unit was to facilitate the traditional almanac makers in updating their astronomical elements.[24]

There was parallel institutional development along with the above individual contribution from Saha. Its reflection was first observed with the establishment of Tata Institute of Fundamental Research (TIFR) at Mumbai in 1945.[25] Its founder Homi J Bhabha followed the scientific vision of Jawaharlal Nehru. Bhabha was personally interested about experimental research on cosmic rays. So, TIFR worked for the same in their major agenda. Here the experiments were sending payloads attached to the balloons into the atmosphere. These experiments later turned into the emergence of space astronomies in India. In fact India's entire space programme was a product of such initial efforts. Alternatively, its initiator Vikram Sarabhai got inspiration from Bhabha for his pioneering works in India's atomic energy programme.[26] Bhabha felt that India move into space research, rocket systems and fuels. He announced the formation of the Space Science Technology Centre (SSTC) on November 21, 1963.[27] However, it is analysed extensively in chapter V specifically on India.

But during independence, India has two observatories – Kodaikanal by Government of India and other at Nizamiah Observatory at Hyderabad. Whereas today, the Indian astronomical establishment has several observatories and research institutions like Indian Institute of Astrophysics,[28] the Raman Research Institute[29] both in Bengaluru, TIFR in Mumbai, Physical Research Laboratory (PRL)[30] in Ahmedabad, Inter-University Centre for Astronomy and Astrophysics (IUCCA)[31] in Pune, the Aryabhatta Research Institute for Observational Sciences[32] in Nainital and Udaipur Solar Observatory[33] in Udaipur. The ISRO also runs a space laboratory in Bengaluru called ISRO Satellite Centre (ISAC).[34] The development of astronomy in modern India ends here but there are some developments in the West also.

ASTRONOMY IN WESTERN COUNTRIES

Since this research study is mainly focussed on India's role in making international legal regulation of private actors in outer space, so the astronomy in India is analysed above in brief as a wide background of this research study. But it does not mean that astronomy was not developed too much in western countries especially Europe. The names of the few astronomers are Copernicus (A.D. 1473-1543), Tyco Brahe (A.D. 1546-1601), Giordano Bruno (A.D. 1548-1600), Galileo Galilei (A.D. 1564-1642) and Johannes Kepler (A.D. 1571-1630). It is Kepler's Laws of Planetary Motion which guide us to think and imagine how a satellite could overcome the force of gravitation.[35]

The above details ensure how human beings achieved the mastery of astronomy over a very long period of time. It follows their subsequent and long cherished dream to step in outer space physically. Hence they applied their vast and enriched knowledge of astronomy with other science and technology disciplines like astronautics. This brings the following development of astronautics.

History of Astronautics

The history of astronautics may be classified as two separate histories – rocketry and space flight. The technology behind the rocket is used later on to develop satellites and finally space shuttle to establish our physical presence in outer space. According to NASA space historian Emme, it further goes that 'the impact of rocket technology upon society, apparent and portentous, challenges the social sciences and the humanities'.[36] Therefore the history of rocketry is assumed to be very significant for this research study. Like the history of astronomy, its history belongs to ancient and modern times.

ANCIENT TIMES

It is very difficult to say whether there was any development in rocketry system in ancient India. The history of technology in India, especially for earlier periods, has not been a favourite topic of historians in general. It remains mainly as an understudied part.[37] Moreover, there has been no major work on the history of science and technology in India like Dr. Joseph Needham's magnum opus on '*Science and Civilisation in China*'. It has huge impact in the academic development of China in the progress of science.[38] Another scholarly view is that certain sciences and arts were kept secretly because its disclosure would abuse and disturb the peace of humankind.[39]

The other reason is the incidence of series of attacks perpetrated on India by so many foreign invaders. They destroyed the books situated in ancient heritage educational hubs. But some were escaped from their hands. These disclose the knowledge of aeronautics. The aeroplanes of different types were manufactured with variety of models. The assembling techniques were explicitly described in these mutilated books. The great scholars like Agatysa, Bharadvaj, Manu and Vishwakarma were considered as the mentors of this knowledge. The modern research revealed the fact that the construction of aeroplanes by ancient Indians was not a myth.[40] There are many examples in Puranic and other epic literatures where ancient Indians proved their efficiency to conquer the air.[41] Bharadvaj's *Vaimanika Sastra* is a rich Indian heritage on aeronautics.[42] Recently, the Chinese Government handed over a Sanskrit manuscript found in Tibetian region. It consists of inter-stellar travel and anti-gravitational flights.[43]

Similarly, the contribution of India is also observed in the evolution of rockets but in different way. India acted as a bridge between eastern and western uses of rocketry. In this view, the evolution of rockets was interconnected with the uses of gunpowder because bamboo tubes filled with gunpowder were thrown to the enemies in China. These fire-arrows were used in China about the middle of the 13th century.[44] In 1232 A.D., rockets first came into the written history at the battle of Kai-Feng in China. The defenders of the city used them against invading Mongol hordes led by the son of Chenghis Khan.[45]

There were two regions, China and Europe, developed with rockets in 13th century. But China probably had earlier history. A depiction of rocket occurred there even in the 10th century. The country used this rocketry in practice.[46] There was research study of formulae for fireworks in Sanskrit work of c.1500. It could be stated from such study that these were transmitted from China to India about c.1400.[47] But it was accepted by historians that crude rockets were fired as military weapons in the 13th century in the Far East, the Near East and Europe.[48]

The above analysis proves the Chinese origin of rockets. But Tipu Sultan of Mysore used the rockets to destroy the artilleries of the British in the battle of Srirangapattam (1792). It was his full credit to draw attention of the West regarding rockets to be used in battles as dreadful weapons popularly known as military or war rockets in the history of rocketry. Indians used the technology of rockets, much before French and English people, through Tipu. The sample was taken to England because Tipu lost the above battle with British. The British conquered their battles against Napoleon with this technology as further developed by artillerist Sir William Congreve during early 19th century. But Congreve's rocket did not hit the target precisely. So rockets were ignored in First World War. Rather such solid fueled rocket was used as civilian basis for life-saving purposes during 1850s. Its popular uses were for harpooning whales and to carry lines of ships.[49]

The above discourses of history guide that the technology of rocketry has been transferred from East to West. Especially the credit of India via Tipu is to showcase the rocket technology before the Western world. Later on the World War influenced this technology transfer too much with the support from Western rocketeers to manufacture and develop the advanced models of rockets in modern times. This comes under modern times.

MODERN TIMES

Three persons were especially significant in accomplishing the transition from the small, gun-powder-fueled rockets of 19th century to the giant, liquid-fueled multistage rockets of the space age. They are Konstantin E. Tsiolkovsky in Russia, Robert H. Goddard in the United States and Hermann J. Oberth in Germany.[50] They worked independently to develop the theoretical foundation of rocket propulsion. But during the time of Tsiolkovsky (1890's), one German law student Hermann Ganswindt published his ideas and calculations about rockets. His ideas were ignored during that time.[51] But it was the German Society for Space Travel which picked up the notions of Goddard and Oberth regarding space. The Society then initiated serious rocket work in Germany. Simultaneously, the British Interplanetary Society did the same work followed by the American Rocket Society later.[52]

Ultimately, it was Goddard who successfully launched the world's first liquid-fueled rocket in 1926. Unfortunately, his work was criticised in the newspaper. He became silent about his works rest of his life. Though he did not want the publicity but registered so many patents on rockets. Goddard offered to develop rockets for the military during World War II. But the US Government showed no such interest in the technology. The people recognised his work posthumously through the publications brought by his wife.[53]

Besides Goddard, the German rocket scientist Hermann J. Oberth played a meaningful role to develop the rocketry. His doctoral dissertation on rocketry in the University of Heidelberg was too much utopian as per the opinion of the authority and not accepted. But he published his work in 1923 having title '*The Rocket into Planetary Space*'. Many German scientists and engineers including Wernher von Braun were attracted by his work. The World War II broke in 1930s. The United States, the then Soviet Union, Japan and the United Kingdom manufactured rockets and guided missiles of all sizes and shapes for this war. But Germany took the lead in the advancement of rocket research.

The Treaty of Versailles[54] supported this advancement. Rockets were not under banned items as per this Treaty. It happened due to lack of consciousness about the technology of rocketry. Captain Dronberger of the German military force was ordered to develop liquid fuel rockets where Oberth and Wernher von Braun were in the team. Then Hitler rose to power in 1933. The political support from Hitler boosted up Germany to develop liquid-propellant rocket which had a design range of 275 kms, popularly known as Vengeance Weapon 2 or V -2. These were successfully launched in 1942. Thus Von Braun and his team could rapidly surpass Goddard's research efforts. A vast new rocket experimental station at Peenemunde on the Baltic Sea became functional to develop rockets during April 1937. Von Braun was its technical director. This is the starting point of the modern rocketry as military ballistic missile.[55]

The above scenario was changed after the end of World War II when Von Braun's team of rocket scientists surrendered to the Americans. Many German rocket scientists including Braun moved to US with a dream of spaceflight. Later Oberth joined him. Thereafter America was enriched through Peenemunde technical archives and much of V-2 hardware. The Soviets captured some V-2 rockets and obtained the assistance of a number of V-2 technicians. Hence, ultimately these two countries carried on the responsibility to develop rockets further. By 1949, both had atomic weapons, but these were heavy and bulky. It would need an enormous rocket to carry them. But America relied more on aircraft to drop atomic weapons and so concentrated to develop winged cruise missiles. Rocket developments were decided for small warheads, if required. Unlikely Soviet Union's work concentrated on developing the large rockets that would be needed to carry nuclear weapons from one continent to other.[56]

While the space technology was used for weapons development during the post-World War days but some visionaries like Arthur C. Clarke kept their dreams alive through their writings. He wrote articles on mining the Moon in 1951. The rocket scientists like Braun published '*The Mars Project*' in 1952. It was the first serious technical study of a human expedition to Mars. Walter Disney also promoted space travel in the mid-1950s through his popularised television shows.[57]

IGY Programme

The above activities related with rocketry and its development went on both theoretically and practically. But in the midst of all these activities, another totally new science related development to study the mother Earth and its surrounding environment was taken up. This was International Geophysical Year (IGY) programme during 1957-58. One of the most significant outcomes was manufacturing rockets for scientific experiments within its own programme. India was involved with this programme from the very beginning. Therefore, IGY is required to analyse below.

Scientific Background of IGY

The International Geophysical Year (IGY)[58] could not be explained without its historical significance. The two International Polar Years (IPY) - the first one (1882-83) and the second one (1932-33) were followed by IGY. Their purpose was same – to study the atmospheric changes, both ordinary weather and electrical weather. But in the second IPY, radio has already been invented. So the radio waves were used as an additional means of studying the electrical weather in the ionosphere.[59] The American physicist L.V. Berkner proposed to hold a third IPY later in 1950 because scientific data was needed from the whole world.[60]

Accordingly a draft was submitted to the Joint Commission on the Ionosphere which was linked with three Scientific Unions - for radio science (URSI), geodesy and geophysics (IUGG) and astronomy (IAU). Finally, it was recommended as a project to the International Council of Scientific Union (ICSU). ICSU adopted it and appointed a Special Committee, CSAGI, to organise the project in 1953. CSAGI decided that the 18 months from July 1, 1957 to December 31, 1958 would be observed as International Geophysical Year (IGY). It was decided in October 1954 at Rome in the meeting of scientists gathering from 40 countries. There were 67 IGY committees in the enterprise. These committees sent their own programmes along with scientists to the meetings to plan the final programme. Each IGY committee was very specific about their programme.[61]

Significance of IGY

The scientific background signified the beginning of IGY programme in two ways: (i) a great proposal was made for a common study of our planet by all countries for the benefit of everybody; and (ii) the first coordinated international scientific study ever made of the physical phenomena of the earth and its atmosphere. There is one interesting note that cosmic rays were added as new one to make experiments along with all the subjects studied in the last two IPYs. All were related with each other. So it was necessary to study them simultaneously with that of Sun. 14 scientists, called Reporters, were engaged in special duties to coordinate and lead the developments of the separate parts of the enterprise. Two parts affected more than one of the scientific branches. Their number and title were: (1) World Days and Communication and (11) Rockets and Satellites.[62] The rockets and satellites part revealed the sub-merged concept of space programme within

IGY. Therefore the evolution of space programme within IGY was silently introduced.

Evolution of Space Programme within IGY

The first IPY was confined with the observation at the ground level. In the second IPY, balloons were used to extend the height about six miles. But USA's expectation was at higher levels in the IPY proposal by means of rockets. The rockets captured in Germany during World War II were used primarily. Later these were manufactured.[63]

Unlikely in balloon era, the rocket era faced a new problem. There was excellent skill needed to observe the properties of the atmosphere because of speed of the rockets. It passes through air very swiftly. In 1954, there was consideration for high-level atmospheric exploration by small earth satellites. The US Committee finally took decision to launch satellites in the programme during 1955. But the USSR Committee took the same decision in 1956 when US already had started to build up satellites and the mechanism for launching.[64]

A conference on the Rockets and Satellites was held in Washington D.C. in the month of September and October 1957. It was attended by the countries like US, USSR, Canada, UK, France, Australia and Japan who had included the rocket launching in their programme. The other participating countries had taken decision that they would be observer of the satellites with the reception of its signals. So, it was proved that only USA and USSR have the capability to manufacture satellites all over the world.[65]

Moreover, though the launching could be performed by the two countries above but it would require international cooperation from other countries for accurate tracking of the satellites. The plans of US and USSR to launch the satellites were discussed. Others shared their plans and interacted how to get the best scientific uses of the satellites. On the evening of October 4, 1957, before the final day of the conference, USSR made the history to launch IGY satellite to outer space. The USSR sent another bigger IGY satellite with a dog named Laika on November 3 of the same year. A third in the series was on May 15, 1958. The plan for US IGY satellite was successful on January 31, 1958. They sent another three in the same year.[66]

It is conceived from above that IGY was another gateway for developing the rocketry followed by launching of satellites. But the above significance of IGY at the beginning had deep impact when it came to the individual countries.

Impact of IGY

The impact of IGY programme was the division of countries all over the world amongst two groups –Group I and Group II. Group I enlisted those countries that had space programmes or activities well before IGY. Here the countries listed are Australia, Canada, China, the Federal Republic of Germany (FRG), France, Japan, the USSR, UK, USA. At the end of 20th century, these countries took part in several international organisations that operate and regulate space activities.[67]

Moreover the countries were participating and contributing members of United Nations Committee on Peaceful Uses of Outer Space (UNCOPUOS). But more relevant to this research study is that these countries got stimulus from IGY for their space industrialisation occurred much later on. This industrialisation has ultimately paved way for private actors, whatever be their capacity and performance, to pursue activities in outer space.[68] Unlike Group I, the Group II consisted of those countries which were active in space activity during or shortly following IGY. Here the list followed Argentina, Austria, Belgium, Brazil, Burma, Chile, Czechoslovakia, Denmark, Ecuador, Ethiopia, Finland, Ghana, India, Indonesia, Iran, Ireland, Israel, Italy, Mexico, Norway, Philippines, Peru, Portugal, Rhodesia and Nyasaland, Romania, Spain, Sweden, Switzerland, the Netherlands and the Union of South Africa. Some of these countries later on just lost the momentum of space activities for different reasons. These are till now backward in space technology.[69]

But some countries like India have remarkable achievement through continuous efforts. India's progress in launching technique is internationally acclaimed in the commercial market whereas no other country from this group achieved this height.[70] Moreover, IGY was the first organised entry of Indian science into global level.[71] Thus the IGY programme corroborates this research study to realise how much it is significant in studying the role of India to develop its space programme. However the development within India itself is analysed later in chapter V.

Now this research study reaches at the point where the histories of astronomy as well as astronautics are briefly opened up. The history of astronautics shows that the requirement of rockets and satellites has increasing demand—both in advanced and developing countries in space technology. This increasing demand is from both angles—civil angle through IGY and military angle through making of Intercontinental Ballistic Missiles (ICBMs). This increasing demand of technology regime through manufacturing and launching rockets and satellites to outer space attracts the legal regime because there is general saying that law follows technology. But how and in which way? The answer lies below.

EVOLUTION OF LAW WITHIN ASTRONAUTICS

The brief history of rocketry showed that the countries were mainly interested to use this rocket technology for military purposes. It could be said that it was more sophisticated weapon than canons or other firearms used in those days. Therefore rockets were products of World War.[72] But side by side there was parallel development of thoughts whether spaceflight could be possible through rocket. This brought another kind of rivalry between the countries, mainly the US and the then Soviet Russia, to reach the outer space first as a pride of the nation. It started with the launching of '*Sputnik*' during IGY. Therefore the space law jurist C. Wilfred Jenks rightly pointed out that "the human beings could not hope to avoid confusion and frustration or to keep power politics out of space unless scientific cooperation and political understandings are translated into firm legal obligations".[73] So, it was a natural way to think about regulating these activities which first came to the mind of United Nations just after the launching of 'Sputnik'. Even during pre-sputnik space era, there were astounding scholars who thought about regulating the space.

The pre-sputnik space law development was related with the controversy who owned the space and how high was state sovereignty in airspace.[74] This new problem over sovereignty in outer space indicated the evolution or requirement of law within astronautics. This started hue and cry as already in IGY programme. This evolution or requirement was mainly west centric though exception always lies. The simple reason is that the western countries are maximum in number out of group I countries of IGY. These were strong in space activities during IGY programme. In case of group II countries including India, the situation was full of different problems like absence of technology, colonisation etc. Anyway the western countries dominated this part of legal history which is expanded below.

Let it be cleared first that according to Willy Ley 'it was not the pioneers of space travel but lawyers, especially those engaged in international law, realised the legal problems at an early date'.[75] A Belgian lawyer Emile Laude published first commentary on space law in 1910. But Laude was not sure about the use of term 'space' which would be above air. He mainly focussed on the problem of the ownership and use of the hertizian (radio) waves.

Then Second World War made a long gap. A senior member of Soviet Union Ministry V.A. Zarzar presented a paper in 1926 on Air Law. His query was all about nature and extent of national sovereignty beyond airspace. His view was that there would be a requirement of distinct legal regime to interact this upper zone. The logic was that the high-altitude flight and interplanetary communication would be free in this zone from control by subjacent states.[76] Then it was Vladimir Mandl who published his work in 1932 titled '*Space Law – A Problem of Spaceflight*'.[77] According to the same Ley:

> "Dr. Mandl's study tried chiefly to show that existing legislation – he used strictly codified German law as the means of the presenting his case – covered most of the foreseeable legal problems. But Dr. Mandle failed to establish a unified legal view. This was done (as far as I know for the first time) during a lecture delivered at the first Hayden Planetarium Symposium on Space Travel (October 12, 1951) by Oscar Schachter of the legal departments of the United Nations. Schachter took the position that open space should be regarded like the open sea, as not belonging to any power and available to the use of all."[78]

Besides Mandl, there were other scholars like E. Korovin from Russia who presented a paper in 1933 on '*Conquest of the Stratosphere and International Law*' in an air law conference. His arguments were in favour of state sovereignty over air-space. But he argued for unlimited state sovereignty on the grounds of safety and military security. Later he himself changed his view. The Earth rotated with fast velocity and so the cosmic space changed from time to time. Therefore sovereignty in the cosmos could only be enforced with lightning speed and continuous movement.[79]

In 1952, Alex Meyer published '*Legal Problems of Spaceflight*' in the Annual reports of the British Interplanetary Society. The paper titled '*International Law and Activities in Space*' was published by C. Wilfred Jenks in 'The International and Comparative Law Quarterly', January, 1956.[80] Welf Heinrich, Prince of Hanover, published the first doctoral thesis in space law. Basically his work was an influence of Meyer. He argued extensively that space beyond the atmosphere must be considered free both on technical grounds. The reason cited was that the law of nature supported it. Also, it was for better legal construction and policy.[81]

Another paper written by American jurist John Cobb Cooper was published with the title '*The Russian Satellite- Legal and Political Problem*' within two weeks of the launching of sputnik. His legal proposition was that the sputnik incident had really challenged the traditional sovereignty concept of states over its airspace. Though the sovereignty of each state was fully protected over its airspace but the confusion occurred to define the legal status of outer space. It remained a problem during the above IGY programme. Ultimately, he did not provide any solution but passed over the problem to UN for some serious initiative near future.[82]

Though Ley stated above that lawyers mainly engaged in international law realised the legal problems first, but there were scholars from non-legal background also who contributed for explaining the view of sovereignty in outer space. In case of science fiction writer Arthur C. Clarke, he acknowledged the upper limit on state sovereignty in the interests of development of space science and its applications during his lecture at British Interplanetary Society in 1946.[83] According to Lyall, "Being unfamiliar of the works of Mandl, Clarke also observed that action would be needed to forestall extraterrestrial imperialism and consequent conflict."[84] Andrew G. Halley, the rocket scientist cum lawyer, was another person who extensively travelled all over the world to deliver lectures and wrote papers to develop space law. The compilation of his work was ultimately published in his book titled '*Space law and Government*'. But his thought on space law was triggered from his meeting and conversation with another rocket scientist Dr. Theodore Von Karman.[85] Therefore, the persons outside the legal field were involved in the process of development of space law.

It is mentioned in the earlier paragraph that there was exception of this western centric evolution of space law. So it follows the Indian paper titled '*An Attempt to Determine the Sovereignty in Outer Space*' by R. C. Hingorani during 1957. His argument was that launching of satellites during IGY was common benefit to all countries. So, it could not be objected in raising question about sovereignty as explained in air law. Moreover, space could not be owned because it existed in vacuum. Therefore, all controversies over outer space would be solved likely.[86]

It is analysed from above that the scholars from legal as well as non-legal backgrounds contributed for conceptualising the legal regime of outer space within the domain of astronautics. Its main reason was to determine sovereignty in outer space or to fix the upper limit of airspace. This was the history of evolution of law within astronautics.

History of Developing International Space Law

The above preliminary phase of evolution of law existed up to the launching of Sputnik. Then it was United Nations who took the mantle to develop space law. Its initiative encouraged other organisations later on including the non-governmental organisations like International Institute of Space Law (IISL) to promote space law. But these organisations were established for their own purposes.

DEVELOPMENTS WITHIN UNITED NATIONS FRAMEWORK

The establishment of United Nations was a smoothing impact of World War II. So any incident which would attract the disturbance of international peace and security came under its agenda of discussion in its General Assembly. The incident related with launching of 'Sputnik' on October 4, 1957, was attracted by UN for the same reason. There were two phases of this development – one Pre-UNCOPUOS (United Nations Committee on Peaceful Uses of Outer Space) and another Post-UNCOPUOS.

Pre-UNCOPUOS Period

The first General Assembly resolution related with outer space activities was passed on November 14, 1957. It was related with disarmament and stated that 'the joint study of an inspection system designed to ensure that the sending of objects through outer space should be exclusively for peaceful and scientific purposes.'[87] The two super powers of space technology, USA and USSR, stated their purpose for space expedition separately. Both sides maintained its purpose peaceful. In 1958, President Eisenhower stated that the outer space should be dedicated only to the peaceful uses of mankind. In the same year, the Soviet Government also proposed a plan on prohibiting the use of outer space for military purposes. Each state had to give one undertaking to launch rockets only in accordance with international programme as well as within the commitments of UN Framework.[88]

The above General Assembly (GA) resolution was followed by another GA resolution adopted in 1958 which stated 'recognising the common interest of mankind in outer space and ..... that it is the common aim that the outer space should be used for peaceful purposes only'[89], expressing the wish 'to avoid the extensions of present national rivalries into this new field'.[90]

It was anticipated by UN that space would be further utilised for causing disturbances in international peace and security. The rivalry between two superpowers, United States and the then U.S.S.R. would be main cause in this regard. There were no other reasons to adopt these resolutions. The post-world war situation was very cool. But the political goals of the United States, Great Britain and France and on the other hand, those of the Soviet Union were diametrically opposed.[91]

This led to Cold War which continued over a period of 40 years. The historic event of '*Sputnik'* launching happened during Cold War period. Both the USSR and the United States had tried to work on building of intercontinental ballistic missiles (ICBM) using existing rocket technology. The incident of '*Sputnik'* proved that the USSR would be able to use outer space in launching such missiles.[92] This was the very birth of space law within UN Framework. The following paragraphs analyse further development.

In 1958, the United Nations General Assembly (UNGA) decided to establish an ad-hoc Committee on the Peaceful Uses of Outer Space. It has 18 member states including India. All these activities were placed through a General Assembly resolution under the title 'Question of Peaceful Uses of Outer Space'.[93] The purpose of this Committee was to carry forward the outer space activities and research peacefully. There were two demands – (1) highest international cooperation with all states that had no capabilities of outer space activities and (2) to find out the legal problems which may arise to pursue such activities. But the conflicts existed amongst the member states on the dominance of one state to another. Therefore India did not participate initially.[94]

Anyway the Committee established 2 subcommittees – one technical and another legal. The legal committee decided to focus some legal problems. These problems were detected on priority and non-priority basis. There were six priority legal problems. Rests were problems in distant future. The recommendations of the Committee were the following: (i) to follow the UN Charter and the Statute of ICJ in outer space activities; (ii) to study the regulations related with sea and air extensively in order to determine the space regulation; and (iii) not to frame a comprehensive code of space law as it is neither desirable nor practicable.[95]

These findings were prepared in June 1959. But due to the difference in opinions followed by boycotting the Committee, the General Assembly First Committee met to discuss the findings during December 1959 and to consider establishing the permanent outer space committee.[96] The permanent committee was adopted by the UNGA resolution 1472 (XIV) of December 12, 1959. This committee was 24 member states. It is named as United Nations Committee on the Peaceful Uses of Outer Space (UNCOPUOS).[97]

Post-UNCOPUOS Period

The above Committee first met in 1961 because of the indifference in opinion amongst the members. An important resolution was passed which stated that 'International law, including the Charter of the United Nations, applies to outer space and celestial bodies.'[98] Besides the two subcommittees above, the United Nations has a separate United Nations Office for Outer Space Affairs (UNOOSA)[99]. Both these Sub-committees meet annually - Technical Committee in between January to February and Legal Committee in between March to April and prepare their final report after deliberations. Finally the UNCOPUOS sends this report with recommendations to the UNGA. The review of the whole work is done by the Political Committee of the UNGA and accordingly a resolution is to be adopted in General Assembly.[100]

In this manner, the UN becomes the forum for drafting of outer space legislations for the peaceful uses of outer space. Here the role of UN is mainly significant to build the foundation of space law through five space law treaties. A brief examination of the *travaux preparatory* of these treaties is followed below.

The Legal Subcommittee formulated a set of principles in the form of a draft declaration. Later it was adopted as UNGA resolution 'Declaration of Legal Principles Governing the Activities of States in the Exploration and Use of Outer Space'.[101] This Declaration basically was an attempt to enact legal principles for outer space activities in a formalised manner. This resolution represented a major turning point in the development of international space law. It was resulted basically from an understanding between the then only two space powers - the Soviet Union and the United States. The basic rules were to be observed not only by themselves but by all states in the exploration and use of outer space. It followed their agreement on the Nuclear Test Ban Treaty.[102] There was scarcely any consultation with other members of the COPUOS.[103] Though the UNGA resolution is legally non-binding nature but it is the first and probably the most important early normative framework for space activities.[104] The most significant for this research study from this resolution is that all private entities will carry out outer space activities subject to state's authorisation and supervision.

The Outer Space Treaty, 1967, which is the Magna Carta of outer space activities, is a follow-up of the above UNGA declaration in 1963.[105] In June 1966, the USSR submitted a text of draft treaty on principles governing the activities of states in the exploration and use of outer space and other celestial bodies.[106] The United States submitted a counter proposal for the treaty text. These two proposals were considered in the legal sub-committee during 1966. A working group of the Sub-committee was established to discuss both proposals. It extracted a series of articles on which agreement could be reached.[107] The Sub-committee took the matter in its next session later in the same year. The proposals were made by the member states but no final agreement was reached. Later on the 'Treaty on Principles Governing the Activities of States in the Exploration and Use of Outer Space, including the Moon and Other Celestial Bodies' was finally achieved on an agreed text. This text was adopted by the General Assembly.[108]

The next space law treaty was the Rescue Agreement (Agreement on Rescue of Astronauts, the Return of Astronauts and the Return of Objects Launched into Outer Space) as adopted by the UNGA resolution 2345 (XXII) in 1968. It was the product of the first fatal accident in space exploration in 1967. On January 27, 1967, three United States astronauts died when fire broke out on board Apollo I before take-off. On April 24, Colonel Vladimir Kamorov of the Soviet Union perished in Soyuz I on landing.[109] This treaty was historical in the sense that the General Assembly for the first time made request to one of its Sub-committees to prepare the text of a multipartite treaty. The Soviet Union took the major initiative behind this treaty.[110]

The other space treaties are the Liability Convention (Convention on International Liability for Damage Caused by Space Objects) as adopted by UNGA resolution 2777 (XXVI) in 1972; Registration Convention (Convention on Registration of Objects Launched into Outer Space) as adopted by UNGA resolution 3235 (XXIX) in 1975 and Moon Agreement (Agreement Governing the Activities of States on the Moon and Other Celestial Bodies) as adopted by UNGA resolution 34/68 in 1979.[111]

All these treaties were made for specific purposes to pursue activities in outer space beside the Outer Space Treaty, 1967 which holds the common umbrella over all the others. Though the UN made all these treaties but its implementation was different in different countries. The status of each treaty shows different reports. The status of these treaties is very significant to analyse the domestic space law of different countries in chapter IV.

Table 1: Status of Space Law Treaties[112]

Instrument	Parties	Signatories	IGO Declaration
Outer Space Treaty	101	26	Not Applicable
Rescue Agreement	91	24	2
Liability Convention	88	23	3
Registration Convention	56	4	2
Moon Treaty	13	4	--

It is very transparent that the effects of all the treaties in the development of space law are not same. The significance of the first one i.e., the Outer Space Treaty is maximum. The last one, the Moon Treaty, has the minimum effect. The latest status of Registration Convention is 60 parties with 25 signatories.[113] The latest status of Moon Treaty is 15 parties with 11 signatories.[114] India has been ratified all the treaties besides the Moon Treaty where it is a signatory only.[115] It was signed on January 18, 1982.[116]

The major significant development of space law within UN Framework is examined above but there are other developments through five declarations and legal principles out of which the UNGA resolution 1962 (XVIII) of 1963 is already mentioned above. Four others are: (i) the Principles Governing the Use by States of Artificial Earth Satellites for International Direct Television Broadcasting[117] (resolution 37/92 of December 10, 1982); (ii) the Principles Relating to Remote Sensing of the Earth from Outer Space[118] (resolution 41/65 of December 3, 1986); (iii) the Principles Relevant to the Use of Nuclear Power Sources in Outer Space[119] (resolution 47/68 of December 14, 1992); and (iv) the Declaration on International Cooperation in the Exploration and Use of Outer Space for the Benefit and in the Interest of All States, Taking into Particular Account the Needs of Developing Countries[120] (resolution 51/122 of December 13, 1996).

All these are related with application of space technology in particular domain like first for using artificial earth satellites for direct television broadcasting; second for the application of data from remote sensing satellites; third for using of nuclear power sources, and the last one for exploration and use of outer space especially for the needs of the developing countries. They are legally non-binding in nature. But these guidelines serve the soft regulatory purposes for the specific uses of space technology where there are no space related regulations. In case of such existing regulations, these are additional one.

The other development besides treaties is the United Nations Conference on the Exploration and Peaceful Uses of Outer Space (UNISPACE) under COPUOS. There were three such conferences till now all at Vienna during 1968, 1982 and 1999. The most relevant to this research study is UNISPACE III titled as 'Space Benefits for Humanity in the 21st Century'.[121] The private industry representatives were present in UNISPACE III. It means that the business community has crucial role to develop the space technology along with its applications. Moreover as mentioned in the introduction that the Governments have sort of fund as well as expertise to develop the space projects. The final message from this conference states 'the private sector is playing a major role in the development of space technology and making a major contribution to the economic development of many countries is something that the United Nations recognises and is keen to encourage.'[122] Therefore the trends of development within UN itself directed towards pro-commercialisation and pro-privatisation.

DEVELOPMENTS OUTSIDE UN FRAMEWORK

The above developments of space law within UN were mainly to maintain international cooperation and peace on pursuing activities in outer space. But the organisations concerned with astronautics like International Academy of Astronautics (IAA) or International Astronautical Federation (IAF) contributed a lot in the domain of space law while working on their own field. Both the organisations have non-governmental status. The other two make focus exclusively on law – one International Institute of Space Law (IISL) solely on space law and another International Law Association (ILA) as a part of international law. All the four organisations have permanent observer status in UNCOPUOS.[123] Besides these four major organisations, there are several others including some purely private bodies that have direct and indirect impact to develop space law. But for the time being the analysis below is confined within the four major organisations.

Firstly, it was the International Academy of Astronautics (IAA) founded in 1950 shortly after World War II. The basic purpose was to transfer the technology of rocketry from warfare to spaceflight. It came to limelight in 1955 during the 6th International Astronautical Congress (IAC) at Copenhagen. Here Soviet Union and the United States announced its national programme to launch artificial satellite to celebrate International Geophysical Year (1957-58). There are several committees in the IAA established for studying and developing different aspects of astronautics. A committee was set for scientific legal liaison. It was established in 1962 to make liaison with International Institute of Space Law (IISL). The discussions were welcomed from the members of IISL and other IAA committee members. Also, the cooperation from the non-members were sought for to develop a multidisciplinary approach of astronautics.[124]

But till 1975, the effective dialogue between scientists and lawyers had not been made though it was the main purpose of the committee. Hence the committee was reorganised and its membership was regularly reviewed. After that it was an effective body of discussions of scientists, technologists and lawyers on international non-governmental basis. The committee had roundtables on different issues like definition of outer space on the basis of scientific factors, legal problems likely to arise from space station operations, scientific and legal aspects of remote sensing. In these roundtables, the eminent international lawyers like Manfred Lachs and Vladimir Kopal were involved.[125]

Like IAA, the International Astronautical Federation (IAF) is another organisation. The IAF is one of the oldest organisations outside UN for the development of astronautics. It was established in the year 1951 to promote the dialogue between East and West. The reason was that the two superpowers in space did not want to make any dialogue in the cold war scenario though there was tremendous development in rocketry. It was a non-governmental and non-profit making international organisation which encouraged the development of space based activities for the benefit of humankind.[126] When the IAF was formed in the early 1950s, the IAF did not expressly address the need for nor contemplate that it would have a role in the development of space law. Thereafter, the scientific community and national militaries worked diligently to address the challenges of space flight during 1950's. The lawyers were beginning to interact publicly about their views on emerging legal problems.[127]

IAF's annual conference called International Astronautical Congress (IAC) is the largest gathering of space communities from different disciplines like science, technology, law, trade etc. till now. There is a motivation behind conducting the IAC. With the advancement of rocket technology, the general feeling has been changed. Rockets were not used only as weaponries but it could be used for an instrument of peaceful research.[128] This motivation has formalised the idea of IAC. So first few IACs are assumed to be very significant to develop space law.

Table 2: Significant IACs & Concerned Developments[129]

IAC No.	Year	Place	Developments
1	1950	Paris	Recognition for the need of a worldwide organisation to promote the achievement of spaceflight for peaceful project.
2	1951	London	Primary scientific interest for artificial satellite vehicles.
3	1952	Germany	Oberth presented historical paper that later on formed the basis of worldwide space cooperation
4	1953	Switzerland	Japan, being the first Asian country to send observer.
7	1956	Rome	Social scientists contributed.
8	1957	Spain	Legal problems for spaceflight first seriously considered under the Presidentship of Haley, being the first social scientist to hold this position.
9	1958	Netherlands	Space problems related with science, technology and social science are divided.
10	1959	London	1. Indian Astronautical Society admitted as voting member. 2. Steps taken to establish International Institute of Space Law.
11	1960	Sweden	1st Colloquium on outer space held.

Besides Argentina, all representatives were from European countries in 1st IAC. The Society for Space Research in Germany and British Interplanetary Society (BIS) played the main role. Though the international cooperation was sought from the beginning amongst the two super powers in space but the Russians did not participate in the IAF until the announcement of USSR's satellite program in 1955. The 2nd IAC was just the official inauguration of this organisation. The American Rocket Society joined here. The rocketeer Oberth presented the paper in 3rd IAC '*Private Research in Astronautics*' which later on formed the basis of world cooperation. Over 450 experts in natural and social sciences attended the meetings in 7th IAC.[130] The following IACs were practically responsible for the development of space law.

In 1957, the IAF held its 8th session in October after the incidence of launching of Sputnik. Andrew Haley, a lawyer, was elected as President and for the first time a person from social science took this post. This IAC was important for the development of space law. The representatives were impressed by the fact that the legal problems would be a serious concern for the space flight. The peace of the world was also threatened. The division of space science, space technology and social science relating to space problems were framed during 9th IAC. In 10th IAC organised by British Interplanetary Society in London in 1959, the Indian Astronautical Society was admitted as voting member of IAF. Also steps were taken to establish the International Institute of Space Law within the framework of the IAF. In the 11th IAC one day space law colloquium was conducted.[131]

The places of first few IACs were in western countries according to **Table 2**. Therefore the development of space law was mainly influenced in its formative years by western thoughts and according to their self-interests. The IAC was held till now outside European and American countries like Japan, India, China, South Korea and South Africa.[132] It discloses the fact that these countries have optimum infrastructure in space which could be compared to international level along with quality. Therefore this research study would focus more on these Asian countries in chapter IV.

However, the IAF cultivated space law as a part of its other programmes whereas the International Institute of Space Law (IISL)[133] dedicated for the development of space law since beginning. This organisation name speaks for itself. It has been established in the year of 1960. But the legal framework for astronautics has been started in 3rd IAF Congress during 1952. The comprehensive study of space law problems by an official body of the IAF was proposed by Haley in 1954. But it was in the discussion stage for some time. In 1956 during the 7th IAC in Rome, there was presentation and discussion of two basic papers on space law – one by Haley and another by Aldo Armando Cocca of Argentina. In 1957, the 8th IAC took the formal step to study space law. The decision was taken within few hours of the launching of *Sputnik* I. Later on Haley started the world tour through his lectures to build up consciousness about space law. The problem was basically the jurisdiction of air space and outer space.[134]

The other contribution in IAC on behalf of IISL is the Colloquium on the Law of Outer Space as shown in **Table 2**. It is hosted by IISL each and every year which is most effective at present to develop space law keeping pace with space technology. It was an integral part of the 9th IAF Congress in The Hague. The Hague Colloquium was basically an anticipation of the discussions in the UN Ad hoc Committee on the Peaceful Uses of Outer Space in 1959. A permanent Legal Committee was established in this Colloquium to make a draft proposal for an international agreement on space legal problems. A resolution was also passed in the IAF to communicate the Secretary-General of UN that the IAF would cooperate in any matter with UN in the field of astronautics. There were many leading jurists in this committee.[135]

The next year 10th IAF Congress in London replaced this Committee by a new organisation, International Institute of Space Law (IISL). The working groups were constituted in 1960 and their services were offered to the UNCOPUOS which was established in 1959. The Institute's activities besides the annual colloquium are Manfred Lachs Moot Court Competition for students interested to pursue space law study and research, cooperation with UN, the teaching of space law throughout the world and publications of the Institute and disclosing information of space law through its website.[136]

The last but not the least is the International Law Association (ILA)[137]. It is the oldest organisation for the development of international law and was established in 1873.[138] It has different committees. The Committee for space law was made in 1959 under the chairmanship of C. Wilfred Jenks. The committee first submitted its report on many topics of space law in 1963.[139] Since 1990, the space law committee has a permanent observer status in COPUOS and its two subcommittees. Also the report is sent annually to the COPUOS.[140]

The space law committee works permanently between the biennial conferences of ILA. It always keeps in touch with the other committees in ILA such that international law and comparative law are at the very root of law of outer space. ILA takes part in cooperation activities with public and private international organisations like the Permanent Court of Arbitration on the drafting of rules for dispute settlement procedures in international space law. ILA has contacts with a number of national space agencies in both industrialised and developing countries. Within the COPUOS, this Committee participates in United Nations experts' meetings on promoting education in space law. Also, it takes active participation in the work of the IISL, IAA and the European Centre for Space Law (ECSL) and the Ibero-American Institute of Air and Space Law.[141] During 2012 biennial conference at Sofia (Bulgaria), this Committee passed the resolution on considering the legal aspects of privatisation and commercialisation of space activities. The resolution recommended a model law on national space legislation.[142]

Conclusion

History of space regulation did not originate without science following technology. More specifically, the philosophers, scientists and other different experts having well-versed knowledge on the different aspects of celestial bodies first put their untiring, indomitable spirit to explore the mystery of the unknown cosmos. It took too long period to prove and establish a simple fact because of the society and its consciousness about the scientific development. Some great scholars already explored few celestial incidents much before the societal consciousness came into existence. Their works came into light later on.

Another problem related with different geographical locations. The epicentre of scientific and technological development was shifted from one geographic location to another due to different reasons like world wars. Historically speaking, the western countries got the opportunity finally to keep this momentum of development in right direction.

In case of India, it was once very strong in astronomy but later on deflected from its top position. One of the reasons was rise of many western scholars in astronomy compared to India. Additionally, the flavour of colonialism imposed by the British rulers affected the progress of development of general science and technology including astronomy in India. The country revived its old glory since post-independence period.

The knowledge of astronomical developments reflected on the progress of space technology, i.e. astronautics. The real development of rocket technology, a part of astronautics, took place during the World War period especially World War II. There were parallel developments in both the fields – Intercontinental Ballistic Missiles (ICBMs) and rockets for spaceflight. Some group of scientists like Von Braun, Goddard was in favour of utilising the rocket technology for space flight from the very beginning of their research on rockets. They preferred to fulfill the long cherished dream of human beings to reach the outer space.

Their initiative got additional favour through a totally different scientific programme i.e. International Geophysical Year (IGY). The manufacturing rockets followed by satellites got priority to satisfy the scientific purpose of IGY during 1957-58. There was legal controversy over IGY programme because the satellites would break the traditional norm of sovereignty over airspace on orbiting the Earth.

The above controversy was fueled up when IGY programme gave birth of the Sputnik era with the launch of 'sputnik' on October 4, 1957. The scholars from legal and non-legal background started to write extensively about the limits of airspace or legal boundary between airspace and outer space. Additionally, the United Nations along with other organisations started to think warfare of different kinds in outer space with the commencement of this new era. The reason was that this historic incident took place in the aftermath of World War II. The UN thought that the space race would endanger the situation of cold war that was going on between the two superpowers in space—the then USSR and the United States. Accordingly the UN formed the regulations for space activities that were adopted through different treaties, declarations and principles.

Later on with expanded activities related with outer space, there were so many organisations outside UN framework like IAA, IAF, IISL and ILA who also felt the legal need to regulate outer space activities. They followed UN in this regard. These organisations are mainly non-governmental organisations. Moreover there were participations from private actors for the activities within these organisations. The expanded activities were shared by these actors along with states. The ultimate effect was privatisation to increase the commercial revenue of state.

The changing scenario was also reflected in the programme of UN. The message from the last United Nations Conference on Peaceful Uses of Outer Space, 1999 (UNISPACE III) mentioned the role of private actors in developing the space technology. Moreover, the resolution adopted during 2012 ILA Biennial Conference had once again acknowledged their importance.

There are few queries coming up from this acknowledgement. Like where and how many private actors for outer space activities are stepped in and functioned nationally or internationally? How much their potential would be as compared to state actors? What are their commercial interests at present or in the near future? This research study would like to make an attempt to seek the answers of these queries in the next chapter.

Notes

1. Sarma, Nataraja, *India – A Hub of Ancient Astronomy,* In J.V. Narlikar (Ed.), *Science in India* (New Delhi: Viva Books, 2009), p. 221.
2. Ohashi, Yukio, *The Mathematical and Observational Astronomy in Traditional India*, In J.V. Narlikar (Ed.), *Science in India* (New Delhi: Viva Books, 2009), p. 77.
3. Kay, G.R., *Hindu Astronomy Ancient Science of the Hindus* (New Delhi: Cosmo Publications, 1981), pp. 1-3, 5-6.
4. Hardin, Garrett, *Exploring New Ethics for Survival the Voyage of the Spaceship Beagle* (New York: The Viking Press, 1972), p. 22.
5. Sen, S.N., . *A Survey of Source Materials,* In D.M. Bose et al., (Eds.), *A Concise History of Science in India* (New Delhi: Indian National Science Academy, 1971), p. 16.
6. Kochhar, R. and Narlikar, J., *Astronomy in India a Perspective* (New Delhi: Indian National Science Academy, 1995), p. 1.
7. Gupta, Mohan, *Astronomical Observations in the Vedas,* In G.C. Pande (Ed.) *A Golden Chain of Civilisations: Indic, Iranic, Semitic and Hellenic up to c. 600 BC* (New Delhi: Centre for Studies in Civilizations, 2007), pp. 663-715.
8. See n. 2. pp. 4-29.
9. Thapar, Romila, *History of Science and the Oikoumene,* In S. Irfan Habib and Dhruv Raina (Eds.), *Situating the History of Science- Dialogues with Joseph Needham* (New Delhi: Oxford University Publication,1999), p. 25.
10. Sen, S.N., *Astronomy,* In D.M. Bose et al., (Eds.), *A Concise History of Science in India* (New Delhi: Indian National Science Academy, 1971), p. 92.
11. See n. 7, pp. 20-21
12. See n. 2, pp. 94-95.
13. See n. 10, pp. 25-29.
14. See n. 7, p. 98.
15. Sriram, M.S. and Ramasubramanian, K., *Contributions of Nilakantha Somayaji to the Kerala School of Astronomy,* In J.V. Narlikar (Ed.), *Science in India* (New Delhi: Viva Books, 2009), p. 180.
16. Kochhar, R. and Narlikar, J., *Astronomy in India: Past, Present & Future* (Pune: Inter-University Centre for Astronomy and Astrophysics), p. 11.
17. Ansari, S.M. Razaullah, *Reception of Indian Astronomical Treaties and Handbooks in Sanskrit by Muslim Scholars of Medieval India,* In J.V. Narlikar (Ed.), *Science in India* (New Delhi: Viva Books, 2009), p. 252.
18. Alvi, M.A. and Rahman, A., *Jahangir – The Naturalist* (New Delhi: National Institute of Sciences in India, 1968), pp. 136-140.
19. See n. 10. pp. 101-102. See also Kaye, G.R.,*The Astronomical Observatories of Jai Singh,* (Varanasi: Indological Book House, 1973), pp. 88-90.
20. See n. 15, pp. 20-33.
21. Narlikar, Jayant V. and Kochhar, Rajesh K., *Post-Independence Indian Achievements in Astronomy*, In J.V. Narlikar (Ed.), *Science in India* (New Delhi: Viva Books, 2009), pp. 287-312.

22. Ibid.
23. Ibid., pp. 35-37.
24. See n. 10. pp. 39-41. See also n. 20. Narlikar and Kochhar, 2009 p. 38-40.
25. Tata Institute of Fundamental Research at http://www.tifr.res.in/index.php/en/ (Accessed January 05, 2013).
26. Chowdhury, I. and Dasgupta, A., *A Masterful Spirit Homi J. Bhabha 1909-1966* (New Delhi: Penguin Books, 2010), p. 242.
27. Anderson, Robert S., *Building Scientific Institutions in India: Saha and Bhabha* (Montreal: Centre for Developing-Area Studies, McGill University, 1975), p. 82.
28. Indian Institute of Astrophysics at http://www.iiap.res.in/ (Accessed January 5, 2013).
29. Raman Research Institute at http://www.rri.res.in/ (Accessed January 5, 2013).
30. Physical Research Laboratory at http://www.prl.res.in/ (Accessed January 5, 2013).
31. Inter-University Centre for Astronomy and Astrophysics at http://www.iucaa.ernet.in/ (Accessed January 5, 2013).
32. Aryabhatta Research Institute for Observational Sciences at http://www.aries.res.in/ (Accessed January 5, 2013).
33. Udaipur Solar Observatory at http://www.prl.res.in/~uso/ (Accessed January 05, 2013).
34. ISRO Satellite Centre at http://www.isro.org/isrocentres/isac.aspx (Accessed January 5, 2013).
35. Ptolemy, *The Almagest*, Vol. I-V, Translated by R. Catesby Taliaferro et al., (Chicago: Encyclopedia Britannica Inc., 1952), pp. 1-4, 541-842, 845-851.
36. Emme, Eugene M., *History of Rocket Technology* (Detroit: Wayne State University Press, 1964), p. 1.
37. Alam, Ishrat, *Technology and Economic Progress in Medieval India, 2011*. In Prabhat Patnaik (Ed.), *Excursus in History Essays on Some Ideas of Irfan Habib* (New Delhi: Tulika Books), p. 196.
38. Agarwal, D.P., *Harappan Technology and Its Legacy* (New Delhi: Rupa & Co., 2009), pp. 13-15.

    In the preface of this book, Prof. M.G.K. Menon, the ex-chairman of Indian Space Research Organisation, states "India has had a long history of civilisation going back several thousand years. In the global mind this civilisation is largely associated with spiritualism, philosophy and religiosity. There is also an appreciation of great traditions that have continued today: of performing arts in dance and music; of magnificent works in architecture, sculpture, painting.... However, over the last couple of centuries the image has been significantly one of poverty: For many, it is a land of magicians and snake-charmers; of wild animals like tigers and elephants; of medicants and mystics. The image is changing today with India is moving powerfully into the knowledge economy and becoming a power to reckon with.

    For all these reasons, the overall effort relating to writing of the history of science and technology in India has been a limited and scattered effort.

    Subsequent forward note by Rajiv Malhotra in this book (p. xx) 'Amartya Sen (1997) "A similar history of India's science and technology has not been attempted, though many of the laments have been well discussed in particular studies........The need for a work like Needham's has remained unmet."
39. Raghavan, V., *Yantras or Mechanical Contrivances in Ancient India* (Bangalore: The Indian Institute of Culture, 1952) at http://www.iiwcindia.org/transactions/transaction10.pdf (Accessed July 30, 2013).

40. Ibid., See also Khanolkar, G.D., *Walchand Hirachand Man, His Times and Achievements* (Bombay: Walchand Hirachand Company Ltd., 1969), pp. 374-375.
41. Dikshitar, V.R. Ramachandra, *War in Ancient India* (Madras: Macmillan & Co. Ltd., 1994), p. 275.
42. At http://www.aryabharati.org/vimaniksas/vimaniksas.asp?ln=en&bk=01&pt=a&pg=000(Accessed July 30, 2014)
43. Sekhar, J. Chandra and Prasad, Gangadhar M. (Eds.), *Eternally Talented India 108 Facts* (Hyderabad: Vivekananda Life Skills Academy, 2008), p. 74.
44. Needham, Joseph, *The Grand Titration Science & Society in East and West* (London: George Allen & Unwin Ltd, 1969), pp. 18, 20. See also Hall, A. R., *A Note on Military Pyrotechnics, 1956*. In Charles Singer et al., (Eds.), *A History of Technology* (Oxford: Clarendon Press), vol. 2, p. 120.
45. Pendray, G. E., *The Man Who Ushered in the Space Age*, 1948. In Esther C. Goddard and G. Edward Pendray (Eds.), *Rocket Development Liquid-Fuel Rocket Research 1929-1941* (New York: Prentice Hall Inc), p. xiii; See also Brooks, Peter W, *Aeronautics, 1958*. In Charles Singer et al., (Eds.), *A History of Technology* (Oxford: Clarendon Press), vol. 5, p. 180.
46. Habib, Irfan, *Technology in Medieval India c 650-1750* (New Delhi: Tulika Books, 2008), pp. 88-90.
47. Gode, P.K., *History of Fireworks in India: between A.D. 1400 and 1900* (Bangalore: Indian Institute of Culture, 1953), pp. 12-14.
    'In search of a text I was fortunate enough in discovering a section on the manufacture of specific fireworks in a Sanskrit work called the *Kautukacintamani* by Gajapati Prataparudradeva of Orissa (A.D. 1497-1539), the reputed author of some works on *dharmasatra* like *Sarasvativilasa* etc............The list of ingredients of pyrotechnic mixtures used in India along with other accessories for the manufactured fireworks c. A.D. 1500 speaks for itself. It is possible to suggest that the Chinese formulas for the manufacture of fireworks were brought to India some time about A.D. 1400 and then modified by the use of Indian substitutes for Chinese ingredients, not all of which may have been then available in India. The main pyrotechnic ingredients like sulphur, saltpetre, charcoal, powder of iron etc. had to be retained in the Indian formulas as they were the very basis of pyrotechny; they were available in India from early times.'
48. Braun, W.V. and Ordway, F. I., *Space Travel* (New York: Thomas Y. Crowell Company, 1975), p. 5.
49. Ghosh, A., "Tipu Sultan: A Pre-British Engagement with Modern Technology," *Journal of the Asiatic Society*, vol. 49, no. 4, 2007. p. 15; See also Griffiths, J., *Spaceflight*, 1990. In Ian McNeil (Ed.), *An Encyclopedia of the History of Technology* (London: Routledge), pp. 862-863. See also Michaelis, Anthony R., *Space Technology*, 1978. In Trevor I. Williams (Ed.), *A History of Technology* (Oxford: Clarendon Press), vol. 7, no. 2, p. 859.
50. Dornberger, Walter R., *The German V-2*, 1964. In Eugene M. Emme (Ed.), *The History of Rocket Technology* (Detroit: Wayne State University Press), p. 30.
    'The history of technology proves that when the time is ripe, people are thinking about or working on the same problems in almost all civilised countries. Since the early 1920's, with the development of inexpensive, mass-produced light metals, highly efficient oxidizers which could be handled, and reliably accurate electronic equipment,

three fundamentals were available for the revival of ancient art of rocketry. So we see in 1930, private groups, inventors, and engineers in many countries were working on rocket propulsion, even designing and fusing first samples of liquid-fuelled rockets. Experimenting in the United States was Professor Robert H. Goddard, in Romania Professor Herman Oberth, in Russia Konstantan E. Ziolkovosky, in Germany Max Valier, Engineer Johannes Winkler, Rudolf Nebel, and others.'

51. Temple, William F., *The True Book about Space-Travel* (London: Frederick Muller Ltd., 1954), p. 58; See also Ley, W., *Rocket, Missiles and Men in Space* (New York: The New American Library, 1969), pp. 115-124.
52. See n. 36. p. 5.
53. See n. 45. Pendray, p. xi. See also n. 49. Michaelis, pp. 862-863.
54. At http://www.history.com/topics/world-war-i/treaty-of-versailles (Accessed March 13, 2014).
55. Haley, Andrew G., *Space Law and Government* (New York: Appleton-Century-Crofts, 1963), pp. 344-345; See also Dornberger, Walter S., *The German V-2*, 1964. In Eugene M. Emme (Ed.), *The History of Rocket Technology* (Detroit: Wayne State University Press), p. 156; Griffiths, J., *Spaceflight,1990*. In Ian McNeil (Ed.), *An Encyclopedia of the History of Technology* (London: Routledge), pp. 649-651. Also Lee, Asher & Stockwell, Richard E., *Soviet Missiles*, 1959. In Asher Lee (Ed.), *The Soviet Air and Rocket Forces* (London: Weidenfeld & Nicolson), pp. 146-153.
56. Ibid, Griffith. See also Ray Spangenburg and Diane K. Moser, *Wernher von Braun: space visionary and rocket engineer* (Hyderabad: University Press, 1999), pp. 74-82.
57. Angelo, Joseph A., *Space Technology* (New Delhi: Pentagon Press, 2009), pp. 12-13.
58. Chapman, S., *IGY: Year of Discovery* (The University of Michigan Press: Michigan, 1959), p. 11.

    'Among the ancient Greeks some philosophers taught that all things are compounded from four elements – earth, water, air and fire. In the great study of the planet earth and the sun that is known as the IGY, all four of these so-called elements were involved. The major aim of the IGY was to improve our knowledge and understanding of the earth and its rapid changes. To do this it was essential also to improve our knowledge and understanding of the sun and its changes. Thus IGY was a study of the earth and sun.'
59. Ibid., p. 12. See also Wilson, J. Tuzo, *IGY the Year of the New Moons* (London: Michael Joseph Ltd, 1961), pp. 28-34.
60. Ibid., Chapman, p. 101.
61. Ibid., pp. 101-102.
62. Ibid.
63. Ibid., pp. 104-106.
64. Ibid.
65. Ibid.
66. Ibid., See also Eisenhower, Dwight D., *The White House Years Mandate for Change 1953-1956* (London: Heinemann, 1963), p. 492; See also Marshack, Alexander, *The World of Space the Story of the International Geophysical Year* (New York: Dell Publishing Co. Inc., 1958), pp 5-10; Mitra, A.P., *Indian IGY Programme – Achievements* (New Delhi: Indian National Science Academy, 1958), p. 46.
67. Doyle, S. (Ed.), *The International Geophysical Year Initiating International Scientific Space Co-operation* (Paris: International Astronautical Federation, 2012), pp. 27-28, at http://www.iislweb.org/docs/2012_IGY.pdf (Accessed January 06, 2013).

68. Ibid.
69. Ibid.
70. Ibid.
71. Mitra, A. P., "India in Global Science: Are We Ready for it?" *Journal of the Asiatic Society*, vol. 49, no. 2, p. 9.
72. See n. 52, Griffiths. pp. 651-652.
73. Jenks, C. Wilfred, *Space Law* (London: Stevens & Sons, 1965), p. 39.
74. Hingorani, R.C. (Ed.), *International Law through United Nations* (Bombay: N.M. Tripathy Pvt. Ltd., 1972), p. 172.
75. See n.51, Ley. p. 547.
76. Doyle, Stephen E., *Origins of International Space Law and the International Institute of Space Law of the International Astronautical Federation* (San Diego: Univelt, 2002), pp.1-5, at http://www.iislweb.org/docs/Origins_International_Space_Law.pdf (Accessed January 6, 2013).
77. Kopal, V., *The Life and Work of Professor Vladimir Mandl—A Pioneer of Space Law, 2011*. In Corinne M. Contant Jorgenson (Ed.), *Proceedings of the 53rd Colloquium on the Law of Outer Space* (Washington: American Institute of Aeronautics and Astronautics), pp. 18-20.
78. See n. 73.
79. Korovin, E., *International Status of Cosmic Space* (Moscow: International Affairs, 1958), p. 55.
80. See n. 67. pp. 31-32, 46. See also Lyall, F. and Larsen, Paul B., *Space Law: A Treatise*, (Surrey (England): Ashgate, 2009), pp. 5-6.
81. Ibid. Doyle. pp. 32-34.
82. Cooper, J. C., "The Russian Satellite- Legal and Political Problems," *The Journal of Air Law and Commerce*, vol. 24, no.4, 1957, p. 383.
83. Galloway, Eilene, *The Community of Law and Science, 1959*. In Andrew G. Halley and W.H. Hanover (Eds.), *First Colloquium on the Law of Outer Space The Hague 1958 Proceedings* (Vienna: Springer-Verlag), p. 123.
'In 1946 Arthur C. Clarke wrote "The Challenge of the Spaceship", he counseled that "Morals and ethics must not lag behind science, otherwise the social system will breed poison which will cause its own destructions."
84. See n. 80, Lyall and Larsen, p. 8.
85. See n. 55, Haley.
86. Hingorani, R. C., "An Attempt to Determine Sovereignty in Upper Space," *Kansas City Law Review*, vol. 26, no. 1,1957, pp. 5-12.
87. General Assembly Resolution 1148 (XII) of November 14, 1957, para I (f).
88. See n. 73, pp. 219-224.
89. General Assembly Resolution 1348 (XII) of December 13, 1958.
90. Ibid.
91. McDougall, Walter A., *The Heavens and the Earth: A Political History of the Space Age* (New York: Basic Books Inc.,1985), pp. 41-62.
92. Hobe, S., *Historical Background*, 2009. In Stephen Hobe et al., (Eds.), *Cologne Commentary on Space Law* (Cologne: Carl Heymanns Verlag), vol. 1, pp. 3-4.
93. UNGA Resolution 1348 (XIII) on December 13, 1958.
94. See n. 55, Haley. pp. 313-317.
95. Ibid.

96. Ibid.
97. http://www.oosa.unvienna.org/oosa/SpaceLaw/gares/html/gares_14_1472.html (Accessed January 15, 2013).
98. UNGA Resolution 1721 on December 20, 1961.
99. United Nations Office of Outer Space Affairs, at http://www.oosa.unvienna.org/ (Accessed January 15, 2013).
100. http://www.oosa.unvienna.org/oosa/en/COPUOS/cop_overview.html (Accessed January 15, 2013).
101. UNGA Res 1962 (XVIII), Dec 13, 1963.
102. UNGA Resolution 1962 (XVIII) of December 13, 1963 provides that not to station in outer space any objects carrying nuclear weapons or other kinds of weapons of mass destruction not only by the Soviet Union and the United States but also by other states.
103. See n. 92, Hobe. p. 12.
104. Ibid.
105. Cheng, Bin, *Studies in International Space Law* (Oxford: Clarendon Press, 1997), p. 217.

    'The 1967 Treaty is the first and doubtless also the most important of these five treaties. The impetus behind the conclusion of this treaty was the successful 'soft' landing by the Soviet Union of its automatic station Luna IX on the moon on February 3, 1966, after three failures the previous year. Speaking from his ranch in Texas on 7 May 1966, President Johnson announced that the United States, which had hitherto opposed the development of international space law through treaties, would seek a treaty through the United Nations to prevent any nation from claiming sovereignty over the moon or any other celestial bodies and that the exploration thereof would be for peaceful purposes only.'
106. UN Doc A/6352 (June 16, 1966).
107. See Working Group Paper L.1 to L.9.
108. UNGA Res 2222 (XXI) (December 19, 1966) 'Treaty on Principles Governing the Activities of States in the Exploration and Use of Outer Space, Including the Moon and Other Celestial Bodies'.
109. See n. 49. Michaelis, p. 855.
110. See n. 99, *Travaux preparatories* of Rescue Agreement.
111. http://www.oosa.unvienna.org/oosa/en/SpaceLaw/treaties.html (Accessed January 15, 2013).
112. Status of International Agreement Relating to Activities in Outer Space as on January 1, 2012, at http://www.oosa.unvienna.org/oosa/en/SpaceLaw/treatystatus/index.html (Accessed January 15, 2013).
113. http://treaties.un.org/pages/ViewDetailsIII.aspx?&src=TREATY&mtdsg_no=XXIV~1 &chapter=24&Temp=mtdsg3&lang=en (Accessed November 28, 2013).
114. http://treaties.un.org/pages/ViewDetailsIII.aspx?&src=TREATY&mtdsg_no=XXIV~1 &chapter=24&Temp=mtdsg3&lang=en (Accessed November 2013).
115. UN Document A/AC.105/C.2/2012/CRP.3
116. http://disarmament.un.org/treaties/t/moon (Accessed November 28, 2013).
117. Principles Governing the Use by States of Artificial Earth Satellites for International Direct Television Broadcasting, AT http://www.oosa.unvienna.org/oosa/en/SpaceLaw/gares/html/gares_37_0092.html (Accessed January 20, 2013).
118. Principles Relating to Remote Sensing of the Earth from Outer Space, at http://www.

oosa.unvienna.org/oosa/en/SpaceLaw/gares/html/gares_41_0065.html (Accessed January 20, 2013).

119. Principles Relevant to the Use of Nuclear Power Sources in Outer Space, at http://www.oosa.unvienna.org/oosa/en/SpaceLaw/gares/html/gares_47_0068.html (Accessed January 20, 2013).
120. Declaration on International Cooperation in the Exploration and Use of Outer Space for the Benefit and in the Interest of All States, Taking into Particular Account the Needs of Developing Countries, at http://www.oosa.unvienna.org/oosa/en/SpaceLaw/gares/html/gares_51_0122.html (Accessed January 20, 2013).
121. http://www.un.org/events/unispace3/ (Accessed January 20, 2013).
122. Ibid.
123. http://www.oosa.unvienna.org/oosa/en/COPUOS/members.html (Accessed January 20, 2013).
124. International Academy of Astronautics, at http://iaaweb.org/content/view/154/270/ (Accessed January 22, 2013). See also 25 IAA / IISL Scientific-Legal Roundtables at International Astronautical Congresses http://www.iislweb.org/docs/25years%20IAA_IISL%20Roundtable.pdf (Accessed January 22, 2013)
125. Ibid.
126. 60 Years of the International Astronautical Congress, at http://www.iafastro.com/index.php/about/history/iaf-60th-anniversary (Accessed January 22, 2013).
127. See n. 55, Haley pp. 354-361.
128. See n. 55, Haley.
129. See n. 55, Haley; Also see n. 76, pp. 23-40. See n. 80, Lyall & Larsen.
130. See n. 55, Haley.
131. See n. 71, Lyall & Larsen.
132. http://www.iafastro.org/events/iac/past-iacs/ (Accessed October 15, 2013)
133. International Institute of Space Law. http://www.iislweb.org/ (Accessed January 25, 2013).
134. See n. 52. Haley.
135. Ibid.
136. Ibid.
137. International Law Association. http://www.ila-hq.org/ (Accessed January 25, 2013).
138. Ibid.
139. See n. 55. Haley.
140. A/AC.105/C.2/103. p.2 file:///C:/Users/DELL/Downloads/ila_report_for_copuos_8-19_april_2013_v1.pdf (Accessed February 05, 2013).
141. UN Document A/AC.105/C.2/100.
142. Resolution No. 6/2012. http://www.ila-hq.org/en/committees/draft-committee-reports-sofia-2012.cfm (Accessed January 25, 2013).

II. Private Actors in Outer Space

Introduction

The history of space regulation enlightened that the UN showed interest to develop some kind of soft regulation after launching of Sputnik because states were the main actors in outer space. This scenario gradually has changed especially in the countries already tagged as space super powers or group II countries in IGY. These super powers have started the commercialisation of space to increase its return on investment. To satisfy this purpose, many private initiatives have been welcomed. The UN through UNISPACE III and the non-governmental organisations like ILA have recognised their role.

But these private actors have lacked the legal infrastructure within the existing state-centric regime of international space law. At the first instance, the meaning of non-governmental space activities is not stated in the Outer Space Treaty itself. Therefore the legal meaning of 'private actors in outer space' is to be examined first. Then there is descriptive analysis of private actors in different sectors of space activities along with Indian scenario to know why, how and where such actors diffuse the state-centric domain. It further facilitates to get details about their numbers that are exponentially increased in different sectors of space activities; because these increasing figures demand their international legal regulation ultimately. Some legal issues come up by default during this analysis. These are only mentioned here to examine critically in the next chapter.

Meaning of Private Actors in Outer Space

It is mentioned in the introduction of this research study that the space activities were fully state-centric. The text of international space law treaties follows this trend; because the period when such treaties were established, none but states were the only actors in outer space. The factors behind it were high cost and complex technologies of space development. These two key factors were beyond reach for any actors besides state. In short, the state during this period played the role of single actor and regulator in space activities. But the scenario has been changed gradually. The role of state as actors has been slowly diminished.[1] The reason follows that the private actors like national and multinational firms having advanced technology take initiative to launch their privately built instruments into outer space. Their purpose would be to gather economic benefits from the potential yields of outer space. This is called commercialisation of space.[2] The other explanation of this development is that free enterprise does not exist in the long run where there is no possibility of profit.[3]

Howsoever, these private actors are mainly incorporated as companies – the national companies. They are subject to national laws of the country of their registration. Their structure is sometimes complicated.[4] Example—the state becomes the major shareholder like French national space agency CNES holds major share in French private launching company 'Arianespace'.[5] The government control exists by default in such companies.

The complicacy may be further extended on interpreting the word 'privatisation' - a product of 1980s. This word introduced in 1983 only into the pages of a standard dictionary.[6] Its most simple and ordinary interpretation is the transfer of ownership from public to private sectors. But its critical interpretation adds liberalisation coming through privatisation. Therefore the process of privatisation may or may not be involved with liberalisation. One example is that private monopoly could exist in a country when the ownership of a public entity was transferred to private entity. In case of telecommunication industries, a part of space industry, there exist different types of privatisation. One type is private sectors' participation without privatisation or liberalisation as in the case of the Peoples' Republic of China and Saudi Arabia. The other type is liberalisation without privatisation in Finland e.g. Telecom Finland is cent percent state owned.[7]

Alongside this analysis, space activities having commercial interest are not distinctly separated from those having public interest. It is not easy to differentiate clearly between the functions of the private and public (state) sectors. Some enterprises perform dual role like performing public service but free to provide commercial operations. The private enterprises in commercial space activities may depend on the public (state) sectors like hiring of launchers, leasing of communication channels etc. In reverse way, the public sector may depend on the private sector for the supply of technology and equipment according to commercial contract between them.[8]

It is sanguine from above that the private actors in outer space may co-exist with state actors within the regulation of later or the case may be vice-versa. Their inter-dependency with each other varies from one country to another. The state policy mainly decides it. Now it is time to look forward how the space law treaties would react against this changing scenario? The answer is most probably laid down in Article VI of the Outer Space Treaty. The relevant portion of this Article states

> "states are internationally responsible for national activities in outer space, including the Moon and other celestial bodies, whether such activities are carried on by governmental agencies or by non-governmental agencies........The activities of the non-governmental entities in outer space, including the Moon and other celestial bodies, shall require authorisation and continuing supervision by the appropriate State Party to the Treaty........"

This is the only provision where the existing state-centric space law treaties find some place or justification for actors in outer space not to be from governments. The *travux preparatoires* of this Treaty stated that it was the Soviet who wanted to restrict the space activities to states only excluding private entities. But USA was interested to extend the provision of the Treaty to private entities. Therefore, Article VI was drafted after long drawn negotiation.[9]

There are other aspects which provide that the textual and historical construction of this Article in conjunction with its other Articles. All these allow us to speak not about a principle of 'free private enterprise'. It is about the indirect recognition of a state's right to permit space activity as an exception by non-governmental legal entities. There are two conditions attached with this exception: (i) the state bears international responsibility for their activity, and (ii) the state authorises and constantly supervises this activity which ensures that it conforms to the provisions of the Space Treaty.[10] But the forms of authorisation and supervision are not specified. Even no condition is prescribed for this authorisation though state indirectly supervises the activity.

It may be better explained if the Outer Space Treaty is compared with the Law of the Sea Convention. Both regime deals the area like outer space and high seas which belongs to Common Heritage of Mankind. Unlikely, the Law of the Sea Convention prescribes some internationally recognised principles to be followed by states engaged in deep sea-bed mining that is outside national jurisdiction of a state. It is also to be noted from Article VI that 'non-governmental entities' are not defined. It is assumed that the private companies are included here.[11]

All the confusions and anomalies rose in explaining the words 'private actors in outer space' are caused by absence of proper provision in the space law treaties. This is due to lack of consciousness about the futuristic use of outer space by actors besides states.

Different Private Actors

The implication of 'private actors in outer space' is cleared from above. But it is to be analysed now by example taking from so many corporate to small and medium size private space companies even start-ups—first outside India and then from India. This analysis reflects how the private actors in current period take the entry into different domain of space activities like satellite manufacturing, space-craft launching, space tourism etc. It further guides this research study to know the number of private actors in some particular domain. Moreover, it discloses whether this number is created by big corporate or by small start-ups.

There may be the cases that a country like USA is pioneering in a particular domain whereas private actors from other European countries or Asian countries may be interested in other domains. At the outset the interest depends on capacity building of a particular country in three directions—technical, financial and human resources, out of which the last two are analysed in chapter IV (outside India) and V (on India). The first one is beyond the scope of this study.

Therefore the same type of regulation may not be observed or required in these two chapters. In this context, it is not the space activities only but the regulations have been developed in other non-space sectors depending on the concentration as well as legal complexities caused by private actors in those sectors. The concerned institutions or organisations established by the private actors came up to tackle this complexities that are explained in chapter IV and V. In other way, the establishment of institutions or organisations related with specific space sector reaffirms the concentration of private actors in a particular domain of space activities.

The last but not the least, the investment of private actors in a particular sector of space activity confirms that such actors would like to take the leading role on competition with the state actors. So the following analysis on private actors may provide a trend of their activities not only in present time but also in future. Moreover, it tries to demarcate pure state-centric domain, public-private centric domain and purely private domain. In this regard, there is annual report for Satellite Industry Association (SIA) as prepared by Futron Corporation of USA. It was reported how the private bodies have dominated the space markets. India ranked 6th according to its report as a stakeholder in the industry.[12]

With this above analytical background, the few areas that have been developed or are very promising ones are satellite manufacturing, satellite launch services, space tourism, commercial orbital transport systems (COTS), mining of celestial bodies, private space stations, space robotics, space debris removal, commercial remote sensing satellite imageries, satellite communication and broadcasting, solar energy from space etc. Some fall under other or multiple categories also.

Every industry is opened first with manufacturing unit. Thus satellite manufacturing is the major sector. Just like other manufacturing definitions, satellite manufacturing means manufacturing parts, components and subsystems of satellites also. The major actors are depicted below:-

Table 3: Countries & Major Actors in Satellite Manufacturing[13]

Countries	Actors	Beginning Year	Activities
USA	Boeing Defence, Space, Security Ltd.	2002	Boeing 601 best-selling satellite model since 1987.
As above	Lockheed Martin	1995	More than 900 satellites built.
Europe & India	Astrium Satellites (Now Airbus Defence & Space)	2006 (Astriun) 2014 (Airbus)	(i) All SPOT series satellites manufactured for CNES. (ii) Galileo.

Russia	Joint-Stock Company 'Information Satellite Systems Reshetnev Company'	2008	Built $2/3^{rd}$ of Russia's Orbital Constellation.
Germany	OHB System	1980s (space division started)	From sub-system of satellites to leading satellite producers.
Europe (France, Italy, Belgium, Spain) & USA	Thales Alenia Space	2007	Produced more than 100 satellites.

The American company Boeing Ltd. is an aerospace giant from the very beginning but its space unit Boeing Defence, Space & Security Ltd.[14] has come into existence later as shown in the above Table. The Company built different types of spacecraft from the very beginning. Its offices, activities and products exist all over the world.[15] This company has significant business impact in India through Boeing (India) Ltd. that is further explained in chapter V. In spite of being an American company, its products are popularly accepted like a domestic company in the respective countries. Therefore, the presence of Boeing for a long time all over the world indicates that satellite manufacturing is a very lucrative area for private actors. Lockheed Martin[16] is another American giant to add in this list. This company has also a great demand from the international space market.[17]

Table 3 mentions that Astrium Satellites have now been changed as Airbus, Defence & Space.[18] The earlier one, Astrium was the first European company in the manufacturing of a spacecraft.[19] It has branches all over the world on capturing the market for 40 years.[20] The company built many European satellites besides the multi-mission SPOT satellites.[21] All five SPOT satellites (from SPOT-1 to SPOT-5) were built under the prime contractorship of Astrium.[22] The SPOT 6 was launched in 2012[23] and subsequently, SPOT 7 in 2014[24] by Indian Space Research Organisation (ISRO). It is observed that the Company built the sensitive satellites like SPOT for CNES. This example signifies that state activities are performed by the private actors. It is one kind of backdoor privatisation in governmental agencies like CNES. There is another example from Astrium UK that is prime contractor for manufacturing satellites for European Space Agency (ESA).[25]

Sometimes this Company builds satellites for another private actor. In case of the telecommunication satellite HYLAS 1, UK telecommunication company Avanti Communications Plc. is the customer of Astrium Satellite. The ISRO is also a partner with EADS Astrium in this case.[26] Here ISRO builds up public-private partnership. The three satellites for British telecommunication company *Inmarsat*[27] were built with Astrium as the prime contractor.[28] In the Helios programme, Europe's first military optical reconnaissance system, the French Ministry of Defence procurement agency DGA and the CNES, selected Astrium as prime contractor for the satellites.[29] This proved that government entrusted on private actors for sensitive space projects of the country. Lastly Astrium built Galileo, the European satellite navigation system.[30] The last two examples – Helios and Galileo confirm that this company seats in the key areas of national as well as international space projects. It proves that private actors have penetrated deeply in global space market on producing the equivalent work or sometimes better than the state actors.

Besides the contributions from individual companies, there is a joint venture between two private actors from **Table 3** like the JSC Information[31] from Russia and Thales Alenia[32] from Europe in 2011 for Russian telecommunication satellites. The future target of this joint venture is to develop the new products of satellite for Russian as well as international market.[33] So the private actors from different countries work together for capturing big markets. The alternative argument may exist here. The infrastructure of maximum companies could not be equivalent to that of a state to manufacture a satellite. So for effective privatisation of the major domain of space activity i.e. satellite manufacturing, there are joint ventures, mergers between private companies. The case of OHB System[34] was interesting because how a German company changed its status from manufacturing sub-systems of satellites to produce a whole unit of satellite. It is an example of increasing dominance of comparatively small private actors in large unit of space activities i.e. satellite manufacturing. The small and medium companies follow the corporate giants in this sector. The following Table reflects it.

Table 4: Countries & Small/Medium Actors in Satellite Manufacturing[35]

Countries	Actors	Beginning Year	Activities
UK & USA	Surrey Satellite Technology Limited (SSTL)	1985 (UK) 2008 (USA)	From University to a commercial company.
USA	Generation Orbit Launch Services Inc.	2011	Dominating micro and nano satellites.
Japan	Mitsubishi Heavy Industries Limited	1964	Developed KIBO, Japanese experimental model in ISS.
As above	IHI Corporation	2000	Developed engine in Cygnus spacecraft launched to ISS.
Netherlands	Dutch Space	2002	Prime contractor of robotic arm which was the major European contribution to the ISS.
Russia	RSC Energia	1946	Producer of Sputnik 1.
Argentina	INVAP	1976	Only Latin American company certified by NASA.

The case of Surrey Satellite Technology Limited (SSTL)[36], a private company based in UK could be cited differently from others in **Table 4**. It is a best example of contribution of academia into industry. An inspiring story about establishment of a private space company was cooked in the laboratory of a British University. Perhaps the requirement of some University Acts of India to get the services from Indian services in chapter V may be followed from the example of University of Surrey which started such initiative: the first of its kind. SSTL was established in 1985 to transfer the result from research for building a commercial enterprise. But the situation is totally different now. The 99 per cent of share is owned by Astrium BV and only 1 per cent by the University.[37] The further achievement is to acquire 40 per cent of the global small satellite market since it was purchased by Airbus Defence and Space (formerly EADS-Astrium).[38] A foreign branch ultimately opened in USA. This branch will manufacture its own spacecraft and system for the US market within few years.[39] The SSTL has paved way how an academic institution like University became a popular industry stake holder in space commerce.

The Mitsubishi Heavy Industries Limited (MHI)[40] is a unique case in **Table 4** not only from Japan but also from Asia. The commercial profile in space was raised since 2011 when it was merely a commercial supplier of the above Boeing Ltd. Now it became the prime contractor of JAXA, national space agency of Japan, over the years in manufacturing different satellite units.[41] The contribution of this company is such that it has impact on developing space related regulation in Japan to be analysed in chapter IV. Here it is observed that JAXA being a state actor depends on the biggest private actor MHI in Japan. The implication is that state is willing to build-up private space industry and so it became the prime customer by default at the beginning. The journey of IHI Corporation[42] in **Table 4** started towards space business on establishing IHI Aerospace Co. Ltd. but till now it confines within manufacturing satellite engines.[43]

Out of others in **Table 4** like Generation Orbit Launch Services Inc.[44], Dutch Space[45], and INVAP,[46] the RSC Energia[47] has a golden history in Russia. It became a corporation now on changing its status from an old state actor. The manufacturing of *Sputnik 1* was its output at the beginning. Now it manufactures highest level of complex scientific and engineering parts of satellite.[48] Russia was once totally dead against the private space activities during the drafting of Outer Space Treaty shown in the previous chapter.[49] But emergence and present status of this company now prove the changed scenario of the same country.

The satellite manufacturing is full of private actors from big one like Boeing to small one INVAP as enlisted in **Table 3** and **4**. In this view, space manufacturing industry dominated by private actors is a positive indication of self-reliant private industry in any country. The data from the Tables indicate that the private dominance is in USA followed by Europe whereas Japan is almost the lone survivor from Asia. In case of India, it is the Hindustan Aeronautics Ltd. (HAL) that is a government company.[50] But whatever is their size and place of business, IPR safeguard is required at the first instance by default.

The manufacturing of satellites speeds up the same towards outer space through launching services that is known as satellite launching. Their list is following.

Table 5: Countries & Actors in Satellite Launching[51]

Countries	Actors	Beginning Year	Activities
France	Arianespace	1980	First totally independent international infrastructure in launching being a French company.
Russia	Eurockot Launch Services	1995	Major contribution to develop launching facility at Pelestick, the first spaceport within Russian territory.
As above	International Launch Services	1995	Launched Intelsat 23 satellite in 2012. Provide services to ESA, Europe & Africa.
As above	ISC Kosmotras	1997	Customers are international i.e. from state space agencies and other private actors from Europe, Asia & Africa.
Switzerland	Sea Launch AG	1995	Increased capacity of payloads with reducing launch costs as launching from equatorial area in the sea.
Euro-Russian Organisation	Starsem	1996	Mixture of big private actors like Astrium, Arianespace & Russian Federal Space Agency.

Arianespace[52], a French company, is the first and foremost name from **Table 5** in the launch services provided by private actor. It discloses from the website of the company that not only the private actors but also maximum national space agencies have preferred launching by Arianespace. ISRO has launched so many satellites especially the heavier one through Arianespace.[53] The shareholders of this company are scientific, technical, financial and political entities from 10 different European countries including some national space agencies. CNES, the French space agency, is the major shareholders in Arianespace.[54] In 2003, Arianespace joined with Boeing Launch Services and Mitsubishi Heavy Industries (MHI) to create the Launch Services Alliance. The purpose was to provide customers with flexible, reliable and on-time delivery to orbit. This alliance is one of the best examples of conglomeration of multinational corporate. The recognition of this company goes beyond the country when France, the country of its incorporation, granted independent launch operator status to Arianespace through French Law on Space Operation specifically made for this purpose in 2010.[55] This incidence is nothing but a historic win of private-centric era over the age-long traditional state-centric era in launching sector.

The other private launching companies stand nowhere in comparison with Arianespace's performances. Others are only coming up in **Table 5**. Out of them, Eurockot Launch Services[56] was attached later with the EADS to get patronage. There are two parent companies behind the scenario – one Khrunichev Space Centre and EADS. Both Eurockot and EADS invested a large amount at Plesetsk Cosmodrome[57] in Russia (to be the first in Russian territory) for developing the launch services.[58] Eurockot has customer like ESA.[59] This Company exemplifies that there are patronages from big companies to comparatively small one. The presumption is that the former would like to survive from the fierce competition on patronising the later. The other interesting observation is that after satellite manufacturing by RSC Energia,[60] a corporation in Russia, the country again entrusted on private actor in launching industry to develop their first spaceport at the historic place Plesetsk[61].

The case of International Launch Services[62] (ILS) is different in the context of shareholding. Khrunichev, the Russian government company, became the majority shareholder of ILS.[63] This type of privatisation has already been observed in case of Arianespace.

ISC Kosmotras[64] is International Space Company Kosmotras under Russian Law. The customers are not only state space agencies but commercial companies from different parts of the world. It launched satellites like NIGERSAT-2 and X (2011) for Nigeria, CRYOSAT -2 for ESA (2010), DUBAISAT-1 (2009) for UAE, THEOS for France (2007), OICETS, INDEX for Japan (2005) and TIUNGSAT-1 for Malaysia (2000).[65] Its customer profile reflects that the company launched satellites from all over the world. Though the company is formed under domestic law but the services are much international of its kind. The activity is domestic but impact is international. So this case may be an indication why international legal regulation is required for a Russian private actor.

The service of Sea Launch AG[66] of **Table 5** has reduced launch costs because of its mobile sea platform on the equator.[67] Due to this speciality in launching procedure, there are four major subcontractors of Sea launch – Energia Logistics United States, Energia Logistics Russian Federation, S.P. Korolev Rocket and Space Corporation and lastly, Boeing Commercial Space Company.[68] The low profile Sea Launch AG hires the service of comparatively high profile space companies to provide comprehensive service finally to its customers. It could be said that interdependency amongst different private actors is the corporate mantra of survival of low profile actors.

Strasem[69] is special of its kind because of mixture of corporate and national space agency simultaneously to increase the volume of business. So the European-Russian Organisation has put effort to transform this Soyuz rocket company for international sales of launch vehicles.[70] Therefore such privatisation encourages private actors through the infrastructure developed by state.

It is seen that Arianespace has paved way of privatisation to its extreme but the other companies of **Table 5** are developing within their small infrastructure. Their customers are state space agencies. But sometimes it is a mix-up between state and other private companies. Also there are mergers of companies. The satellite launching is directly linked with the liability issue in case of any failure or default in launching that causes injury to the human beings or the surrounding environments. Moreover, it attracts safety issue at the ground level. These issues are concerned with launching by default.

When the satellite launching is commercially viable, then transportation to the orbits like International Space Station (ISS) has been started by the private commercial actors. This incidence of Commercial Orbital Transportation Services (COTS) have already been referred in the introduction of this research study. Unlikely the above two sectors of space activities, COTS are yet to develop but there are few companies that performed in reality at present. The following Table has the list of these companies.

Table 6: Countries & Actors in COTS[71]

Countries	Actors	Beginning Year	Activities
USA	Space X	2002	First cargo transport to ISS in 2012 and after.
USA	Orbital Science Corporation	1982	Cygnus spacecraft sent to ISS for transporting cargo in 2012.
Isle of Man (UK)	Excalibur Almaz	2005	Proposed for transportation of human & cargo to LEO & other places in outer space.
USA	XCOR Aerospace	1999	Strong lobbyist for amending the Commercial Space Launch Act in 2004.

In **Table 6**, Space X (Space Exploration Technologies Corporation)[72] is now the most leading commercial transport company since 2012 when its Dragon spacecraft delivered cargo to the ISS according to its contract with NASA. It is to be noted here that NASA itself has no transportation system for ISS and the disaster of Columbia has practically forced the national space agency for planning alternative solution to carry astronauts or cargo transportation for ISS.[73] So, it is under contract with Space X to shift its risk or burden to a most promising private actor in the national space industry. This company has further planned to carry crew in another agreement with NASA. Besides the NASA missions, Space X is developing its rocket Falcon for heavy launch so that it could enter into the commercial launching market.[74] Unlike Arianespace, Space X is pioneer of private actors that really performs in outer space. The march to be self-reliant in its overall space activities is followed on developing its own commercial launcher. It presumes that Space X would carry bigger responsibility in future days on behalf of all private actors in USA. This responsibility could be sometimes more than that of a state.

Orbital Science Corporation (OSC)[75] is next in order of **Table 6** that had also achievement in COTS delivering cargo to ISS according to contract with NASA.[76] This company is a close competitor of Space X. These two companies are till now in this sector that have already performed the service contract from NASA. The rest of **Table 6** are in process of COTS.

Excalibur Almaz[77] (EA) is an international commercial space transport company based in the Isle of Man that is heaven of private space companies. This place is set for facilitating private space companies to be explained in chapter IV of this study.[78] XCOR Aerospace[79] was one of the leading voices for the Commercial Space Launch Amendments Act of 2004 to be analysed in chapter IV.[80] Just like other transport companies on earth, the liability will be imposed if the companies of **Table 6** fail to transport the space objects to the specific destination (orbit) within the scheduled time period. Also, the issue of safety comes into play especially to human spaceflight.

It is observed from above that launching industry is well developed to place the satellite in the required orbit. Moreover, the era of COTS has been enriched with different private actors. Now some private companies make plan to extend this entire technological prowess for commercial entertainment in zero gravity environment of outer space like tourism in outer space called space tourism.

Table 7: Countries & Actors in Space Tourism[81]

Countries	Actors	Beginning Year	Activities
USA	Virgin Galactic	1999	Almost ready for sub-orbital tourism flights in the coming year.
As above	Space Adventures	1998	Dennis Tito, the first private space tourist in 2001.
Sweden	Spaceport Sweden	2007	Extension of Virgin Galactic in Europe.
UK	ShipinSpace Ltd.	2013	Proposed ticketing price less than Virgin Galactic.

Virgin Galactic Ltd.[82] is the most authentic company from **Table 7** till now which made for space tourism though it faced a fatal accident recently. This incident may badly impact the future progress of its schedule.[83] The Company has started to develop spaceport in the southern part of New Mexico and the new name of this place became *Spaceport America.* This is the first private spaceport in the world.[84] It discloses a fact that the innovation in space activities like space tourism has expanded the other activities ancillary to the main activity of private actors. Here it is developing a private spaceport that is really a need of the hour. In brief, this company gets credit to accept the challenge in state-centric space era and has totally adventured space with their self-reliant private infrastructure especially developing first private spaceport in the world. This kind of daring activity could not even be imagined in the earlier state-centric regime.

The case of Spaceport Sweden[85] is a very interesting one in concern with Virgin Galactic. The former had signed off an agreement with the later in 2007. According to the agreement, Virgin Galactic will use the spaceport at Kiruna (Sweden)[86] for space tourism. It would be the first spaceport outside USA for Virgin Galactic.[87] Therefore the American company Virgin has extended its business wing to Europe with the formation of another European company. The private actors in some challenging and highly expensive area of space activities like space tourism could only survive if they are not confined within a single country. Here it would require some wealthy passengers from all over the world.

Another company in **Table 7**, Space Adventures[88] has vision to go beyond space tourism. It wants to open up the resources of space for all humankind. The plan is to grow its estimated industry over US$10 billion over the next several years.[89] The world's first private space tourist, Dennis

Tito, made his dream successful in 2001 through its service.[90] It is exhibited from **Table 7** that ShipinSpace Ltd.[91], a European start-up has claimed that their facility is better than that of the Virgin Galactic and XCOR.[92]

The presumption from the above that space tourism is going to face fierce competition in near future because of increasing number of private actors and their low-pricing policies to attract more customers. But for the time being it appears to be just opening up another space venture by private actors only. However, the activity of space tourism attracts lots of legal issues like tourism anywhere under the Sun starting from liability, environment, safety, financial, corporate social responsibility and ethics.

Space tourism is for very short term existence of human beings in outer space whereas the ISS had been placed by the countries in outer space since 1998.[93] Like ISS, there is totally private initiative to develop private space stations in near future. There are approximately two companies below right now with this giant initiative. It is listed below.

Table 8: Countries & Actors in Private Space Stations[94]

Countries	Actors	Beginning Year	Activities
Russia	Orbital Technologies	2010	Proposed commercial experiments in private space station.
USA	Bigelow Aerospace	1999	Proposed only.

Orbital Technologies[95] was founded to open space station for private enterprises unlike ISS that was made by state actors. It was established to bridge the historical successes of the Russian space industry with other entrepreneur start-up companies.[96] The Company came into focus because of its building and launching of Commercial Space Station (CSS). The company will lead the private sectors to commercialise the human spaceflight program in Lower Earth Orbit (LEO).[97] RSC Energia is a partner in making CSS to be utilised by professional crews, private citizens as well as corporate researchers interested in conducting their scientific programs onboard the world's first commercially available human spaceflight platform.[98] This company is a best example of private commercial initiative for permanent habitation in outer space within a space station. Moreover, another Russian private actor RSC Energia made partnership with this company for attracting more private and corporate bodies as the customer of private space station.

The other one from **Table 8** is Bigelow Aerospace[99] that is engaged to build orbital space module which will be placed at high altitude to circle the earth for many years. The primary focus is on providing clients like groups of nations, companies and even individuals with the opportunity to lease area space and resources in their orbital space module.[100] Its historic first commercial space station will open up extraordinary opportunities for countries across the globe. Now-a-days, it is status of a country to send their citizens into outer space i.e. human spaceflight is prestige of a nation and so highly deserved to all nations. But smaller countries like Singapore or UAE have no immediate human spaceflight programme. Therefore they could think of this company. Therefore a whole state may depend on a private company that is not incorporated from the state itself in the present case. Moreover, the microgravity environment represents a new arena for commercial R&D. It will be strongly established as demand grows and the on-orbit industry matures.[101] So many state as well as private actors could plan their microgravity research through private initiative.

IPR is a leading issue from the activities of the companies in **Table 8** because the place within such space station would be used for many path-breaking innovative research activities in near future.

It is shown from the above that the satellites are manufactured and launched. But these became dead functionally at the end of their life cycle or may be malfunctioned before their schedule term finished. Then these useless bodies collide with the functioning one to create debris in outer space. These are called as space debris.[102] The number of satellites have increased in outer space since the launching of Sputnik. Therefore the states have started to take this issue of space debris seriously. The private actors also take the entry to remove the debris. There is only one in this category.

Table 9: Country & Actor in Space Debris Removal[103]

Country	Actor	Beginning Year	Activities
Italy	D-Orbit	2008	Developed the device to remove satellites at the end of their operational life.

D-Orbit provides the solution for space pollution. The satellite insurers could calculate the insurance cost in a better way.[104] The company is interlinked with different kind of private actors i.e. space insurers and the insurance business would be facilitated by their service. It relates with sovereignty, IPR and liability issues that are explained in next chapter.

Space Robotics is very new initiative comparative to others in the activities above. Its simple meaning is use of robots in the activities of outer space. Besides any actor, whether state or private, would require robots because of life-risk and uncertainty of space adventure along with cost-effective planning of all outer space experiments and projects.

Table 10: Country & Actor in Space Robotics[105]

Country	Actor	Beginning Year	Activities
USA	Astrobiotic Technology Inc.	2008	Application of Robots in outer space

Astrobiotic Technology Inc. was founded by a Carnegie Mellon professor. Its deliverables are space robotic technology and planetary missions.[106] Like University of Surrey through SSTL in satellite manufacturing, pure academics here also gave birth to private actors through space commerce. The IPR issue is relevant here.

The above space activities are facilitated in outer space itself whereas there are some activities in outer space for which the benefits are enjoyed solely on earth. These are mining of celestial bodies, solar energy from space, commercial remote sensing satellite imageries, satellite communications and broadcasting.

The mining of celestial bodies are extracting resources from Moon and asteroid. This topic is very hot now-a-days because it attracts the private wealthy entrepreneurs below. But the activities are yet to start though European Space Agency (ESA) has already landed on a comet in 2014.[107] Their list shows below.

Table 11: Countries & Actors in Celestial Mining[108]

Countries	Actors	Beginning Year	Activities
USA	Shackleton Energy Company	2007	Developed technology for Moon mining.
As above	Planetary Resources	2010	Proposal for Asteroid mining.
As above	Deep Space Industries	2013	Proposal for in-orbit fueling on mining asteroids.

As above	Moon Express	2010	Proposal for extraction of Moon resources through robotic spacecraft.

The Shackleton Energy Company[109] was established to develop the technologies for mining the Moon.[110] But the leader in this sector from **Table 11** till now is Planetary Resources[111] that is engaged with upcoming mining activities.[112] The people behind this company are very interesting to analyse for the present study. They created new industry not new company. Its investors are Chief Executive Officer (CEO) of Google; one attached with Microsoft Corporation previously; a real estate developer in USA. The advisors of this company are renowned Hollywood film director; a former Chief Technical Officer of Microsoft; a Professor of space law. The CEO is founder director of Space Adventures, a space tourism company above.[113] The presence of such persons signify that the high-innovation risky expensive space activities are not the agendas of any state now-a-days. Rather the big corporate along with their successful and innovative key people are interested about breathtaking activities in space or deep space. That is why such type of private space initiative has evolved in this sector. Another one Deep Space Industries[114] would like to draw attraction to in-orbit customers in near future like supplying energy fuel on mining asteroids in outer space.[115] Unlike other companies in **Table 11**, the company would like to pursue its future through in-orbit business in outer space itself.

Another interesting fact is that the funding of Moon Express[116] came from NASA and Google Lunar X Prize competition. It will start its first mission on 2015.[117] So Moon Express is also funded by NASA like Space X contract with NASA. Here the national space agency itself is interested to pass over its high-risk to the small but potential companies or start-ups to promote the national agenda. This highly sophisticated technical space activity is confined within USA according to **Table 11**. Sovereignty and proprietary rights are involved with celestial mining. The details are explained in chapter III.

Like extracting resources from celestial bodies, solar energy from outer space could be utilised in near future to meet the energy crisis on earth. It is very expensive and complex space commercial venture till now. There are many initiatives including research going on to capture this energy to utilise as a power resources of the satellites like Solar Powered Satellites (SPS) as well as the ways to utilize this energy on earth. The SPS concept was originally proposed by Dr. Peter Glaser of Arthur D. Little Co. of Boston.[118] The single company highlights this domain till now.

Table 12: Country & Actor in Space Solar Energy[119]

Country	Actor	Beginning Year	Activities
Europe	EADS Astrium	2006	Developed technology for Moon mining.

EADS Astrium is also looking the venture of space based solar energy. The legal issue is IPR.

When some companies put their efforts on bringing back the celestial resources from outer space to earth, then some are with the business of releasing the satellite imageries of earth taken from outer space through remote sensing technique used for commercial purposes. These imageries are called commercial satellite imageries.

Table 13: Countries & Actors in Commercial Satellite Imageries[120]

Countries	Actors	Beginning Year	Activities
USA	Digital Globe	2001	Data imageries attracted by big corporates like Google, Microsoft etc.
Europe	Astrium (now Airbus Defence & Space)	2006	Agreement with Google to supply imageries.
USA	Skybox Imaging Ltd.	2009	World high-resolution image provider.
Spain	Zero2Infinity	2009	To enable cost efficient access to near space with zero environmental impact flying solutions.
Germany	RapidEye	1998	The combination of large-area coverage, frequent revisit intervals, five multispectral bands, and high resolution makes RapidEye products superior within the remote sensing industry.

The Land Remote Sensing Policy Act, 1992, that is analysed in chapter IV brought the private companies in USA to enter the satellite imaging business. Its effect was establishment of Digital Globe[121] in **Table 13** that is a leading global provider of commercial high-resolution earth imagery products and services.[122] This company launched world's high-resolution commercial satellite, QuickBird in 2001 for pursuing its business. It started business networking in government and commercial markets. There was agreement to provide high-resolution imagery to Keyhole Corporation that was subsequently acquired by Google and the key component in making Google Earth.[123]

Besides these activities, there was announcement of a number of agreements with other companies expanding the availability of high-resolution imagery to online portal, navigation, location based system (LBS). It was with Google for providing high-resolution satellite imagery for Google Earth and Google Map; Microsoft to provide high-resolution satellite and aerial imagery for the Virtual Earth Platform; Oracle using satellite imagery for its customers and Nokia for use of imagery in Nokia Location Services available on compatible Nokia devices.[124]

Due to these huge demands from such corporate customers, the Digital Globe and GeoEye, two leading providers of earth observation (EO) and geospatial analysis, merged into one company since January 2013. This combination will provide a more comprehensive solution for geospatial information and services.[125] It is very significant to observe how the well-known corporate and their tie-up flourish the business of satellite imageries commercially. The service of Digital Globe is expanded with the business collaboration with Google, Microsoft, Nokia and Oracle. Finally, there is a merger with another company GeoEye.

Astrium,[126] a European company has made an agreement with Google Inc. to supply the high-resolution imageries for developing different Google products and services including Google Maps and Earth.[127] The Skybox Imaging Ltd.,[128] Zero2Infinity[129] and RapidEye[130] could not be compared with the commercial potential of Digital Globe but they are serving the increasing demands in this sector. The legal issues like sovereignty, national security become imbalanced in the era of high-resolution commercial remote sensing satellite imageries. The issue of ethics also comes into limelight to be explained in the next chapter.

There is another kind of satellites besides remote sensing satellites above. This is called communication satellites which are placed in geosynchronous orbit or Clark's orbit[131] after the name of its inventor Arthur C. Clarke.[132] Satellite communications have become the first truly worldwide space business. There are different organisations like national consortia, multinational corporations, international governmental organisations and private domestic corporations which have shown interest in this business.[133] But the following analysis is confined within private domestic corporations which is the present requirement of this research study.

Table 14: Countries & Actors in Satellite Communications[134]

Countries	Actors	Beginning Year	Activities
USA	COMSAT	1962	1st private firm to take responsibility from NASA.
Europe	INTELSAT	2001	Largest provider of satellite services throughout the world.
As above	INMARSAT	1999	World's first global satellite mobile satellite system

The US Communication Satellite Act was passed in 1962 with the initiative of AT&T and Hughes's Aircraft. Its effect was Communication Satellite Corporation or COMSAT.[135] This private firm COMSAT took the responsibility of NASA to exploit the satellites built, launched and operated by NASA itself.[136]

The International Telecommunication Satellite Organisation (INTELSAT)[137] being established in 1964 as an intergovernmental organisation as well as the first satellite commercial provider became a private company in 2001. Being merged with PanAmSat Holding Corporation in 2006, it becomes the largest provider of fixed satellite services throughout the world.[138] The International Maritime Satellite Organisation (INMARSAT)[139] was converted to a private company in 1999.

INMARSAT was the first of the International Satellite Organisations (ISO) moving towards privatisation.[140] The privatisation of satellite communications was basically a global move to implement the UNGA Res 1721 of 1961 to provide communication by satellite on non-discriminatory basis. Its implementation through privatisation is easier for a state because the burden of responsibility for financing is shifted from the state. Additionally, competition makes the telecommunication industry to reach at the lowest level of customers anywhere in the globe.[141] The legal hurdles are primarily like dispute settlement.

There are some private actors (companies) that promote space commerce differently as well as uniquely. Sometimes space is one of the sectors with other non-space sectors in their commercial ventures. These are the circumstances below.

Table 15: Countries & Actors in Miscellaneous Space Activities[142]

Countries	Actors	Beginning Year	Activities
Canada, USA, Russia	MDA Corporation	1969	Global communications; Surveillance & intelligence systems.
USA	Space Angels Network	2006	To attract private investment in space industry.
Isle of Man (UK)	Cavendish Trust Company Limited		Provide all-inclusive solutions to the international space companies from Isle of Man.
Europe	Satec Underwriting	1993	Face international space risk through space insurance.
USA	Nanoracks Ltd.	2008	Agent for cost-effective programme in ISS on behalf of governmental (NASA) & private customer.
USA	Sierra Nevada Corporation	2008	Focus on microsatellites & human spaceflights.
As above	Paragon Space Development Corporation	2008	Provider of environmental controls for extreme and hazardous environments.
As above	Celestis Inc.	1982	Memorial spaceflights to orbits, Moon & Deep space.
Europe	Euroconsult	1992	Consulting & analyst firm for space activities globally.
South Korea	Satrec Initiative Ltd.	1999	Supplier of Earth Observation Data.
UK	Treemetrics	2005	Watchdog of inventory of forests.

The MDA Corporation[143] is in joint collaboration with Canadian government in functioning of RADARSAT-2, the remote sensing satellite system. MDA owns the satellite and ground segment and has exclusive rights to distribute data from RADARSAT-2.[144] So MDA being a private body holds control over the national remote sensing satellite system that is not only used for commercial purpose but also for national security and defence purpose.[145] Space Angles Network[146] is to connect investors with entrepreneurs through a worldwide network.[147] This company practically supports to increase the number of private actors in outer space. So its target is to connect the entrepreneurs with investors. The issue of financing that is highlighted in next chapter III is concerned with the activities of Space Angles Network.

The case of Cavendish Trust Company Limited[148] is confined within Isle of Man that is an off-shore place specially created for private space activities. This is explained in chapter IV. The company provides all-inclusive solutions to the international space companies which will be operated from or covered by the jurisdiction of Isle of Man. The present situation in space business is that 34 leading satellite companies are represented from this place. The turnover is increased from £62 m (2008) to £1.6bn (2012-14).[149] Space commerce is over flourished here. Sometimes it is needed for any high-investment business.

Alongside the High-investment business like space has high-risk. This is where Satec Underwriting[150] makes entry to **Table 15.** It, being one of the members of International Union of Aerospace Insurers is a European underwriting agency dealing with international space risk. This agency has joined with Lloyd's Coveholder since 1997.[151] Now Lloyd is not a company but an international insurance market to promote the insurance companies.[152] In this view Satec underwrites on behalf of companies like financial institutions, telecommunication companies and private investors related with their commercial ventures in space. Satec underwrites Lloyd's Syndicates Satellite Risks in the International Space Insurance Market.[153] Therefore the private actors are not only established for providing finance to other actors but also the insurance for space commerce is provided by them.

Nanoracks Ltd.[154] acts as a mediator company for performing experiments of NASA and other private actors in ISS. The advantage of such system is to decrease the cost of experiment if it had been directly conducted by the party. Paragon Space Development Corporation[155] puts another effort to decrease the space tourism cost through its innovative high-altitude balloon flight that has nearly zero-gravity experience.

There is another exciting example for development of private actors in case of Space Services Inc.[156] (SSI) of America. It arranged the first ever privately financed launch into outer space in 1982. Later on the situation of the company has created the technical, financial, and legal or regulatory foundation for the commercial space industry of today. NASA purchased its launch services in 1989 for launching Starfire 1. The company claimed that this was the first purchase of NASA for launch services.[157] It delivered services to ISS on working with Nescafe Japan in 2001.[158] SSI facilitates to build private commercial regime in USA during the nascent era of private-centric regime. It is very interesting that Nescafe which is popular to the world not for space activities has been working with SSI.

Therefore there is enough opportunity for the private actors to approach any actors from different sectors. This is not likely found in the beginning era of space law dominated by states. It is further noted that SSI's Advanced Systems Division was made for establishing and to entrepreneur the companies to investigate new commercial opportunities in space weather and remote telecommunications' applications. Basically the government or any company could hire this commercial service to test its space systems on earth or the effects of space weather on its space system or to test remote telecommunications previously from earth.[159] This facility promotes space commerce with low risks.

It means that private actors having small potential in financial resources as well as technological infrastructure could plan for investing on space business. Additionally, SSI serves to study the non-traditional space markets like corporate sponsorship and public participation.[160] So any private actors like small start-ups and companies could make advance feasibility study to their return on investment from commercial market. Therefore it is very much acceptable to welcome such services not only in America but also all over the world.

Euroconsult,[161] an international consulting and analyst firm based in Paris, has its consultancy service in the four core area as per the following: (1) business strategy support, (2) government policy support, (3) commercial due diligence, and (4) operations management services[162] Each of the four categories above are equally important to develop the space industry within and outside (private) the government.

There are some companies in every country to take the pioneering role for other private actors in future. The case of Satrec Initiative Ltd.[163] of South Korean private company is like this in **Table 15**. It was established by the same group of people who has first built the South Korean satellite following the commercialisation of space technology in the country.[164] This country is now full of private actors to be discussed in the subsequent part concerned with South Korea in chapter IV. But this company paved way of privatisation in the country. The examples of Celestis[165] and Treemetrics[166] as shown in **Table 15** are very unique of its kind to spread the private actors in different innovative ways. Sierra Nevada Corporation[167] is associated with small satellites.

As these activities are varied in nature, the legal issues like sovereignty, national security, liability, environment, corporate social responsibility and dispute settlement come into play.

In the background of different private actors in varied space sectors, **Table 16** surmises below the number of actors against each space sector and their places of business all over the world. But there is a caution that the numbers are ever changing and moreover the list of companies in each sector above is not all inclusive. Moreover the miscellaneous sector covers more than one sector.

Table 16: Comparison of Space Sectors against Total No. & Regionwise No. of Companies[168]

Space Sectors	Total No. of Companies	Regionwise No. of Companies
Satellite Manufacturing	13	USA (4), Latin America (1), Europe (7), Asia (3) including India (2).
Satellite Launching	6	Europe (6).
Commercial Orbital Transportation Services	4	USA (3), UK (1).
Space Tourism	4	USA (2), Europe (2).
Private Space Station	2	USA (1), Europe (1).
Space Debris Removal	1	Europe (1).
Space Robotics	1	USA (1).
Celestial Mining	4	USA (4).
Solar Energy from Outer Space	1	Europe (1).
Commercial Satellite Imageries	5	USA (2), Europe (3).
Satellite Communications	3	USA (1), Europe (2).
Miscellaneous	11	USA (6), Europe (5), Asia (1).

It is indicated from **Table 16** that satellite manufacturing is at the top and other sectors are declining in number especially where space technology reaches cutting-edge like space robotics etc. However, it verifies from **Table 16** that it is indeed the sunrise era of private actors because their effort maximise their numbers in core area of space sector i.e. satellite manufacturing and it is followed by another core area launching.

Private Actors in India

Unlike above, the situation in India is totally different. The different types of privatisation is already observed in different countries within the meaning of 'private actors in outer space'. It is in this context to be analysed first what type India has followed generally since its independence. India followed a broad economic policy just after independence according to its first Prime Minister Jawaharlal Nehru. According to him, it was the state's responsibility to carry forward the big investments which ultimately would turn India into an industrial power.[169]

In this process private sector should play minor but supportive role to make profit in their respective businesses. This policy was followed subsequently. The government took the monopoly over most assets and decided on its own for their use. So the private sector was compelled to pursue their activities as little more than an extension of the state. There was no independent decision from their side over uses of labour, capital or raw material. It was also a fact that there were state-mandated marketing and distribution restrictions in some industries.[170]

Afterwards it was noted in outline by the Industrial Policy Resolution adopted by the Indian cabinet in 1956. The impact was drastic negative influence on private sector. Their smaller, supportive but independent role under Nehru's economic policies was missing after 1956. The state control was increased to such an extent that every phase of activity of private sector had requirement of compulsory approval from government. The system of creation of a compulsory licencing system started. It was known as the 'licence raj' failing which no private industry could survive.[171]

At the end the economic reform took place in 1991 and three buzz words of this era were - competition, entrepreneurship and the beginnings of world-class infrastructure. Its effect was that state control of economic activity ended.[172] A large scale disinvestment had occurred. It is treated as privatisation. Now like other countries above, there are three different patterns of this disinvestment. First is considered by few that disinvestment in a 'non-government company' is privatisation. The second is accepted by many that the popular meaning of privatisation is the holding of less than 51 per cent share by the government enterprises and rest by private participation. The third option is already noted within the meaning of private actors that change of ownership and control by the government company which holds a minimum share-holding or no-share-holding.[173]

With these background thoughts and strategic planning for privatisation in Indian context, there are no such intense space activities outside ISRO like European countries and USA. The big projects like Chandrayaan–I[174] and Mangalyan[175] have shown some light to the private actors. There were about 125 companies including private ones associated with year long Mangalyan programme.[176] Therefore the private actors have worked under different situations in India. It is also to be noted here that India's modern space programme was started very late compared to the western countries. Moreover India's space programme is people-centric and application-centric.[177] However, two categories of companies exist in India—(i) first category like other countries is always the domestic companies and (ii) second category is the foreign companies or international companies that have branches and also interested to spread their space business in India. These two types are analysed below.

DOMESTIC COMPANIES

It starts with the domestic companies that are engaged with their activities for ISRO projects. The national space agency has started partnership with the domestic industries since the decade of 70s. There were about 250 technologies developed by ISRO transferred to different industries by 2000. A technology transfer cell has been established.[178] They manufacture space products like – satellite manufacturing, satellite parts and components, satellite technology, launch vehicle, space applications etc. In all these classification, ISRO is the major customer of the following companies in India.[179]

Table 17: Actors, Places & Activities in India[180]

Actors	Places	Activities
Walchandnagar Industries Ltd.	Pune	Manufactured – (i) rocket motors of SLV-3, ASLV, PSLV and GSLV programs; (ii) equipments of satellites like ROHINI, SROSS, IRS, G-SAT.
Larsen and Toubro (L & T)	Mumbai	Developed large maraging steel rocket motor cases and complex launch structures and facilities.
Bharat Heavy Plate and Vessels Ltd.	Vishakapatnam	Manufacturer large space chamber facility.
International Marketing & Services	Bengaluru	Manufacturing like spacecraft mechanisms, space technologies, propulsion systems of satellites; Satellite technology; Producer of liquid propellant; Space Capsule Recovery Experiment.
International Pvt. Ltd.	As above	Satellite Parts & Components.
Axon Interconnectors and Wires (P) Ltd.	As above	As above.
Unified Electro-Tech Ltd.	As above	Satellite Parts & Components; Space Applications.
Advanced Micronic Devices Ltd.	As above	Satellite Parts & Components; Space Capsule Recovery Experiment.
Jyoti Electronics	Ahmedabad	Satellite Parts & Components; Space Applications; Satellite Application; Space Capsule Recovery Experiment; Payloads.
Progressive Engineers	Mumbai	Satellite Parts & Components.
Astra Microwave Products Ltd.	Hyderabad	Space Applications.
TATA Advanced Materials Ltd.	Bengaluru	Launch Vehicle & its Parts; Satellite applications; Payloads.
Captronics System & Virginia Panel Corporation	As above	Launch Vehicles & its Parts.
Fenwick & Ravi	As above	As above.

Vantage Technologies	Chandigarh	As above.
MTAR Ltd	Hyderabad	As above.
NOCIL (a part of Mafatlal group)	Mumbai	Manufacturing Solid & Liquid Propellants.
Andhra Sugar	Tanuku	As above.
Premier Explosives Ltd.	Hyderabad	Lessee for supplying explosives, fuels & management to ISRO.
Godrej & Boyce Mfg. Co. Ltd.	Mumbai	CS, VIKAS and STEERING engine for PSLV & GSLV; Payloads; Space Transportation Systems.
Komoline Aerospace Ltd.	Ahmedabad	Satellite Applications; Payloads.
Magma Machining Pvt. Ltd.	As above	Space Applications.
Accord Software & System (P) Ltd.	Bengaluru	Space Capsule Recovery Experiment.
Nova Integrated Systems Ltd. (a fully owned subsidiary of TATA Advanced Systems Ltd.)	Hyderabad	Manufacturing Payloads.
Aarjay International (P) Ltd.	Bengaluru	As above.
BrahMos Aerospace Ltd.	Thiruvananthapuram	Missile Development (same technology used in development of rocket).
Valeth Hightech Composites	Chennai	Producing High Silica based tiles as heat shields in spacecraft.
Earth2Orbit Ltd.	Mumbai	Private consultancy in space activities.

The name of Walchandnagar Industries Ltd. (WIL) came first because of its historical contribution towards developing aircrafts. It was established by Walchand Hirachand Doshi who was one of the pioneering industrialists during British period. One of the greatest industrial achievements of Walchandji was the establishment of Hindusthan Aeronautics Ltd. (HAL) at Bengaluru.[181] The above air age of the company[182] extended to the space age when WIL started their aerospace business in 1971 with the satellite launch programmes of ISRO.[183] The **Table 17** shows some of its activities. The critical machinery used in Chandrayaan-1 has supplied by it. In 2012, Agni-V, India's first Inter-Continental Ballistic Missile (ICBM) has developed with its technical support.[184] The recent business deal with ISRO is that it will provide the machines to this company to make products for ISRO. So India's national space agency will purchase equipment worth about Rs. 30 crore for use by Walchandnagar Industries Ltd. to make rocket components.[185]

Out of the companies listed in **Table 17**, there are some big corporates in India. These are Godrej & Boyce Mfg. Co. Ltd.,[186] TATA Advanced Materials Ltd.[187] and Larsen and Toubro[188]. The Godrej was assigned to build landmark VIKAS engine in PSLV after developing it by ISRO. But it took long time to develop and then transfer technology to the private actors. So, ISRO from the very beginning have made Godrej and MTAR[189] as industry partner for fabricating cryo-engine, the most developed stage of rocket engine.[190]

The status of maximum private actors within **Table 17** is just like ordinary Indian companies. But some of them have already performed incredible works for which India could now think and plan better in reality for further development of private space industry. The example could be drawn from earlier period. The manufacture of solid and liquid propellants was assigned to NOCIL Ltd. (a part of Arvind Mafatlal group)[191] and Andhra Sugars Ltd.[192] respectively by ISRO in the early 80's.[193] This Table discloses that the Space Capsule Recovery Experiment (SRE) which is must for any human spaceflight was assigned to the companies not so much known to the public like International Marketing & Services (IMS)[194], Advanced Micronic Devices Ltd.,[195] Jyoti Electronics[196] and Accord Software & System (P) Ltd.[197] The same International Marketing & Services (IMS)[198] exported its products to US sources. The products were used to develop a range of hybrid rocket motors that powered SpaceShipOne used for space tourism.[199] The Valeth Hightech Composites[200] perhaps the latest of smaller companies' partnership with ISRO when it has contributed for its upcoming uncrewed manned mission.[201]

There are two companies in **Table 17** that contributed differently. The first is BrahMos Aerospace Thiruvananthapuram Ltd. (BATL);[202] its significance is slightly different in developing other private actors or contributing as private actor itself. It is engaged with missile industry or military space industry[203] according to **Table 17**. But the same technology which is used in launching a rocket is applicable for launching a missile. So it could be treated as ancillary space industry whereas Brahmos Ltd. is treated as indirect private actor in the present context of the study.[204] The second is Earth2Orbit Ltd.[205] **Table 17** shows that it serves as consultant to the domestic as well as international space activities. Its one of the visions is to 'lead India in the emerging world of private enterprise for space exploration and utilisation'.[206] Therefore these private actors have potential to perform major space works but contributions are in different directions.

The contributions from other companies in this Table like Aarjay International Pvt Ltd.,[207] Axon Interconnectors and Wires (P) Ltd.,[208] Unified Electro-Tech Ltd.,[209] Syatron Technologies (P) Ltd.[210] and Progressive Engineers,[211] Astra Microwave Products Ltd.,[212] Captronics System & Virginia Panel Corporation,[213] Fenwick & Ravi,[214] Vantage Technologies,[215] Komoline Aerospace Ltd.,[216], Nova Integrated Systems Ltd.,[217] a fully owned subsidiary of TATA Advanced Systems Ltd., Bharat Heavy Plate and Vessels Ltd.,[218] and Magma Machining Pvt. Ltd.[219] do not have less importance in developing the domain of private actors in India.

The names of companies in **Table 17** are many but very few are common to the people. All are contributed to the different projects of ISRO and sometimes they have served for other countries within a very small capacity as their websites reflect. Some companies are start-up companies but their prospects are very high as the ISRO projects are gradually expanded.

There is other category of companies related with aerospace[220] industries like Sanghvi Aerospace (P) Ltd.[221] at Ahmedabad. The users of its product are ISRO with others. There are some companies in this category at Bengaluru Aerospace Park like Dynamatic Aerospace, AK Aerotek Software Centre Pvt. Ltd., Symmetric Technologies Pvt. Ltd., Sakthi Aerospace, Pinaka Aerospace Solutions Private Ltd. and UTC India.[222] These aerospace companies may not be like their counterparts in foreign countries like Boeing Ltd. Their contribution for the time being mainly in aviation sector but their future object is to relate outer space with their activities. Such types of domestic private actors are in rise.

There are licencee private companies with ISRO that has transferred 290 technologies to Indian industries to which licences were issued to make production and market the products. There are in total 500 small, medium and large scale industries having partnership with ISRO.[223] Some of them already mentioned above. Annexure II reflects such transferred technologies used in commercial applications. Some of these technologies also have applications in non-space sectors.[224] Thus there is every possibility to commercialise these spin-offs fully through these private entities in future. It is only a matter of time to frame the suitable policy made by the government.

Albeit the above possibilities or uncertainties, the very recent procedural development as planned by ISRO is that there would be an entity comprised of public and private sectors that would build up the satellites and rockets instead of ISRO. It is not the prerogative of space agency now to build these space products. A five-year time line has been set for this purpose. Additionally, ISRO would like to institutionalise the production of rockets and satellites with the support from industry.[225]

FOREIGN COMPANIES INTERESTED IN INDIA

Besides these domestic companies, there are some foreign companies having branch offices in India. The Indian telecommunication sectors are already packed up with so many foreign private companies having branches in India.

EADS DS INDIA is a subsidiary of EADS (now changed name is Airbus Defence & Space) that is a global aerospace company. EADS DS is mainly associated with defence in India. It has offices both in New Delhi and Bengaluru.[226] Now due to the business short fall in Europe, EADS has changed its strategy to consolidate its defence business with space business. There is another reason that both businesses have some common market. Like when a customer is approached to the company for wide-area surveillance, its low-flying satellites will serve the purpose of customer. This strategy is applied in India to promote the business of this company. It has engineering centres at Bengaluru for Airbus Defence & Space. Also the company has subcontractors in India. In a nutshell, India is one of the sleeping giants when it comes to space and defence activities. Previously, the company has never treated India as a market like now.[227]

The Thales Alenia group from satellite manufacturing sector **(Table 3)** has branch in India. It was incorporated in 2003 as Thales India Pvt. Ltd. The contribution is till now in avionics sector supplying the latest trends to a wholly owned subsidiary of Larsen & Turbo (L&T) of **Table 17** according to joint venture between the two companies.[228] There is one interesting note that this company is interested in joint venture with so many local industries like subsidiary of L&T. The Thales group is more familiar in space business all over the world. So it may be presumed that the present activities ultimately lead to space sector in India. The company may welcome joint venture for this purpose.

There is Virgin Ltd. that has initiated space tourism through its sister concern Virgin Galactic as explained above. India has till now the market focus of this company through its two sectors (i) airline business—Virgin Atlantic and (ii) Virgin Mobile (India) Ltd.,[229] a cellular telephone service provider company in a joint venture with Tata Teleservices. Its airline business is so dynamic in India that Indian market takes place just after its US airline market.[230] Virgin Produced (India) Ltd. that relates with the entertainment industry of India has stepped in very recently.[231] According to the statement of Richard Branson, owner of the company,

> "At Virgin, we try to infuse everything we do – whether it's in the music, travel, or telecommunications industry – with a sense of entrepreneurialism, innovation and fun."[232]

The above analysis shows how much Virgin along with its CEO, Branson, is interested to expand their business in India. They get only one space tourist from India till now.[233] Perhaps the presumption may not be wrong to see the company in near future to expand its facilities for space tourism from the land of India itself. The legal issue like dispute settlement is the most significant in this category because of the recent legal complexities observed from the investment of foreign telecommunication companies in India.[234]

Conclusion

There are so many private actors in different capacity pursuing their activities in outer space. The explanation of the meaning of 'private actors in outer space' has link with general privatisation concept. But the interpretation of the word 'privatisation' varies from country to country. However, according to Article VI of the Outer Space Treaty, all these activities must be supervised and authorised by the concerned state.

It starts with satellite manufacturing and continues with other space activities. The private uses of space also bring two categories of companies: first category involves directly with outer space and second interacts with space applications on earth. Building private space station, removing space debris etc. fall in the first category while the second category utilises the satellite imageries or data as resources for different commercial activities on earth. The numbers are more in second category for the time being. Moreover, the activities like space tourism share the platform of earth and space both.

The fact observed from above is that the technologies are developing day by day. The private entities set their feet to accept these technological challenges to grasp more international commercial market space. Additionally the national space agencies, both from India and abroad are the prime customers of the private actors in outer space. It is further observed that there are many mergers and take-overs of companies. These indicate the future survival of the private space industry from steep competition.

Simultaneously the big corporate like Boeing Ltd., Airbus Defence and Space has expanded their business from home country to foreign countries. This trend is followed by the smaller ones like Surrey Space Technology Ltd. Some companies would like to be self-reliant in one space sector e.g. the space tourism companies are now developing not only the spacecraft but also their own launchers. The reason is that it will be cost-effective and expand the scope of business beyond space tourism. In short, the whole scenario communicates the strong message from private actors to pursue the activities in outer space. Therefore this research study is assumed to be more justified through these actors' immense potentials as well as performed activities.

In this context, the sharp contrast is observed over commercialisation and privatisation between developed and developing countries in space. The major and maximum private actors are from USA and European countries. The developing countries roll down with low profile where space industry is just like sunrise industry. Moreover, as explained above, the stages of privatisation differ from country to country since it depends upon the strategy and policy of the state besides the development of self-reliant space technology. In the case of China, being a superpower is not so privatised like other Asian countries; because state's dominance is present everywhere in the country. Unlikely, Japan has made it possible through its multinational company Mitsubishi Heavy Industries Limited or IHI Ltd.

In this regard, the history of privatisation in India indicates that the industrial sectors have freed from state monopoly since 1991. At the first instance, ISRO has taken the opportunity for commercialising space in India through their business wing ANTRIX. Then due to increasing workload and to bring the innovation and efficiency more to ISRO itself, it has started to invite Indian private companies to show their excellence.

The process of attracting domestic private actors is different like providing licence to the companies for some specific space technology related product. But it has to be specially mentioned here that these private actors do not work independently without ISRO. The main reason is that ISRO is the major buyer of space products developed by them. The major buyer of space products from Walchandnagar Industries Ltd. is none other than ISRO itself. Only the Indian telecommunication sectors walk along in the line of true sense of privatisation. However the Indian list follows from big corporate like Godrej & Boyce, TATA and Walchandnagar Industries Ltd. to small start-ups.

Alongside some foreign companies like Airbus Defence & Space, Thales Alenia and Virgin Ltd. are also eagerly interested to pursue their business in India to satisfy the national demand, and space is within their upcoming business agenda. Overall it is just tip of the beginning of the regime dominated by private actors in India.

All the above details of so many private actors in outer space along with their commercial activities would definitely require some enactment to regulate them like any other industry. It will otherwise lead to a legal chaos between the commercial tie-up of state and private actors at the first instance and then within that of the private actors themselves. Already some legal issues have emerged by default while analysing the different categories of space activities. The private actors in outer space face these issues. Therefore the circumstance demands for critical analysis of such issues that follows the next chapter.

Notes

1. Latipulhayat, A., *Privatisation of Space Law: Negotiating of Commercial Benefit-Sharing Issues in the Utilisation of Outer Space, 2013*. In Corinne M. Contant Jorgenson (Ed.), *Proceedings of the International Institute of Space Law 2012* (The Hague: Eleven International Publishing), p. 247.
2. Reijnen, G.C.M., *Utilisation of Outer Space and International Law* (Amsterdam: Elsevier, 1981), p. 107.
3. Dula, Art, "Private Sector Activities in Outer Space", *The International Lawyer*, vol. 19, no. 1, 1985, p. 187
4. Fawcett, J.E.S., *Outer Space New Challenges to Law and Policy* (Oxford: Clarendon Press, 1984), p. 37.

5. Carminati, Giugi, "French National Space Legislation: a Brief "Parcours" of a Long History," *Houston Journal of International Law*, vol. 36, no. 1, 2014, pp. 5-6.
6. Reddy, Y.V., *In Foreword Note of T.T. Ram Mohan, Privatisation in India Challenging Economic Orthodoxy* (London: Routledge Curzon, 2005), p. 15.
7. Latipulhayat, Atip, Privatisation of Telecommunications in the Developing World: a Lesson Learned or Burden Imposed, In Corinne M. Contant Jorgenson (Ed.) Proceedings of the 48th Colloquium of the Law of Outer Space, Washington: American Institute of Aeronautics and Astronautics, 2006, pp. 425-426.
8. See n. 4, p. 38.
9. Cheng, Bin, "Article VI of the 1967 Space Treaty Revisited: 'International Responsibility', 'National Activities' and 'The Appropriate State' ", *Journal of Space Law*, vol. 26, no. 1, 1998, p. 14.
10. Vereshchetin, V. S. et al., *Outer Space: Politics and Law* (Moscow: Progressive Publishers, 1981), p. 118.
11. See n. 4, pp. 41-42.
12. Futron's Report at http://www.sia.org/wp-content/uploads/2012/05/FINAL-2012-State-of-Satellite-Industry-Report-20120522.pdf (Accessed February 13, 2013)
13. Data are taken from websites of concerned companies and details are provided within analysis.
14. Boeing Defence, Space & Security at http://www.boeing.com/boeing/bds/ (Accessed April 7, 2013).
15. Boeing Company at http://www.boeing.com/boeing/defense-space/space/bss/factsheets/601/601fleet.page? (Accessed February 13, 2013).
16. Lockheed Martin Ltd. (Space Division) at http://www.lockheedmartin.com/us/what-we-do/space.html (Accessed April 7, 2013).
17. Lockheed Martin at http://www.lockheedmartin.com/us/products/a2100.html (Accessed February 15, 2013).
18. Airbus Defence & Space at http://www.space-airbusds.com/ (Accessed April 7, 2014).
19. file:///C:/Users/DELL/Downloads/EADS_GIF%202012_FA_ASTRIUM.pdf (Accessed February 15, 2013).
20. http://www.space-airbusds.com/media/document/astrium-broschure-digital_neuertitel-2607.pdf (Accessed February 15, 2013).
21. http://www.space-airbusds.com/en/programme/spot-603.html (Accessed February 15, 2013).
22. http://www.astrium-geo.com/en/143-spot-satellite-imagery (Accessed February 15, 2013).
23. Astrium SPOT at http://www.astrium.eads.net/en/programme/spot.html (Accessed February 15, 2013).
24. http://www.isro.org/scripts/milestones.aspx (Accessed July 1, 2014)
25. http://www.astrium.eads.net/en/programme/sentinel-5-precursor.html (Accessed February 15, 2013)
26. http://www.astrium.eads.net/en/press_centre/astrium-primed-hylas-1-is-commissioned-in-orbit.html (Accessed February 20, 2013)
27. http://www.inmarsat.com/about-us/ (Accessed February 25, 2013)
28. http://www.astrium.eads.net/en/press_centre/astrium-built-inmarsat-4-satellite-system-receives-sspi-2010-industry.html (Accessed February 25, 2013)
29. http://www.astrium.eads.net/en/programme/helios-i.html (Accessed February 25, 2013)

30. http://www.astrium.eads.net/en/programme/galileo.html
31. JSC-Information Satellite System at http://www.iss-reshetnev.com/?cid=history (Accessed April 7, 2013).
32. Thales Alenia Space at http://www.thalesgroup.com/Press_Releases/Markets/Space/2013/First_batch_of_four_O3b_satellites_ready_for_shipping_to_launch_site/ (Accessed April 14, 2013).
33. http://www.thalesgroup.com/Press_Releases/Markets/Space/2013/Thales_Alenia_Space_and_ISS_Reshetnev_create_Joint_Venture_in_Russia/ (Accessed April 14, 2013)
34. OHB Systems at https://www.ohb-system.de/competencies.htm (Accessed April 07, 2013).
35. Data are taken from websites of concerned companies and details are provided within analysis.
36. Surrey Satellite Technology Ltd. at http://www.sstl.co.uk/ (Accessed April 14, 2013).
37. SSTL at http://www.sstl.co.uk/About-SSTL/Management---Ownership (Accessed April 14, 2013).
38. Svitak, Amy, "Aiming for the Stars," *Aviation Week & Space Technology*, vol. 176, no. 24, 2014, p. 116.
39. http://www.sstl.co.uk/Downloads/SSTL-Brochure-pdfs/SSTL-25-years-brochure (Accessed April 14, 2013).
40. Mitsubishi Heavy Industries Limited, at http://www.mhi.co.jp/en/products/space_index.html (Accessed April 14, 2013).
41. https://www.mhi-global.com/news/products/space.html (Accessed April 14, 2014).
42. IHI Limited. http://www.ihi.co.jp/en/products/aeroengine_space/rocket_system/satellite_propulsion/index.html (Accessed April 14,2013)
43. http://www.ihi.co.jp/en/company/history/index.html (Accessed April 15, 2013).
44. http://www.generationorbit.com/about.html (Accessed April 14, 2013).
45. Dutch Space at http://www.dutchspace.nl/pages/press/content.asp?id=307&P=6_1&PURL=%2Fpages%2Fhot%2Fcontent%2Easp%3Fid%3D283&PNAME=Hot+at+Dutch+Space (Accessed April 14, 2013).
46. INVAP at http://translate.google.co.in/translate?hl=en&sl=es&u=http://www.invap.com.ar/&prev=/search%3Fq%3Dinvap%26hl%3Den%26biw%3D1280%26bih%3D699&sa=X&ei=26FqUdnZF4L_rAfZjYHIBw&sqi=2&ved=0CDIQ7gEwAA (Accessed April 16, 2013).
47. RSC Energia at http//www.energia.ru/english/ (Accessed April 14, 2013).
48. http://www.energia.ru/en/corporation/history_rsc.html (Accessed April 16, 2013).
49. See n. 9.
50. http://www.hal-india.com/HAL-Congrats-ISRO.asp (Accessed April 15, 2013).
51. Data are taken from websites of concerned companies and details are provided within analysis.
52. Arianespace at http://www.arianespace.com/index/index.asp (Accessed April 15, 2013).
53. http://arianespace.com/news-feature-story/2013/9-26-2013-G-Shivanna.asp (Accessed April 15, 2014).
54. See n. 5.
55. Arianespace at http://www.arianespace.com/about-us/milestones.asp (Accessed April 15, 2013).
56. Eurockot Launch Services at http://www.eurockot.com/ (Accessed April 15, 2013).

57. http://www.russianspaceweb.com/plesetsk.html (Accessed April 16, 2013).
58. Eurockot launch Services at http://www.eurockot.com/about-us/business-profile/ (Accessed April 16, 2013).
59. http://www.eurockot.com/missions/manifest/ (Accessed April 16, 2013).
60. See n. 47.
61. See n. 57.
62. International Launch Services at http://www.ilslaunch.com/ (Accessed April 15, 2013).
63. International Launch Services at http://www.ilslaunch.com/about-us/ils-legacy; See also http://www.ilslaunch.com/about-us/ils-milestones; Also at http://www.ilslaunch.com/newsroom/news-releases/ils-proton-launch-success-intelsat-23-provide-enhanced-capacity-americas-euro. (Accessed April 16, 2013).
64. ISC Kosmotras at http://www.kosmotras.ru/en/company/ (Accessed April 15, 2013).
65. ISC Kosmotras at http://www.kosmotras.ru/en/zapuski/ (Accessed April 16, 2013).
66. Sea Launch AG at http://www.sea-launch.com/ (Accessed April 15, 2013).
67. Sea Launch AG at http://www.sea-launch.com/missions-q1-past_launches.aspx (Accessed April 16, 2013).
68. http://www.sea-launch.com/about-q11324-Sea_Launch_Contractor_Roles__Responsibilities.aspx
69. Starsem at http://www.starsem.com/ (Accessed April 15, 2013).
70. http://www.starsem.com/starsem/starsem.html (Accessed April 15, 2013).
71. Data are taken from websites of concerned companies and details are provided within analysis.
72. Space X at http://www.spacex.com/ (Accessed April 17, 2013).
73. http://www.spaceref.com/news/viewnews.html?id=955 (Accessed April 17, 2013).
74. Space X at http://www.spacex.com/company.php (Accessed April 17, 2013).
75. Orbital Science Corporation at http://www.orbital.com/About/CompanyBackground/ (Accessed April 18, 2013).
76. Malik, T., Private Cygnus Spacecraft Launches on Maiden Space Station Voyage. *Space.Com,* September 18, 2013, at http://www.space.com/22843-private-cygnus-spacecraft-launch-space-station.html (Accessed September 19, 2013); See also https://www.orbital.com/CompanyOverview/History/ (Accessed September 19, 2014).
77. Excalibur Almaz at http://www.excaliburalmaz.com/ (Accessed April 17, 2013).
78. Excalibur Almaz at http://www.excaliburalmaz.com/0001_Overview.html (Accessed April 17, 2013).
79. XCOR Aerospace at http://www.xcor.com/ (Accessed April 17, 2013).
80. XCOR Aerospace at http://xcor.com/overview/index.html (Accessed September 19, 2013).
81. Data are taken from websites of concerned companies and details are provided within analysis.
82. Virgin Galactic at http://www.virgingalactic.com/ (Accessed April 17, 2013).
83. http://www.virgingalactic.com/statement-from-virgin-galactic/ (Accessed November 20, 2013).
84. Virgin Galactic at http://www.virgingalactic.com/overview/ (Accessed April 17, 2013).
85. Spaceport Sweden at http://www.spaceportsweden.com/ (Accessed April 17, 2013).
86. Spaceport Sweden at http://www.spaceportsweden.com/mission/ (Accessed April 17, 2013).
87. http://www.flightglobal.com/news/articles/swedish-spaceport-awaits-government-go-

ahead-316843/ (Accessed April 17, 2013).

88. Space Adventures at http://www.spaceadventures.com/ (Accessed April 17, 2013).
89. Space Adventures at http://www.spaceadventures.com/index.cfm?fuseaction=about_us.welcome (Accessed April 17, 2013)
90. http://www.spaceadventures.com/index.cfm?fuseaction=Our_Vision.welcome
91. ShipinSpace Ltd. at http://shipinspace.com/ (Accessed April 17, 2013).
92. Messier, Doug (2013), Space Tourism Startup SHIPinSPACE Receives $7.8 Million Investment at http://www.parabolicarc.com/2013/08/26/shipinspace-announcement/ (Accessed October 20, 2013).
93. http://www.nasa.gov/audience/forstudents/k-4/stories/what-is-the-iss-k4.html (Accessed October 20, 2013).
94. Data are taken from websites of concerned companies and details are provided within analysis.
95. Orbital Technologies at http://orbitaltechnologies.ru/ (Accessed October 20, 2013).
96. Orbital Technologies at http://orbitaltechnologies.ru/en/our-mission.html (Accessed April 18, 2013).
97. http://orbitaltechnologies.ru/en/purpose-of-the-commercial-space-station.html (Accessed April 18, 2013)
98. http://orbitaltechnologies.ru/en/news/orbital-technologies-and-rsc-energia-to-launch-world-s-first-commercial-space-station.htm (Accessed April 18, 2013)
99. Bigelow Aerospace at http://www.bigelowaerospace.com/ (Accessed October 20, 2013).
100. Bigelow Aerospace at http://www.bigelowaerospace.com/faq.php (Accessed April 18, 2013)
101. http://www.bigelowaerospace.com/beam_media_brief.php (Accessed April 18, 2013)
102. http://www.globalcomsatphone.com/hughesnet/satellite/space_junk.html (Accessed April 18, 2013)
103. Data are taken from websites of concerned companies and details are provided within analysis.
104. D-Orbit at http://www.deorbitaldevices.com/site/about-us/ (Accessed April 25, 2013).
105. Data are taken from websites of concerned companies and details are provided within analysis.
106. Space Robotics at http://www.astrobotic.com/about/ (Accessed April 25, 2013).
107. http://rosetta.jpl.nasa.gov/news (Accessed November 18, 2014).
108. Data are taken from websites of concerned companies and details are provided within analysis.
109. Shackleton Energy Company at http://www.shackletonenergy.com/ (Accessed April 18, 2013).
110. Shackleton Energy Company at http:// www.shackletonenergy.com/ (Accessed April 18, 2013).
111. Planetary Resources at http://www.planetaryresources.com/ (Accessed April 18, 2013).
112. Planetary Resources at http://www.planetaryresources.com/2012/04/faq/ (Accessed April 18, 2013).
113. Ibid.
114. Deep Space Industries at http://deepspaceindustries.com/ (Accessed April 18, 2013).
115. Deep Space Industries at http://deepspaceindustries.com/business/ (Accessed October 3, 2013).

116. Moon Express at http://www.moonexpress.com/ (Accessed April 18, 2013).
117. http://moonexpress.com/ (Accessed April 18, 2013).
118. Finch, E.R. and Moore, A.L., *Astrobusiness a Guide to the Commerce and Law of Outer Space* (New York: Praeger, 1985), p. 13.
119. Data are taken from websites of concerned companies and details are provided within analysis.
120. Data are taken from websites of concerned companies and details are provided within analysis.
121. Digital Globe at http://www.digitalglobe.com/ (Accessed April 18, 2013).
122. Digital Globe at http://www.digitalglobe.com/about-us/overview (Accessed April 19, 2013).
123. http://www.digitalglobe.com/about-us/history#/quickbird-is-launched (Accessed April 19, 2013).
124. http://www.digitalglobe.com/about-us/history#/the-growth-of-the-business (Accessed April 19, 2013).
125. http://www.digitalglobe.com/about-us/history#/a-new-era (Accessed April 19, 2013).
126. Astrium (now Airbus Defence & Space) at http://www.space-airbusds.com/ (Accessed April 18, 2014).
127. Astrium to provide new satellite imagery for Google Maps and Google Earths at http://www.astrium.eads.net/en/press_centre/astrium-to-provide-new-satellite-imagery-for-google-maps-and-google-earth.html (Accessed September 30, 2013).
128. Skybox Imaging Ltd. At http://www.skyboximaging.com/ (Accessed April 18, 2013).
129. Zero2Infinity at http://www.0ll00.com/ (Accessed April 19, 2013).
130. RapidEye at http://blackbridge.com/rapideye/ (Accessed April 19, 2013).
131. Arthur C Clarke predicted first in 1945 that there was an orbit at a distance of 35,786 km (approximately) in space over the equator, which has the same rotational speed like Earth. This was the first conception of geostationary orbit. All the communication satellites are in this orbit.
132. http://www.tnmoc.org/sites/default/files/Extra-Terrestrial%20Relays2.pdf (Accessed April 19, 2013).
133. Goldman, N. C., *Space Commerce Free Enterprise on the High Frontier* (Massachusetts: Ballinger Publishing Company, 1985), p. 58.
134. Data are taken from websites of concerned companies and details are provided within analysis.
135. COMSAT at http://www.comsatsystems.co.in/ (Accessed on 25 April, 2013).
136. Reijnen, G.C.M., "Outer Space Law and Private Enterprise in Outer Space: An International Perspective," *Houston Journal of International Law*, vol. 2, no. 1, 1979, p. 66.
137. INTELSAT at http://www.intelsat.com/ (Accessed April 25, 2013).
138. INTELSATat http://www.intelsat.com/about-us/our-history/2000s/ (Accessed April 25, 2013).
139. INMARSAT at http://www.inmarsat.com/ (Accessed April 25, 2013).
140. http://adsabs.harvard.edu/full/1999ESASP.442.127S (Accessed April 25, 2013)
141. Lyall, F., "On the Privatisation of INTELSAT," *Journal of Space Law*, vol. 28, no. 2, 2000, pp. 101,106.
142. Data are taken from websites of concerned companies and details are provided within analysis.

143. MDA Corporation at http://www.mdacorporation.com/corporate/index.cfm (Accessed April 17, 2013).
144. Jakhu, Ram S., *Regulation of Space Activities in Canada,* In Ram S. Jakhu (ed.) National Regulation of Space Activities, 2010, p. 96.
145. Ibid., p. 97.
146. Space Angels Network at http://www.spaceangelsnetwork.com/about/ (Accessed April 25, 2013).
147. Space Angels Network at http://www.spaceangelsnetwork.com/about/ (Accessed April 25, 2013).
148. Cavendish Trust Company Limited at http://www.cavendishtrust.com/independence/ (Accessed April 25, 2013).
149. Cavendish Trust Company Limited at http://www.cavendishtrust.com/space-and-satellite-services/ (Accessed April 25, 2013).
150. SATEC Underwriting at http://www.satecgroup.eu/chi-siamo/la-storia-2/?lang=en (Accessed April 25, 2013).
151. SATEC Underwriting at http://www.satecgroup.eu/chi-siamo/la-storia-2/?lang=en (Accessed April 25, 2013).
152. Llyod at http://www.lloyds.com/lloyds/about-us/history/innovation-and-unusual-risks/pioneers-of-travel (Accessed April 25, 2013).
153. http://www.satecgroup.eu/spazio/?lang=en (Accessed April 25, 2013).
154. Nanoracks Ltd. at http://nanoracks.com/about-us/our-history/ (Accessed April 25, 2013).
155. Paragon Space Development Corporation at http://www.paragonsdc.com/paragon_background_09.php (Accessed April 25, 2013).
156. Space Services Inc. at http://www.nameastarlive.com/aboutDetails.asp (Accessed April 25, 2013).
157. Space Services Inc. at http://www.nameastarlive.com/aboutDetails.asp (Accessed April 25, 2013).
158. Ibid.
159. Space Services Inc. Advanced System Division at http://www.spaceservicesinc.com/advanced_systems_division.asp (Accessed April 25, 2013).
160. Ibid.
161. Euroconsult at http://www.euroconsult-ec.com/ (Accessed April 25, 2013)
162. Euroconsult at http://www.euroconsult-ec.com/ (Accessed April 25, 2013)
163. Satrec Initiative Ltd. at https://www.satreci.com/eng/ds1_1.html?tno=4 (Accessed April 25, 2013).
164. Satrec Initiative Ltd. at https://www.satreci.com/eng/ds1_1.html?tno=4 (Accessed April 25, 2013).
165. Celestis at http://www.celestis.com/about.asp (Accessed April 25, 2013).
166. TreeMetrics at http://www.treemetrics.com/about/ (Accessed April 25, 2013).
167. Sierra Nevada Corporation at http://www.sncorp.com/about_snc.php (Accessed April 25, 2013).
168. Data are provided by Tables 3-15.
169. Chase, Aaron, *India an Investor's Guide to the Next Economic Superpower* (Singapore: John Wiley & Sons (Asia) Pvt. Ltd., 2006), pp. 8-11.
170. Ibid.
171. Ibid.

172. Ibid.
173. Reddy, Y. Venugopal, *Privatisation in India, 1989;* In V.V. Ramanadham (Ed.), *Privatisation in Developing Countries* (London: Routledge), p. 183.
174. http://www.isro.org/satellites/chandrayaan-1.aspx (Accessed April 1, 2014)
175. http://www.isro.org/mars/home.aspx (Accessed October 1, 2014)
176. http://www.business-standard.com/article/news-ians/indian-industry-to-make-rockets-satellites-isro-chief-114111901291_1.html (Accessed November 22, 2014)
177. http://indianexpress.com/article/india/india-others/we-dont-have-any-doubt-about-our-cryogenic-engine-the-capability-of-india-to-launch-heavier-satellites-has-now-been-established/ (Accessed April 01, 2014)
178. Rao, U.R., *India's Rise as a Space Power* (New Delhi: Foundation Books, 2014), p. 189.
179. The names of the companies are taken from exhibitor catalogue of Bengaluru Space Expo 2012.
180. Ibid. Data are also taken from companies' websites.
181. Piramal, G. and Herdeck, M., *India's Industrialists*, vol. I, (Washington D.C.: Three Continents Press Inc., 1985), p. 393.
182. Khanolkar, G.D., *Walchand Hirachand Man, His Times and Achievements* (Bombay: Walchand Hirachand Company Ltd., 1969), p. 375.
"Walchand's prodigious exertions allowed the knowledge of astronautics, first born of Indians thousands years ago but thereafter lying buried, to be reborn in India under a fresh form. By founding the Hindusthan Aircraft Company, Walchand ushered the air age into India's industrial field'.
183. http://www.walchand.com/wp-content/uploads/2013/01/Milestone-v2.pdf (Accessed April 25, 2013).
184. http://www.walchand.com/business-area/aerospace/ (Accessed April 25, 2013).
185. Ramesh, M., ISRO to fund Walchandnagar's equipment worth Rs. 30 crore, 2014 at http://www.thehindubusinessline.com/news/isro-to-fund-walchandnagars-equipment-worth-30-cr/article6705011.ece (Accessed December 20, 2014).
186. Godrej & Boyce Mfg. Ltd. at http://www.godrejandboyce.com/ (Accessed April 30, 2013).
187. TATA Advanced Materials Ltd. at http://www.tamlindia.com/ (Accessed April 30, 2013).
188. Larsen & Tourbo Ltd. http://www.larsentoubro.com/lntcorporate/LnT_Offerings/Offering.aspx?res=P_CORP_BOFF_CEPS_FARS&sbu=71 (Accessed April 30, 2013). See also n. 116, pp. 190-191
189. MTAR Ltd. At http://www.mtar.in/businessSegments/indianspace_program.php (Accessed April 30, 2013).
190. See n. 178, p. 188.
191. NOCIL Ltd. at http://www.nocil.com/ (Accessed April 30, 2013).
192. Andhra Sugars Ltd. http://www.theandhrasugars.com/ (Accessed April 30, 2013).
193. See n. 178, p. 190.
194. International Marketing and Services at http://www.ims-indiabiz.com/space.html (Accessed April 25, 2013).
195. Advanced Micronic Devices Ltd. at http://www.amdlcorp.com/ (Accessed April 30, 2013).
196. Jyoti Electronics at http://www.jyotimicrosystems.com/ (Accessed April 25, 2013).
197. Accord Software & System (P) Ltd. Ahttp://www.accord-soft.com/ (Accessed April 30, 2013).

198. See n. 194.
199. Ibid.
200. http://www.valeth.com/about-us.html (Accessed November 29, 2014).
201. http://economictimes.indiatimes.com/tech/smaller-companies-partner-for-isros-precursor-to-first-manned-mission/articleshow/45320222.cms (Accessed November 29, 2014).
202. http://www.brahmos.com/content.php?id=1 (Accessed October 30, 2013).
203. http://www.thespacereview.com/article/2626/1 (Accessed October 30, 2014).
204. http://indiatoday.intoday.in/story/indian-missile-programme-space-launch-vehicles/1/259177.html (Accessed October 30, 2013).
205. Earth2Orbit at http://www.earth2orbit.com/ (Accessed April 30, 2013).
206. http://www.earth2orbit.com/company/vision&manifesto.html (Accessed April 30, 2013).
207. Aarjay International (P) Ltd. at http://www.aarjay.com (Accessed April 25, 2013).
208. Axon Ltd. At http://www.axon-cable.com/ (Accessed April 25, 2013).
209. Unified Electro-Tech Ltd. at http://www.unified.co.in/ (Accessed April 30, 2013).
210. Syatron Technologies (P) Ltd. at http://syratron.com/ (Accessed April 28, 2013).
211. Progressive Engineers at www.progressiveengineers.net/ (Accessed April 25, 2013).
212. Astra Microwave Products Ltd. at http://www.astramwp.com/ (Accessed April 30, 2013).
213. Captronics System at http://www.captronicsystems.com/ (Accessed April 30, 2013).
214. Fenwick & Ravi at http://far.co.in/ (Accessed April 30, 2013).
215. Vantage Technologies at http://www.indiamart.com/vantage-technologies/#profile (Accessed April 30, 2013).
216. Komoline Aerospace Ltd. At http://www.komoline.com/ (Accessed April 30, 2013).
217. NOVA Integrated System Limited at http://www.novaintegrated.com/ (Accessed April 30, 2013).
218. Bharat Heavy Plate and Vessels Ltd. at http://www.bhelviz.co.in/ (Accessed April 30, 2013).
219. Magma Machining Pvt Ltd. At http://magmamachining.com/Profile.html (Accessed October 30, 2013).
220. http://www.nasa.gov/centers/langley/news/factsheets/FS-2001-09-68-LaRC.html (Accessed April 30, 2013)
221. Sanghvi Aerospace (P) Ltd. At http://www.sanghviproducts.com/saero.html (Accessed October 30, 2013).
222. http://bangaloreaerospacepark.com/facilities/aerospace-companies.html (Accessed October 30, 2013).
223. http://www.isro.gov.in/ttg/technologytransfered.html (Accessed April 30, 2013)
224. Ibid.
225. http://www.business-standard.com/article/news-ians/indian-industry-to-make-rockets-satellites-isro-chief-114111901291_1.html (Accessed November 23, 2014).
226. http://www.defenceandsecurity-airbusds.com/web/guest/opportunities-in-india (Accessed April 30, 2013)
227. Enders, Tom, In Defence, India is a Sleeping Giant, Says EADS Global Chief. *The Economic Times*, November 20, 2013, p. 6.
228. https://www.thalesgroup.com/en/india/about-us; https://www.thalesgroup.com/en/india/what-we-do (Accessed April 30, 2014)

229. http://www.virginmobile.in/ (Accessed November 20, 2013).
230. Sanjai, P.R. & Deshpande, A., Virgin Atlantic has no plans of investing in any Indian carrier for now: Craig Kreeger, 2013. http://www.livemint.com/Companies/ZjAg0UJBkIkpEC4RyNeVPI/Virgin-Atlantic-has-no-plans-of-investing-in-any-Indian-carr.html (Accessed November 20, 2013)
231. http://economictimes.indiatimes.com/news/news-by-industry/media/entertainment/entertainment/virgin-proudced-to-enter-indian-entertainment-market/articleshow/26048795.cms (Accessed November 20, 2013)
232. http://www.virgin.com/news/introducing-virgin-produced-india (Accessed November 20, 2013).
233. http://www.santhoshgeorge.com/space_mission.php (Accessed November 20, 2013).
234. http://www.business-standard.com/article/pti-stories/telecom-industry-in-india-is-a-mess-says-vodafone-india-chief-114091100773_1.html (Accessed August 21, 2014).

III. Legal Issues

Introduction

This research study has examined the historical background of space regulations. The examination has revealed how the private actors have placed themselves within the state-centric domain of outer space. Alongside this historical development, their credibility and sustainability for pursuing space activities in the long run is not questionable at all after detailed analysis of their nature and characteristics of activities in the previous chapter. It is much assured now that such actors would take the lead in near future along with the states. Some legal issues follow this new commercial turning; these are primarily like sovereignty, national security, liability, intellectual property rights (IPR), financing, environment, ethics, corporate social responsibility, safety and dispute settlement etc.

Some legal issues like sovereignty, national security, liability and environment exist already in state-centric space era. Only these issues become more vigorously intense in touch with the private actors whereas the issues like IPR, ethics and corporate social responsibility are assumed to be directly linked up with the legal development of private actors in outer space.

Out of all these issues, some like property rights, environmental protection of outer space are for short-term issue whereas the governance of large space societies (specifically for private actors in this study) is long-term issue.[1] It is more than obvious that the first category occurs very shortly or already in existence. The present study is undoubtedly concerned with these short-term issues. Moreover, it is not that these are the only one because many more new problems will also emerge with the advancement of technology expanding the nature and scope of man's utilisation of outer space.[2] Therefore there may be other issues and sub-issues related with this legal development. But to remain within the scope and objective of the present study for the time being, only the primary short-term issues are critically reviewed.

Legal Issues for Private Actors

The **Table 18** below depicts how the legal issues are concerned with activities of private actors explained in previous chapter.

Table 18: Space Sectors & Concerned Legal Issues[3]

Space Sector	Legal Issues
Satellite Manufacturing	IPR.
Satellite Launching	1. Liability 2. Safety.
COTS	As above.
Space Tourism	1. Liability 2. Environment 3. Safety 4. Corporate Social Responsibility 5. Ethics
Private Space Stations	IPR.
Space Debris Removal	1. Sovereignty 2. Liability 3. IPR.
Space Robotics	IPR.
Celestial Mining	1. Sovereignty 2. Proprietary Rights.
Space Solar Energy	IPR.
Commercial Satellite Imageries	1. Sovereignty 2. National Security 3. Ethics.
Satellite Communications	Dispute Settlement.
Miscellaneous	1. Sovereignty 2.National security 3. Liability 4. Environment 5. Corporate Social Responsibility 6.Dispute settlement.

SOVEREIGNTY & PROPRIETARY RIGHTS

The first and foremost issue is sovereignty and proprietary rights. The public international law stands with the sovereignty of states since its evolution. The domain of space law could not be escaped from it on being ventured by the private actors. The following analysis begins with the interpretation of sovereignty within traditional public international law and then within the provisions of space law treaties as the major concern of this study relates with outer space.

The legal scholars interpreted the term 'sovereignty' differently. It was the French philosopher Jean Bodin who used the written word 'sovereignty' for the first time in the 16th century (1576) in his famous work on '*Six lives la Republiqe*'. The Book I Chapter 8 had discourse on sovereignty.[4] According to him sovereignty was "the absolute and perpetual power of a commonwealth". He was attracted because it was the central theme in his writing on the commonwealth which meant just a government with sovereign power. Interestingly, none defined it earlier.[5] Vattel observed the sovereignty as an external status of the state through which it maintained the independence towards other states.[6] Kelsen argues sovereignty as a quality of the state and how the citizens would be best ruled.[7] They have interpreted sovereignty with their own logics. The realisations as well as arguments of these scholars mainly reflect the societal norms and customs during their life time.

With the passage of time, the sovereignty is vested in the people and exercised by its state and its various organs. Its simple meaning now turns into power of the state to control over its people, resources and institutions. This very power is generally executed within the limits of territorial boundaries of a state including its land, territorial water and adjacent air space. In this context, some of the important cases of ICJ highlighting sovereignty are like - (I) Right of Passage case[8] for passage over land; (ii) Anglo-Norwegian Fisheries case[9], Corfu Channel case[10], North Sea Continental Shelf case[11] for passage through water; and (iii) Nicaragua case[12] and Aerial Incident of 1999 case[13] between Pakistan vs India for passage through airspace. In all these landmark cases of ICJ, the sovereignty of a state tags with territoriality of the state. But there is exception as ruled by the Permanent Court of International Justice (PCIJ) in the Lotus Case.[14] It was decided in this case that State's exercise of jurisdiction outside the territorial waters was based on sovereignty.[15]

The above paragraphs highlight sovereignty in general within the norms of international law. In the present context, much concern is expected how sovereignty is reflected within the text of space treaties under the framework of United Nations. The Article II of the Outer Space Treaty states:

> "Outer space, including the Moon and other celestial bodies, is not subject to national appropriation by claim of sovereignty, by means of use or occupation, or by any other means."

So outer space is an international region where there is no possibility of concept of a state or combination of states. Moreover, there is no lower boundary of outer space either in international law or space law per se. The boundary problem has been raised at the very initial phase of space law and it remains unsolved till now. This issue is reflected within Annexure II of report of 52nd session of Legal Sub-Committee in 2013. The participation of private sectors is newly added concern behind solving the old problem now.[16] Although the dimensions of state sovereignty above its territory are limited but its boundaries especially the inward boundary of outer space need not necessarily be defined.[17] This boundary problem has created other problems in the past like Bogota Declaration[18] of 1972 where eight territorial countries claimed that the geostationary orbit to be part of their national sovereignty. Moreover besides the Article II above, the term 'sovereignty' is not mentioned in the text of other treaties. There are many places of the text of space law treaties where it is mentioned that the rules of space law are according to the provisions of international law.[19] So space law is based on the principle of sovereignty.[20]

With this very brief background of sovereignty in international law as well as international space law, it shows two sides of the same coin simultaneously. One side seems to be not subject to sovereignty whereas opposite side subject to sovereignty. In this view, sovereignty is neither necessary nor sufficient for solving the problems created by space age.[21] Therefore when the space technologies are used for commercial satellite imageries of the earth or satellite communication for direct television broadcasting, the principle of sovereignty is jeopardised as shown in **Table 18**. The states having advanced remote sensing satellite technology can easily get information well in advance about the territory of other states which are less developed in such technology. The commercial information related with economic benefit like natural mineral reserves is siphoned out from the territory of the state without its permission on violating the principle of sovereignty. To safeguard the sovereignty of each state, there are 'Principles of Remote Sensing' established in 1986 as made by UN General Assembly resolution. But the very text of these principles does not cover the commercial remote sensing.[22] So there is no regulation for commercial remote sensing in the provisions of international space law.[23]

The above anomalies related with sovereignty continue with recent enthusiasm regarding mining of celestial bodies like Moon or Asteroid. So, celestial mining is concerned with sovereignty and proprietary rights as shown in **Table 18**. The much discussed and debatable issue of water in the Moon brings sovereignty in the new dimension like proprietary rights over the minerals or water.[24] According to the Outer Space Treaty (non-appropriation principle)[25] or Moon Treaty (Common Heritage Principle)[26], there could not be any extension of national sovereignty in outer space.

If these outer space resources had been brought out to earth, no private company dealing with these mining procedures can vehemently claim the ownership. But how a private company, on investing huge amount, would be disclaimed over ownership of such celestial resources is really a tough legal challenge. Accordingly USA has outlined the Asteroid Act very recently though the discussions and debates are going on in the concerned departments. It is proposed to have proprietary rights over resources found from celestial bodies.[27] It was most surprisingly initiated from the pressure of private companies interested in celestial mining.[28] This problem was further discussed in a roundtable of the Hague Institute for Global Justice. The private sector representatives like the Planetary Resources or Deep Space Industries in **Table 11** argued that there should be new agreement or regime based on the state practice of the Outer Space Treaty. Alternatively, it was proposed how such celestial mining would be accommodated in the existing framework of the Outer Space Treaty.[29]

NATIONAL SECURITY

The next serious concern is national security after going through the legal hurdles for sovereignty and proprietary rights over the private actors' commercial ventures. It is mentioned in the introduction of this research study that utilisation of space is always a strategic issue; because a state can better be governed from outer space through the high-end space technology. And this strategy is always entangled with the national security of the very particular state.

So national security is better supervised from outer space through remote sensing satellites. Therefore **Table 18** highlights national security issue on disseminating commercial satellite imageries. This process follows through directly by the defence or reconnaissance satellites though it is a different aspect whether spying from outer space is permitted or not.[30] No states, in general, would like to give up its control over outer space activities to any other authority. The government of any state controls its space activities directly or indirectly. But this scenario has been slowly changing with the commercialisation of satellite imageries provided by private companies. They use high-resolution imageries for civil purposes.[31] Hence it is a challenge for any government to liberalise the space sectors to the private bodies without compromising the national security of its territory.

In this background, the private company Google Inc. has violated the norms for national security of India through Google Map on disclosing vital military installations, core of *Apsara* nuclear reactor, sensitive areas of the Hindon airbase, ammunition depots, markings of hangers meant for specific fighter jets, warships in naval dockyards and much more. The satellite imagery generally available on Google Earth or through any other remote sensing satellites can only give a viewer a vague idea of structures and objects. But Google shows specific sensitive (with respect to national security) areas of the Apsara reactor within the Bhabha Atomic Research Centre (BARC) and air force's base station at Hindon.[32] This problem of Google is not only in India but other countries have also faced this problem earlier but then again in different ways.[33]

Furthermore, the above analysis of national security influences the privacy of the citizens of any country. The high-resolution photographs expose the activities of citizens in their private domain.[34] It goes further that Location-Based-System (LBS), a technological application of Geographical Positioning System (GPS), where the LBS provider informs anybody about the local geographical information. Whether it is legitimate?[35]

LIABILITY

Besides the issues like sovereignty and national security, liability is also another issue of legal discomfort in the state-centric era. An effort is made first to analyse how liability is reflected within the texts of space law treaties. The Article VII of the Outer Space Treaty[36] makes provision for liability. It imposes on or hits the states only. There is separate international liability regime for space activities with enactment of the Convention on International Liability for Damages Caused by Space Objects 1972 (Liability Convention). This Convention also mentions liability for the damages caused by space objects as launched by the state.[37] It was unthinkable and beyond imagination during the period of establishment of both these instruments of space law that one day private actors could pursue the activities in outer space. So the issue of liability is always attached to the state only. The states are not only responsible but also liable for the activities pursued by any non-governmental entity. But the space law treaties are silent about the liability of private actors directly.

This general explanation of liability within the provisions of space law has faced some lacuna with the increasing number of participation of private actors. Additionally such actors though remain engaged with different activities related with outer space but there are certain key areas where they encounter heavily with liability regime. These areas are till now according to **Table 18:** (i) space launching – already started (**Table 5**) and (ii) space transportation (**Table 6**) which just commences with the introduction of SPACE X's transportation to ISS during 2012.

There is active engagement of private entities in launch activities. The private companies earn profits. But if the damage occurs during or after launch, the launching company is not liable. Rather it is the launching state as defined in Article I of the Liability Convention. Under such a legal framework, a state should be held responsible for the activities of private entities registered in its territory that procures a launch in a different state. It is immaterial whether the host state has knowledge or involvement in such launch.[38] Moreover, it is neither feasible nor fairly justified to make the states responsible because increasing number of private entities is engaged in space activities.[39] The Liability Convention has not considered the individual liability of private bodies. In case of a space, object has been transferred whether by sale, lease or secured financing to private operators in countries that is not launching states, then how the liability will be imposed on private satellite operators. It is totally unfair to still hold the original state liable in such cases.[40]

It is mentioned above that private space transportation is yet to begin except the case of SPACE X and Orbital Science Corporation as shown in **Table 6**. But there is every possibility to start as explained in previous chapter. There is high probability to make a loss to customer like failure to place the goods in an orbit effecting their destruction in space or on earth, or, to place the goods in an improper orbit. A customer in private space transportation service can also be prejudiced by further unreasonable delay of a launch.[41]

The above issues are directly provided within text of the space treaties whereas the followings are not like that. The reason is high-level commercialisation which attracts IPR first.

INTELLECTUAL PROPERTY RIGHTS

The protection of Intellectual Property Rights (IPR) will play an important role to attract private actors. The main emphasis is on the right of invention. Invention is the key tool to promote commercial exploitation of outer space.

But there are two types of IPR – one where space is used and the other is in discoveries made in space e.g. within the ISS.[42] It is the first type which is more significant for this research study; because states are mainly involved in ISS till now. The previous chapter shows that there is an increasing shift of space activities from state-owned to private commercial activities in different sectors like satellite based remote sensing, direct broadcasting, research and manufacturing in micro-gravity environment etc. In this scenario, the World Intellectual Property Organisation (WIPO) has observed:

> "Not only is the new participation of commercial sector increasing, but the privatisation of entities is equally increasing as in the cases of Inmarsat or Intelsat. In general, those non-governmental entities are more conscious of their 'property', both in tangible and intangible forms. Further, due to financial and technical resources which are required to realise space projects, collaboration with the private sector is not alien to many of the state-owned space agencies today. Licencing contracts are concluded between governmental space agencies, between governmental agencies and private companies, and between private companies. Such private financing has to be motivated by the expectation that the R&D investment could be recovered in the future. Thus, the acquisition and protection of intellectual property rights would have a positive effect on the participation of the private sector in the development of outer space activities and on further development of space technology in general." [43]

It has been further observed by WIPO that space would require huge investment. So a legal framework is necessary to maintain smooth and healthy competition in the era of private space activities. The intellectual property protection would confer exclusive rights. These in turn carry competitive benefits to the right holders in two ways. It could be either by concluding a licencing agreement or by excluding competitors from using a given technology. In other words, the overall image of the company may be enhanced by IPR created in the company itself. For example, the technical competence of a company will be proved by the acquisition of patents. Moreover, in a case of combination of various high-technologies, the possibility of licencing intellectual property has another advantage like allowing to negotiate a cross-licence with other parties.[44]

In this context, the other reason to attract IPR is that the huge investments in space sector like satellite manufacturing in **Table 3** draws attention of economic forces which in turn control the law of the marketplace. As a result some international diplomatic commitments may yield to economics. So, the protection of IPR is too much required in case of satellite manufacturing. The two are linked with each other in **Table 18**. Furthermore, there may be a tendency of aggressiveness on the part of IPR owners in the field of space activities due to high technology, high risk and high potential gains. The example may be cited from **Table 8** in concern with private space station that is really a hub for micro-gravity research. The very small production in such environment undoubtedly has immense innovative value in R&D.[45] So, **Table 18** has nexus between IPR and private space station. However, it may further lead to increased litigation or aggressive licencing campaigns. The overall situation makes it difficult for a newcomer to enter the marketplace because maximum of them are not prepared to pay a substantial amount as a fee for acquiring third party licences. The particular difficulty is to assess the potential applicability of third party IPR.[46]

The above scenario directs that the IPRs are established and protected by national or regional law of the concerned countries based on the principle of territoriality. Different national laws apply to different regulations. On the other hand, international space law does not provide any solution to solve IPRs issue.[47] This leads to a vacuum for IPR laws for outer space especially in private dominated space industry.

FINANCING

The imposition of IPR already brings the financing problem of new private actors to start their commercial space ventures. The major economic hurdle arises from financing all private space activities that require high-value investment with high risk. It is just for an example to attach this issue in space tourism as shown in **Table 18.** So space financing is really a tough job for any organisation including the government. Here financing includes leasing and insurance. The principal difficulty of a financer is the security on its investment. In case of any space disaster, how the resources invested will be returned back?

To redress the above question, the International Institute for the Unification of Private Law (UNIDROIT) has adopted a Protocol known as the Convention on International Interests in Mobile Equipment on Matters

Specific to Space Asset. It was observed at the final proceeding of the Convention according to Article XXXIV of the Protocol. It shall not affect states' rights and duties under the existing space law treaties and the legal instruments of the International Telecommunication Union (ITU). Whether the draft of final Space Protocol fully respects this public law supersession clause may be the subject of subsequent scrutiny. The objective is to lower the cost of space asset financing by way of facilitation. Whether the new legal regime will achieve its cost saving objective and whether it will improve present space asset financing remain to be seen. Major commercial satellite operators are unconvinced of the need for the new legal instrument. Advocates, however, believe that the space protocol will be a valuable tool for small satellite operators and start-up companies. Moreover it will make the industry more competitive.[48]

Another view is that the early conclusion and adoption of the UNIDROIT space assets protocol will facilitate the expansion of space commerce and trade to the economic benefit of a wide range of states and companies. But there are some critical economic issues that have not yet been resolved. The other international bodies like the United Nations Commission on International Trade Law (UNCTAD) and the World Trade Organisation (WTO) could contribute to the UNIDROIT in this and other areas relating to outer space.[49]

The present status of this Space Protocol is not satisfactory because it was open for signature more than a year since 2012. Only four states have signed but no instruments of ratification have been deposited whereas ten signatories are required to enter the Protocol in force. The reason is that commercial space industry did not welcome the new draft of the Protocol from the very beginning. The industry groups like Satellite Industry Association and the European Satellite Operators Association thought that the new draft will create more uncertainty and risk into satellite finance. Therefore a second look of the new draft is well deserved.[50]

ENVIRONMENT

The financial feasibility of private actors bring fresh legal challenge in the space industry. But this research study belongs to the current era of global sustainable environment. It also flares up some legal debates related with the environment in outer space. In this context, there are two types of space missions like the robotic (e.g. space robotics in **Table 10**) and human missions for exploration of celestial bodies (e.g. celestial mining in **Table 11**). Even the activities of human being like space tourism in **Table 7** or memorial spaceflights of Celestic Inc. (**Table 15**) for sending a symbolic portion of cremated remains to outer space are one form or other would cause environmental problem.[51] These will affect the concerned natural environment in two reciprocal ways. In one way, the human beings and other instrumental facilities with equipments will need protection from potentially harmful environmental elements like radiation, temperature and even dust. In the reciprocal way, the celestial environment will need planetary protection to have the less impact from the activities of human beings and machine.[52]

However, this broader impact of environmental assessment of outer space gets less priority when the issue of space debris threatens the ongoing activities in final frontier. In fact, space environment is not so agitated before the burning problem of space debris comes up. The general concern was cornered earlier because space was not so crowded like earth during the launching of sputnik and afterwards. Therefore, environmental awareness was not a key issue when the space treaties were made.[53] Even environmental protection is remarkably limited in OST.[54] The Article IX of OST only prescribes environmental safeguards. The relevant part of Article IX of OST states

> "...States' Parties to the Treaty shall pursue studies of outer space, including the Moon and other celestial bodies, and conduct exploration of them so as to avoid their harmful contamination and also adverse changes in the environment of the Earth resulting from the introduction of extraterrestrial matter...."

This provision is so broad that it subjugates the very purpose.[55] Moreover, it refers the environment only on Earth and not in outer space. Hence the Article VII (1) of the Moon Agreement further provides that:

> "In exploring and using the Moon, State Parties shall take measures to prevent the disruption of existing balance of its environment, by its harmful contamination through the introduction of extra-environmental matter or otherwise."

This Agreement has minimum number of ratification as mentioned earlier. Overall there is tendency of casual treatment for safeguarding the environment throughout the space treaties. Gradually the situation becomes totally changed. There are many cases of environmental hazards out of which the recent one occurred in Russia.[56]

In this background, space debris was considered for discussion for the first time in 31st session of Scientific and Technical Sub-committee of UNCOPUOS in 1994. Since then it was technically studied and at its 33rd session in 1996, this Subcommittee adopted the technical report on space debris and distributed it in the 39th session of Legal Subcommittee in 2000.[57] When the Scientific and Technical Subcommittee, one division of Subcommittee, well-established the fact of space debris, then it became an agenda in the Legal Subcommittee.[58] This legal agenda is equally important to develop the international legal regulation for private actors in outer space which is examined below.

The legal anxiety is caused from the vast expansion of modern space activities. This expansion is continued with speedy environmental degradation like other large-scale industries. Moreover, the ideology of any business including space is pact with the maximisation of economic profit. Alongside the objectives of any business make value with waste reduction, risk management, pollution control and energy efficiency. These objectives should not deter the growth of business. Rather they should enhance growth. But it is impossible to maintain the optimum balance to reach the goal.[59]

The above problem is a general one but there is specific issue to regulate the space environment in case of private actors. While the commercial space industry grows up in size, the other side of this development is that these commercial actors largely follow the reasoning of their investments. Though it is true for other commercial industries but here the problem is quite different. The environmental impacts of space activities involve a period of time which is considerably longer than any other time-frame of investment decisions. Like the policies for removing space debris may take a decade or a century or even more. Hence, it may be the case that the benefits of investment to reduce space debris will not be enjoyed by the investor but the subsequent investors will get the benefits.[60] In such a complex situation, why a private actor in outer space will invest to protect space environment, is really a point of serious consideration. Therefore it is a legal challenge to satisfy these actors first why they invest and then how they invest for sustainable space environment.

ETHICS

The ethics of private actors may be an area where it relates with environment and all earlier issues. The current era of space activities indicates high-level space commercialisation which enhances the competition of return on investment basis. The different stake-holders of the government itself as well as the private actors come up to take the lead of this competition. Sometimes this competition amongst the private actors goes on with their shoestring budgets. The purpose is that everybody would like to sustain in space industry and to hold their position at the top. In other words, the space industry will not survive without this competition in the long run.

The example of this competition is realised in selling the space products like commercial high-resolution satellite imageries as mentioned in **Table 13**. Sometimes such imageries are sold out at exorbitant cost on exploiting the poor customers from the developing countries. Even such imageries are offered when the low-priced medium range resolution data are needed in case of studying natural resources.[61] The question arises whether such type of practices will be prevailed? So space industry is vulnerable on the ground of ethics. That is why **Table 18** shows the connection of ethics with commercial satellite imageries.

The case of space tourism in relation with ethics is that the ordinary tourism activities under the Sun sometimes violate the code of ethics in the name of entertainment. Similarly, tourism in outer space could violate the ethics of outer space and so it relates with space tourism in **Table 18**.

In this context, it is already realised that ethics has been violated on earth by the very nature as well as activities of human beings in different activities even in ordinary circumstances. Hence the next question follows whether the human beings will do the same mistake in outer space? Whether the ethical violation is permitted in ongoing and near future commercial space activities especially by the private actors?[62] What role the private actors would play to maintain the ethics? Lastly, what will be the code of ethics?[63] There is till now no international legal regulation to satisfy all these queries. But a Sub-commission within the framework of UNESCO was established on the ethics of outer space.[64] It was recommended by this Sub-Commission on the ethics of outer space that ethics would precede and guide the law. The legal framework of space activities would be blended by ethics.[65]

CORPORATE SOCIAL RESPONSIBILITY (CSR)

It is perhaps the ethics that bring to some extent to think over the human society, in which and for which, the big private actors function. The multinational corporate like Boeing Ltd. is the best example. This very idea conceptualises the Corporate Social Responsibility (CSR) in outer space though the CSR is not a new domain in corporate sectors.[66] Besides the large multinational corporations, there are space venturists or entrepreneurs who have also a vital role to fulfill their respective CSR. It is a well-known fact that the private space actors have huge investment in their business with the expectation of high return along with risk. But some actors have overcome this risk to achieve finally its financial target. Such actors have to consider CSR for the following reasons.

There are some private companies where the governments are behind the screen to promote their business activities into the space sector. So these companies are getting different advantages from the government, sometimes enjoying the contracts from the government itself. According to **Table 6**, SPACE X and Orbital Science Corporation are such type of companies that are engaged with commercial space transport in US with the contract from NASA itself.[67] Their activities are confined with NASA's contract till now but the future plan will definitely be on making contract outside NASA.[68] All of them have flourished their business initially with seed money from the Federal Government through NASA. Then depending on the success of these projects from NASA, commercial offers may come from other customers. Since the users have to bear ultimately a heavy price to enjoy the benefits of space technology, so it is not possible for every user or community of users to pay the amount for the services rendered by Space X and others.

Virgin Galactic provides opportunity to make experiments in outer space to researchers, teachers and students. The company's space shuttle SpaceShip Two will be used for this purpose. There are two categories — one is directly engaged with sending these researchers to outer space and the second category is only for sending their payloads.[69] **Table 18** correlates corporate social responsibility with space tourism. Here the query comes whether they would be charged at the same rate with commercial space tourists?

The reply is little bit tricky if such customers in these commercial spaceflights had been from developing countries in space. First of all, whether they would be allowed as a part of CSR and then, whether extra-amount for IPR would be exempted? They should be treated differently if the research purpose is non-commercial. There may be other concerns in future where the big private space companies could express their CSR. Till now there is no international legal regulation to make CSR compulsory for corporate in outer space.

SAFETY

This is unlike other issues above. The major disasters have already occurred with the several space shuttles leaving behind the precious lives of astronauts. The earlier experience was with the disaster of Columbia and Challenger. The Columbia space shuttle broke up in 2003 killing seven astronauts.[70] But the disaster of Challenger space shuttle has changed NASA killing seven crew members in 1986.[71] The other serious concern has been observed very recently during the launching of China's Chang'e 3 spacecraft which was for the purpose of soft landing on Moon. The debris created from the launching has wrecked many nearby houses in the village locality.[72]

Therefore the safety related with space activities is going to be more crucial area in the era of private human spaceflight especially crucial issue in space tourism as shown in **Table 18**. The safety involves launching site processing, ground safety, launch safety (**Table 18** thus tags launching with safety), sub-orbital safety, orbital safety, returning vehicle safety and may be many more.[73] Another concern is that all the above disasters happened under the regime of non-commercial space exploration. Now under the era of commercialisation followed by privatisation, safety becomes first and foremost criteria in the upcoming days which are analysed below.

The private enterprises have involved with sub-orbital space tourism flights as explained in the previous chapter. So the situation would change abruptly with the increasing number of sub-orbital tourism flights. There is no system to regulate this upcoming traffic in sub-orbits or beyond. It is not a problem in earlier periods. This would increase possibility of collision with the sub-orbital flights with each other or any space objects. Even these vehicles may collide with aircrafts in airspace while moving towards or coming down from outer space.[74] Therefore International Civil Aviation (ICAO) has placed one of the tentative agendas on 'safety management and systems engineering' in their upcoming symposium during March 2015 jointly held by United Nations Office of Outer Space (UNOOSA).[75]

Another problem is that these sub-orbital flights have to undergo a wide range of technical approaches like single or multiple stages to orbit, vertical or horizontal landing systems, and both solid and liquid-fueled propulsion systems. Moreover there are involvement of spaceport, aircraft and balloon-launched spacecraft. Some have abort and escape systems whereas others do not. Overall the safety features of these various launch systems are totally diverse. The upcoming steep competition in space tourism transforms this diversity into more complex because of cheaper charging of spaceflight tickets. The complexity is mainly due to effort for low-pricing tickets without compromise in safety. Along with this, there are dozens of spaceports being developed around the world under the jurisdiction of different national laws of the respective countries. The safety standards and regulations that govern spaceports, and, launch and re-entry operations vary widely. There are government licenced as well as non-licenced spaceports by the governments.[76]

It is noted that a uniform safety standard under different technical systems within different jurisdictions is very difficult to maintain. The approaches of different countries are different. There are constant efforts from the UNCOPUOS and the International Civil Aviation Organisation (ICAO) to regulate private space ventures and space tourism enterprises. In spite of these sincere efforts, the regulation of safety is so severe in nature that the International Association for the Advancement of Space Safety (IAASS) was established as a non-profit organisation in 2004. The observer status was granted in 2010 at UNCOPUOS.[77] Finally, there are no common safety standards and procedures for space operations at present. Therefore none is equally protected all over the world from the risks attached with launching, over-flying and re-entering space vehicles.[78]

DISPUTE SETTLEMENTS

The last but not the least issue is dispute settlement which may entangle with any issues above. Any space sectors as mentioned from **Table 3** to **15** could face disputes though satellite communication through private telecommunication companies is a matter of great discord in India. So this sector is linked with dispute settlement in **Table 18**. It remains in both the era of space activities whether it is state-centric or private-centric. Moreover, disputes in general are natural within the process of commercialisation. But why it is necessary to think about the mechanism for settlement of disputes specifically in the present context? The space activities are becoming more and more complex but not always expensive compared to its spin-off benefits. It also involves more desperate actors. The technological impact is on the larger section of the society. Further the interdisciplinary nature of space activities is related with other disciplines like physics, economics, trade, diplomacy, information technology and engineering. So, it requires a specific system of dispute settlement system.[79]

Besides the above analysis, the other explanation is that there is no corresponding procedure for the resolution of dispute in the law of outer space to the Protocol's mandatory dispute resolution process by Arbitral Tribunal or by ICJ. Similarly the COSPAR planetary protection policy does not include any enforcement or dispute resolution process. If consultations between states pursuant to the Outer Space Treaty are not successful or refused, states may resort to diplomatic means or other procedures to search a peaceful resolution of a dispute.[80] Such diplomatic means or other procedures unfortunately do not necessarily guarantee that the dispute will be resolved peacefully.

In case of disputes for private entities, there are three types of problems as following: Firstly, state versus private where the complication will arise when the private entities are from different states and so more than one national law will apply including the dispute settlement mechanism of that state; Secondly, Inter-Governmental Organisation (IGO) versus private where the complexity depends on whether the private entity in question falls within the jurisdiction of the member state of the IGO; and lastly, private versus private. In case of private versus private entity, it is a matter of national law and national court. But nature of space and space activities is international. So, is it feasible to allow the national law system to solve disputes having international character?[81]

In case of state versus private dispute, it storms ISRO, the national space agency of India, for the first time over the case leading to arbitral proceedings of ANTRIX-Devas deal. Here ANTRIX Corporation is the commercial wing of ISRO whereas Devas Ltd. is a private company incorporated outside India.[82] Following is some existing way out of disputes raised from space activities.

Under the existing provisions of space law, the OST[83] provides some relevant textual wording asking for cooperation, mutual assistance and consultations but no rules on actual dispute settlement.[84] Next is the Liability Convention which refers Claims Commission[85] for damage caused by space object. But it has no binding effect. There is surprisingly no provision for settlement of disputes in any other space law treaties.[86]

Besides the provision of space law, there are few initiatives taken by other bodies like ICJ, the ILA and IISL. In the 50th year's celebrations of ICJ, there was session on dispute settlement on new dimensions of international law. It was proposed that disputes related with space activities may be considered as a matter of special Chamber of ICJ.[87] In UNISPACE III Technical Forum in 1999, it was recommended that existing arbitration rules should be considered for disputes between private enterprises themselves, and also, between state and private enterprises.[88] The 1984 Paris Convention (61st conference of ILA) proposed the possibility of establishment of a new International Tribunal for Space Law.[89] The 68th ILA conference in 1998 slightly changed the ILA Draft Convention of 1984 for giving effect of commercialisation and privatisation. The Article 10 of this Draft allowed the private parties of sovereign states in the process of settlement of disputes related to space activities.[90]

The following **Table 19** compares the significance of these issues both in state-centric and private-centric regimes as explained above.

Table 19: Significance of Legal Issues in State & Private-Centric Regime[91]

Legal Issues	Significance For Regime	
	State-Centric	**Private-Centric**
Sovereignty & Proprietary Rights	Traditional.	Severe Intensity.
National Security	Topmost Priority.	Followed according to state's policy.
Liability	Solely Liable.	Traditionally borne by concerned states but appears to be individually liable in upcoming days.
Intellectual Property Rights	Traditional.	Severe intensity or better say much needed for private actors only.
Financing	Not so much attracted.	Must Need.
Environment	Traditional Care.	Very endangering & sensitive.
Ethics	Not considered at all	Immediate attention needed.
Corporate Social Responsibility	As Above.	Must look after agenda.
Safety	Serious One.	More serious and attention needed.
Dispute Settlement	Traditional.	More complex and much attention needed.

The analysis from **Table 19** discloses that the existing legal issues from state-centric regime are at different heights or impacts in the regime of private actors whereas some issues like environment, ethics caused mainly by the introduction of numerous private actors in state-centric regime become very much legally vulnerable. The final resultant is that regulation of these issues for private actors are more deserved than state actors but the process of regulation becomes more complex unlike in the purely state-centric regime.

Conclusion

There are so many issues analysed above which would require international legal regulation for private actors in outer space. Some issues have already been drawing attention by space law scholars since the beginning of post-sputnik space age. The issues like sovereignty, national security, liability were much discussed but environment and dispute settlement were comparatively less talked about. Their reflections were drafted accordingly in the text of state-centric Space Treaties. Compared to these issues, the new ones like IPR, financing, ethics, corporate social responsibility (CSR), safety are legal parameters for increased participations of private actors in outer space.

In this scenario, advancement in space technology further implies much opportunity for investment by the private actors in this final frontier with the expectation of high return on investment. It introduces a different type of competition amongst the private actors in many space-faring countries. This new trend is observed in the case of celestial mining. It is till now an innovative action plan made by the private companies mainly to haunt the precious resources in the cosmos. This very recent plan would require re-imagining the traditional concept of sovereignty not only in space law but also international law as well. Its regulation is most deserved one much before possessing such resources from outer space. So, USA has already outlined its proposed Asteroid Act as the most current development in its domestic space law framework because of lobbying by the private companies in USA planned for celestial mining.

On shifting focus from sovereignty to national security that is purely strategic from the inception of sputnik age, the difficulty arises to keep uniform balance over national security in the era of private commercial high-resolution satellite imageries. These imageries are owned by the private actors like commercial satellite imaging companies. Its applicability is for reconnaissance purposes subject to the orders made by their high-valued customers. The Google Ltd. has started their commercial venture through these imageries. International law although is silent about espionage through such reconnaissance satellites.

The next issue after national security is liability that becomes more intensive with the commercial space era than the state-centric era. The existing Space Treaties provide that the liability is ultimately borne by the state. There is no direct liability on private actors within the existing legal regime. But with the increased number of participation from such actors, some scholarly views have expressed deep concern whether the same tradition would be justified with the increasing number of private actors? Whether such system will be continued for adding more financial burdens on the states? Sometimes the states are not genuinely liable in case of any default made by the private parties.

It is discerned that states have already faced legal problems over these issues. The private actors only fuel up these issues. But the issue like IPR does not directly dealt by the existing provisions of international space law. IPR is attracted much more by the private actors. Moreover this issue makes their participation more strong and dynamic. But the difficulty arises in case of new entrants to space industry. They may face steeper competition from their business because of incurring additional cost for IPR. Therefore to what extent IPR should be permitted is a future legal challenge to the private actors themselves.

The next issue relates with problems of financing where unlike IPR all the private actors needed optimum financing for high-value investment on the space objects like satellites. The UNIDROIT has drafted the Space Protocol but the big private companies in the satellite industry have disagreed with this draft.

The debate over this feasibility of financing is also noted in environmental sustainability of space activities. The recent problem is faced from increasing number of space debris that endangers the space objects owned by the private actors launched into outer space. Though it is the main mantra of any business now-a-days to be environmentally sustainable but to clean up the space environment, it may take number of years. Therefore any private actor will think twice before planning to invest on environmental measures in outer space. The outcome of this investment may not be enjoyed by the very actor.

The next issue connects with ethics. The private actors have high-value investment. So it is a natural expectation that the investment returns will not be compromised in any way. Therefore there is every possibility to violate or ignore the ethics of the business for good returns on investment. This issue is a very new outcome as a result of the activities by privatised space industry.

Another issue is lined up i.e. Corporate Social Responsibility (CSR). The point is immaterial within the concept of CSR whether state is ultimately responsible for national activities in outer space according to Article VI of OST. CSR is required because the return on investment is huge. Thus the private actors have some social responsibility like sponsoring the academics, non-commercial R&D works related with space technology. There is no regulation or code of conduct in this regard.

Another new issue is safety that is more entangled with human spaceflight or space tourism. This problem is developing now. It would require experience over lots of technical experiments to be conducted in different phases of space activity; both in ground and outer space environment.

The last one is dispute settlement that is more obvious in the private era of space activities. It is also developing because till now the international disputes are more or less settled down well before it turns into complex. The disputes in functioning the ISS are settled at preliminary level though these are disputes between states, and outside the scope of this research study. The disputes with private actors exist mainly in the telecommunication industries.

In a nutshell, the above legal hurdles challenge the present domain of private actors in outer space for their dynamic participation as well as further development. Therefore this research study would now look forward for critical legal analysis of space regulations in different countries including India. It would also search critically whether these issues have been at all covered within the existing domestic legal instruments related with space activities or any additional issues exist? How these issues are treated in these legal instruments? Hence the next two chapters would make an effort in this regard – first one with space regulations outside India and next in India itself.

Notes

1. Nanda, Ved, International Law in the Twenty-First Century, In Nandasiri Jasentuliyana (Ed.), *Perspectives on International Law* (London: Kluwer Law International, 1995), p. 110.
2. Gorove, S., "International Space Law in Perspective – Some Major Issues, Trends and Alternatives," In Recueil Des Cours 1983 Vol. III. (The Hague: Martinus Nijhoff Publishers, 1983), p. 359.
3. Data are provided from earlier Tables.
4. Ibid., p.360, See also Bodin, Jean, *On Sovereignty: Four Chapters from the Six Books of Commonwealth*, Julian H. Franklin (ed. & translated) (Cambridge: Cambridge University Press, 1992), p. x.
5. Ibid., Bodin, p. 1.
6. Reijnen, G.C.M., *Utilisation of Outer Space and International Law* (Amsterdam: Elsevier, 1981), pp. 7-8.
7. Kelsen, H., *Principles of International Law* (New York: Rinehart, 1952), pp. 438-444.
8. Right of Passage Case, at http://www.icj-cij.org/docket/index.php?sum=278&code=poi&p1=3&p2=3&case=32&k=ce&p3=5 (Accessed April 30, 2013)
9. Fisheries Case at http://www.icj-cij.org/docket/?p1=3&p2=3&k=a6&case=5&code=ukn&p3=0 (Accessed April 30, 2013).
10. Corfu Channel Case at URL:http://www.icj-cij.org/docket/index.php?p1=3&p2=3&k=cd&case=1 (Accessed April 30, 2013)
11. North Sea Continental Shelf Case at http://www.icj-cij.org/docket/index.php?sum=295&code=cs2&p1=3&p2=3&case=52&k=cc&p3=5 (Accessed April 30, 2013)
12. Nicaragua Case at http://www.icj-cij.org/docket/index.php?sum=367&p1=3&p2=3&case=70&p3=5 (Accessed April 30, 2013)
13. Aerial Incident Case of 10 August 1999 at http://www.icj-cij.org/docket/index.php?sum=585&p1=3&p2=3&case=119&p3=5 (Accessed April 30, 2013)
14. The Case of the S.S. Lotus at http://www.icj-cij.org/pcij/serie_A/A_10/30_Lotus_Arret.pdf (Accessed April 30, 2013)
15. Delupis, I., *International Law and the Independent State* (Essex (Great Britain): Gower Press Ltd., 1974), p. 23.
16. http://www.oosa.unvienna.org/pdf/reports/ac105/AC105_1045E.pdf pp. 33-34 (Accessed September 12, 2013).
17. Lachs, M., "The International Law of Outer Space," In *Recueil Des Cours 1964*, vol. III, (The Hague: Martinus Nijhoff Publishers, 1964), pp. 13-44.
18. See n. 2.

    'It was the October 1975 during the 30th session of the U.N. General Assembly that Colombia first claimed geostationary orbit above its national territory. The claim was predicted on the argument that the geostationary orbit was not included in the concept of outer space alluded to the Outer Space Treaty of 1967. Colombia reiterated its stand at the next session of the General Assembly in 1976. Similar stands were taken by Ecuador and Panama. In November, 1976, the eight equatorial countries (Brazil, Colombia, Congo, Ecuador, Indonesia, Kenya, Uganda and Zaire) met in Bogota to hammer out the legal position of geostationary orbit. Their conference was ended on December 3, 1976, with what is known as Bogota Declaration.'
19. Art III of the Outer Space Treaty states 'State Parties to the Treaty shall carry on activities in the exploration and use of outer space, including the moon and other celestial bodies,

in accordance with the international law, including the Charter of the United Nations, in the interest of maintaining international peace and security and promoting international co-operation and understanding.'; Art XII of the Liability Convention; Art. II of the Moon Treaty.

20. Matte, N.M., *Aerospace Law* (London: Sweet & Maxwell, 1969), p. 52, See also n. 2 for Gorove & n. 6 for Reijnen.
21. Beresford, S.M., *The Future of National Sovereignty, 1960;* In A.G. Haley and W.H. Hanover (Ed.), *Second Colloquium on the Law of Outer Space London 1959 Proceedings* (Vienna: Springer-Verleg), p. 8.
22. Principle I states 'the term "remote sensing" means the sensing of the Earth's surface from space by making use of the properties of electromagnetic waves emitted, reflected or diffracted by the sensed objects, for the purpose of improving natural resources management, land use and the protection of the environment.'
23. Murthi, KRS., "Commercial Availability of High Quality Remote Sensing Imageries: Legal Issues," *Singapore Journal of International and Comparative Law*, vol. 5, no. 1, 2001, pp. 149-155; See also Filho, J.M., *A Remote Sensing Convention for the Advancement of Space Law*, 2004. In Corinne M. Contant Jorgenson (ed.), *Proceedings of the 46th Colloquium on the Law of Outer Space* (Washington: American Institute of Aeronautics & Astronautics), p. 65.
24. Husby, E., "Sovereignty & Property Rights in Outer Space," *Journal of International Law & Practice*, vol. 3, no. 1, 1991, pp. 359-372; See also Lewis, John S., *Mining the Sky Untold Riches from the Asteroids, Comets and Planets* (New York: Basic Books, 1996); Brearley, A., "Mining the Moon: Owning the Night Sky?" *Astropolitics*, vol. 4, no. 1, 2006, p. 46; Pop, V., *Who Owns the Moon? Extraterrestrial Aspects of Land and Mineral Resources Ownership* (Bucharest (Romania): Springer, 2009), p. 20.
25. Art II of the Outer Space Treaty.
26. Art XI of the Moon Treaty.
27. https://www.congress.gov/bill/113th-congress/house-bill/5063 (Accessed November 22, 2014)
28. http://www.spacepolitics.com/2014/07/29/panel-sees-asteroids-act-as-step-in-right-direction-for-space-property-rights/ (Accessed November 22, 2014)
29. http://thehagueinstituteforglobaljustice.org/index.php?page=News-News_Articles-Recent_News-Space_Mineral_Resource_Governance_&pid=138&id=330 (Accessed December 3, 2014)
30. Falk, Richard A., In Ronald J. Stanger (Ed.), *Essays in Espionage and International Law* (Ohio: Ohio State University Press, 1962), pp. 6-9,

    'International law was generally silent about espionage....Thus the problem of espionage in the contemporary world challenges a legal analyst to develop a new conceptual apparatus that is able to cope with the transformed character of international relations....existence and development of international legal standards applicable to aerial espionage performed in the course of cold war follows space espionage. This subject matter is important today because it bears directly and ambiguously upon the hopes for disarmament and the fears of a nuclear surprise attack.'
31. Rao, M. and Murthi, KRS., "Keeping up with Remote Sensing and GI Advances—Policy and Legal Perspectives," *Space Policy*, vol. 22, no. 4, 2006, pp. 262-273.
32. Vijay, T., Drawing the line on Google, *The Hindu*, May 8, 2013, p. 11.
33. Bostwick, H., Google Street View Privacy Issue Raised Again, 2011, at https://www.

legalzoom.com/articles/google-street-view-privacy-issues-raised-again (Accessed September 12, 2014).

34. See n. 23, Murthi.
35. Cho, G., *Geographical Information Science- Mastering the Legal Issues* (Chichester (England): John Willy & Sons Ltd., 2005), p. 287; See also Cuijpers, C., "The Legal Angle of Geo-info," *GIS Development*, Vol. 13, no. 8, 2009, p. 38.
36. Article VII: 'Each State Party to the Treaty that launches or procures the launching of an object into outer space, including the moon and other celestial bodies, and each State Party from whose territory or facility an object is launched, is internationally liable for damage to another State Party to the Treaty or to its natural or juridical persons by such object or its component parts on the Earth, in air space or in outer space, including the moon and other celestial bodies.'
37. Article II: 'A launching State shall be absolutely liable to pay compensation for damage caused by its space object on the surface of the earth or to aircraft in flight.'
38. Lee, Ricky J., "Reconciling International Space Law with the Commercial Realities of the Twenty-first Century," *Singapore Journal of International and Comparative Law*, vol. 4, no. 1, 2000, p. 229.
39. Zhao, Yun, *Space Commercialisation and the Development of Space Law from a Chinese Legal Perspective* (New York: Nova Science Publishers, 2009), p. 46.
40. Larsen, Paul B., "Future Protocol on Security Interests in Space Assets," *Journal of Air Law & Commerce*, vol. 67, no. 2, 2002, pp. 1091-1092.
41. Deem, Charles L., "Liability of Private Space Transportation Companies to Their Customers," *Insurance Counsel Journal*, vol. 51, no. 3, 1984, p. 349.
42. Lyall, F. and Larsen, Paul B., *Space Law: A Treatise* (Surrey (England): Ashgate, 2009), p. 124.
43. Issue paper prepared by International Bureau of WIPO, April 2004. http://www.wipo.int/export/sites/www/patent-law/en/developments/pdf/ip_space.pdf (Accessed June 17, 2013).
44. Ibid.
45. http://www.businesswire.com/news/home/20120308006183/en/Medusa-Space-LLC-Acquires-Microgravity-Enterprises-Intellectual#.VHtaRjHF8v0 (Accessed June 17, 2013).
46. Smith, Bradford L., *New Initiatives in Intellectual Property Law for Space Activities, 2001*. In Corinne M. Contant Jorgenson (Ed.), *Proceedings of the 43rd Colloquium on the Law of Outer Space* (Washington: American Institute of Aeronautics and Astronautics), pp. 189-190.
47. Traa-Engelman, H.V., *The Need for A Uniform Law System Protecting Intellectual Property Rights in Outer Space*, 2009. In Corinne M. Contant Jorgenson (Ed.), *Proceedings of the 51st Colloquium on the Law of Outer Space* (Washington: American Institute of Aeronautics and Astronautics), p. 38.
48. Brief Report of the Final Space Protocol by Paul B. Larsen, at http://www.iislweb.org/docs/2012_unidroit.pdf (Accessed July 25, 2013).
49. Kaul, Ranjana, *International Space Law: Future Outlook*, 2012. In Arvind Gupta et al., (eds.), *Space Security Need for Global Convergence* (New Delhi: Pentagon Security International), p. 55.
50. http://www.americanbar.org/content/dam/aba/publications/air_space_lawyer/ASL_V26N1_sundahl.authcheckdam.pdf (Accessed July 25, 2013).

51. Fawkes, S. (2007), Space Tourism and Carbon Dioxide Emissions, at http://www.thespacereview.com/article/813/1 (Accessed July 25, 2013).
52. Sterns, P. and Tennen, L.I., *Should There Be An Environmental "Code of Conduct" for Activities in Outer Space?* In Corinne M. Contant Jorgenson (Ed.), *Proceedings of the 53rd Colloquium on the Law of Outer Space* (Washington: American Institute of Aeronautics and Astronautics, 2011), p. 268.
53. Manson, Harold Craig, "The Impact of International Outer Space Commerce on the Environment," *Texas International Law Journal*, vol. 26, no. 54, 1991, p. 553.
54. Fawcett, J.E.S., *Outer Space New Challenges to Law and Policy* (Oxford: Clarendon Press, 1984), p. 32.
55. See n. 53, p. 550.
56. http://mobiletoi.timesofindia.com/mobile.aspx?article=yes&pageid=20&sectid=edid=&edlabel=CAP&mydateHid=03-07-2013&pubname=Times+of+India+-+Delhi&edname=&articleid=Ar02005&publabel=TOI(Accessed July 5, 2013).
'Russian rocket carrying 3 sats blows up after lift-off....The rocket contained 172 tonnes of highly toxic heptyl propellant...Toxic clouds would probably not reach the town of Baikonur some 60 km away as it was raining, authorities instructed locals to stay at home and not to open windows, and ordered to close shops and public catering.'
57. Space Debris Mitigation Guidelines of the Committee on Peaceful Uses of Outer Space, at http://orbitaldebris.jsc.nasa.gov/library/Space%20Debris%20Mitigation%20Guidelines_COPUOS.pdf (Accessed July 10, 2013).
58. Interview with Mazlan Othman, Director of the Office for Outer Space Affairs, at http://www.un.org/apps/news/newsmakers.asp?NewsID=43 (Accessed July 10, 2013)
'Before something comes to the Committee, there has to be a very strong scientific foundation, and this can be dealt with by the scientific and technical subcommittee. Then, when those issues are pretty much resolved, we can take them on to the legal subcommittee. Space debris is such an issue. We discussed space debris from the scientific point of view for years after which we were then confident enough to come up with guidelines. And now the legal subcommittee is looking at which countries are enforcing space debris mitigation.'
59. Chatterjee, P. and Finger, M., *The Earth Brokers: power, politics and world development* (London: Routledge, 1994), p. 8.
60. Greenberg, Joel S., *Economic Principles Applied to Space Industry Decisions* (Virginia: American Institute of Aeronautics and Astronautics, 2003), p. 381.
61. Rao, U. R., *The Role of Ethics in the Decision-Making Strategies Such as Technological Feasibility*, Cost-Benefit Ratio, 2000, p. 67, at http://unesdoc.unesco.org/images/0012/001220/122048e.pdf (Accessed July 10, 2013).
62. Livingston, David M, *The Ethical Commercialisation of Outer Space*, 2000, at http://www.spacefuture.com/archive/the_ethical_commercialization_of_outer_space.shtml (Accessed July 10, 2013).
63. Sachdeva, G.S., "Commercial Order of Outer Space: Quest for Ethical Values," *Indian Journal of International Law*, vol. 51, no.1, 2011, pp. 21-41. See also Livingston, David M., The Ethical Commercialisation of Outer Space, 1999, at http://www.spacefuture.com/archive/the_ethical_commercialization_of_outer_space.shtml (Accessed July 30, 2014).
64. Gilbert, Juan M. F., *Law and Ethics of Outer Space*, 2001. In Corinne M. Contant Jorgenson (Ed.), *Proceedings of the 43rd Colloquium on the Law of Outer Space*

(Washington: American Institute of Aeronautics and Astronautics), p. 14.
65. http://unesdoc.unesco.org/images/0012/001220/122048e.pdf. p. 80. (Accessed July 10, 2013).
66. Ekweozoh, Irene, "Shifting Focus from State Responsibility to Corporate Responsibility: Finding an Ethical Approach to Inclusive Outer Space Governance", Presentation delivered on May 30, 2014 at the 2nd Manfred Lachs International Conference on Global Space Governance, Montreal, Canada, 2014. http://www.mcgill.ca/iasl/sites/mcgill.ca.iasl/files/mlc-2014-ekweozoh.pdf (Accessed June 3, 2014).
67. http://www.spacex.com/about (Accessed July 11, 2013)
68. http://www.orbital.com/ (Accessed July 11, 2013)
69. http://www.virgingalactic.com/research/ (Accessed October 14, 2014).
70. Colombia Disaster, at http://www.space.com/19436-columbia-disaster.html (Accessed July 3, 2013)
71. Challenger Disaster, at http://www.space.com/18084-space-shuttle-challenger.html (Accessed July 3, 2013)
72. http://www.spacedaily.com/reports/China_space_launch_debris_wrecks_villagers_homes_report_999.html (Accessed December 10, 2013)
73. Jakhu, R.S. et al., The Need for an Integrated Regulatory Regime for Aviation and Space ICAO for Space? (New York: Springer, 2011), pp. 71-99.
74. Tronchetti, Fabio, "Using Air Traffic Control Rules as a Model to Manage Sub-orbital Traffic: a Proposal," *Asian Journal of Air & Space Law*, vol. 2, no. 2, 2012, p. 224.
75. http://www.icao.int/Meetings/SPACE2015/Pages/Programme.aspx (Accessed September 30, 2014).
76. Pelton, Joseph N., The International Challenges of Regulation of Commercial Space Flight, 2010; In Joseph N. Pelton and Ram S. Jakhu (Eds.), *Space Safety Regulations and Standards* (Oxford: Elsevier), pp. 289-300.
77. International Association for the Advancement of Space Safety. http://iaass.space-safety.org/ (Accessed July 3, 2013)
78. See n. 73, p. xii.
79. Goh, G.M., *Dispute Settlement in International Space Law: A Multi-Door Courthouse for Outer Space* (Leiden: M.N. Publishers, 2007), p. 3.
80. Williams, Sylvia M., *Dispute Settlement and Space Activities: A New Framework Required?* In Corinne M. Contant Jorgenson (Ed.), *Proceedings of the 39th Colloquium on the Law of Outer Space* (Washington: American Institute of Aeronautics and Astronautics, 1997), pp. 61-67.
81. Dunk, F. G. Von Der, *Space for Dispute Settlement Mechanisms-Dispute Resolution Mechanisms for Space?* A Few Legal Considerations. In Corinne M. Contant Jorgenson (Ed.), *Proceedings of the 44th Colloquium on the Law of Outer Space* (Washington: American Institute of Aeronautics and Astronautics, 2002), pp. 442-452.
82. http://www.thehindu.com/news/international/world/devas-investors-take-antrix-to-arbitration-court-in-the-hague/article4718339.ece (Accessed July 30, 2014).
83. Article III and IX of OST.
84. Bockstiegel, K.H., "Proposed Draft Convention on the Settlement of Space Law Disputes," *Journal of Space Law*, vol. 12, no. 2, 1985, p. 136.
85. Article XIV of the Liability Convention.
86. Diederiks-Verschoor, I.E. H., "The Settlements of Disputes in Space: New Developments," *Journal of Space Law*, vol. 26, no. 1, 1998, p. 42.

87. See n. 80, p. 64.
88 Proceedings of the Workshop on Space Law in the Twenty-First Century http://www.oosa.unvienna.org/pdf/publications/st_space_02E.pdf (Accessed June 28, 2013).
89 See n. 80, p. 63.
90 ILA Conference Resolution 2000. file:///C:/Users/DELL/Downloads/RESspace%20(1).pdf (Accessed June 28, 2013).
91 Data are provided from analysis of legal issues.

IV. Space Regulations Outside India

Introduction

The previous chapter makes an attempt that there are legal issues where international legal regulation is required for private actors in outer space. But the space law treaties are the only soft regulations at international level till now. Hence the countries especially space faring ones, have faced problems to regulate the above issues to promote such actors within their national jurisdiction. This circumstance follows in framing the national space legislations for domestic space activities. Its main purpose is commercial development of private actors.[1] Albeit very few countries have comprehensive national space legislation. Here the issues analysed in the previous chapter are assumed to have some reflections.

It is also to be mentioned that the regulations include policies and institutions to develop such regulations besides these national space legislations. In this view, policies generally are framed first, then legislations, and last institutions. Therefore the following analysis is based on these three themes. The present analysis further confines within few countries because national space activities of many countries are still in its nascent stage even at the state level. So the very conception of private actors in outer space is a day dream just like achieving the goal of self-reliant space technology in those countries. So the following analysis sometimes just introduces the promising countries in space activities. It is most expected that their current space activities would face similar circumstances in near future.

ASIA

This research study has prime focus on India. So let the analysis be started with countries from Asian region. Though many theoretical concepts of astronomy have developed from the Asian region as reflected in chapter I but the very few Asian countries like China, India and Japan have crossed some milestones through their national space programmes. **Table 20** shows the Asian picture.

Table 20: Space Related Regulations in Asia[2]

Countries	Policies	Legislations	Institutions
China	I. Three White Papers 1. Chinese White Paper on Space Activities, 2000 2. Chinese Space Activities, 2006 3. Chinese Space Activities, 2010 II. Interim Measures on the Administration of Permits for Civil Space Launch Projects III. The 11th Five-Year Program for National Space Development	Nil	1. The Commission of Science, Technology and Industry for National Defence (COSTIND). 2. China National Space Administration (4 Departments but 2 relevant here). (i) Department of General Planning. (ii) Department of Foreign Affairs.
Hong Kong	Nil	The Outer Space Act 1986 (Hong Kong) Order 1990	Executive Council
Singapore	Nil	Nil	The Office for Space Technology and Industry (OSTIn).
Japan	1. Basic Plan on Space Policy 2009 2. Basic Plan on Space Policy 2013	1. Basic Space Law 2008 2. The Radio Law 3. The Space Activities Act (In-process)	1. Strategic Head Quarters for Space Policy 2. JAXA 3. The Society of Japanese Aerospace Companies (SJAC)

Republic of Korea	National Space Development Mid- and Long-Term Basic Plan 1996 (i) Mid-Term Plan (2006-2010) (ii) Long-Term Plan (2011-2015)	1. Aerospace Industry Promotion Act, 1989 2. The Space Development Promotion Act 2005 3. The Space Damage Compensation Act 2008	1. Korea Aerospace Research Institute (KARI) (Independent Organisation since 1996) 2. KARI, affiliated institution of Korea Research Council of Fundamental Science & Technology since 2008
Pakistan	1. National Space Policy (In-Process) 2. Pakistan's Space Vision 2040	Telecommunication (Reorganisation) Act, 1996	1. Pakistan Space and Upper Atmospheric Research Commission (SUPARCO) 2. Research Society of International Law (RSIL)
Thailand	Nil	Nil	1. Information and Communication Technology Ministry 2. The National Committee on Space Policy 3. Thai Space Agency (Future regulator)
Philippine	Nil	1. The Constitution of 1987 2. Philippine Space Act of 2012	Philippine Space Commission (PSC)
United Arab Emirates (UAE)	EIAST Strategic Plan 2011-13	Nil	Emirates Institution for Advanced Science & Technology (EIAST)

Republic of Kazakhstan	Nil	Law of the Republic of Kazakhstan on Space Activities, 2012.	National Space Agency of Kazakhstan (Kazcosmos)

China is the most promising one in Asia leading the space activities not only in Asia but also in the world at present. The Registration Convention was acceded on December 12, 1988.[3] Chinese White Paper on Space Activities 2000[4] framed it keeping its national security intact as well as promoting space industrialisation. In this regard this White Paper would like to enact laws and regulations following its existing state policies, laws and other regulations. Also, it highlights international cooperation and peaceful uses of outer space for civilian programme and societal development. It stresses on IPR. The space debris issue is also a serious concern and the state has extended international cooperation to mitigate the issue. But the country never returns back from state's supervision over space activities.[5] The White Paper remains silent about the scope of private actors that implies more monopoly by the state.

The next White Paper, Chinese Space Activities 2006 prescribes for consideration of national security and environment while building the national space industry.[6] The Chinese Space Activities 2010, the last one till now, acknowledges the importance of national security. This document is also blueprint for space debris. This Paper stresses on innovation in space science and technology. It attracts the issue of IPR later on. Like earlier Papers, it is silent on private space activities. Finally, all the White Papers have failed to develop the infrastructure for space legislation in China.[7]

The Interim Measures on the Administration of Permits for Civil Space Launch Projects adopted in November, 2002 concerns with the licencing of launching services by the private enterprises. It is applicable for all space-crafts launched within the territory of China but the purpose will not be military. The Commission for Science, Technology and Industry for National Defence (COSTIND) is the supreme authority to grant the licence after satisfying that the prescribed procedure is followed by the private enterprise. It implies that China shows its sovereign authority to issue the required licence for launching through COSTIND. This Commission is also in charge of national defence or security of the country. As described in the previous chapter within issue of financing, the provision for third party insurance and other necessary licences for launching a space object are must for getting the permit to launch.[8]

The 11th Five-Year Programme for National Space Development released by COSTIND in 2007 prescribes that the country will make national space law without mentioning any time frame. Also, the policy will be built-up for space industry to provide incentives for using domestic space products like domestic satellites, remote sensing data and rockets. It will forward further towards commercialisation and privatisation.[9]

Besides policies, **Table 20** guides this research study about regulation through institutions in China. It is already mentioned that COSTIND is at the top, and China National Space Administration (CNSA) is a part of COSTIND. The CNSA is in charge of the enforcement of national space policies as well as organising the space science and technology along with space industry. It appears that department of general planning and that of foreign affairs out of four departments of CNSA may regulate to some extent the space activities of the country.[10]

The Chinese authorities have the strict confidential policy regarding their space activities as a whole. This bars to get detailed information for regulation.[11] There is lastly one fact that the country is not interested to promote private actors or such actors may exist under full autonomy of the government. It is quasi-privatisation that is observed in other industrial sectors of China.[12] So the regulations both existing and upcoming follow this trend.

Though once upon a time, Hong Kong was under China but it is not under the administration of Mainland China now. Its liberal market is flooded with private enterprises having businesses with modern technology. In this regard, space technology is not an exception. The private companies, in fact, are engaged with telecommunication services in Hong Kong. The Registration Convention was acceded in the same date as China.[13] The Outer Space Act 1986 (Hong Kong) Order 1990 was applied to this territory before its entry to the People's Republic of China in 1997. The four space law treaties (except the Moon Treaty, 1979) have effect on Hong Kong on ratification by the United Kingdom.[14]

After taken over by China in 1997, the Outer Space Act (Hong Kong) Order 1990, as shown in **Table 20** was considered as the foundation of the present Outer Space Ordinance (Cap. 523). This Ordinance is the main constitutional document to launch and operate a space object and other activities in outer space. Two companies were granted licence as per this Ordinance. The incorporated companies in Hong Kong are APT Satellite

Company Limited and Asia Satellite Telecommunications Company Limited. According to this Ordinance, two licences are required to launch a satellite. The licences were granted by the Hong Kong's Chief Executive to procure the launch and operation of the satellite. According to the prescribed provisions, the space activities will not disturb in any way public health or the safety of persons or property as well as keeping the international obligations of China with a strong focus on national security of China and Hong Kong. But the Outer Space Ordinance is more restricted with procuring and launching of satellites. As a result, the growing trend of expansion of space activities with more inclination towards privatisation requires Hong Kong to balance public international law and private domestic law simultaneously.[15] The Table shows no policies to regulate but under the Basic Law, the Executive Council has power to advise the Chief Executive mentioned above to make any important policy decisions.[16] Therefore, the Chief Executive has enough power to regulate the private actors in outer space.

Besides Hong Kong, another business hub in Asia is Singapore. **Table 20** has no mention of policies or legislations to regulate the private actors. But there is institution like the Office for Space Technology and Industry (OSTIn) formed by the Singapore Government in August 2012. Its sole purpose is to regulate the private actors to develop the space industry.[17] The different types of space activities include satellite technology development, satellite remote sensing applications, and satellite communication services.[18] Singapore Technologies Electronics[19], a unit of defence conglomerate Singapore Technologies Engineering Ltd., has already performed the works for observation satellites. Moreover, there are huge possibilities to use the economic resources to start space tourism from Singapore using the Changi Airport. Only there would be a great expectation for favourable laws with tax incentives.[20] It is presumed from the analysis that space is a sunrise industry in Singapore where legislations will be developed supporting the issue of financing for space activities.

Unlike the above countries, Japan has developed strong base on regulating the space. The Registration Convention was acceded on June 20, 1983.[21] Japan's initiative to legislate national space law started with the transfer of H-IIA rockets by Japan Aerospace Exploration Agency[22] (JAXA) to Mitsubishi Heavy Industries (MHI) in April 2007. It was followed by introducing another private actor, Mitsubishi Electronics. These incidents brought the thrust to develop the space related regulations in the country.[23]

From the angle of policy initiative as depicted in **Table 20**, it brought up the Basic Space Plan of June, 2009.[24] Its subsequent and recent follow-up was 'Basic Plan for Space Policy' established by the Strategic Headquarters for Space Policy of Japan on January 25, 2013.[25] It offered an overall picture and plan for the next five years i.e. 2013-2017 Japanese Financial Year. This policy prescribed the government to create an environment such that the private actors including new entrepreneurs would be encouraged to develop national space industry.[26]

The legislative impact was 'Basic Space Law' made by the Japanese Government in 2008.[27] This only space legislation prescribed the commercialisation of research and development following promotion of space industry[28] and that of space development by private enterprises. The necessary steps taken are for tax and other financial support to boost investment from the private enterprises.[29] So the issue of financing is highlighted here. The environmental measures are taken for conservation and protection of environment.[30] There is a new initiative to ensure close cooperation between different sectors like universities, private businesses etc.[31] The significance of this Article is to legalise the process of human resource development within domestic space law framework. The regime of private actors would require such type of legal provision to furnish in the market. The legislation is to be made not only in accordance with international space law treaties but also for the utilisation of the private sectors.[32] So this provision obligates the state to make legislation for private actors.

Another Bill on the Legislation of Space Activities is in process. It covers mainly the authorisation as well as liability risk sharing regime. All commercial launches have certain involvement of JAXA with authorisation from government.[33] Therefore the state's sovereignty controls any launching by private actors. The second concerns with liability. Though it is different kind of liability but liability risk-sharing regime is the core of legal risk management in space activities. Like the safety at different levels as stated in the previous chapter, it covers liability concerning with different levels like launch, re-entry and satellite operation in orbit. But liability risk-sharing regime includes channeling the liability, financial responsibility, requirements of space operators like insurance etc. and government indemnifications.[34] Moreover, the third party indemnification regime already exists in the country for commercial launches by the companies like MHI.

Therefore, JAXA will pay the damage caused by the launch if it exceeds the third party insurance.[35] Thus the forthcoming Space Activities Act will guide Japan's future initiative regarding privatisation and commercialisation of space business.

Besides this upcoming Act, the Radio Law at present is the single most important domestic law. Here any non-governmental space activities are authorised and continuously supervised by the state.[36]

Table 20 shows that the institutional regulation is assigned to the Strategic Head Quarters for Space Policy under the Cabinet and JAXA. But after implementing the above Basic Space Law 2008, JAXA is the main regulatory institution taking charge from other governmental institutions.[37] So, it would contribute to the space policies specified in the Basic Plan. The national space agency is competent to give advice to the private enterprises on their request. Now the Prime Minister, the head of the Cabinet Office along with the Minister of Economy, Trade and Industry, the Minister of Education, Culture, Sports, Science and Technology, and the Minister of Internal Affairs and Communications are all in cooperation with JAXA to regulate the space industry.[38] The Society of Japanese Aerospace Companies (SJAC),[39] an organisation representing Japanese aerospace industry since 1952 has put effort to regulate the promotion of aerospace industrial policies.[40]

On comparison with national space activities of above space giants like China and Japan, the country South Korea, officially known as Republic of Korea, is not famous as space-faring country; neither has it drawn the attention of international space market through its private actors. The Registration Convention was acceded on October 14, 1981.[41]

The Korean Aerospace Research Institute[42] (KARI) was established in 1989 under the control of government's wing, Ministry of Education, Science and Technology (MEST). There is also National Space Committee under the President to review the policy of MEST. The KARI has responsibility for national space development plan though the focus is on satellite development and launch vehicle technology. The country established its first National Space Development Mid- and Long-Term Basic Plan in 1996 (**Table 20**). The plan was for basic activities in space up to 2015. The latest version of the plan divided the period into mid-term (2006–2010) and long-term (2011–2015).[43]

Though the government is the main actor but private actors exist in the form of domestic companies like Korea Aerospace Industry Co. (KAI),

Korean Air, Hanwha, Doowon Heavy Industrial, Daewoo Heavy Industries and Machinery. The ROTEM, Korean Air, Hankook Fiber, Hanwha, Doowon Heavy Industrial and Samsung Techwin are KARI subcontractors for the development of the Korean Sounding Rocket and Space Launch Vehicle Program.[44] This development of technology related industry is parallel to that of space law since the establishment of KARI. Therefore to analyse the development of South Korea's national space legislation, the concerned development of space technology, industry and activities is very much required.[45] At the outset it is to be noted that the private enterprises do not get much financial support from the government as the space sector is monopolised by the national research institution. Technology transfer from government research institution to private sector is lacking.[46]

Alongside these policies, there are three legislations as shown in **Table 20**. The first one was Aerospace Industry Promotion Act in 1989 followed by Space Development Promotion Act in 2005 which was revised twice in 2008 and 2009,[47] and lastly, Space Damage Compensation Act, 2007.[48]

The Aerospace Industry Promotion Act, 1989, provides the financial support for manufacturing space-crafts and satellites according to Article 12. There is a provision for designating and supporting specified businessmen. But Article 13 prescribes that these aerospace businessmen could lend the state-owned facilities and also can enjoy the benefits derived from it.[49] The implication is that the legal hurdles for financial resources which are subject of UNIDROIT Space Protocol could be bypassed here; because the aerospace businessmen would enjoy the benefit of lending the state-owned facilities with the benefits derived from them. It is a totally new endeavour within the issue of financing.

The Space Development Promotion Act 2005[50] is targeted to promote and safeguard the national space industry because huge investment along with high risk is related with any space project. The provision for domestic registration of space object is reflected in Article 8. It supports the sovereignty issue. Also, according to Article 11, state's sovereignty is reflected on issuing launching licence by the state for a launch vehicle; Article 14 provides the liability of a person for damage from space accident; Article 16 is a little way ahead for dispute settlement in space accidents on establishing space accident investment commission; Article 18 provides support for private space development projects. The supportive measures from the Minister of Science and Technology are tax incentive, financial support etc. It extends towards the increase of investment on research and development of the private sector; Article 21 is for the national security issue along with space development programmes.[51] Therefore the analysis shows that this Act covers many legal issues like sovereignty, national security, liability, financial and dispute settlement.

The Space Damage Compensation Act, 2008[52] is also known as Space Liability Act, 2008. The separate Act for compensation is established for knowing the exact damage and limiting the liability to protect the aggrieved parties in case of damage through space activities. It is unique in this sense. It deals with direct injury but not indirect one. Hence Korea has one added legal advantage to solve the liability issue in more strategic way. It would bypass the conflicting disputes in this regard.

The above KARI is behind the regulation through institution. But since 2008 it is not an independent institution but an affiliated body under Korea Research Council of Fundamental Science & Technology.[53]

The following Asian countries, though most promising in space, but besides Kazakhstan, none has national space legislation like above countries.

Pakistan has till now ratified all the five major space treaties including the Moon Treaty, 1979.[54] The Registration Convention was signed and ratified on December 1, 1975 and February 27, 1986.[55] The Moon Treaty was acceded on February 27, 1986.[56] Pakistan is amongst the very few countries that have ratified the Moon Treaty, 1979. The draft of national space policy has been prepared and submitted to the government where the regulatory regime would cover the issuance of licence to satellite operators.[57] The National Telecommunication Policy is being drafted by the Ministry of Information Technology. It is an effort to connect terrestrial operators with satellite operators.[58] Pakistan's Space Vision 2040, has been announced where the state has put many progrmmes and agendas. These are to be fulfilled in due course of time.[59]

The principal space organisation is the national space agency of Pakistan known as Pakistan Space and Upper Atmospheric Research Commission (SUPARCO).[60] It was established in 1961, and got the status of commission in the year 1981.[61] There was a SUPARCO's national conference on space during 2012 where space law was a part of the schedule of the programme. The conference report exhibited that the local laws of Pakistan would be developed to make it compatible with international space law first. Then this development would support commercialisation and privatisation for making a sustainable space industry through these regulations.[62]

Moreover, space related matters are governed by different legislations and rules belonging to different areas of domestic law. The SUPARCO lacks constitutional and legal mandate to regulate and control space activities following the implementation of space policy. The reason is that SUPARCO is functioning under the administration of Federal Government but the legislation power is with the Provincial Governments. The Pakistan Telecommunication (Reorganisation) Act, 1996, is the only domestic Act that supports to some extent to regulate the telecommunication activities within Pakistan. Section 4(a) provides that the Pakistan Telecommunication Authority (PTA) regulates partly the conduct of satellite service providers.[63] Pakistan has just started to regulate its space programme through its national space agency SUPARCO. It conducted international space conference in 2014 like 2012 with a panel discussion on space law.[64] Besides SUPARCO, the Research Society of International Law (RSIL)[65] has started interaction with SUPARCO for developing regulation.[66] But it is not clear how far it put effort to regulate the private actors because 'Pakistan does not have space legislation and regulatory framework in place as such'.[67]

Thailand is not famous for space activities like the above Asian countries but there is a development on space law in Thailand as decided by the National Committee on Space Policy in its recent meeting. It has acknowledged the guideline for space affairs development of Thailand as proposed by the Information and Communication Technology Ministry earlier. These two bodies – one is Committee and other is Ministry—are the institutions in Thailand to regulate the space activities presently. But the Thai Space Agency will be the future regulator. However the guideline is composed of strategies which focus on (1) development of space affairs for the national security, (2) development of space law and international cooperation, and (3) commercialisation of space.[68] It encapsulates from above that Thailand is prepared for making or changing the domestic law as suitable for space industry keeping its national security intact. Also, the country would like to be a leader in commercial space sector.

Philippine is one of the Asian countries where there is no indigenous space technology. In spite of that the state has drafted a Bill for an Act for creating and establishing a space agency. The Act shall be known as

Philippine Space Act of 2012. Moreover, the Moon Treaty was signed on April 23, 1980 and ratified on May 26, 1981.[69]

The brief provisions of the Bill on Philippine Space Act, 2012 are: section 2 provides the declaration of the policy that follows the policies and mandates in the 1987 Constitution. Here two points are relevant in the present context – one is needed 'for maintaining sovereignty of the state' and other is 'the recognition of the indispensable role of the private sector with the encouragement of private enterprise and provision of incentives to investments.'[70]

Moreover section 4 of this upcoming Act provides the establishment of the Philippine Space Commission (PSC) whose objective is keeping national security intact as well as to promote the peaceful use and exploration of space that is also the purpose of all the UN space treaties.[71] Section 5 provides protection of IPR.[72] Section 12 states to take financial initiative by the prescribed authority like incentives to be needed for investments, e.g. tax exemptions, tariff cuts, etc. for promotion of public-private partnership of space exploration.[73] Therefore, the issues of sovereignty, national security, IPR and financing are to be reflected within its future Space Act.

There are no countries from the Arab region till now. Therefore this research study takes one Arab country, United Arab Emirates (UAE). UAE adopted the Registration Convention on November 7, 2000.[74] The Emirates Institution for Advanced Science & Technology (EIAST) is the regulatory body behind developing and promulgating space law in UAE. It was established in 2006 by the Decree of Dubai Government.[75] The corresponding Act is 'Law Relating to the Establishment of the Emirates Institution for Advanced Science & Technology'.[76] One of the strategic objectives of the EIAST Strategic Plan 2011-13 is 'Participating in the drafting and execution of local, regional and international space related laws and regulations, to enhance the state's sovereignty in outer space affairs'.[77] Therefore UAE is also going to draft the space related regulations to carry forward its sovereignty in outer space matters. There is no special mention for regulating private actors.

Unlike the above Asian countries, the credit of Kazakhstan goes for having the Baikonur cosmodrome. It is the most dynamic spaceport in Asia. Russia uses this spaceport mainly for its launches. The National Space Agency of Kazakhstan is called as Kazcosmos. Its one of the major function is to regulate and coordinate Kazakhstan's space activities and to prepare the space-related legislature.[78] So Kazcosmos is the regulatory institution related with space activities in the country. The Registration Convention was acceded on January 11, 2001,[79] whereas the Moon Treaty was acceded on January 11, 2001.[80]

The Law of the Republic of Kazakhstan on Space Activities, 2012, is itself made for commercial space activities according to Article 1(7).[81] The Constitution of Kazakhstan and other legislative Acts of the country are applicable to the space activities of the country according to Article 2(1). Any international treaty ratified by this Republic is applicable.[82] Article 3 prescribes that the principles of implementation of space activities are through environmental safeguards, compliance with the international law norms in the field of space activities.[83] The Articles 11 and 12 are a proof of state's sovereignty because space objects must be registered by the state that has right also; state has control in the field of space activities. It reflects that Kazakhstan has adopted the Registration Convention in its domestic law.[84] The safety issue is provided in the chapter 5. Article 29 regulates the ecological condition of the environment in the region where space activities are conducted.[85] The regulation for private actors is not specifically mentioned but this domestic space legislation covers the activities of private actors in the country. It is found that the issues of sovereignty, environment and safety are duly acknowledged to pursue the space activities.

AFRICA

Unlike Asian countries, there are very few African countries that have some global exposure for space activities. South Africa is leading one following the others like Nigeria etc. As a programme of international cooperation to develop the infrastructure in non-space-faring states, International Astronautical Congress (IAC) was held at South Africa for the first time in 2011. Previously, the United Nations Office of Outer Space has conducted a workshop on space law in Nigeria during 2005.[86]

Table 21: Space Related Regulations in Africa[87]

Countries	Policies	Legislations	Institutions
Whole Africa			African Leadership Conference on Space Science & Technology (ALC)
South Africa	National Space Policy, 2008	1. Space Affairs Act, 1993 2. South African National Space Agency Act, 2008	1. Ministry of Trade & Industry 2. SA Council for Space Affairs 3. SA National Space Agency
Nigeria	1. National Space Policy, 2001 2. National Geo-information Policy, 2003	1. Nigerian Insurance Act, 2003 2. The Communications Act, 2003 3. Copyright Act, Cap 68, Laws of the Federation, 1990. 4. Fire Arms Act, Cap146 5. National Space Research & Development Agency Act, 2010	National Space Council (established in June 2013)

There is African Leadership Conference on Space Science & Technology (ALC) that is very encouraging to develop space related regulation for private actors in this region. It has pro-institution status in regulating private actors. This is noted from the following analysis. It is a biennial conference that was first held in 2005. Each time the conference was held on different parts of Africa. The goal of this Conference is to make Africa vibrant in space science and technology. Only the African member states can contribute with the two exempted category out of which one is non-member state represented by a private company.[88] The 2nd ALC at South Africa introduced specific theme like space law in 2007. The 4th ALC conducted session on space law for its capacity development within Africa with the support from UNOOSA.[89]

It was observed in 2nd ALC that there were very few African states that were acceded to the international space law treaties and a small number of states of Africa involved in the activities of Legal Subcommittee of COPUOS. The recommendation was to consider developing national space legislation for African countries that would like to develop space activities. Other recommendation was to extend African partnerships in space law where practitioners, academicians and policy makers all should join.[90] The recommendation from the 4th ALC was to consider domestic legislation.[91] This brief descriptive analysis of the development of space law through ALC would bring an overall promotion of space law in African countries.

It is observed that the development of space law within ALC was first started from the conference at South Africa. Not only that, South Africa has leading role in African region where the comprehensive national space law exists. South Africa has ratified the Outer Space Treaty in 1968 and the Rescue Agreement in 1969. The country commenced domestic parliamentary processes during 2007 to ratify the Convention on Registration of Objects Launched into Outer Space (1975) and the Convention on International Liability for Damage Caused by Space Objects (1971).[92] Finally, the country adopted the Registration Convention on January 27, 2012.[93]

With this very brief introduction about South Africa, the concerned policy is National Space Policy, 2008 that is a national policy made for promotion of domestic space industry.[94] In fact domestic space industry is the corner stone of this policy. One of the objectives of this policy states promoting and implementing a regulatory environment to enhance the industrial participation. It emphasises to build human capital. Moreover, the private space industry would require support from government to perform the outsourced works of the later. Similarly, government should be the buyer of private bodies. The public-private partnership is required ultimately to develop the industry made of private actors.[95] South Africa is committed to pursue any private space activity in accordance with international treaties. Any space activities undertaken by the private actors are compulsorily under the provisions of the Space Affairs Act, 1993.[96]

The main legislation is the Space Affairs Act of 1993[97] that provides the South African Council for Space Affairs under the authority of Ministry of Trade and Industry to issue licences for pursuing space activities according to section 11. The licence is issued on satisfying the obligations under the provisions of international space law. The licencing procedure follows national security as well as safety standards.[98] Therefore on issuing licence by the Council, the Act promulgates sovereignty of the state in outer space activities. It does not allow any private actors to neglect national security and safety standard.

The South African National Space Agency Act, 2008[99] focusses on sovereignty, national security and safety whereas the objective of the National Space Agency is to build-up an environment friendly space industry according to section 4 of South African National Space Agency Act 2008.[100] So, the environmental issue is considered within the Act establishing national space agency. It gives effect to environment as the year of establishment is not old i.e., 2008. Lastly, the regulation through institution grows with Ministry of Trade & Industry, South African Council for Space Affairs and National Space Agency as explained above.

Nigeria is another country where there exist some regulations related with space. The realisation of Nigeria's vision to become a space-derived data producer and service provider was realised with the establishment of National Space Research & Development Agency[101] (NASRDA) in 1999, and the subsequent launch of Nigeria's first earth observation satellite Nigeria-Sat-1 in September 2003.[102] The country acceded to the Outer Space Treaty in 1967 and the Liability Convention in 2005. It ratified the Registration Convention in 2009, and the Rescue Agreement in 1973.[103]

The National Space Policy, 2001, focusses on defence and security of Nigeria as one of the objectives of the policy. There is a provision for National Space Council chaired by the President of the country, which is responsible for framing policy guidelines. Chapter 8 deals with the commercial aspects where its objective is to attract foreign industries to boost up the domestic private industry.[104] Therefore though the country still remains in the preliminary stage of space activities but it focusses on defence and security. Moreover, the initiative to attract the foreign industries is indirect way of financing the private space industry in Nigeria.

There are other domestic statutes related with communications, insurance, IP, and last not the least, for export controls. The provisions of Nigerian Insurance Act, 2003, the part of re-insurance for assets like satellites has to be underwritten by the foreign insurance companies with domestic underwriters in Nigeria.[105] It is also an attempt to solve the high value investments by private actors in outer space. This would support space assets financing initiated by UNIDROIT Space Protocol as explained in chapter III.

The Communications Act, 2003, is made to engulf the private actors for establishing state's sovereignty. The Communications Act of 2003 has imposed the sole and exclusive power to Nigerian Communications Commission to manage and administer the radio frequency spectrum for communications sector. The Commission has to grant licence to regulate the use of the said radio frequency spectrum.[106] Therefore the private actors related with communication industry have to get the licence from government through Nigerian Communications Commission.

The IPR relates with remote sensing data only. It follows the National Geo-information Policy, 2003, and the Copyright Act, Cap 68, Laws of the Federation, 1990.[107] Moreover, Fire Arms Act, Cap 146 regulates the use, import and export artillery, and rocket weapons. These weapons come under the category of space launch vehicles.[108]

National Space Research and Development Agency Act, 2010, established the National Space Agency in 2010. Its objective is to promote the participation of private actors in the national industry. According to section 9, on recommendation from the Agency, the above mentioned licence for communication business will be issued by the Commission. The conditions are that the licencee follows the international obligation of the state and the activity will not disturb the public health or safety of the persons or property. Also, it will not hamper the national security of Nigeria. The licencee has to safeguard the environment such that its activity will not contaminate the outer space in any way.[109] Moreover, it is prescribed for granting of licence to persons or corporate body for activities relating to satellite data.[110] This Act supports the national security issue. The most legal significance is to consider the contamination in the outer space which is not dealt by the existing international space treaties. It is an on-going problem especially with the experiments and activities on Moon and other celestial bodies.

The National Space Council as mentioned above is the institution through which the regulation is developed. There is a representative from private sector in this high-powered Council.[111]

The rests like Australia, Europe and American countries have developed the space related regulations in different forms as well as different purposes. It follows below:

AUSTRALIA

Table 22: Space Related Regulations in Australia[112]

Policies	Legislations	Institutions
Satellite Utilisation Policy, 2013.	Space Activities Act, 1998.	1. Department of Industry 2. Space Co-ordination Committee (SCC) (Established in 2013)

It starts with the commonwealth country, Australia first; because the country has comprehensive space legislation since 1998. India, the prime focus of this research study, is also a commonwealth country. Australia is a party to all five international space treaties.[113] This commonwealth country shares the international platform through the United Nations Space Conventions, Missile Technology Control Regime.[114] The Registration Convention was acceded on March 11, 1986.[115] The Moon Treaty was acceded on July 7, 1986.[116] So the country is more legally advanced.

Australia has the Satellite Utilisation Policy 2013.[117] It focusses on national security issue and economic well-being. But the role of private actors is not mentioned directly.[118]

The Space Activities Act, 1998, is a comprehensive space legislation amended in 2010. The issue of sovereignty is followed up by the objective of the very Act where it states for implementation of certain obligations as imposed by UN space treaties according to section 3.[119] The requirement of launching permit according to section 18 also means upholding sovereignty by the state for private space activities. Even sovereignty is exhibited in the case of granting an overseas launch certificate on condition that Australian foreign policy is followed as prescribed under section 35.[120] The national security issue is reviewed as a part of requirement of launch permit as prescribed under section 18.[121] Section 63 prescribes that liability for damages caused by the state object is borne by the country like the provisions of state-centric space law treaties. But provision for adequate compensation for damages is made in the objective of the Act. The safety issue is prescribed within sections from 50 to 52.[122]

There is provision for safety officer who works to look after the launching safety. The officer works as instructed by the Minister-in-Charge. Safety clearance is necessary to get the launch permit. There is requirement for environment clearance to launch the space objects as usual. Section 18 provides this.[123] The financial issue is considered by many sections of the Act like possessing sufficient funding by the licence holder to launch the space object according to section 18. Then insurance is covered by the holder of launch permit or authorised actor. The same private actor has to satisfy to pay damages to the third party as prescribed under section 48. Also, it is the onus of the holder to bear the insurance on behalf of the Commonwealth against any liability that the country might incur to pay compensation for the above damage under the same section.[124]

The issue of dispute settlement covers the cases like reviewing any decisions of the Minister on filing an application before Administrative Appeals Tribunals under section 61.[125] The jurisdiction of the Federal Court is to hear and determine the actions following the damage. It is within purview of section 72.[126] The section 75 has provision for Claims Commission as prescribed in the Liability Convention. The Space Coordination Office (SCO)[127] within the Department of Industry is the institution behind making regulation.

The analysis reflects that the legal issues for private actors like sovereignty, national security, environment, safety, liability, dispute settlement are all covered within the provisions of this Act. The country does not want to lose its sovereignty even for launching beyond its territory. On interacting with the issue of liability, the private actor, being licence holder of the launch, has to bear the insurance cost on behalf of the state itself for any damages which have imposed liability on the state. It is a positive deviation from the state's liability to pay compensation because state bears the liability in the forefront on behalf of damages caused by the private actor. The dispute resolution follows to solve the disputes over government authority's decision through Administrative Appeals Tribunal and damages through the Federal Court system. But this does not undermine the provision of Claims Commission in the Liability Convention. Therefore Australia's domestic space regulation has considered the maximum legal issues for private actors in outer space.

The research study is now advanced towards the developed countries in space. These are European countries followed by American countries out of which USA is the most leading one.

EUROPE

Table 23: Space Related Regulations in Europe[128]

Countries	Policiies	Legislations	Institutions
European Space Agency (ESA)	European Space Policy, 2007.	Nil	1. The Space Council. 2. European Centre for Space Law (ECSL).
European Union	Draft of International Code of Conduct for Outer Space Activities, 2008, 2014.	Nil	Nil
Russian Federation	Nil	Law of the Russian Federation on Space Activity 1993.	Russian Federal Space Agency (ROSCOSMOS).
Ukraine	Nil	1. Decree of the President of Ukraine on NSAU. Establishment, 1992 2. Law of Ukraine on Space Activities, 1996. 3. Decree of the President of Ukraine "On provision about NSAU", 1997. 4. Law of Ukraine on State Support of Space Activities, 2000. 5. Law of Ukraine on State (National) Space Program of Ukraine 2003-2007. 6. Decree of the President of Ukraine on Space Industry Development, 2005.	National Space Agency Ukraine (NSAU).

France	European Space Policy, 2007.	French Space Operation Act, 2008.	Space Committee established in 1989 under two Ministries – Ministry of Defence & Minister of Industries. But CNES's task to implement & coordinate space policy.
Germany	1. European Space Policy, 2007. 2. German Space Strategy, 2010.	German Act on Satellite Data Security 2007.	German Aerospace Centre (DLR).
United Kingdom	European Space Policy, 2007.	Outer Space Act, 1986.	1. Department of Business, Innovation and Skills (BIS). 2. British National Space Centre (BNSC) since 1 April 2010. 3. Ofcom.
The Netherlands	European Space Policy, 2007.	Law Incorporating Rules Concerning Space Activities and the Establishment of a Registry of Space Objects, 2007.	Netherlands Space Office (NSO) established in 2009 reporting to the steering committee made of the Ministry of Economic Affairs, Ministry of Education, Culture and Science, Ministry of Transport, Public Works and Water Management.
Norway	European Space Policy, 2007.	Act on Launching Objects from Norwegian Territory etc. into Outer Space, 1969.	Norwegian Space Centre (NSC) under the Ministry of Trade, Industry & Fisheries.

Spain	European Space Policy, 2007.	Royal Decree Establishing the Registry of Objects Launched into Outer Space, 1995.	National Institute of Aerospace Technology (INTA in Spanish).
Sweden	European Space Policy, 2007.	Act on Space Activities (1982:963).	Swedish National Space Board (SNSB).

The main European countries are Russian Federation, Ukraine, UK, Germany and France where first three countries have comprehensive space legislation as shown in **Table 23**. But to study India's role in the next chapter, it is assumed that the domestic regulations of Russian Federation, France and Germany are more important for analysis. Russia has a long term friendship through space technology with India since the development period of the cryogenic engine of rocket though it was unsuccessful due to American embargo.[129] In the case of France, the French Government is very much interested for joint space venture with India. Not only that, as mentioned in chapter II, ISRO's bunch of satellites have launched through the private French company, Arianespace from French Guiana.[130] The study of Germany is relevant because of its historical background in the development of modern rocketry as explained in chapter I. Then other European countries are just followed.

In this background, the above analysis could not be started without explaining the contribution of European Space Agency (ESA) and that of European Union (EU). Now it is to be noted that ESA being an intergovernmental organisation of 20 member states where some of them are under EU and vice-versa. Moreover, ESA links legally with EU through a Framework Agreement made in 2004. But two are independent organisations. They have developed jointly a common space policy.[131] So the most effective and strategic influence of ESA is that it could take part in any space activities on utilising and coordinating the different resources of its member countries which they individually do not perform. The member states of the two organisations interact at ministerial level in the Space Council.[132]

This Council is made by the representatives of member states in the High-level Space Policy Group (HSPG). This Council is acting as regulatory institution though European Centre for Space Law (ECSL). It is totally dedicated to contribute in the regulatory mechanism for private actors.[133]

A resolution was passed in Space Council during 2007. This resolution was backed by the 29 European countries to have a European Space Policy. This strategy is a basic vision to invoke the issues like security and defence etc.[134] Moreover, the ESA has declared on making a notification that rights and obligations of the Registration Convention are to be followed. The notification was received by the UN on January 2, 1979.[135]

It is appeared that European Space Policy 2007 is basically a vision for building strong strategy on issues like security and defence. Since national security is a strategic issue of all states, the ESA being established as an organisation of European states keeps security and defence to its top priority. Moreover, upholding the rights and obligations of the Registration Convention implies the very existence of sovereignty of the state in activities related with outer space.

The European Union like ESA could not keep away from regulating the space activities for its member states. It introduced a preliminary draft titled as European Union's International Code of Conduct for Outer Space Activities in 2008. This is a multilateral initiative taken by EU for increasing number of governmental and non-governmental entities in outer space. The purpose is- (i) to protect the space assets from the collision with ongoing increase of space debris; (ii) to regulate the crowding of geo-stationary orbits; and (iii) to keep balance with saturated radio-frequency spectrum along with the intentional threat of disruption etc.[136]

The draft Code followed from the UNGA resolution 61/75 of December 6, 2006, and 62/43 of December 5, 2007, on 'Transparency and Confidence-building Measures in Outer Space Activities'. The last draft was released on March 31, 2014, that would be discussed again in open-ended consultations during May 2014, at Luxembourg.[137] This legally non-binding Draft has included the safety, security and sustainability of outer space activities. The challenges for further discussion are like space debris for security, safety and sustainable development of outer space. All international space law treaties and the norms of international law are to be complied.[138] But there are lots of criticisms earlier especially from USA.[139]

In spite of this criticism, its relevancy with this research study is that this Code of Conduct is made for the safety, security and sustainability of the outer space environment. The increasing threats of space debris disturb the safety and security of space assets in outer space. Therefore this draft Code of Conduct is complement to international law. Also, it is complementary to the international legal framework regulating outer space activities.[140] So the environmental issue is dealt within this draft.

Before analysing the regulations of the countries shown in **Table 23**, it is to be mentioned here that the Russian Federation and Ukraine are outside the ESA.[141]

Once upon a time it was Soviet Union—the one and only country in outer space in Europe besides USA. With the passage of time the earlier Soviet has been reshaped geographically and politically. This situation influences the current trend of space activities along with its development of domestic space law in Russia. In this scenario, the Law of the Russian Federation on Space Activity, 1993, the main domestic Act is to be examined to know how many legal issues are reflected within it.

It was enacted on August 20, 1993, by the Supreme Council of the Russian Federation. The country has made this first law to regulate the space activities since 1960s.[142] First it attracts licencing of space activity according to Article 9 of the Act.[143] Its critical examination discloses about licencing for private actors whether they are organisation or private citizen or even both from foreign countries but under the jurisdiction of Russian Federation. It is applicable for certain space activities provided under sub-article 2. Everything related with licencing shall be regulated by the legislation of Russian Federation. The violation by the private actors while pursuing any space activity shall be punishable under the same legislation.[144] It means that the state does not allow any space activity not prescribed by domestic Acts. So there is no question of any activity bypassing the sovereignty of Russian Federation.

The next relevancy relates with solving problem of financial burden like parallel initiative taken up later on through the UNIDROIT Space Protocol. It is Section III titled as economic conditions of space activities. The relevant portion of Article 12 expresses that the republican budget of Russian Federation appraises the financing of space activity carried through state customers. It is distributed amongst the contractors. This does not prevent the state customers and the contractor to approach for financing through their own resources. [145] Therefore the process of financing opens the door in two ways – one primarily by the state itself and the other by owned resources. The state further provides guarantees, soft credits, tax exemptions and other necessary privileges to the private actors like organisations and citizens who are engaged with the space projects.[146] Hence so many opportunities inspire the domestic contractors and citizens to become involve with the space activities as carried by the Federal space programme of Russia. Furthermore, to take recourse for solving the financing impediments, the participation in space activities is opened up for foreign countries. The foreign investments in space activity of organisations and citizens of the country are guaranteed to invest in space activities outside the country. In case of total loss of such investments, their assets or their intellectual or any other property compensates the loss according to Article 12 (4).[147]

Another system unlike the other countries exists to finance the space activities by the private actors themselves with the support from the Russian Space Fund.[148] The Article 13 (2) states

> "The assets of the Russian Space Fund shall be provided by: .... part of the profit received by organisations and citizens at the expense of tax exemption granted in connection with space activity; insurance payments made by organisations and citizens involved in space activity in the form of obligatory or voluntary insurance; voluntary contributions of Russian and foreign organisations and citizens."[149]

Thus the private actors like organisations and citizens contribute to the Space Fund from their profit generated from the above exemption of tax, insurance payments and voluntary payments by the domestic as well as foreign organisations and citizens. The utilisation of this fund according to Article 13 (3) is also to settle the liability from risk entangled with space activity and to remove the post-accident scenarios from such activity.[150] It is indeed a source of financing even after establishment of business by private actors.

Besides financing the private actors, the IPR regime is prescribed by Article 16.[151] The effects of use and transfer of space technology is regulated by the IPR as prescribed in Article 16 (1) of the legislation of Russian Federation.[152] The Article 16 (2) prescribes that the contractor has only obligation to create space technology with or without the state order. The contractor is not responsible to transfer technologies to the customer unless it is specified by the agreement between the contractor and customer.[153] Even if IPR is not prescribed by the legislation of Russian Federation then also the solution for property rights depends on the agreements between the interested organisations and citizens according to Article 16 (3).[154] But there are some classifications on IPR as provided by Article 16 (4) which states

> "The property rights over the physical product created in outer space shall belong to the organisations and citizens possessing property rights in the components of space technology, with the use of which such product has been created, unless otherwise specified by relevant agreements. The property rights over the information product created as a result of space activity shall belong to the organisations and citizens that have created such information product, unless otherwise specified by relevant agreements. The property rights of other organisations and citizens participating in space activity, in particular by providing transportation and other services, shall be stipulated by relevant agreements."[155]

It is clearly stated here that the property rights for physical products created in outer space, say in International Space Station, remains with the private actors for their ownerships in the components of space technology. If any information product is created as a consequence of space activity, it shall belong to the private actors who have created these products unless the agreement directs otherwise. But the private actors who supply transportation and other services have to seek their property rights in space activities by the concerned agreements. Hence the analysis of IPR shows that the private actors are covered widely through different kinds of space activities.

Another issue safety is mentioned after IPR in the Act. The Article 22(1) prescribes that the organisations and citizens engaged in space activity will consider about the safety measures. It is obligation to ensure all the measures. The Russian Space Agency and the Ministry of Defence of the country are in the charge of providing information in case of any threat to the private actors on request by the later. But the national space agency has obligation in reverse way to inform the private actors in case of public safety and the environment.[156]

Apart from safety, another major legal concern is liability for private actors. The liability for damage according to Article 30 concerns that it is the private actors who are responsible for fault or in proportion to their fault being caused by damages on a space object of the state or on property on board of such object by another space object. The party affected by such damage may claim for compensation from all the private actors or any of them. Similarly, in a reverse way, the private actor who has indemnified for the damage shall have right of recourse to prove its fault false.[157] The Article 30 (4) prescribes that liability of the private actors is limited to the insured amount as provided in contracts of insurance of space technology and risks related with space activity. If the compensation of damage surpluses the insured amount, then the measures will be taken on adjusting the property of the private actors as prescribed in the legislation of Russian Federation.[158]

The regulation through institution is mainly done by Roscosmos, the federal space agency. It organises implements and coordinates the commercial space projects.[159]

The overall analysis proves that Russian Federation develops its legal infrastructure for outer space activities along with its expertise space technology. Moreover many legal issues for private actors are reflected. Out of these the mechanism for re-investment of profit exempted from tax etc. is really a legal innovation and unique all over the world. In spite of this strong legal effort to solve the legal hurdles for private actors, there are several amendments of the above Act and the latest was in December 2006. But after the collapse of Soviet Union, the new initiative has been commenced not only to cover the general issues of space activities but also to regulate new licencing procedures for space activities as well as to make new norms to regulate certain space activities. Besides these specific laws, the general laws like the provisions of the Civil Code, intellectual property regulations are also applicable to space activities. But the Russian Federation Regulations are still lack of regulating provisions for private sector participation.[160]

Russian Federation is followed by Ukraine in **Table 23** because of their common ancestral country-origin i.e., Soviet Russia. It shared about one-third of the former Soviet Union' space potential after the collapse of the later.[161] Therefore Ukraine has insisted in its space policy to return back the commercialisation of its Soviet-heritage space industry. The national space policy states the expansion of the presence of Ukrainian enterprises on the global space market.[162]

It has signed and ratified the Registration Convention on July 11, 1975, and September 14, 1977, respectively.[163] The Article 62 (5) of the Constitution of Ukraine, 1996, states that 'the foundations of space activities shall be exclusively defined by the laws of Ukraine'.[164] The main legislations for regulating space activities in Ukraine are: (1) Decree of the President of Ukraine on NSAU (National Space Agency Ukraine) Establishment, 1992; (2) The Law of Ukraine on Space Activities, 1996; (3) Decree of the President of Ukraine "On provision about NSAU", 1997; (4) The Law of

Ukraine on State Support of Space Activities, 2000; (5) The Law of Ukraine on State (National) Space Program of Ukraine 2003-2007 approved in 2002; and (6) Decree of the President of Ukraine on Space Industry Development, 2005.[165]

These are all in Ukrainian text besides the Law on Ukrainian Space Activities, 1996, that is in English. This Act is more or less comprehensive space legislation. Moreover, it is the backbone made by the Parliament for regulating space activities and for further development of space legislation.[166] National security is to be safeguarded according to Article 3.[167] Sovereignty is distinctly maintained through state regulation that is one of the principles of space activity as per Article 4.[168] The issue of sovereignty is again prescribed through licencing system for state regulation and management of space activities according to Article 5.[169] Article 8 prescribes environment protection, safety, compliance with the requirement of IPR related with space activities.[170] According to Article 9, the violation of international norms and standards regarding pollution of outer space shall be prohibited and restricted in connection with space activity in Ukraine.[171]

Like other countries, licencing to the private actors comes under Article 10 and it is the most important area for state's regulation of space activities.[172] It is must for pursuing any space activity within Ukraine and outside the country if it comes under the jurisdiction of Ukraine. The Ukrainian National Space agency issues the licence.[173] In spite of the fact that NSAU is the licencing body, the State Committee of Ukraine on Regulatory Policy and Entrepreneurship acts as a specialised body on licencing issues.[174]

The provision of financing for space activity is mentioned under Article 11 when state is a customer. It comes from a special item in the Ukrainian National Budget. But there is a provision for contractors to perform the works. Therefore the state actors like private entities would be the ultimate beneficiary of this financing system.[175] Unlike Russian Federation, the financing system is monopolised by the state itself. Registration of space facilities is mandatory and Cabinet of Ministers approves it before entering into the State Register of Space Facilities of Ukraine as per Article 13.[176]

The settlement of disputes is made according to Article 14 in the Court of Ukraine unless otherwise mentioned in the international treaties where Ukraine is a party.[177] The safety is supervised by the state having focus on public and environmental safety according to Articles 15 and 16.[178] Ukraine shall maintain according to Article 17 all international obligations in the field of space activity and bear all international responsibility under general recognised norms of international law as well as international treaties.[179] Article 24 enforces compulsory insurance for space activity in Ukraine. Article 25 prescribes that the liability for damage and compensation shall be payable as per Ukrainian legislation.

Once again national security is invoked for pursuing space activities as per Article 26.[180] The analysis of the Act discloses the fact that Ukraine follows the Russian Federation to some extent in solving the issue of sovereignty, national security, financing, safety, liability and dispute settlement.

The above National Space Agency Ukraine (NSAU) is the main regulatory institution to frame space policy in the country. The Article 4 of the Law on Ukrainian Space Activities, 1996, prescribes that state is interested to commercialise the space activities and in this regard the state supports to attract investment in national space activities.[181] Therefore NSAU takes the regulating role also to promote the private actors.

The next in **Table 23** is France that is one of Europe's most advanced space nation though it has no such glorious history like Russian Federation. France started their space activities in 1960. Its national space agency, National Centre for Space Studies (CNES), is very powerful in modern technological expertise. The space sector is occupied by large scale industrial activities through some 100 small and medium size enterprises. There exist three large groups like EADS, Safran and Thales Alenia Space.[182] The last one has approached the French Government to relax the restrictions on commercial sale of imageries below 50 cm resolution because of high-demand of high resolution imagery all over the world. The government also understood it. Its implication is that the private actors have more influence to change the regulation for high-imageries in the country.[183]

In this scenario, the country signed the Registration Convention on January 14, 1975, and ratified it during the same year on December 17.[184] France signed the Moon Treaty on January 29, 1980, with a reservation that Article 3 (2)[185] of the Treaty on 'any threat or use of force' could not be interpreted in any other manner than as provided under UN Charter. It is simply an affirmation in the Moon Treaty.[186] This brief background facilitates to review critically the single domestic space law in France till now. The Act known as French Space Operation Act (FSOA) was passed by the Parliament of France in 2008. It is the first uniform law of its kind in the country and the last adopted in Europe.[187]

French Space Operation Act, 2008, is a new Act that covers all space operations besides human spaceflights, suborbital flights, command of space probes and sounding rockets and balloons. These are covered by other French laws and case specific agreements.[188] There was government monopoly through CNES for all space activities before its enactment. Basically this Act excites the private sectors. So the new legal framework has introduced the provisions of international space treaties and accords ratified since late 1960s. Its main objective is to mitigate the technical risks associated with space activities without any compromise with the competitiveness of the private contractors. The reason behind it is that the government has provided a guarantee to compensate the damages to people, property or the environment. The CNES is overall in charge of safety of all space activities. The Minister-in-Charge of space will approve the authorisation finally to perform the space activity. Therefore this Act provides opportunity to the private operators on guaranteeing access to the space market. It raises the safety standards to its excellence.[189] The preliminary analysis follows that the legal issues are reflected within the Act.

Article 2 of the Act provides three cases where authorisation from the administrative authority is required for pursuing space operations. Firstly, any operator having French nationality or not would like to launch any space object from the territory of France or return any space object to national territory comes under the French jurisdiction; Secondly, the case consists of any French operator who wants to launch the space object from foreign state or an area not under the jurisdiction of France and lastly, any natural person having French nationality, being an operator or not, wants to procure the launching of a space object.[190] This provision clearly proves that France does not share its sovereignty with any private actors whether French national or foreign national, and whether the space operation is from territory of France or outside its jurisdiction. But the case of jurisdiction outside France is only for French national.

Moreover, the conditions for authorisation according to Article 4 prescribes national security clause. It also attracts the issues of safety and environment. The administrative authority will check the moral guarantee going beyond the financial and professional guarantee.[191] So the issue of ethics as analysed in chapter III is slightly covered here.

Another provision under Article 12 is for registration of launched space objects. It is repetitively mentioned earlier that registration of space objects represents the sovereignty of the state.[192] The liability is provided under Article 13. The operator is liable absolutely to the third party for damages both in ground and airspace as per Article 13 (1). The same operator is liable for fault based in outer space according to Article 13 (2).[193] Therefore it is adoption of the provision of Article III of the Liability Convention, 1972. But the provision of liability takes the 1972 Liability Convention in broader perspective. The French government will be liable in the operator's place for damages occurring after one year period unless it is not a case of willful misconduct. Moreover, the liability of an operator is limited to Euro 60 million.[194]

The IPR issue is promulgated in Article 22. Article L. 611-1 of the Intellectual Property Code is applicable for all inventions made or used in outer space unless otherwise mentioned in an international agreement where France is a party.[195] Lastly, this country is famous for high-resolution remote sensing imageries SPOT imageries from the very beginning. Its reflection is within Article 24 of the Act where the competent administrative authority has power to restrain the space-based data operators if these data are harmful in the ground of national security, foreign policy and international commitment of France.[196] Therefore the country again restricts the private actors related with the space-based data to keep its sovereignty in the forefront.

The regulation through institution is maintained by CNES but there is a Space Committee established in 1989 under the co-leadership of Minister of Defence and that of Industries.[197]

Germany follows France in **Table 23**. It signed and ratified the Registration Convention on August 27, 1975, and May 12, 1977, respectively.[198] The country is a party to all the international space treaties. But the obligation lays only to the state not the private actors in space according to Article 25 of the German Constitution. This Article bars these treaties to consider them as general rules of international law. In this legal scenario, the country adopted German Space Strategy in 2010. Prior to this Strategy, there are legislations like 'Law Governing the Transfer of Responsibilities for Space Activities' of 1998 and the 'Act on Safeguarding Security Interests in Distribution of High Resolution Satellite Data' of 2007. But the first one is purely administrative legislation to allow German Aerospace Agency as authority to pursue any national space activities.[199] The second one follows below.

The German Act on Satellite Data Security, 2007, prescribes that German authorities are permitted to restrict the dissemination of data through high-resolution satellite imageries if the data are vulnerable to national security of Germany as well as the security of the other states. Also, the data are restrictive in nature if the foreign policy does not permit.[200] Therefore the issue of national security is considered as high priority in national legal framework.

Germany launched its space strategy in 2010. Formation of national space law is an agenda within this space strategy.[201] It has proposed to attract private investment in space sector and to develop the private enterprise business model. A dependable legal framework is an essential need of the country. This idea has come from the above Satellite Data Security Act where Germany has established commercial markets in the earth observation data.[202]

Similarly, the Federal Government works on to draft a German Space Act which will provide a clear and comprehensive legal framework especially for commercial and private space activities. It is also in response to Germany's obligation under international law. The upcoming law will provide a clear legal infrastructure where science and industry will have joint role in Germany. The Federal Government would also like to persuade the European Union and other partners in Europe to frame such type of legal framework through which a competitive model of space industry will arise.[203] Moreover, in this process of formulation of space Act, Germany will stick to its obligations to approve and supervise the space activities as prescribed by space law treaties.[204] So, the country extends its sovereignty over private space activities.

The German Aerospace Centre, DLR, is one regulating institution but the Federal Ministry of Economics and Technology is in charge of national space activities.[205]

The domestic space regulation of UK is the next in **Table 23**. It is assumed to have preference to analyse the case of India in next chapter because the British colonised India. So the major sources of Indian laws including its constitution have background from the English Acts and regulations. Hence it is assumed to be necessary to go through the UK's domestic space legislation. Moreover, there is a Memorandum of Understanding (MoU) between ISRO and United Kingdom Space Agency (UKSA) in 2011.[206] The country signed and ratified the Registration Convention on May 6, 1975, and March 30, 1978, respectively.[207]

The Outer Space Act, 1986, is the only domestic Act that is specifically made according to its preamble to provide licence and conferred other powers on the Secretary of State for launching and operations of space objects by the private actors in the form of persons.[208] So the preamble makes it clear that the state holds sovereignty over space activities. Like other domestic space legislations, Section 3 (1) provides for licencing of space activities and the conditions of licencing is followed in Section 4 (2). The conditions are more or less same like other countries. These are no threats on national security of UK and space activity not harmful for public health or safety of a person or property.[209]

The environmental issue is reflected in Section 5 (2) (e) (1) as it states 'prevent the contamination of outer space or adverse changes in the environment of the earth'. The licencee as a term of licence does not allow any space activities which contaminates the outer space or makes any negative effect in the environment of earth. The very Act includes Moon and other celestial bodies within the definition of outer space according to Section 13 (1).[210] So the Article IX of the Outer Space Treaty is reflected on considering environment of earth.

The provision of Section 5 (2) (e) (iv) reiterates the national security clause. The provision of insurance on behalf of the licencee exists for damage or loss suffered by third parties as per Section 5 (2) (f).[211]

But the provision of Section 5 (2) (f) is much ahead of time because it has already considered space debris issue. The text of this section states 'governing the disposal of the payload in outer space on the termination of operations under the licence and requiring the licencee to notify the Secretary of State as soon as practicable of its final disposal'.[212] It means that the licence issued under this Act has already prescribed the provision for disposal of payload in outer space. When the operation for which the payload is launched to outer space is dispensed with, then the licencee has to notify the Secretary of the State at the earliest after final disposal. This step is strongly supportive to remove the defunct payloads from the orbit at initial stage. It is one kind of measure to mitigate the space debris legally.

The issue dispute resolution according to section 9 of this Act comes in different way. A justice of the peace has conferred rights to issue warrant if a person contravenes any condition of licence issued by the Secretary of State.[213] The Act has put relief to UK government and its taxpayers from some liabilities arising from the private organisations or individual.[214] Therefore the Outer Space Act, 1986, has already made domestication of space activities legally on imposing the issues of sovereignty, national security, environment, dispute settlement within the text of the Act.

The regulation of space activities through institution was first made by the Department of Business, Innovation and Skills (BIS) till it discharged its responsibility to British National Space Agency (BNSC) during 2010.[215] Moreover, there is Ofcom (Office of Communications) that is government approved communications regulator in UK. It supports in making policies related with telecommunications.[216]

The space regulation of UK remains incomplete without mentioning the case of Isle of Man where four out of 10 world's top satellite companies have existed. The island is a British crown dependency. But it is not part of the UK or the EU. The self-government exists. The parliament makes its own laws. Through a special agreement with UK Government, the later takes its defence and external affairs.[217] This island has two important organisations related with space – Space Data Association and International Institute of Space Commerce. The first one is the association for satellite data operators formed for better sharing of space environment and radio frequency spectrum, whereas the second one is the think tank for space economics.[218]

The Government is a pro-space government that has facilitated a number of private operators. It offers orbital slots and launch services through the UK Space Agency. The Communications Commission is the authority to issue licences and regulates every telecommunications here as per Telecommunications Act, 1984.[219] But as the Island is Crown-dependent, any company registered in Isle of Man for pursuing space activities must apply to the British Secretary of State via British National Space Centre for an operation and space licence.[220]

Moreover, there are other facilities like zero tax on space and satellite business; no insurance premium tax; lawyers specialised in space law; a large number of qualitative firms to finance the space activities and excellent services from the insurance companies to deal with high value risk.[221] In deed the space commerce of Isle of Man supports to establish a new type of company called International Space Company (ISC) which is just anticipated. There would be no income tax liability for space ventures. Additionally if an ISC makes revenues of 51 per cent of its business in space, the non-space income would also be exempted from tax. The reason is that there is till now no space company operating exclusively in outer space.[222] The case of Isle of Man is an idle example till now to start and continue a dedicated private space industry anywhere. The legal facilities not only attract the financing but encourage the small private actors tremendously.

The above European countries are advanced in developing space regulations compared to the others in **Table 23**. But this does not undermine the regulations of others because all of them come under ESA and EU.

The country, Netherlands, though not famous for its space activities but holds the leading position developing space law in Europe and outside through its old prestigious academic institution, International Institute of Air & Space Law, Leiden.[223] The Netherlands has started making national space legislation on enacting 'Law Incorporating Rules Concerning Space Activities and the Establishment of a Registry of Space Objects' in 2007. But long before that, the Netherlands has ratified the Outer Space Treaty (1967) on entering into force in 1969. Later the Rescue Agreement (1968) was approved by the Dutch Parliament in 1980 followed by the Liability Convention (1972) and the Registration Convention (1975). The Moon Agreement (1979) has 13 parties till now including the Netherlands.[224] The country has adopted the Registration Convention on January 26, 1981, through accession.[225] The Moon Agreement was signed on January 27, 1981, and ratified on February 17, 1983.[226] This small legal background follows the critical examination of the only domestic space Act - Law Incorporating Rules Concerning Space Activities and Establishment of a Registry of Space Objects, 2007.[227]

The Act has provision for licencing of space activities as per Section 3. The conditions are also the same like safety of persons and goods, protection of environment in outer space, financial security and the national security of the state. Since the Act was enacted in 2007 much later than other European countries' space Acts, therefore it prescribes for the environment in outer space. Section 3 (4) refers liability for which the Minister of Economic Affairs will consider the maximum possible cover. Also the due concern is provided to cover it by insurance.[228]

The liability of the licence-holder is up to the insured amount according to Section 12.[229] This is one kind of benefits to develop the infrastructure of private actors in outer space. The registration of space objects is included in the provision of Section 11. The licence-holder shall provide all information to the registry as maintained by the Minister of Economic Affairs.[230] It is implementation of Registration Convention in domestic laws of Netherlands and sovereignty of the country is established with the space activities. The enforcement of the Act that is one kind of dispute settlement is covered by chapter 5 of the Act from Sections 13 to 23.[231]

One scholarly view from the country itself is the Act that it is difficult to say in advance what the private actors within the country could do with the next application of licence. But the 2007 Space Activities Act is a basic law for all practical purposes even for the high-level comprehensive legislation.[232] The institution for regulation is Netherlands Space Office (NSO) and steering committee made of the Ministry of Economic Affairs, Ministry of Education, Culture & Science and Ministry of Transport, Public Works & Water Management.[233]

The next is Norway in **Table 23**. It has Norway Space Centre (NSC), a government agency, under the Ministry of Trade and Commerce. It was founded in 1987 when Norway became the member of European Space Agency.[234] The country adopted the Registration Convention on June 28, 1995.[235] The private space industry in Norway is full of 40 companies from small to big ones. Telecommunications is the largest industry where Telenor and its subcontractor Kongsberg Norspace exist. Others are Kongsberg Defence & Aerospace, Presens and Gamma Medica.[236] That is why the domestic space Act of Norway is important for this study.

The Act on Launching Objects from Norwegian Territory etc. into Outer Space, 1969, is the single-most Act till now. This Act prescribes that the permission from the Ministry is required to launch any object into outer space. The place may be within Norwegian territory, Norwegian vessels or aircrafts according to Section 1 (a) and (b). But the provision in Section 1 (c) is not like other countries i.e. permission is required to launch from 'Areas that are not subject to the sovereignty of any state, when the launching is undertaken by a Norwegian citizen or person with habitual residence in Norway.'[237] It implies that sovereignty of the country extends to the areas of common heritage of mankind e.g. high-seas. But it is only for citizens or persons with habitual residence in the country. The Norwegian Space Centre under the Ministry of Trade, Industry & Fisheries is the regulatory institution.[238]

Spain is not full of private actors like Norway in **Table 23** but the country has old history in aerospace. The National Institute of Aerospace Technology (INTA in Spanish) was created in 1942, but the space has been developed later on. It provides technical advice and services to institutions and government agencies and industries.[239] It is also the regulatory institution. Spain has till now no space law as such except a Royal Decree No. 278/1995 has been passed in 1995 giving effect the establishment in Spain of the Registry of Objects Launched into Outer Space as provided for in the Convention adopted by the United Nations General Assembly in 1974.[240] The Registration Convention has been acceded on December 28, 1978.[241] The country has Royal Decree establishing the registry of objects launched into outer space which was passed in 1995. Any launching from Spain or procuring country's facility or with the Spanish facility shall be entered in the Spanish Registry for space objects as per Article 5 of the Act.[242] It means that principle of sovereignty is followed in space activities.

Like Spain, the territory of Sweden is also not famous in space activities in Europe. The Swedish National Space Board (SNSB), a central governmental agency under the Ministry of Education and Research, is in charge of national and international activities related with space and remote sensing.[243] Sweden, being a member of ESA, is pursuing its space programme through ESA's activities. Also the country has bilateral cooperation with others.[244] It signed and ratified the Registration Convention on June 9, 1976.[245] Sweden has a competitive space industry.

With these briefs about the Swedish space activities, the country has still now the Act on Space Activities (1982:963). It prescribes that licence is must for anybody besides the state to pursue space activities within Sweden. The licencing requirement according to Section 2 is also needed for a Swedish natural or juridical person to pursue space activities anywhere. Swedish state will reimburse the authority that has faced damage from the activities of persons who carried space activities on behalf of the state. It is as per undertakings in international agreements.[246] The case of Sweden is also like the above state practice to regulate the space activities through state's machinery though Sweden is full of private space companies as listed in the website of SNSB.[247]

This ends the critical analysis of domestic space law in Europe which follows advanced domestic legislations in American countries specially USA.

AMERICA

The American countries especially USA is always advanced in space science and technology. To analyse the study over India, the Latin American country like Brazil will come first than USA because it is within the BRIC (Brazil, Russia, India, China) countries. There is another Latin American country, Argentina, where national space legislation is developing. Therefore the following analysis starts with Latin American countries. **Table 24** shows the scenario of Latin American countries.

Table 24: Space Related Regulations in Latin America[248]

Countries	Policies	Legislations	Institutions
Brazil	Nil	1. The licencing of private enterprises to prepare launching operations from Brazilian territory, 2001. 2. The authorisation of private enterprises to carry out launching operations on Brazilian territory, 2002. 3. General Regulation of Space Safety, 2007.	Brazilian Space Agency (AEB).
Argentina	Nil	National Decree No. 125/95, Establishment of the National Registry of Objects Launched into Outer Space (July 25, 1995).	1. National Commission on Space Activities (CONAE) (National Space Agency). 2. National Communications Commission (CNC).
Venezuela	Nil	1. Agency Law Bolivarian for Space Activities. 2. Constitution of Venezuela. 3. Organic Law of Science, Technology and Innovation.	Agency Law Bolivarian for Space Activities since 2008.
Mexico	Outline of Mexico Space Policy, 2011.	Act Establishing the Mexican Space Agency, 2010.	Mexican Space Agency.

The space activities in Brazil have commenced with the enactment of a Presidential decree number 51.133 of August 3, 1961.[249] Brazil signed and ratified 3 international space treaties (i) The Outer Space Treaty, 1967; (ii) The Rescue Agreement, 1968; and (iii) The Liability Convention, 1972. The Registration Convention, 1975, was acceded on March 17, 2006, but not the Moon Treaty, 1979.[250] The Brazilian space law relevant for this study was passed at the beginning of 21st century for promoting commercialisation.[251] The Acts passed are (1) The licencing of private enterprises to prepare launching operations from Brazilian territory, 2001; (2) The authorisation of private enterprises to carry out launching operations on Brazilian territory, 2002; (3) The Brazilian-Ukrainian Treaty signed in 2003, to create a bi-national venture to exploit commercial launchings from the Alcantara Launch Center (CLA) and the Bye-law for this new enterprise adopted in 2006; and (4) General Regulation of Space Safety, 2007.[252]

The first two regulations were approved by the Brazilian National Space Agency, AEB. Its effect is that the licencing followed by authorisation is mandatory for any private entities interested to launch from Brazil. So the government indirectly controls the private launching activities in Brazil.[253] Sovereignty is not diffused with the entry of private actors in outer space just like other countries. AEB is the regulatory institution here.

Like Brazil, another Latin American country, Argentina, adopted its national space law through its National Space Plan.[254] The government has major control over private space activities. Liability issues arising from space activities are governed by general responsibility provisions contained in the Civil Code. Argentina does not yet have regulations governing earth observation services or intellectual property created in outer space or related to space endeavours. The Constitution of Argentina or Federal Congress does not provide the norms related with space activities. The state's national space agency, National Commission on Space Activities (CONAE), and the National Communications Commission (CNC) are the two bodies making regulatory norms related with space activities. Argentina ratified the Outer Space Treaty, the Liability Convention, the Rescue and Return Agreement, and the Registration Convention.[255] It signed the Registration Convention on March 26, 1975, and ratified it May 5, 1993.[256]

In this background, the country passed one decree in 1995—The National Decree No. 125/95, Establishment of the National Registry of Objects Launched into Outer Space (July 25, 1995).[257] This decree established the provision to have a national registry of objects launched into outer space.[258] It is the implementation of Article II of the Registration Convention, 1972.

So the Federal government does not lose its control over the space activities by the private entities.

The following Latin American countries are not significant in space legislation. They are coming up. But the case of Colombia is totally different and that is why it is not depicted in **Table 24.**

Colombia joined COPUOS in 1959. The National Council of the Space was created in the middle of 1970s under the Ministry of Foreign Affairs that is responsible for representing Colombia relating to space subjects at the UN. This country is the main supporter of Bogota Declaration in 1976 where the equatorial countries claimed the territorial ownership of the geostationary orbit situated just over the equator.[259] The country signed but not ratified the Outer Space Treaty, the Rescue Agreement and the Liability Convention but signed the Registration Convention and Moon Treaty. The Colombian Space Commission, called CCE, was created to regulate the space activities by the Presidential Decree 2442 in July 2006. At present the Colombian Air Force undertakes the Executive Secretariat up to 2014.[260]

In this background, the Colombian Government is in process of thinking over new space regulation to frame a basis for its new outer space policy in accordance with international law. The reason is that Article 101 (3) of the Colombian Constitution states that the segment of Geostationary Orbit over Colombia is part of its national territory. This Article is in contrast with international law because the Article 2 of the Outer Space Treaty prohibits any claim of sovereignty over outer space. Hence no country will take interest to cooperate with Colombia in space activities at present.[261]

Now the country was interested to purchase a telecommunication satellite. It got failed because any satellite manufacturing company had to bear heavy restrictions and contractual liability rules under domestic law of Colombia. Since the Liability Convention is not ratified, the responsibility sharing between the state and a private actor does not fulfill in Colombia.[262] The case of Colombia proves that the state holds the sovereignty for space activities but not in outer space that is common heritage of mankind. No country could make it possible to develop national space legislation without ratifying the international space treaties.

The country, Venezuela, is also not famous for space activities in **Table 24.** The Inter-ministerial Commission for the Exploration and Peaceful Uses of Outer Space (2004), Venezuelan Presidential Commission for the Peaceful Use of Space (2005) and Venezuelan Foundation Space Centre

(CEV) (2005) were the institutional backing for the establishment of Bolivarian Agency for Space Activities (ABAE) during 2008 to expand the space activities in Venezuela.[263] It is an autonomous body under the Ministry of Science and Technology. All the matters relating to space policy development and peaceful use of outer space are within its jurisdiction.[264] The Agency Law Bolivarian for Space Activities is the decree establishing the ABAE. [265] It states that ABAE will generate rules and regulations related with space activities. According to Article 3, the formation of rules and regulations would require the issues of national regulatory principles of sovereignty, security and comprehensive defence of the nation.[266] Therefore the national space agency is established to regulate the issues like sovereignty and national security. The other supportive legislations for national space activities are Constitution of Venezuela[267] and Organic Law of Science, Technology and Innovation[268].

The last is Mexico in **Table 24**. Like other countries, its space legislation has commenced from the very inception of the Act establishing its national space agency, Mexican Space Agency (AEM) that was established in 2010.[269] Mexico signed the Registration Convention on December 19, 1975, whereas ratification came on March 1, 1977.[270] The Moon Treaty was acceded on October 11, 1991.[271]

In this scenario, Mexico has Act Establishing the Mexican Space Agency, 2010. Here the constitution of Mexico was followed.[272] The constitution of any state reflects the sovereignty of that state. So this Act shows the dominance of state's sovereignty in national space activities. Besides this Act, there is newly framed policy outline.

The general outline of Mexico's Space Policy, 2011, will be developed by the Mexican Space Agency. One of the strategic objectives of this policy is to articulate the private sectors to ensure the national sovereignty through space activities. The national development plan 2007-2012 stands on rule of law and security, environment sustainability with other driving factors. The general lines of the space policy are: (i) guidance to the state in the matter of formulation and implementation of national space programme to preserve the national sovereignty and national interests in the exploration and exploitation of space and (ii) to develop Mexico's space industry in accordance with the National Safety Act. The protection of sovereignty and national security are the main criteria.[273]

Canada and United States are the only two space-faring countries in North America. **Table 25** depicts North America.

Table 25: Space Related Regulations in North America[274]

Countries	Policies	Legislations	Institutions
Canada	Nil	1. Canadian Space Agency Act, 1990. 2. Remote Sensing Space Systems Act, 2005. 3. Constitution Act, 1867 4. Telecommunications Act. 5. Broadcasting Act. 6. Radio-communications Act.	Canadian Space Agency (CSA).
USA	1. National Space Policy, 2010. 2. National Space Transportation Policy, 2013.	1. Commercial Space Launch Act, 1984. 2. Land Remote Sensing Policy Act, 1992. 3. Commercial Space Act, 1998. 4. Commercial Space Launch Amendment Act, 2004.	1. The Office of Legislative & Intergovernmental Affairs coordinate between NASA & US Congress on legislative affairs. 2. Subcommittee on Science & Space of US Senate Committee on Commerce, Science, and Transportation. 3. Subcommittee on Space of US House Committee on Science, Space & Technology. 4. The Space Policy Institute, George Washington University. 5. Numerous Non-governmental bodies like L5 Society.

Canada ratified all the international space treaties except the Moon Agreement, 1979. It signed the Registration Convention on February 14, 1975, and ratified it on August 4, 1976.[275] These treaties were implemented in some form of specific laws or with a small amendment in existing laws. So there are reflections of few specific laws exclusively regulating certain aspects of space activities. Other regulations of general application which have been amended are adopted to cover different aspects of space activities without any constitutional challenge. Moreover, the basic provisions of the Constitution Act, 1867, are applicable to regulate the space activities in Canada. The general clause in Section 91 of the Constitution provides the base for regulating space activities that are under the jurisdiction of Federal Parliament in Canada. It has exercised legislative authority over the regulation of domestic space activities. The specific areas are telecommunications and broadcasting by satellite. The Acts are Telecommunications Act, Broadcasting Act and Radio-communications Act.[276]

The main domestic Act is Canadian Space Agency Act, 1990, establishing national space agency. It has provision according to Section 9 for granting loan to any person in respect of the commercial exploitation of space science and technology. The prescribed Minister (Minister of Industry, Science and Technology) who grants the loan has the capability to be guarantor of such loan repayment.[277] It is beneficial to the private actors because the Minister plays the role of the granting authority and guarantor of such loan payment simultaneously.

In this scenario, there is no comprehensive space legislation to regulate the space activities in Canada. The Remote Sensing Space Systems Act was passed in 2005, to promote the private use of high-resolution data by private entities keeping intact the national security of Canada. Though the data are for use by private entities but the government holds the control through licencing system.[278] Therefore, Canada sticks to national security clause with the promotion of the high-resolution data by private actors. The Canadian Space Agency plays the regulating role as an institution for private actors.

Lastly, it is United States that is most pioneering one not only to commercialise but privatise the space activities. It is observed from **Table 16** that the majority of the private actors in outer space hail from this country. United States ratified all international space treaties beside the Moon Treaty, 1979. The Registration Convention was signed on January 24, 1975, and ratified on September 15, 1976.[279]

There are two policies - first National Space Policy released in 2010[280] followed by National Space Transportation Policy 2013. The last but one principle of this policy interprets sovereignty and proprietary rights in different way.[281] There shall be no national claims of sovereignty in outer space according to Article II of the Outer Space Treaty. So, USA would like to consider the space systems of all nations to have rights of passage through and conduct of operations without interference. According to this policy, purposeful interference is infringement of nation's right. The meaning of 'purposeful' is not explained within the policy.[282] The reason for inclusion of this principle is to claim the proprietary rights over resources found from celestial mining. The private companies in USA as observed in chapter II has started this endeavour. Therefore, the government has included such texts within its policy. It may be assumed that outline of the Asteroid Act became strategically possible with such supportive arguments.[283] But the fallacy is that much opportunity and scope along with time would be required to accept this explanation on case to case basis in future.

Besides this different way of explanation of sovereignty, the preamble of this policy considers the environment in outer space to be treated properly. The preamble states that the outer space environment becomes gradually damaging in nature from the increasing activities of space faring nations. The probability of collision is high in such type of environment. [284] The explanation of the word 'irresponsible' is presumed to attract the issue of ethics of the private actors as highlighted in chapter III. This irresponsibility is observed in the increasing number of private actors leading to the requirement of international legal regulation of ethics. It is also prescribed in the subsequent parts of this policy to preserve space environment and responsible uses of space. USA has started the industry standard and policies like the United Nations Space Debris Mitigation Guidelines.[285] These Guidelines are one kind of international soft regulations to mitigate the space debris legally. Therefore, it is indicated that the private actors will follow the guidelines while participating in national industrial development.

Apart from the issues of sovereignty and environment, the policy is on commercial space guidelines.[286] The guideline is related with this research study through financing issue. For the purpose of this policy, the word 'commercial' refers to space goods, services or activities provided by private actors.[287] These actors carry the major investment risk and responsibilities for their activities. Their commercial ventures are based on market profit and optimal return on investment. They would require a good market for these commercial goods, services or activities.[288] Therefore this policy concerns with the requirement of legal capacity to offer these goods or services to the existing or potential non-governmental customers.

To liberalise the commercial private actors in the market economy, the policy decides to minimise the regulatory burden for their activities. This would require timely and responsive licencing of space activities.[289] Moreover, the analysis discloses that the financing of space projects for delivering these goods or services will ultimately come from the market if the legal provision for making such market exists. It is very unique and innovative legal policy step in this regard. The other aspect is that the policy supports the use of incentives like prizes or competitions in promoting the commercial space sector.[290] The example lies with the Google's X prize. These incentives facilitate financing to the new start-ups.

The Federal Government has released another policy on November 21, 2013. It is based on transportation to outer space. This policy follows the above space policy but the focus is on safety issue. [291] The commercial human spaceflight conducted by the private companies comes up in USA as shown in **Table 6** and so this policy was framed. The Secretary of Transportation has imposed the following duties:

> "Seek to ensure that the regulatory environment for licencing commercial space transportation activities is timely and responsive, and addresses current market and industry developments;
>
> Support continuation of the current liability risk-sharing regime for US commercial space transportation activities, including provisions for the conditional payment of excess third-party claims by the United States Government; and
>
> Advocate internationally for the adoption of United States Government safety regulations, standards, and licencing measures to enhance global interoperability and safety of international commercial space transportation activities."[292]

So this policy adds value to the existing safety requirement as enacted in the existing space legislations. USA insists that the other countries will adopt these requirements. Thus its effectiveness will increase globally.

There may be another reason for enhancing its global effectiveness. 'Space transport' is an Sub-sector under the Sector 'Transport Services' in the services sectoral classification list of General Agreement on Trade in Services (GATS).[293] Its implication is wider in the sense that if two WTO member countries take any service sector in their specific commitment of schedule, then one country could access this service sector of another country and vice-versa.[294] Therefore the same rule is applicable for space transport. It is appeared from **Table 6** that USA is ready for space transport. So the country would like to internationalise its National Transportation Policy on adopting US Government's safety regulations first in other countries. Safety is the key issue in commercial space transport as explained in chapter III. Then it would take space transport in its specific commitment of schedule depending on other factors.

The National Space Policy, 2010, liberalises the private actors to pursue their space activities in general whereas the National Space Transportation Policy, 2013, provides more facilities and supports from the Federal Government to the same actors in the commercial space transportation. Additionally, USA has framed the strategy to impose their national transportation policy globally to introduce its domestic legal framework within future international legal framework in the sector of commercial space transportation.

There are a few legislations in USA besides these policies. The Commercial Space Launch Act, 1984,[295] is the first of its kind to promote private actors in the country. The launch services provided by the private actors is in conformity with the national security as well as foreign policy interests of the country. Also the launching activity shall not be against the public health and safety, and even safety of the property according to section 2.[296] The provision of section 6 obligates that the Secretary of Transportation will issue a licence for launching vehicle or operating a launch site. No person is allowed to pursue such activities without such licence. Moreover, licence is required for similar activities outside USA for its own citizens.[297] The requirement for licence, according to section 8, shall satisfy the safety measures, national security and foreign policy of US. The Secretary has the only power to transfer the licence to other party as per section 7.[298]

But the supreme power of Secretary to deal the whole licencing procedure shall be subject to judicial review as provided in chapter 7 of title 5, United States Code. It is prescribed in section 12.[299] There is provision under section 16 for liability insurance whose amount is to be considered by the Secretary and it is in parlance with the international obligations of USA.[300] The provision of section 20 repeats the national security issue again through indirect way. It provides that the Secretary of Transportation shall consult with the Secretary of Defence on all matters related with issuance or transfer of licence that affects the national security of USA.[301]

So, the analysis facilitates that USA, though, highly interested to promote the private actors but the state would like to regulate these actors through its state's functionaries like the Secretary of Transportation. It is the Secretary who is in charge of issuing licence on satisfying some conditions. In this regard, the national security interest is the priority. But there is process of dispute settlement against the order of Secretary which is subject to judicial review. The provision for liability insurance supports the significance of liability in the regime of private actors.[302]

The chronological list of Acts next follows Land Remote Sensing Policy Act, 1992.[303] It encourages the private actors like companies to pursue business with remote sensing data related with earth acquired through satellite imageries. The Act specifically relates with the Federal Government's Landsat system for land remote sensing imageries. The Act provides another legal instrument for licencing of private space activity. Here it is private remote sensing space systems.[304]

Section 201 prescribes that the Secretary of Commerce is authorised to licence the private actors to operate private remote sensing space systems.[305] Like other countries, there are some licencing requirements according to section 202. The operation of the private remote sensing system shall preserve the national security of USA. Section 202 (b) (2) provides that the unenhanced data or raw satellite data collected by the satellite shall be available to the country that is sensed by the remote sensing satellite as soon as the data are available. It is basically domestication of the provisions of the Principles of Remote Sensing, 1986, maintaining the full regards of the sovereignty of other countries under whose jurisdiction the satellite data falls.[306]

But the provision of section 202 (b) (3) prescribes the disposition of any satellite in space after termination of operations under the licence. It shall be done in a manner 'satisfactory to the President'.[307] Though this Act relates with the land remote sensing data but it takes care about the environment in outer space on disposing the satellite when its operation will be over. The meaning of 'satisfactory to the President' is not provided. Therefore, it may raise debates and arguments.

The other conditions clearly show that the state is the supreme authority that makes command over any issues for licencing through the Secretary. Moreover, the Secretary has the power to seek an injunction or similar judicial determination from USA's District Court if any private actors say licencee violates the condition of licence according to section 203.[308] Just like the above Act, section 507 is addressed for consultation from the Secretary of Defence by the Secretary of Commerce on the grounds of national security.[309]

It is observed from the analysis that the high-resolution satellite imageries produced by the private owned satellites are examples of violation of the sovereignty of the sensed country jeopardising the national security of the same country. But USA makes legal provision to protect the sovereignty of other countries with the private licence holders' entry into this domain. In this regard USA does not make any compromise with its national security. The other issue relates space environment which remains clean after its termination of operation.

The next is Commercial Space Act, 1998,[310] to encourage the commercial space industry. The issue of national security is prescribed to sustain the global positioning system (GPS) according to section 103(b).[311] Safety standards are maintained in all uses of space.[312] Regarding space transportation by commercial private actors, the Federal Government shall acquire the space transportation services from such actors if it is not inconsistent with the national security objectives.[313] Therefore national security and safety are not compromised in anyway.

Though there is a common mention of safety in 1998 and 2004, but it is more pertinent for amended Act in 2004,[314] for commercial space launch that includes the commercial human spaceflight. After the analysis of Commercial Space Act 1998, safety becomes continuously more important issue for private actors in outer space. The Commercial Space Launch Amendment Act, 2004, is basically an amendment of the above Commercial Space Launch Act, 1984. It follows the same trend because this Act was passed for promoting the development of the emerging commercial human space flight industry.[315]

Thus it indicates that the human spaceflight is solely dependent on the issue of safety. The development could not be achieved in this area unless and until the safety requirement is continuously improved on legal basis. The holder of licence has the duty to inform the space flight participants about the risks of the launch and re-entry including the safety record of the launch or re-entry vehicle type. Moreover, the Secretary of Transportation has also the same obligation separately to inform the space flight participants. But the safety requirement may not be such that it shall go against the obligations of the state regarding national security.[316]

The institutional regulation is performed by The Office of Legislative & Intergovernmental Affairs coordinate between NASA & US Congress on legislative affairs,[317] Subcommittee on Science & Space of US Senate Committee on Commerce, Science, and Transportation[318] and Subcommittee on Space of US House Committee on Science, Space & Technology.[319] Alongside these state regulatory bodies, there are so many non-government institutions. The Space Policy Institute of George Washington University, being a private institute, contributed to the development of policy regulations for space activities including the private actors since 1987.[320] The L5 Society was very proactive and biggest lobbyist against signing of the Moon Treaty by the country.[321]

The following Table shows how the legal issues are attracted by different countries for regulating the private actors in outer space.

Table 26: Countries & Their Legal Issues[322]

Countries	Legal Issues
China	Sovereignty, National Security, IPR, Environment, Dispute Settlement.
Hong Kong	Sovereignty, National Security, Safety.
Singapore	Financing.
Japan	Sovereignty, National Security, Liability, Environment, Financing.
Republic of Korea	Sovereignty, National security, Liability, Environment, Financing, Dispute Settlement.
Pakistan	Sovereignty.
Thailand	National security.
Philippine	Sovereignty, National Security, IPR, Financing.
UAE	Sovereignty.

Republic of Kazakhstan	Sovereignty, Environment, Safety.
South Africa	Sovereignty, National Security, Environment, Safety.
Nigeria	National Security, Financial, IPR, Environment, Safety.
Australia	Sovereignty, National Security, Environment, Safety, Liability, Dispute Settlement.
ESA	National Security.
EU	Environment, Security.
Russian Federation	Sovereignty, Financing, IPR, Safety, Liability.
Ukraine	Sovereignty, National Security, Finance, Safety, Liability, Dispute Settlement.
France	Sovereignty, National Security, Safety, Environment, Ethics, Liability, IPR.
Germany	National Security.
UK	Sovereignty, National Security, Environment, Dispute Settlement.
The Netherlands	Sovereignty, National Security, Liability, Environment, Dispute Settlement.
Norway	Sovereignty.
Spain	As above.
Sweden	As above.
Brazil	As above.
Argentina	As above.
Venezuela	Sovereignty, National Security.
Mexico	Sovereignty, National Security, Environment, Safety.
Canada	National Security.
USA	Sovereignty, National Security, Liability, Financing, Environment, Safety, Dispute Settlement.

It is shown from **Table 26** that the issue of sovereignty is regulated by all the countries though it may sometimes not show against each country. This issue is by default attached with the regulation of private actors because till now it is the states that regulate the private actors. The other issues against each country are merely information based on the regulations of different countries. But this does not mean to ignore or undermine other issues in each state. These may be sub-issues or sub-merged or may be upcoming ones in the future regulatory instruments.

Conclusion

The framing of domestic space regulations for private actors has different approaches and connotations in different parts of the world. Therefore instead of focussing the legal issues individually over different countries, there is country wise analysis of national regulations that interact with these issues: directly or indirectly. The regulations are maintained by policies first, then legislations and lastly, institutions. To this endeavour, the non-space-faring countries' common pursuit is to develop their indigenous space capabilities with their existing national science and technology infrastructure. But countries sometimes seek for international cooperation from other space-faring countries depending on the situation. The purpose is to develop national space infrastructure that ultimately attracts the private actors at domestic level.

With this background trend in global technological development, the above analysis discloses that all the countries, more or less, follow a common strategy to develop its domestic legal regulations for private actors. First follows the UN space law treaties to implement them fully or partly in their regulatory system. Then next step is to address the concerned provisions from their constitutional law in support of this implementation. Moreover, the countries consider the legal issues like sovereignty, national security, IPR etc. in making their effort to develop regulations. But the reflection of these legal issues within the domestic space law instruments varies from country to country; because space is a strategic agenda for any country. Therefore majority of the states has foremost focus on national security issue.

In addition to it some have preference for issues like financing to promote space commerce in making national space legislation. Its first reflection is noted when an Act establishing national space agency has been initiated or passed; or the concerned Bill has been drafted; or some related preliminary legal initiatives have been duly considered in any country. Perhaps, it may not be wrong to presume that institutionalise international space law in different countries like international environmental law is itself a part of developing regulation for private actors.[323]

Therefore the Act establishing the national space agency reflects sometimes the issues like sovereignty, national security and environment besides the routine administrative regulations of such space agencies. Therefore the regulations outside India are done with policies, legislations and lastly, institutions. But sometimes it is space legislation that has been firstly made in a country. There is mention within it that some policy would be framed. Similarly some legislation has been made to establish the institution i.e. national space agency. The object or purpose of such legislation is to make space related policies and other legislations.

The regulations of private actors through institutions are followed in different countries in different ways. But mainly it is first regulated on establishing the national space centres like national space agencies, institutes of national repute related with space or national societies related with space activities.

In this scenario, this research study first concentrates on Asia because India is the prime focus at the end. Then it subsequently follows Africa, Australia, Europe and lastly, America. The Asian countries besides China, India and Japan are rarely recognised at international level for their national space activities. In spite of their lack of such space technology, some Asian countries like Hong Kong, Singapore, Republic of Korea, Pakistan, Thailand, Philippine, United Arab Emirates (UAE) and Republic of Kazakhstan have started their effort for regulating private actors in outer space. It is a part of building their national space infrastructure. The cases of Republic of Korea and Republic of Kazakhstan are much advanced in this regard. The same scenario is observed in non-space-faring states in African and South American region. The European countries jointly under EU and ESA are benefited because of the collaborative march of the ESA and European Centre for Space Law (ECSL) in developing uniform space regulation. Its recent example is developing 'International Code of Conduct for Outer Space Activities' made by EU.

However, China though a leading Asian space country does not have any comprehensive national space legislation till now but it is in the process to develop such legislation. Presently, the White Papers take care of the regulatory roles on reflecting the issues like sovereignty, national security, IPR, environment (on considering space debris issue) and dispute settlement. But there is view that these White Papers fail to develop the infrastructure for space legislation in China. The China National Space Administration is the main regulatory institution under the Commission of Science, Technology and Industry for National Defence (COSTIND).

Besides China, there is another space giant in Asia i.e., Japan. It is awaiting for the full-fledged space law for private entities though Japan's Basic Plan for Space Policy as well as forthcoming Space Activities Act

their common space agency i.e. European Space Agency (ESA) along with the dynamic European Centre for Space Law (ECSL). The ECSL is an institution developing the space related regulations along with the Space Council. Besides European Union's International Code of Conduct as mentioned above, there is European Space Policy, 2007. The Code of Conduct considers the environment of outer space from the increasing threats of space debris that disturbs the safety and security of space assets in outer space. But the final draft is under the process of discussions and debates. Russian Federation, UK and Ukraine have already comprehensive national space legislation like Australia.

The first is definitely Russian Federation. The Law of the Russian Federation on Space Activity, 1993, provides a more or less a comprehensive legal regime. The creation of the Russian Space Fund is unique in support of financing. It is made from benefits provided to the private actors like the profits generated by the exemption of tax, insurance payments and voluntary payments by the domestic as well as foreign organisations and citizens. The other legal issues are reflected as usual. The Russian Federal Space Agency is the main regulatory institution. The Ukraine, being previously within the former Soviet Union, has comprehensive space legislation like Russian Federation.

The next most dynamic space faring European country is France. The French Space Operation Act, 2008, prescribes the authorisation required for space operations along with its different categories because of the domestic presence of most proactive private actor Arianespace in international launching industry. No operators within the territory of the country and no operators having French nationality outside the country could pursue the space operations without authorisation from the concerned administrative authority of the government. The authorisation is symbol of sovereignty. The administrative authority will also check the moral guarantee besides professional and financial guarantee for issuing the licence required for space activities. It is one kind of attracting the issue of ethics here.

Germany is another country following France because the former has its golden ancient history of rocketry as observed in chapter I. It has German Act on Satellite Data Security, 2007, that regulates only the high resolution satellite imageries. The German Space Strategy, 2010, was established where it was mentioned that German Space Act was in process. DLR, the German Aerospace Centre, has institutional role to develop regulations.

Just like Germany, it is UK which once upon a time was the pioneer of space activities and research through the British Interplanetary Society that exists till now. UK has comprehensive space legislation- the Outer Space Act, 1986, where the provision for space debris is made. It is really a forward looking as well as dynamic legal approach to make the outer space environment clean. The case of Isle of Man is attached with UK. This is an exceptional one because of its special initiative to develop space commerce with space law on introducing measures like zero tax on space and satellite business, no insurance premium tax, a large number of qualitative firms to finance the space activities and excellent services from the insurance companies to interact with high-value risk. The regulatory institution in UK is as usual like above but the Ofcom is the regulatory authority for communications including telecommunications. So, it works like an institution.

The other countries in Europe are though not too much famous for its space legislations but they could not be ignored also like the Netherlands, Norway, Spain and Sweden. The Act on Launching Objects from Norwegian Territory etc. into Outer Space, 1969, has something special. It prescribes that the permission from the government is always required to launch the space objects. Even the permission is required from the area where no country has sovereignty e.g., high sea which is common heritage of mankind (CHM). But this special extension of sovereignty in CHM is only applicable for Norwegian citizen or person with habitual residence in Norway. The national space agency plays the role of regulatory institution but it is National Institute of Aerospace Technology in Spain.

The countries left now are only American countries, both Latin and North. In the former category the countries are mainly Brazil, Argentina, Colombia, Venezuela and Mexico whereas Canada and USA are the only two in the latter category.

Brazil has two Acts like the Licencing of Private Enterprises to Prepare Launching Operations from Brazilian Territory, 2001, and the Authorisation of Private Enterprises to Carry out Launching Operations on Brazilian Territory, 2002. The legal effect is that the licencing followed by authorisation is mandatory for any private entities interested to launch from Brazil. Therefore the state's control of space activities is repeated here again like other countries. Argentina follows Brazil through its National Decree for Objects launched into Outer Space, 1995.

The example of Colombia is totally exceptional compared with countries all over the world. It introduced in its Constitution the provision for claiming and owning the geostationary orbit. But this is totally in contrast with the provisions of space law treaties. Therefore instead of duly considering the issue of sovereignty within its Constitution for space activities, the country has followed reverse state practice that is not permitted under international law. No other countries are interested to make business tie-up for space activities. So this case proves the negative consequence for violating any legal issues as raised in previous chapter.

The case of Canada is that Canadian Space Agency Act, 1990, provides for granting loan to any person in respect of the commercial exploitation of space science and technology. The Minister of Industry, Science and Technology who grants the loan becomes the guarantor of repayment of such loan. Therefore, the financial burden for private actors is one kind of self-enjoyment by the concerned Ministry.

At last it is the mighty in outer space i.e. United States of America that has so many space related legislations along with policies. All these follow directly or indirectly the commercial side of space activities for which the regulation of private actors is the main criteria. The legal issues are also settled within these regulations. In this view, the Commercial Space Launch Act, 1984, signifies this research study with the observation that USA took the legal stand for private actors in outer space long back. For this reason the country has to look back again to amend this Act in 2004, when the issue of safety is the top most criteria in the era of commercial human spaceflight. This is upcoming in the form of space tourism.

The Land Remote Sensing Policy Act, 1992, is mainly the legal check point for violation of two issues like sovereignty and national security of the sensed states through high-resolution satellite imageries. The environment issue is facilitated like disposing the satellite after its operation is terminated.

The next is Commercial Space Act, 1998, where the commercial global positioning system running by the private actors could not be vulnerable to national security. The issue of safety is pressed in pursuing commercial space activities. The commercial space transport operators have to follow the national security restrictions.

Lastly, there are two policies of USA. First, the National Space Policy, 2010, interprets the sovereignty and proprietary rights in different way. There is no sovereignty in outer space for any states according to space law treaties.

So, the countries could enjoy the space systems of all nations to have rights of passage through and conduct of operations without interference. The purposeful interference is infringement of nation's right. USA has brought this text strategically well in advance to legally facilitate the celestial mining. Its more advanced form is conceptualised on establishing the outline of Asteroid Act for discussion and debates in the Parliament of US. The issue of ethics is attracted on warning the irresponsible uses of space environment that increases the probability of collision. The commercial guideline part of this policy is unique in the sense that it mentions the legal creation of market for space goods, services or activities provided by private actors. The consequence will be automatic financing of these actors.

Lastly, the National Space Transportation Policy, 2013, is value addition of the issue of safety as prescribed in other Acts and policies of USA. The simple reason is upcoming commercial human spaceflight to be conducted by the private actors. It also advocates these safety measures to be followed globally to promote the international commercial space transportation activities. USA, being an old super power in space, has institutions from governmental side as well non-governmental side to regulate the private actors.

This is observed from above that different countries consider and implement the legal issues as explained in the previous chapter. The different domestic legal instruments are attracted but their contributions are corroborative in achieving the maximum commercial success through regulations. The last Table of this chapter shows that all these issues are concerned with the space related regulations of different countries but sometimes all issues are not in forefront. The reason may be different. Sometimes one individual country shows special consideration of one issue and provides unique legal solution like financing in Russia. But the issues like sovereignty, national security are considered by all states in pursuing the space activities conducted by the private actors. That is why the legal procedure for launching and authorisation is almost the same in every country. The environmental issue related with Earth is considered in Article IX of the Outer Space Treaty. The same in outer space is also considered later on by Nigeria whose space legislation was established later i.e., in 2010. The legal treatment of space debris issue within national space legislation of UK is another exciting example. The issue of financing of space activities is also prescribed differently by different countries. Safety is considered in general with the launching activities but the era of commercial space transportation attracts this issue especially in the countries where the government is interested to promote such space activities. USA is leading one in this sector. Therefore the issue of safety is highlighted specially in the Commercial Space Launch Amendment Act, 2004. Dispute settlement is common for all states. In comparison with these issues, the issues like ethics, corporate social responsibility are not interacted too much though ethics come indirectly in some countries' space legislations.

The regulation through institution discloses that it is not always the national space agency of a country but also the institutes related with space technology are the background force for establishing space regulations. The examples are cited from Republic of Korea, Saudi Arabia etc. Moreover, there are societies for developing regulations as shown in Japan and USA.

This analytical background for regulating the legal issues for private actors in different countries ends here. Now it is high time for this research study to search and analyse critically similar issues or others, if any, within existing Indian regulations. Therefore this research study would like to make an effort in the next chapter to analyse the space regulations in India.

Notes

1. Vereshchetin, V., *Next Steps in International Law*, 1995. In Nandasiri Jasentuliyana (Ed.), *Perspectives on International Law* (London: Kluwer Law International), p. 477.
2. Data are provided from concerned countries national space agencies' websites and details are within the analysis.
3. http://treaties.un.org/pages/ViewDetailsIII.aspx?&src=TREATY&mtdsg_no=XXIV~1 &chapter=24&Temp=mtdsg3&lang=en (Accessed June 15, 2013).
4. China's Space Activities (White Paper), at http://www.cnsa.gov.cn/n615709/n620681/ n771967/69198.html (Accessed June 15, 2013)
5. Ibid.
6. China's Space Activities in 2006, at http://www.cnsa.gov.cn/n615709/n620681/ n771967/79970.html (Accessed June 15, 2013).
7. Shouping, Li, "The New Development of China's Space Policy," *Asian Journal of Air and Space Law*, vol. 2, no. 1, 2012, pp. 122-123, 130.
8. Zhao, Y., "National Space Legislation in Mainland China," *Journal of Space Law*, vol. 33, no. 2, 2007, p. 432.
9. Ibid., p. 435; See also Lyall, F. and Larsen, Paul B., *Space Law: A Treatise* (Surrey (England): Ashgate, 2009), pp. 479-480.
10. http://www.cnsa.gov.cn/n615709/n620681/n771918/index.html (Accessed June 15, 2013).
11. Pagkratis, Spyros, *European Space Activities in the Global Context, 2011*. In Kai-U-Schrogwl et al., (Eds.), *Yearbook on Space Policy 2009/2010* (New York: Springer Wien), p. 58.

12. http://www.treasury.gov.au/PublicationsAndMedia/Publications/2013/Economic-Roundup-Issue-2/Economic-Roundup/Chinas-unfinished-SOE-reforms (Accessed June 15, 2014).
13. Zhao, Yun, *Space Commercialisation and the Development of Space Law from a Chinese Legal Perspective* (New York: Nova Science Publishers, 2009), p. 169.
14. Ibid.
15. Ibid., pp. 175-176.
16. http://www.ceo.gov.hk/exco/eng/index.htm (Accessed June 15, 2014).
17. http://www.edb.gov.sg/content/edb/en/industries/emerging-businesses/emerging-businesses.html#space (Accessed June 15, 2013).
18. Ibid.
19. Singapore Technologies Electronics Ltd. http://www.stee.stengg.com/ourcompany/aboutus.html (Accessed June 15, 2013).
20. Singapore plots economic lift-off with satellites, spacecraft, at http://www.reuters.com/article/2013/07/23/singapore-satellites-idUSL4N0FN0V920130723 (Accessed June 15, 2013).
21. http://treaties.un.org/pages/ViewDetailsIII.aspx?&src=TREATY&mtdsg_no=XXIV~1&chapter=24&Temp=mtdsg3&lang=en (Accessed June 15, 2013).
22. Japan Aerospace Exploration Agency, at http://www.jaxa.jp/index_e.html (Accessed June 15, 2013).
23. Aoki, S.,"Current Status and Recent Developments in Japan's National Space Law and its Relevance to Pacific RIM Space Law and Activities," *Journal of Space Law*, vol. 35, no. 2, 2009, pp. 369-370
24. Tronchetti, F., *Fundamentals of Space Law and Policy* (New York: Springer, 2013), p. 69.
25. Basic Plan on Space Policy as Established by Strategic Headquarters for Space Policy, Government of Japan, at http://www8.cao.go.jp/space/plan/plan-eng.pdf (Accessed June 15, 2013).
26. Ibid., pp. 9-10. See also Hata S., "Japanese Space Industry's Efforts regarding Long-term Sustainability of Space Activities", presentation on 14 February at 50th Session of the Scientific & Technical Sub-Committee on Outer Space, United Nations, Vienna, 2013. http://www.oosa.unvienna.org/pdf/pres/stsc2013/2013lts-04E.pdf (Accessed June 15, 2013).
27. Basic Space Law, Japan, at http://law.e-gov.go.jp/announce/H20HO043.html (Accessed June 15, 2013).
28. Ibid., Article 4.
29. Ibid., Article 16.
30. Ibid., Article 20.
31. Ibid., Article 21.
32. Ibid., Article 35.
33. Saisho, D., "Liability Risk Sharing Regime of the Bill of Japan's Legislation on Space Activities and its Comparison with the U.S. and French Law", in Corinne M. Jorgenson (ed.), Proceedings of the International Institute of Space Law 2011 (The Hague: Eleven International Publishing, 2012), p. 107.
34. Ibid.
35. Ibid., pp. 112-113.
36. See n. 23.

37. Aoki, S. (2014), "National Space Laws of Japan: Today and Tomorrow", Presentation delivered on November 18, 2014, at the China National Space Administration in UN Workshop on Space Law, Beijing, at http://www.unoosa.org/pdf/spacelaw/activities/2014/pres10E.pdf
38. See n. 25, p. 4. Also see http://www.oosa.unvienna.org/pdf/pres/stsc2013/2013lts-04E.pdf (Accessed June 15, 2013).
39. http://www.sjac.or.jp/en_index.html (Accessed June 15, 2013).
40. http://www.oosa.unvienna.org/pdf/pres/stsc2013/2013lts-04E.pdf, p. 2 (Accessed June 15, 2013).
41. https://treaties.un.org/pages/ViewDetailsIII.aspx?&src=TREATY&mtdsg_no=XXIV~1&chapter=24&Temp=mtdsg3&lang=en (Accessed June 15, 2013).
42. Korean Aerospace Research Institute, at http://www.kari.re.kr/eng/ (Accessed June 15, 2013).
43. Ibid.
44. Hwang, Chin Young, "Space activities in Korea—History, current programs and future plans," *Space Policy*, vol. 22, no. 3, 2006, p. 195.
45. Rhee, Sang-Myon, "Current Status and Recent Developments in Korea's National Space Laws," *Journal of Space Law*, vol. 35, no. 2, 2009, pp. 523-524.
46. Lee, J.J. and Chung, S., "Space policy for late comer countries: A case study of South Korea," *Space Policy*, vol. 27, no. 4, 2011, p. 230.
47. Lee, Yoon, "A Review of the Space Development Promotion Act of the Republic of Korea," *Journal of Space Law*, vol. 33, no. 1, 2007, pp. 123-190.
48. See n. 45.
49. Space Law and Policy in the Republic of Korea presented by Prof. Doo H. Kim. http://www.oosa.unvienna.org/pdf/pres/2010/SLW2010/02-09.pdf (Accessed June 15, 2013).
50. Space Development Promotion Act, 2005, at http://www.oosa.unvienna.org/oosa/en/SpaceLaw/national/republic_of_korea/space_development_promotions_actE.html (Accessed June 15, 2013)
51. Ibid.
52. See n. 45, pp. 533-536.
53. http://eng.kari.re.kr/sub04_04 (Accessed June 15, 2013).
54. International Cooperation http://www.suparco.gov.pk/pages/agreements.asp (Accessed June 20, 2013).
55. http://treaties.un.org/pages/ViewDetailsIII.aspx?&src=TREATY&mtdsg_no=XXIV~1&chapter=24&Temp=mtdsg3&lang=en (Accessed June 20, 2013).
56. http://treaties.un.org/pages/ViewDetails.aspx?src=TREATY&mtdsg_no=XXIV-2&chapter=24&lang=en (Accessed June 20, 2013).
57. Khan, Abdullah, "National Regulatory Framework of Outer Space Activities in Pakistan", Presentation delivered on at the China National Space Administration in UN Workshop on Space Law, Beijing, 2014, at http://www.unoosa.org/pdf/spacelaw/activities/2014/pres16E.pdf (Accessed November 25, 2014)
58. Ibid.
59. Pakistan's Space Programme, at http://www.suparco.gov.pk/downloadables/03-Pakistans-Space-Programme.pdf (Accessed June 25, 2013); See also Address of the Prime Minister. https://www.google.co.in/url?sa=t&rct=j&q=&esrc=s&source=web&cd=5&ved=0CEUQFjAE&url=http%3A%2F%2Fwww.pid.gov.pk%2Fpm%2520speech%2520on%25205-11-2011.doc&ei=sSoYUv-hCcPrrQeb6YCICg&usg=AFQjCNH

Rs5X2im94pnakR_qzIMGQ-WyrMA (Accessed June 25, 2013).

60. Pakistan Space Agency, at http://www.suparco.gov.pk/ (Accessed June 20, 2013).
61. Ibid, Major Programmes, at http://www.suparco.gov.pk/pages/major-programmes.asp (Accessed June 20, 2013).
62. National Space Conference, 2012, at http://www.suparco.gov.pk/downloadables/nsc-2012-event-report.pdf (Accessed June 25, 2013).
63. Murad, Shah, "Regulating Space Activities Emerging Issues & Regulatory Challenges for Pakistan's Space Programme-2040", Lecture delivered on at National Space Conference 2012, Islamabad, Pakistan. http://suparco.gov.pk/downloadables/nsc17.pdf (Accessed November 5, 2013).
64. See n. 57.
65. http://rsilpak.org/ (Accessed November 25, 2014).
66. See n. 57.
67. Ibid.
68. National committee on space policy discusses on Thailand's space affairs development on 13-05-2013, at http://www.thaigov.go.th/en/news-room/item/77613-national-committee-on-space-policy-discusses-on-thailand%E2%80%99s-space-affairs-development.html (Accessed July 2, 2013). See Also Noichim, C., "Thai Space Law: Past, Present & Future Perspectives", Presentation delivered on 18 November 2014 at the China National Space Administration in UN Workshop on Space Law, Beijing, 2014, at http://www.unoosa.org/pdf/spacelaw/activities/2014/pres14E.pdf (Accessed November 25, 2014)
69. http://treaties.un.org/pages/ViewDetails.aspx?src=TREATY&mtdsg_no=XXIV-2&chapter=24&lang=en (Accessed July 3, 2013).
70. HB 6725 Philippine Space Act of 2012, at http://agham.org.ph/house-bill-6725-philippine-space-act-2012/ (Accessed July 5, 2013).
71. Ibid.
72. Ibid.
73. Ibid.
74. http://treaties.un.org/pages/ViewDetailsIII.aspx?&src=TREATY&mtdsg_no=XXIV~1&chapter=24&Temp=mtdsg3&lang=en (Accessed July 5, 2013).
75. EISAT, at http://www.eiast.ae/default.aspx?options={a93e7034-0baa-4e2b-be21721a4b6feb8e}&view=Article&layout=Article&itemId=98&id=28 (Accessed July 5, 2013).
76. http://www.eiast.com/userfiles/EIAST-Law-No-2_2006_English.pdf (Accessed July 5, 2013).
77. EIAST Strategic Plan 2011-2013, at http://www.eiast.ae/default.aspx?options={a93e7034-0baa-4e2b-be21-721a4b6feb8e}&view=Article&layout=Article&itemId=100&id=29 (Accessed July 5, 2013).
78. Kazakhstan's National Space Agency, at http://www.tsenki.com/en/partners_customers/foregn_partners/space_agencies/?ELEMENT_ID=86196 (Accessed July 5, 2013).
79. http://treaties.un.org/pages/ViewDetailsIII.aspx?&src=TREATY&mtdsg_no=XXIV~1&chapter=24&Temp=mtdsg3&lang=en (Accessed July 5, 2013).
80. http://treaties.un.org/pages/ViewDetails.aspx?src=TREATY&mtdsg_no=XXIV-2&chapter=24&lang=en (Accessed July 5, 2013).
81. Law of the Republic of Kazakhstan on Space Activities, 2012. http://www.oosa.unvienna.org/pdf/spacelaw/national/kazakhstan/528-IV_2012-01-06E.pdf (Accessed July 5, 2013).

82. Ibid.
83. Ibid.
84. Ibid.
85. Ibid.
86. United Nations Workshop on Space Law, at http://www.oosa.unvienna.org/oosa/en/SpaceLaw/workshops/index.html (Accessed July 10, 2013).
87. Data are provided from concerned countries national space agencies' websites and details are within the analysis.
88. http://alc2013ghana.com/index.html (Accessed November 15, 2013).
89. Martinez, P., "The African Leadership Conference on Space Science and Technology for Sustainable Development," *Space Policy*, vol. 28, no. 1, 2012, pp. 33-37
90. Martinez, P., "The 2nd African Leadership Conference on Space Science and Technology for Sustainable Development", 2008, at http://www.saao.ac.za/~wgssa/archive/as12/PMartinez2.pdf (Accessed November 15, 2013)
91. Kerrest, A., "Responsibility, Liability and Registration under Space Law Treaties", Conference presentation at the 4th Leadership Conference on Space Science & Technology for Sustainable Development, 2011 at Mombasa, Kenya, 2011, at http://www.unoosa.org/pdf/bst/ALC2010/11_Kerrest_Mombasa_2011.pdf (Accessed November 30, 2013).
92. See n. 90.
93. http://treaties.un.org/pages/ViewDetailsIII.aspx?&src=TREATY&mtdsg_no=XXIV~1&chapter=24&Temp=mtdsg3&lang=en (Accessed July 10, 2013).
94. National Space Policy, 2008. http://www.unoosa.org/pdf/spacelaw/national/safrica/nat-policyE.pdf (Accessed July 10, 2013).
95. Ibid.
96. See n. 94.
97. Statutes of the Republic of South Africa - Trade and Industry No.84 of 1993, Space Affairs Act, 1993, at http://www.oosa.unvienna.org/oosa/en/SpaceLaw/national/south_africa/space_affairs_act_1993E.html (Accessed July 10, 2013).
98. Ibid.
99. South African National Space Agency Act, 2008, at http://www.oosa.unvienna.org/pdf/spacelaw/national/safrica/Act36-2008.pdf (Accessed July 10, 2013).
100. Ibid.
101. National Space Research and Development Agency, at http://www.nasrda.gov.ng/en/portal/ (Accessed July 10, 2013).
102. Boroffice, R.A., "The Nigerian Space Programme: An Update," *African Skies,* vol. 12, pp. 40-45, at http://www.saao.ac.za/~wgssa/archive/as12/boroffice.pdf (Accessed July 10, 2013)
103. http://www.unoosa.org/oosa/en/SpaceLaw/treaties.html (Accessed July 10, 2013).
104. National Space Policy, 2001, at http://www.dawodu.com/space.pdf (Accessed July 10, 2013).
105. Space Economic Readiness- Economical Analysis for Public Funding of Space Technology in Developing African Countries, at http://isulibrary.isunet.edu/opac/doc_num.php?explnum_id=45 (Accessed July 10, 2013).
106. Ibid. See also Momoh, W., "An Overview of Nigerian Space Activity and Space Law," *African Skies*, vol. 12, p. 106. http://articles.adsabs.harvard.edu/cgi-bin/nph-iarticle_query?2008afrsk..12..104m&defaultprint=YES&filetype=.pdf (Accessed July 10, 2013).

107. Ibid.
108. Ibid.
109. National Space Research and Development Agency Act, 2010, at http://nasrda.gov.ng/NASRDA_ACT_2010.pdf (Accessed July 12, 2013).
110. John, Olusoji N. et al., *Legal Regime of Remote Sensing and Geographical Information System in Nigeria*, 2012. In Corinne M. Contant Jorgenson (Ed.), *Proceedings of the International Institute of Space Law 2011* (The Hague: Eleven International Publishing), p. 262.
111. http://www.dawodu.com/space.pdf (Accessed August 10, 2014).
112. Data are provided from Australian Space Agency website and details are within the analysis.
113. http://www.space.gov.au/INTERNATIONAL/Pages/TreatiesandAgreements.aspx (Accessed July 12, 2013).
114. http://www.space.gov.au/INTERNATIONAL/internationalfora/Pages/default.aspx (Accessed July 12, 2013).
115. http://treaties.un.org/pages/ViewDetailsIII.aspx?&src=TREATY&mtdsg_no=XXIV~1&chapter=24&Temp=mtdsg3&lang=en (Accessed July 12, 2013).
116. http://treaties.un.org/pages/ViewDetails.aspx?src=TREATY&mtdsg_no=XXIV-2&chapter=24&lang=en (Accessed July 12, 2013).
117. Satellite Utilisation Policy 2013, Australia. http://www.space.gov.au/Documents/Australia%27s%20satellite%20utilisation%20policy%20-%20version%201.1p%20-%2016%20April%202013.pdf (Accessed July 14, 2014).
118. Ibid. Freeland, Steven, "Australia National Space Law & Space Policy", Presentation delivered on 18 November 2014 at the China National Space Administration in UN Workshop on Space Law, Beijing, 2014, at http://www.unoosa.org/pdf/spacelaw/activities/2014/pres09E.pdf (Accessed November 25, 2014).
119. Space Activities Act 1998 (No. 123, 1998) (as amended, taking into account amendments up to Act No. 8 of 2010), at http://www.comlaw.gov.au/Details/C2010C00193 (Accessed July 12, 2013).
120. Ibid.
121. Ibid.
122. Ibid.
123. Ibid.
124. Ibid.
125. Ibid.
126. Ibid.
127. http://www.space.gov.au/SpacePolicyUnit/NationalSpacePolicy/Pages/default.aspx (Accessed November 20, 2014).
128. Data are provided from concerned websites of ESA, EU and European countries. Details are within the analysis.
129. http://forbesindia.com/article/hindsight/cryogenic-technology-the-india-story/14012/1 (Accessed July 15, 2013).
130. http://www.isro.org/pressrelease/scripts/pressreleasein.aspx?Sep30b_2008 (Accessed July 15, 2013).
131. http://www.esa.int/About_Us/Welcome_to_ESA/New_Member_States (Accessed July 15, 2014).
132. http://www.esa.int/SPECIALS/ECSL/ (Accessed July 15, 2013).

133. Ibid.
134. ESA and the EU, at http://www.esa.int/About_Us/Welcome_to_ESA/ESA_and_the_U (Accessed July 15, 2013).
135. http://treaties.un.org/pages/ViewDetailsIII.aspx?&src=TREATY&mtdsg_no=XXIV~1 &chapter=24&Temp=mtdsg3&lang=en (Accessed July 15, 2013).
136. http://eeas.europa.eu/non-proliferation-and-disarmament/outer-space-activities/index_ en.htm (Accessed May 1, 2014).
137. Ibid.
138. Draft of International Code of Conduct for Outer Space Activities. http://eeas.europa. eu/non-proliferation-and-disarmament/pdf/space_code_conduct_draft_vers_31-march-2014_en.pdf (Accessed May 1, 2014).
139. http://swfound.org/media/83247/icoc_factsheet_may2013.pdf (Accessed October 1, 2013).
140. See n. 138.
141. See n. 131.
142. Hermida, Julian, *Legal Basis for a National Space Legislation* (Kluwer Academic Publishers: Dordrecht, 2004), pp. 101-102.
143. Law of the Russian Federation on Space Activity, 1993, at http://www.unoosa.org/oosa/ SpaceLaw/national/russian_federation/decree_5663-1_E.html (Accessed October 01, 2013).
144. Ibid.
145. Ibid., Article 12.
146. Ibid.
147. Ibid.
148. Ibid., Article 13.
149. Ibid., Article 13 (2).
150. Ibid., Article 13 (3).
151. Ibid., Article 16
152. Ibid., Article 16 (1).
153. Ibid., Article 16 (2).
154. Ibid., Article 16 (3).
155. Ibid., Article 16 (4).
156. Ibid., Article 22 (1).
157. Ibid., Article 30.
158. Ibid.
159. Malkov, Sergey P. and Doldirina, C., *Regulation of Space Activities in Russian Federation, 2010*. In Ram S. Jakhu (Ed.), *National Regulation of Space Activities* (New York: Springer), p. 330.
160. Ibid., p. 332.
161. Malysheva, Nataliya R., *Regulation of Space Activities in Ukraine*, 2010. In Ram S. Jakhu (Ed.), *National Regulation of Space Activities* (New York: Springer), p. 335.
162. Morring, F., "Selling Space Ukrainian Officials travel world to capitalize on Soviet-era capability," *Aviation Week & Space Technology*, vol. 175, no. 38, 2013, pp. 28-29.
163. http://treaties.un.org/pages/ViewDetailsIII.aspx?&src=TREATY&mtdsg_no=XXIV~1 &chapter=24&Temp=mtdsg3&lang=en (Accessed July 28, 2013).
164. See n. 161.
165. Main Laws Regulating Space Activities in Ukraine, at http://www.nkau.gov.ua/nsau/

catalogNEW.nsf/160776743F0D4A37C3256BB30050B196/31F0D0AA62772124C2256F97003C920B?OpenDocument&lang=E (Accessed July 28, 2013).

166. See n. 161, pp. 335-336.
167. The Law on Ukrainian Space Activities, 1996, at http://www.nkau.gov.ua/nsau/pravonsau.nsf/8EE0562C6B91F547C3256A8F00362010/785F24D0FD8DF9CFC22573D3004E6717?OpenDocument&lang=E (Accessed July 28, 2013).
168. Ibid., Article 4.
169. Ibid., Article 5.
170. Ibid., Article 8.
171. Ibid., Article 9.
172. See n. 161, p. 339.
173. See n. 167, Article 10.
174. See n. 161, p. 340.
175. See n. 167, Article 11.
176. See n. 167, Article 13.
177. See n. 167, Article 14.
178. See n. 167, Article 15 & 16.
179. See n. 167, Article 17.
180. See n. 167, Articles 24-26.
181. See n. 161, p. 336.
182. http://www.cnes.fr/web/CNES-en/7405-space-challenges-for-france-and-europe.php (Accessed July 15, 2013).
183. Selding, Peter B. de, "Thales Alenia Space Asks France to Ease Imagery Sale Restrictions", 2013, at http://www.spacenews.com/article/military-space/37148thales-alenia-space-asks-france-to-ease-imagery-sale-restrictions (Accessed September 30, 2013)
184. http://treaties.un.org/pages/ViewDetailsIII.aspx?&src=TREATY&mtdsg_no=XXIV~1&chapter=24&Temp=mtdsg3&lang=en (Accessed July 15, 2013).
185. See Article 3 (2): 'Any threat or use of force or any other hostile act or threat of hostile act on the moon is prohibited. It is likewise prohibited to use the moon in order to commit any such act or to engage in any such threat in relation to the earth, the moon, spacecraft, the personnel of spacecraft or man-made space objects.'
186. http://treaties.un.org/pages/ViewDetails.aspx?src=TREATY&mtdsg_no=XXIV-2&chapter=24&lang=en#EndDec (Accessed July 15, 2013).
187. Carminati, Giugi, "French National Space Legislation: a Brief "Parcours" of a Long History," *Houston Journal of International Law*, vol. 36, no. 1, 2014, p. 4.
188. Ibid., p. 9.
189. A space act and a new foundation for a forward-looking space sector, at http://www.cnes.fr/web/CNES-en/7406-french-space-act.php (Accessed July 15, 2013).
190. French Space Operation Act, 2008, at http://www.oosa.unvienna.org/pdf/pres/lsc2009/pres-04.pdf (Accessed July 15, 2013). Article 2.
191. Ibid., Article 4.
192. Ibid., Article 12.
193. Ibid., Article 13.
194. See n. 187, pp. 14-15.
195. See n. 190, Article 22.
196. See n. 190, Article 24.

197. See n. 189.
198. http://treaties.un.org/pages/ViewDetailsIII.aspx?&src=TREATY&mtdsg_no=XXIV~1 &chapter=24&Temp=mtdsg3&lang=en (Accessed July 15, 2013).
199. Teichert, Sandra, 'Impact of Germany's Recent Space Policy and Progress Towards a National Legislation', 2013; In Corinne M. Jorgensen (Ed.), *Proceedings of the International Institute of Space Law 2012* (The Hague: Eleven International Publishers), pp. 96-99.
200. Ibid. p. 97.
201. German Space Strategy, 2010, at http://www.gwu.edu/~spi/assets/docs/2011-04-29_German_Space_Strategy.pdf (Accessed July 20, 2013).
202. Ibid.
203. Ibid.
204. See n. 199, p. 103.
205. Hobe, S. & Neumann, J., *Regulation of Space Activities in Germany, 2010*. In Ram S. Jakhu (Ed.), *National Regulation of Space Activities* (New York: Springer), pp. 128-129.
206. MOU between ISRO and UKSA in 2011, at http://www.bis.gov.uk/assets/ukspaceagency/docs/mous/mou_indianspaceresearchorganisation2011.pdf (Accessed July 25, 2013).
207. http://treaties.un.org/pages/ViewDetailsIII.aspx?&src=TREATY&mtdsg_no=XXIV~1 &chapter=24&Temp=mtdsg3&lang=en (Accessed July 25, 2013).
208. The Outer Space Act, 1986, at http://www.bis.gov.uk/ukspaceagency/what-we-do/space-and-the-growth-agenda/uk-capabilities-for-overseas-markets/the-outer-space-act-1986 (Accessed July 25, 2013).
209. Ibid., Article 3 & 4.
210. Ibid., Article 5.
211. Ibid.
212. Ibid.
213. Ibid., Article 9.
214. Ibid; Also at http://www.bis.gov.uk/assets/ukspaceagency/docs/osa/outer-space-act-1986.pdf (Accessed July 25, 2013).
215. Mosteshar, Said, *Regulation of Space Activities in the United Kingdom*, 2010. In Ram S. Jakhu (Ed.), *National Regulation of Space Activities* (New York: Springer), p. 358.
216. http://www.ofcom.org.uk/about/ (Accessed July 25, 2013).
217. http://www.spaceisle.com/iom.html (Accessed July 25, 2013). See also Aganaba, T., *Legal Framework in Support of Commercialisation of Outer Space: the Case of the Isle of Man*, 2010. In Corinne M. Contant Jorgenson (Ed.), *Proceedings of the 51st Colloquium on the Law of Outer Space* (Washington: American Institute of Aeronautics & Astronautics), p. 439.
218. http://www.isleofman.com/business-sectors/space/ (Accessed July 25, 2013).
219. Telecommunications Act, 1984, at http://iomcc.im/lib/docs/cc/legislation/telecommunicationsact1984_1.pdf (Accessed July 25, 2013).
220. See n. 217, Aganaba, p. 443.
221. http://www.whereyoucan.com/space (Accessed July 25, 2013).
222. Andrews, William L., "A Mighty Stone for David's Sling: the International Space Company," *Regent Journal of International Law*, vol. 1, 2003, pp. 31-32.
223. International Institute of Air & Space Law, Leiden, at http://law.leiden.edu/organisation/

publiclaw/iiasl/ (Accessed July 26, 2013).

224. Dunk, F. G. Von Der, *Regulation of Space Activities in the Netherlands from Hugo Grotius to the High Ground of Outer Space*, 2010. In Ram S. Jakhu (Ed.), *National Regulation of Space Activities* (New York: Springer), p. 227.
225. http://treaties.un.org/pages/ViewDetailsIII.aspx?&src=TREATY&mtdsg_no=XXIV~1&chapter=24&Temp=mtdsg3&lang=en (Accessed July 26, 2013).
226. http://treaties.un.org/pages/ViewDetails.aspx?src=TREATY&mtdsg_no=XXIV-2&chapter=24&lang=en#2 (Accessed July 26, 2013).
227. Law Incorporating Rules Concerning Space Activities and Establishment of a Registry of Space Objects, 2007, at http://www.oosa.unvienna.org/oosa/en/SpaceLaw/national/netherlands/space_activities_actE.html (Accessed July 26, 2013).
228. Ibid., Section 3.
229. Ibid., Section 12.
230. Ibid., Section 11.
231. Ibid., Section 13-23.
232. See n. 224, p. 244.
233. http://www.spaceoffice.nl/en/The-NSO/ (Accessed July 26, 2013).
234. Norwegian Space Centre, at http://web.spacecentre.no/eng/About/More-about-the-NCS (Accessed July 26, 2013).
235. http://treaties.un.org/pages/ViewDetailsIII.aspx?&src=TREATY&mtdsg_no=XXIV~1&chapter=24&Temp=mtdsg3&lang=en (Accessed July 26, 2013).
236. The Norwegian Space Industry, at http://web.spacecentre.no/eng/Focus-Areas/Industry/The-Norwegian-Space-Industry (Accessed July 26, 2013).
237. Act on launching objects from Norwegian territory etc. into outer space, at http://www.oosa.unvienna.org/oosa/en/SpaceLaw/national/norway/act_38_1969E.html (Accessed July 26, 2013).
238. http://web.spacecentre.no/eng/About/More-about-the-NSC (Accessed July 26, 2013).
239. National Institute of Aerospace Technology. http://translate.google.co.in/translate?hl=en&sl=es&u=http://www.inta.es/&prev=/search%3Fq%3Dspanish%2Bspace%2Bagency%26espv%3D210%26es_sm%3D93 (Accessed July 26, 2013).
240. http://www.unoosa.org/oosa/en/SpaceLaw/national/spain/royal_decree_278_1995E.html (Accessed July 26, 2013).
241. http://treaties.un.org/pages/ViewDetailsIII.aspx?&src=TREATY&mtdsg_no=XXIV~1&chapter=24&Temp=mtdsg3&lang=en (Accessed July 26, 2013).
242. Ibid.
243. Swedish National Space Board, at http://www.snsb.se/en/ (Accessed July 28, 2013).
244. Ibid.
245. http://treaties.un.org/pages/ViewDetailsIII.aspx?&src=TREATY&mtdsg_no=XXIV~1&chapter=24&Temp=mtdsg3&lang=en (Accessed July 28, 2013).
246. Act on Space Activities (1982:963), at http://www.unoosa.org/oosa/en/SpaceLaw/national/sweden/act_on_space_activities_1982E.html (Accessed July 28, 2013).
247. http://www.snsb.se/en/Home/Swedish-Space-Industry/List-of-Companies/ (Accessed July 28, 2013).
248. Data are provided from websites of the concerned countries' national space agencies and details are within the analysis.
249. National Program of Space Activities 2005-2014, at http://www.aeb.gov.br/wp-content/uploads/2013/03/PNAE_INGLES.pdf (Accessed July 28, 2013).

250. Introduction to Space Law. This work collects the summaries of a series of lectures given by Prof. José Monserrat Filho's headquarters INFRAERO - Brazilian Airports in Brasilia in December 1997, at http://www.sbda.org.br/textos/textos.htm (Accessed July 28, 2013). (Translated from Portuguese). Also at http://treaties.un.org/pages/ViewDetailsIII.aspx?&src=TREATY&mtdsg_no=XXIV~1&chapter=24&Temp=mtdsg3&lang=en (Accessed July 28, 2013).
251. Filho, J.M., *Regulation of Space Activities in Brazil, 2010*. In Ram S. Jakhu (Ed.), *National Regulation of Space Activities* (New York: Springer), p. 63.
252. Ibid., pp. 68-69.
253. Ibid., p. 70.
254. National Space Plan (Updated) 2008-2015, at http://translate.google.co.in/translate?hl=en&sl=es&u=http://www.conae.gov.ar/&prev=/search%3Fq%3Dargentina%2Bspace%2Bagency%26newwindow%3D1%26biw%3D1280%26bih%3D699%26site%3Dwebhp (Accessed July 28, 2013)
255. Hermida, Julian, *Regulation of Space Activities in Argentina*, 2010. In Ram S. Jakhu (Ed.), *National Regulation of Space Activities* (New York: Springer), p. 23.
256. http://treaties.un.org/pages/ViewDetailsIII.aspx?&src=TREATY&mtdsg_no=XXIV~1&chapter=24&Temp=mtdsg3&lang=en (Accessed July 28, 2013).
257. http://www.conae.gov.ar/eng/sobre/legislaciones/l12595.pdf (Accessed July 30, 2013). [Translated Document]
258. Ibid.
259. Arenales-Vergara, Oscar A., "Colombia: reasons to create a national space agency," *Advances in Space Research*, bvol. 34, no. 10, 2004, pp. 2209-2214.
260. Colombian Space Commission, at http://translate.google.co.in/translate?hl=en&sl=es&u=http://www.cce.gov.co/&prev=/search%3Fq%3Dcolombian%2Bspace%2Bcommission%26newwindow%3D1%26site%3Dwebhp (Accessed August 3, 2013).
261. Ortiz, Jairo A. Becerra, "A survey of Colombia's new outer space policy: Reforms in Colombian law," *Acta Astronautica*, vol. 63(1-4), 2008, pp. 560-563.
262. Gomez, Camilo G. and Tahclian, *Space Procurement Regulation: The Colombian Space Procurement Act 2010*, 2012. In Corinne M. Contant Jorgenson (Ed.), *Proceedings of the International Institute of Space Law 2011* (The Hague: Eleven International Publishing), pp. 115-117.
263. Bolivarian Agency for Space Activities (Institutional Review), at http://translate.google.co.in/translate?hl=en&sl=es&u=http://www.abae.gob.ve/&prev=/search%3Fq%3DBolivarian%2BAgency%2Bfor%2BSpace%2BActivities%2B(ABAE)%26newwindow%3D1%26site%3Dwebhp (Accessed August 5, 2013).
264. Ibid.
265. Agency Law Bolivarian for Space Activities, at http://translate.googleusercontent.com/translate_c?depth=1&hl=en&prev=/search%3Fq%3DBolivarian%2BAgency%2Bfor%2BSpace%2BActivities%2B(ABAE)%26newwindow%3D1%26site%3Dwebhp&rurl=translate.google.co.in&sl=es&u=http://www.abae.gob.ve/leyes/SANC-%2520LEY-%2520DE-%2520LA-%2520AGENCIA-%2520BOLIVARIANA-PARA-%2520ACTIVIDADES-%2520ESPACIALES-09-08-07.pdf&usg=ALkJrhgpuhyMguY7Lscjv9lcc_nQ7InVWw (Accessed August 5, 2013).
266. Ibid.
267. Constitution of Venezuela, at http://www.abae.gob.ve/leyes/Constitucion.pdf (Accessed

August 05, 2013).

268. Organic Law of Science, Technology and Innovation, at http://www.abae.gob.ve/leyes/mcti-Ley_de_Ciecia_y_Tecnologia.pdf (Accessed August 5, 2013).

269. Mexican Space Agency Background, at http://translate.google.co.in/translate?hl=en&sl=es&u=http://www.aem.gob.mx/&prev=/search%3Fq%3Dagencia%2Bespacial%2Bmexicana%26newwindow%3D1%26site%3Dwebhp (Accessed August 6, 2013).

270. http://treaties.un.org/pages/ViewDetailsIII.aspx?&src=TREATY&mtdsg_no=XXIV~1&chapter=24&Temp=mtdsg3&lang=en (Accessed August 6, 2013).

271. http://treaties.un.org/pages/ViewDetails.aspx?src=TREATY&mtdsg_no=XXIV-2&chapter=24&lang=en#2 (Accessed August 6, 2013).

272. Act establishing the Mexican Space Agency, at http://translate.google.co.in/translate?hl=en&sl=es&u=http://www.aem.gob.mx/&prev=/search%3Fq%3Dagencia%2Bespacial%2Bmexicana%26newwindow%3D1%26site%3Dwebhp (Accessed August 6, 2013).

273. Ibid.

274. Data are provided from websites of the concerned countries' national space agencies and details are within the analysis.

275. http://treaties.un.org/pages/ViewDetailsIII.aspx?&src=TREATY&mtdsg_no=XXIV~1&chapter=24&Temp=mtdsg3&lang=en (Accessed August 6, 2013).

276. Jakhu, Ram S., *Regulation of Space Activities in Canada*, 2010. In Ram S. Jakhu (Ed.), *National Regulation of Space Activities* (New York: Springer), pp. 82-84.

277. http://laws.justice.gc.ca/eng/acts/C-23.2/ (Accessed August 6, 2013).

278. See n. 276. pp. 97-98.

279. http://treaties.un.org/pages/ViewDetailsIII.aspx?&src=TREATY&mtdsg_no=XXIV~1&chapter=24&Temp=mtdsg3&lang=en (Accessed August 06, 2013).

280. National Space Policy, 2010, at http://www.whitehouse.gov/sites/default/files/national_space_policy_6-28-10.pdf (Accessed August 10, 2013)

281. Ibid.

282. Ibid.

283. https://www.congress.gov/bill/113th-congress/house-bill/5063 (Accessed August 10, 2014)

284. Ibid.

285. Ibid.

286. Ibid.

287. Ibid.

288. Ibid.

289. Ibid.

290. Ibid.

291 National Space Transportation Policy, 2013, at http://www.whitehouse.gov/sites/default/files/microsites/ostp/national_space_transportation_policy_11212013.pdf (Accessed November 23, 2013).

292. Ibid.

293. www.wto.org/english/tratop_e/serv_e/mtn_gns_w_120_e.doc p. 7, at (Accessed November 23, 2014). '[11. Transport Services ……D. Space Transport….]'.

294. http://www.wto.org/english/tratop_e/serv_e/guide1_e.htm (Accessed November 23, 2014).

295. Commercial Space Launch Act, 1984, at http://www.princeton.edu/~ota/disk2/1985/8513/851316.PDF (Accessed August 10, 2013).
296. Ibid., Section 2.
297. Ibid., Section 6.
298. Ibid., Section 7 & 8.
299. Ibid., Section 12.
300. Ibid., Section 16.
301. Ibid., Section 20.
302. http://www.gpo.gov/fdsys/pkg/PLAW-108publ492/html/PLAW-108publ492.htm (Accessed August 11, 2013).
303. Land Remote Sensing Act, 1992, at http://thomas.loc.gov/cgi-bin/query/z?c102:H.R.6133.ENR: (Accessed August 10, 2013).
304. Ibid.
305. Ibid., Section 201.
306. Ibid., Section 202.
307. Ibid.
308. Ibid., Section 203.
309. Ibid., Section 507.
310. Commercial Space Act, 1998, at http://www.nasa.gov/offices/ogc/commercial/CommercialSpaceActof1998.html (Accessed August 10, 2013).
311. Ibid., Section 103.
312. Ibid., Sections 103,107,202.
313. Ibid., Section 201.
314. Commercial Space Launch Amendment Act, 2004, at http://www.gpo.gov/fdsys/pkg/PLAW-108publ492/html/PLAW-108publ492.htm (Accessed August 10, 2013).
315. Ibid.
316. Ibid.
317. http://www.nasa.gov/offices/olia/home/#.VIKozTHF8v0 (Accessed August 10, 2013).
318. http://www.commerce.senate.gov/public/index.cfm?p=ScienceandSpace (Accessed August 10, 2013).
319. http://science.house.gov/subcommittee-space-and-aeronautics (Accessed August 10, 2013).
320. http://www.gwu.edu/~spi/about.cfm (Accessed August 10, 2013).
321. http://www.nss.org/settlement/L5news/L5history.htm (Accessed August 10, 2013).
322. Data are provided from Tables 20-25.
323. Desai, B. H.. *Institutionalizing International Environmental Law*. (New York: Transnational Publishers, 2004) p. 131.

V. Space Regulations in India

Introduction

Since this research study is titled as 'Regulation of Private Actors in Outer Space – India's Role', it would require some broader analysis for India unlikely not so much required in the case of countries outside India. The structure of this chapter follows the basic three pillars of regulation – policies, legislations and institutions. The sequence of this chapter begins with policies to regulate private actors. But it was observed in the previous chapter that there were no private actors at first instance in any country. It is also true for India. So the policies were made to make some basic foundation to build national space infrastructure and then subsequently moved forward to regulate the state and private actors. The second sequence connects with almost all existing legislations of India to regulate the space activities of private actors though there is no direct or dedicated space legislation till date. The legislations are informally classified for analysis to be more meaningful. The last sequence relates with regulation for private actors on making institutions.

Policies

Table 27: Policies for Regulations[1]

Departments	Ministries	Policies
Department of S & T (DST)	Ministry of S & T	1. Scientific Policy Resolution, 1958. 2. Technology Policy Statement, 1983. 3. Science & Technology Policy, 2003. 4. Science, Technology & Innovation Policy, 2013. 5. Draft of National Geospatial Information Policy, 2012.

Department of Space (DoS)	Prime Minister's Portfolio	1. Satellite Telecommunication Policy (SATCOM), 2000. 2. Remote Sensing Data Policy, 2011. 3. Industry Participation Policy. 4. Commercialisation Policy. 5. International Co-operation Policy. 6. Human Resource Development Policy. 7. Technology Transfer Policy of ISRO. 8. Intellectual Property Policy of ISRO.
Department of Telecommunications (DoT)	Ministry of Communication & Information Technology	1. National Telecom Policy, 1994. 2. New Telecom Policy, 1999. 3. National Telecom Policy, 2012 (NPT 2012).
Department of Land Resources	Ministry of Rural Development	1. National Rehabilitation and Resettlement Policy, 2007. 2. Draft National Land Reforms Policy, 2013.
Planning Commission	Nil	1. Report of Working Group on DoS in 11th FYP 2007-2012. 2. Report of Working Group on DoS in 12th FYP 2012-2017.

These are categorised above into general science and technology (S &T) policy, reports of Working group on Department of Space (DoS) in 11th and 12th FYP, policies under DoS, polices under Department of Telecommunications (DoT) and Department of Land Resources. These may not be all inclusive. Moreover, these policies are not always directly connected with the regulation of private actors. It may be the case that future of private space activities would be planned according to some of the policies.

The regulation through policy in **Table 27** starts with S&T policy in general. In this category, the Scientific Policy Resolution (SPR), 1958, was the backbone of development of science and technology in India after independence.[2] It is prime mover of any S&T policies framed subsequently in different disciplines including space. Homi J. Bhabha was the person patronised by Jawaharlal Nehru, the then Prime Minister of India, to draft this resolution. The development of S&T would be based solely on nationalistic approach.[3]

The review of SPR expressed that one of its aims was industrialisation which would invite private sectors by default. So, the SPR could be extended to develop the domestic legal regulation for any industrialisation of S&T programme.[4] This extension may find a place for private actors in outer space. In this regard the sovereignty issue from chapter III is more correlated here because the country legitimised its sovereignty in science and technology for the first time on framing this policy resolution in 1958.

Though there were changes in this policy subsequently for different reasons but SPR was the first step to build a science and technological base in India. It happened when the country's S&T base was almost nil just after independence. However, the very characteristic of science policy is a dynamic concept. It is continuously evolved as well as modified. No country has yet succeeded in introducing a comprehensive science policy although many are striving in that direction. The case of India is not an exception.[5]

The subsequent policy was Technology Policy Statement, 1983. This Policy Statement was made in a scenario that was totally different from the SPR. India has achieved industrial base through science and technology development. The key points were technological self-reliance, initiatives for technological co-operations amongst developing countries and legislative framework to protect national technological know-how as industrial property right.[6]

This Policy Statement is very supporting to develop private actors in outer space because it not only stresses on self-reliance but also it states about export of technologies on internationally competitive basis. There may be import of technologies in some sectors but it will be restricted within a certain period. The overall impact is that there is competition amongst the industrial players in India. It is assumed to be very vital for any technology based industry including private space industry. It refers the technological cooperation amongst similar developing countries like India. So it may be an extended base for interacting the domestic and foreign private actors as mentioned in chapter II and IV. Moreover, it was for the first time to think about development of legislative framework for safeguarding national technological achievements. Therefore this policy statement acknowledges the significance of IPR that is one of the issues for private actors in outer space.

The Science and Technology Policy, 2003, follows the next sequence in **Table 27**. The Indian capabilities in different disciplines of S&T were mentioned for the first time within the policy where there was a place of space technology and applications with astronomy and astrophysics. This policy implied and invoked international law. It noticed the ongoing globalisation and the intensely competitive environment. Some of the policy objectives were: (i) implementation of speedy and effective domestic commercialisation related with S&T inventions, and (ii) promoting the international S&T cooperation as key element of international relations of India. It reminds that export of technologies will be facilitated through new policy initiatives and legislation. This policy stated that Indian legislation with regard to patents, copyrights and other forms of IP would facilitate the maximum incentives to be provided for individual inventions as well as to scientific and technological community as a whole. Its purpose was to promote a large scale and rapid commercialisation within India and abroad.[7]

This policy of 2003 indirectly paved way for privatisation; because rapid scale of commercialisation was only possible with effective privatisation. Perhaps this was the background to think about IP laws for the first time. It has already been presumed in chapter III that IPR is an issue in the era of privatisation. This policy also implied that India would like to obey all customary norms of international law in developing its S&T because of its imposition of international law in this sector.

The Science, Technology and Innovation Policy, 2013, was the last one in this series till now. The national development was the prime focus like earlier policies. India declared 2010-20 as a decade of innovation and the government established the National Innovation Council. So this policy stressed on innovations besides S&T. The Policy of 2003 introduced the role of research and development (R&D) in developing S&T whereas this policy indicates the enhancement of private sectors' participation in R&D. The output of R&D would be ultimately commercialised.[8]

The participation in global R&D infrastructure provides Indian industry to feel the sense of global competition in some high-technology areas with spin-off benefits. The purpose is to double India's share of global trade in high technology products which is at present 8 per cent. Therefore a strategic selection of some industry sectors would be made.[9] Since the annual budgets on space sector are increased,[10] so it is presumed that space industry would be one of the items in the selection list. The private actors in outer space from India consequently would participate in this global development.

These polices above are made to develop the foundation of existence of private actors, first in national level and then international level in the domain of S&T, including space. The direction of regulating the private actors is guided by these policies. The stages are commercialisation, industrialisation, research and development, and finally innovation. It is automatic that private actors are introduced in between these stages. So these policies are made to regulate the private actors in outer space as a part. The IPR issue is reflected in these policies because these are concerned with S&T.

The above polices were made under Department of Science & Technology (DST) whereas Draft of National Geospatial Information Policy, 2012, though made under the purview of DST is focussed to geospatial technology that is developed through space technology like satellite imageries.[11] Its regulatory regime is only for the private actors associated with geospatial industry. This would be a national policy on geographic information (GI). This policy being still in drafting stage has recognised the Remote Sensing (RS) Data Policy 2001 and 2011 describing the distribution process of satellite images of different category of users.[12] The 2011 RS Data Policy welcomed private RS satellites and private agencies to acquire or distribute data in India through licencing.[13]

But the criticism is done concerning the lack of clarity on licencing of RS satellites and RS data acquisition, or distribution allowing equal opportunities for private agencies to distribute satellite images data.[14] It refers the importance of industry for national GI development and in this regard, the Association of Geospatial Industries'[15] recommendation to promote the industry for economic and social reason is considered.[16] The draft Policy consists of issues related with sovereignty and proprietary rights, national security, IPR, liability, dispute settlement etc. but these issues are concerned with geospatial data[17] that include the satellite imageries of earth from remote sensing satellites.[18]

The next category of policies in **Table 27** is policies directly linked with space activities besides the above policies under DST. The policies are mainly under the purview of Department of Space (DoS). These are Satellite Communication Policy (SATCOM), 2000, Remote Sensing Data Policy, 2011, Industry Participation Policy, Commercialisation Policy, International Co-operation Policy and Human Resource Development Policy. Out of these the first two are the major polices in two different sectors of space activities – SATCOM in satellite telecommunication and the other relates with remote sensing data captured by remote sensing satellites in outer space. The name of other policies itself indicates the purposes for which they are established.

The Industry Participation Policy is made to boost the domestic industries for national space programmes. The commercialisation Policy is targeted to capture the global commercial market through national space assets, products and services. The International Co-operation Policy is for mutual exchange and sharing the space programmes and other related facilities with international forums. The Human Resource Development Policy is for the purpose of developing and retaining the people associated with such programme through various incentives as well as capacity development in academia through sponsored research.[19] The development of satellite navigational technology by ISRO brings India to be self-reliant in making satellite navigation system though the full-fledged services are still pending. Alongside satellite navigation policy has not been made. It is only mentioned in ISRO report that there is requirement of satellite navigation policy.[20]

The Satellite Communication Policy is applicable only for satellite communication and popularly known as SATCOM Policy.[21] The preamble of this policy states that it is made for communication satellites and ground equipments industry as well as satellite communication service industry in India. It welcomes the private sector investment in national space industry. One of the goals of this policy is to attract more foreign investment that is more concerned with the issue of financing of space activities. The source of FDI is linked with the foreign private actors in space.[22]

The review of this policy clearly discloses that it is a first-stage regulatory framework to open up the domestic private sectors involvement to use infrastructure of the national satellite communication system, Indian satellite (INSAT). The Communication and broadcasting are promoted through this policy to the large scale Indian population as a part to develop national economy. The foreign satellite service where Indian parties are involved through registration or holding equity in such foreign companies is also welcomed. Those who would like to use INSAT infrastructure have preferential treatment. Hence building-up and promoting national space technology through private actors is a unique characteristic of this policy. Lastly, it is proposed to maintain all the provisions of this policy in upcoming regulations in relation with broadcasting and telecommunication.

This analysis specifies that building and developing satellite communication infrastructure strengthens the sovereignty of India.[23]

The second part of SATCOM Policy is titled as the Norms, Guidelines and Procedures for Implementation of the Policy Framework for Satellite Communications in India (Approved by Government in 2000).[24] Out of all the Articles, Article 2 is for non-governmental parties i.e. private actors are implied.[25] Under the sub-heading 'Factors Leading to the Norms', the entry of private sector in both broadcasting and telecommunications are acknowledged.[26] The other factors are concerned with leasing the INSAT system to numerous private operators and to establish numerous Private Global Satellite Communication Systems as an impact of privatisation of INTELSAT and INMARSAT (as explained in chapter II under INTELSAT and INMARSAT).[27] According to the basic guideline to provide the INSAT capacity to commercial sectors, the private user has to maintain the government policy. The INSAT Coordination Committee (ICC) will decide the capacity of allocation for non-government users who are authorised by law to provide various telecommunication services including broadcasting.[28]

Under the sub-heading 'Commercial and Contractual Factors', the organisation created within DoS is authorised to provide the INSAT capacity to non-governmental users for all services except telecommunications which is under Department of Telecommunications (DoT). The INSAT capacity for operations outside India will not be in contrast with the UN/ ITU Constitution, Convention, Treaties, Agreements and Regulations. The policies of Government of India are followed.[29]

The analysis reflects that government does not intend to lose control even in the era of privatisation of global satellite communication systems. The policies of the government have to be followed in every respect but it emphasises on following international treaties, agreements and regulations to enjoy the INSAT capacity for operations outside India.

There is provision for issuing licences or authorisations for establishing Indian Satellite Systems.[30] The authorisation is required from DoS to own and operate Indian Registered Satellite System. This authorisation confirms that the UN Outer Space Treaty and other related treaties to which India is a signatory are maintained in operating the System. Any security related issues are taken into consideration. Also, the System is in consonance with the Space Policy of the government. The authorisation is required by the Wireless Planning and Coordination Wing (WPC) of the Ministry of Communication to operate a Space Station. It follows the existing ITU Radio Regulations. The operating licences will be issued by the system or network.[31] Each system or network is different in India like broadcasting is covered by Ministry of Information and Broadcasting through the Broadcast Act. In case of telecommunications, it is DoT through the Telegraph Act.[32]

Under the sub-heading 'Norms, Guidelines and Procedures to be Followed in Issuing the Licences', the rule for satellite systems for private parties is that registered Indian companies are only permitted to operate Indian Satellite System. The FDI in such a company does not exceed 74 per cent.[33] In case of conflict between two applicants for the satellite system or network, preference is given to the one who look forward to use satellites built in India and/or launched from India. The DOS shall make arrangement to notify the UN about the Space Station after its launch according to the UN convention.[34]

Therefore it is again repeatedly shown that sovereignty of the state is maintained through its functionaries like DoS with the process of authorisation to private actors within and outside India. In this regard, the security issue is duly considered. Moreover, different national Acts like telecommunications act are applicable for the operations of the private actors in the form of licence holders.

Finally, INSAT system has expanded its branches manifold. The number of users (private actors) is increasing in this system. Considering the current situation of satellite communications business in India, it has been proposed in the 12th FYP that the SATCOM Policy, 2000, will be revisited and revised, if required.[35] The SATCOM Policy is fully established for nationalistic approaches and demands. Even it is proposed to utilise national infrastructure in case of service rendered by foreign satellites.[36]

Besides the SATCOM Policy, Remote Sensing Data Policy, 2011, is another major space policy which has been specifically made for remote sensing data managed and/or permitted for acquisition or dissemination in India from foreign and commercial remote sensing satellites.[37] The policy is considered for availability of high resolution data from these satellites. First of all like other policies above, the preamble of this policy mentions that remote sensing data is for development and societal benefit. So the policy has been prima facie made and updated for developmental purpose i.e. not for commercial purpose.[38] The data policy recognises the national interest with national security as a priority that is also one of the legal issues in the context of this research study. The DoS is nodal agency for all steps taken under this policy if not otherwise stated.[39] So whoever be the private actors, all regulatory processes are to be done by DoS according to this policy. Thus sovereignty of state is prevailed through DoS.

Licence is issued or permission is given by the government through DoS.[40] But government has right to impose control over imaging tasks and distribution of data from Indian Remote Sensing Satellites (IRS) or any other remote sensing satellites of Indian origin when it feels that national security or international obligation or foreign policy demands so.[41] The National Remote Sensing Centre (NRSC) of ISRO has exclusive authority to acquire and disseminate all satellite remote sensing data of Indian territory whether data is retrieved from Indian or foreign satellites.[42] The ANTRIX Corporation of DoS has the authority to receive application for grant of licence to acquire or distribute IRS data outside India. Also it has the exclusive authority to consider and decide to grant the licence, on behalf of the government, with appropriate fees. ANTRIX is responsible for further guidance and help to licencees.[43] The government prescribes some conditions to disseminate data better than 1 meter resolution to protect national security of the country. This policy may be reviewed from time to time basis by the government.[44]

Within the report of the 12th FYP, it has been mentioned that the international service providers like Google Earth and Wikimapia have already released the satellite imageries of resolution better than 1 metre in public domain for browsing, visualisation and downloading through internet based services. Therefore the government will review the policy from time to time as prescribed in the policy itself to maintain the technological development along with global trend.[45]

The Remote Sensing Data Policy emphasises that the government holds its control on acquisition or dissemination of data to private parties from IRS. The licencing procedure lies with the government through its nodal agencies like DoS or ANTRIX as the case may be. It is assumed that government would like to maintain the monopoly in the name of national security of India. In fact the high resolution data is a threat to any country including India as explained under the issue national security in chapter III.

ISRO itself follows some policies within its organisation because it is the key division under DoS to produce technological innovation. Therefore besides the policies explained above, there is Technology Transfer Policy according to the sequence shown in **Table 27**. This Policy regulates the facilities provided by ISRO to the private actors in the form of industries and vice-versa .[46] The choice of licencees for this transfer is absolutely done by ISRO but it depends on some reasonable factors.[47] The government would like to transfer the technology for spin-offs in non-space uses. The reason is that returns from spin-off are more than the direct return on investment in the high-tech programmes like nuclear and space. The offer is provided to the private actors in R&D to develop the space activities.[48]

Here the reason for technology transfer is to impose the routine industrial operations and manufacture to others. The further reasons are—to promote globally competitive products and service capability through Indian industries; to spread technological prowess to other high-end areas through technological and industrial development in space; to create the future output for R&D talents and make the way for organisation diversification in future.[49]

Therefore, this policy repeats the general S&T policy above to internationalise the Indian market through Indian industries with global competition. Likewise it considers the future human resources in R&D that is dealt with law in subsequent part of this chapter. There are some guidelines for licencee selection and pricing in the policy. It establishes mechanism to obtain IPRs if the technologies are developed by ISRO on providing protection of interests of its licencees to use its inventions commercially.[50]

It implies that licencee private actors may develop ISRO technology for commercial purposes but IPR will remain with ISRO itself. This policy on one side opens up the gateway for private actors to work with ISRO. The other side insists the same private actors to depend on ISRO for further development of space activities. It appears that the private actors are discouraged from independent value addition to the technology developed by ISRO. The reason of discouragement is the holding of IPR by ISRO. It keeps the monopoly of the government in the long run. Such type of policy definitely affects the development of private actors to lose their interest.

Intellectual Property Policy[51] is also followed by ISRO to regulate the space technology developed and transferred. But this policy is under change. So currently there are no texts available.[52]

There are other departments in **Table 27** like Department of Telecommunications (DoT) that deals with telecommunication policies. There are three policies till now. National Telecom Policy, 1994, is the first one.[53] Its view was that new economic policy of the government could only be implemented when India would be competitive in global market and export. It referred to attract FDI that also stimulates the domestic sector. Here it included the private telecommunication industries. The policy insisted for the highest priority to develop telecom sector in India.[54]

Its objectives were removal of dispute resolution and consumer grievances. It would also like to see India as a major manufacturing base of telecom products as well as exporter. But this policy did not want to compromise anything which affects the defence and security of India. It referred the private investment in value added services like electronic mail, voice mail, data services etc. For the first time in India, the private companies were invited to invest in the telecom sectors with the adoption of this policy by the government.[55]

The next policy change in this sector had happened in 1999 with the introduction of New Telecom Policy, 1999.[56] The government realised that the plan framed in 1994 policy for private companies was not fully implemented. There was no fault from the private companies' side. The government required more satisfactory participation from private sectors.[57]

One of the objectives of this policy was to shape the Indian telecom companies into global one. This policy would like to attract more investment on building the communication network through technological development. The significance of this policy was to distinguish sectors within telecom infrastructure like access providers (cellular mobile service providers, cable service providers etc.), national long distance operator, and other service providers (tele-trading, e-commerce, tele-banking, tele-medicine and tele-education). The SATCOM Policy was referred though it was under the purview of Department of Space (DoS).[58]

All these policies actually interlinked because of inter-dependent technologies like international long distance for communication of data has been used under the existing Internet Service Provider (ISP) Policy. SATCOM Policy is the gateway for this linking. Spectrum management is required as per this policy because of its increasing demand.[59]

The greatest achievement in regulatory regime through this policy is to realise for the first time the necessity of spectrum management. It is now the most challenging one on behalf of the government to balance commercial demands from private actors and government policy in accommodating the same actors in national telecommunication industry. The assumption is that the issues like sovereignty, IPR and safety would be more required to be studied to formulate a policy itself on spectrum management in near future. Its sole purpose is more investment in telecom sectors through privatisation that boosts up the social and economic life in India as well as exporting more telecom products in foreign markets to compete with the global telecom companies.[60] Therefore this policy regulation would like to upgrade commercial potential of India internationally through private telecommunication sectors.

The National Telecom Policy, 2012, (NTP-2012), was made for further regulatory development by the government. The policy statement at the end recognised the role of private sectors in telecom industry and the prevailing competitive markets.[61] These two factors are very much related with this research study for not only sustainable development of the private actors but also to put a thrust to frame the laws more compatible to them. The significance of this thrust in other way round is that the government practically compels to think why, what and how legal problems have been faced by the foreign telecom companies in India. The current post-licencing problems leading to telecom scams and the displeasures of these foreign companies in consequence are the ultimate result.[62]

The rest policies of **Table 27** are not concerned with science and technology not even space i.e., land policies. These policies are primarily under Department of Land Resources. At the outset it is to be mentioned that land along with its acquisition is very sensitive issue in India. Land was a big deal when the first space launching station was established at Thumba. Unless the local people were willing to vacate their lands, it had not been possible to build the national space agency and later today's space industry.[63]

The same story has returned back when the technological prowess of India in launching sector demands that there would be requirement for more spaceport beyond Sriharikota to satisfy the present demand as per the 12th Five Year Plan.[64] This Plan has further proposed to establish the Space Technology Parks at different places in India to cooperate the involvement of industry in national space programme.[65]

The first policy is National Rehabilitation and Resettlement Policy, 2007. The preamble of the policy states that acquisition of private property involuntarily by the state has tremendous effect on the affected population especially the weaker section of the society. Hence there would require a national policy for rehabilitation and resettlement of these people.[66]

The second policy is at draft stage. It is Draft National Land Reforms Policy, 2013. This is till now in the stage of discussion and opinion from public. But this policy would like to address the whole area of land acquisition issues like land bank, reallocation, distribution etc.[67] A large population will be displaced for spaceport or Space Technology Park or SEZ for space activities as proposed above. Then these policies whether rehabilitation of population or land reforms would regulate the land required and acquired by the government first and then to transfer such land on lease or ownership basis to the private actors. There may be the possibilities that acquisition of land ultimately by the private actors would rehabilitate the people on the same place later on as a policy framework jointly made by the government with private actors. This may be for providing jobs to the locals residing before rehabilitation. But the terms and conditions obviously apply. Besides this, the second policy refers Geographic Information System (GIS) to frame the land information record.[68] A part of GIS is developed through satellite imageries.[69] So, the second policy is interconnected with the above draft of National Geospatial Information policy, 2012.

The above are policies to regulate the private actors in outer space. Alongside **Table 27** consists of report on Working Group on DoS in Five-Year-Plan (FYP) as framed by the Planning Commission (PC) of India. These are action plans of the government for five year in each FYP. So these reports prepared under the PC have regulatory effect. It may be said that all policies are framed later on according to these reports. Here the previous (11th FYP 2007-2012) and current (12th FYP 2012-2017) reports are considered in the present context.

The constitution of 11th FYP has proposed enhanced industry participation where the Indian industries would manufacture space products and provide services related with space activities. [70] Also in the area of space communications, the private sectors' role in Indian Satellite System has been highly recommended. To promote the spin-offs from space it has been suggested that human resources would be developed on strengthening academia and building international partnerships.[71] The portion related with industry interface of 11th FYP report mentions the initiative to boost up the industry for the development of space activities.[72] The load on the industries has been gradually increased from developing small workload to the bigger complex workload. The other areas for industry participation are like launch vehicles and spacecraft segment.[73]

Like 11th FYP, Working Group -14, the group on Department of Space within 12th FYP, is working to develop the national space missions. It has made Human spaceflight programme an agenda in this FYP where it is mentioned that the programme would be a big boost to the Indian industries. Basically the human spaceflight agenda will attract new technologies and programmes which promote the scope of industrial communities.[74] The following portion from the industry interface is very relevant.

> "The share of industries in the space budget is expected to increase further in the coming years. The quantum of contracts to Indian industry is expected to grow significantly in view of expected growth in the magnitude of space transportation and satellite system during 12th plan period. The idea is to have industry as a risk sharing partner and this will be achieved by involving industry from the preliminary stage of development of space systems. In addition to this some other innovative business models for increased participation from industries will also be considered during this plan period."[75]

So the Government of India would like to share the risk in space activities with industry. This is a new turn in 12th FYP. Additionally, the technology transfer is the main purpose for promoting space industry which will enable the national industry to venture the business with new technology.[76]

Legislations

The end of regulatory regime through policy brings the same through legislations. It is examined from above that the existing policies effectively related with space are limited within the domain of satellite communication and remote sensing data for earth observation. But India gives effect to international space treaties. Therefore this research study has to examine first the effect of ratification.

India has ratified all the treaties except Moon Treaty, 1979. The Registration Convention was acceded on January 18, 1982.[77] According to the Registration Convention, 1976, Indian registry is maintained at the United Nations based on the information received from the country on launching space objects into outer space. It was maintained since 1975.[78] In brief, India has been complied certain requirements of these treaties like: (i) strengthening international cooperation in space,[79] (ii) registration of objects in UN registry as mentioned above, and (iii) exchanging experience and capacity-building in space technology and applications.[80]

In spite of its ratification, there is no comprehensive space legislation or any sector specific legislation related with space activities in Indian legal framework. Only telecommunication laws were established since pre-satellite era. The further development of these laws' includes satellite communication technology. Also the above space policies like SATCOM Policy, Remote Sensing Data Policy, Industry Participation Policy are the specific regulatory guidelines for pursuing the commercial activities by government as well as private actors.[81] There is further need to develop national space technology infrastructure according to the 'Outcome Budget of the Department of Space, Government of India, 2013-2014'. The need is new SATCOM Policy, Space Navigation Policy and Space Legislation.[82]

In this view, the requirement for enactment or amendment of domestic laws has been already acknowledged according to the communication made by the Cabinet Secretariat during 2011. The 12th FYP has mentioned that an appropriate legislation namely 'Space Act' is required to regulate the expanded space activities through industry, private and international commercial participation. Moreover, though ISRO has made studies on this line but a thorough discussion with all stakeholders concerned would be need of the hour to give effect the national and international developments.[83]

It is observed that the ratification does not provide too much scope for regulating the domestic space activities. There exist only sector-specific space policies or a proposal for 'Space Act'. Therefore the research study tries to make an attempt to examine analytically the existing legislations where there may be linkages or extensions to regulate the private actors in outer space. It also checks whether the legal issues as explained above are highlighted within the text of these legislations.

Before proceeding towards the brief examination of each legislation, there is informal classification as shown in **Table 28** below for better analysis. The reason is that India has achieved the status of space-faring nation through its two space missions – Chandrayaan- I[84] and Mars Orbiter Mission (MOM)[85] whereas it lacks behind in two significant areas—one financing new complex space projects or missions, and other related with human resources to develop such missions. Similarly, the private actors face the difficulty in these areas to open up their space venture in India and then to create a market of their products.

Financing is obviously a lacking zone by default especially in a country like India. It is beyond any arguments to support. The 11th FYP already proposed that human resources were to be developed for promoting better and more spin-offs.[86] The overview of the Budget of Department of Space for 2013-2014, has mentioned the importance of its Human Resource Development Policy.[87] Hence, how the domestic legislations in India are framed to regulate these lacunas for private actors? So the classification is made below.

Table 28: Legislations for Regulations[88]

Categories	**Legislations**	**Different Types**
First (All Time Applicability)	Constitution of India	
	Atomic Energy Act, 1962	
Second (Direct Laws)	Telecommunication Laws	1. Indian Telegraph Act, 1885. 2. Indian Wireless Telegraphy Act, 1933. 3. Telecom Regulatory Authority of India (TRAI) Act, 1997. 4. Information Technology Act, 2000. 5. Communication Convergence Bill, 2001. 6. Cable Television Networks (Regulation) Act, 1995.
Third (Space-extension of Air)	Air Laws	1. Aircraft Act, 1934. 2. Suppression of Unlawful Acts against Safety of Civil Aviation Acts, 1982 3. Anti-Hijacking Act, 1982. 4. National Airports Authority Act, 1985. 5. Airports Authority of India Act, 1994. 6. Foreign Aircraft (Exemption from Taxes & Duties on Fuel & Lubricants) Act, 2002. 7. Airports Economic Regulatory Authority of India Act, 2008.
Fourth (High-end Technology Area)	Biotechnology Law	Biotechnology Regulatory Authority of India Bill, 2013.
	Geospatial Law	1. Draft of Vetting of Images and Geospatial Information for Licencing for National Security (VIGIL) Act. 2. Draft of National Geospatial Data Authority Bill.

Fifth (Acts to finance the private actors)	Fifth (Acts to finance the private actors)	1. Indian Contract Act, 1872. 2. Partnership Act, 1932. 3. Industries (Development & Regulation) Act, 1951. 4. Technology Development Board Act, 1995. 5. Micro, Small and Medium Enterprises Development Act, 2006. 6. Science and Engineering Research Board Act, 2008. 7. Limited Liability Partnership Act, 2008.
	Land Laws	1. Land Acquisition Act, 1894. 2. National Highways Act, 1956. 3. Special Economic Zones Act, 2005.
	Company Laws	1. Companies Act, 1956. 2. Preference Shares (Regulation of Dividends) Act, 1960 3. Securities and Exchange Board of India (SEBI) Act, 1992. 4. Depositories Act, 1996.
	Banking Laws	1. Reserve Bank of India Act, 1934. 2. Banking Regulation Act, 1949. 3. Export-Import Bank of India Act, 1981.
	Insurance Laws	1. Insurance Act, 1938. 2. Insurance Regulatory and Development Authority Act, 1999.
	Foreign Exchange Laws	1. Conservation of Foreign Exchange & Prevention of Smuggling Activities Act, 1974 (COFEPOSA ACT). 2. Foreign Exchange Management Act, 1999 3. Foreign Contribution (Regulation) Act, 2010

	Export-Import Laws	1. Customs Act, 1962. 2. Export (Quality Control & Inspection) Act, 1963. 3. Research & Development Cess Act, 1986. 4. Foreign Trade (Development & Regulation) Act, 1992.
	Revenue Laws	1. Income Tax Act, 1961. 2. Central Boards of Revenue Act, 1963.
	Environmental Laws	1. Air (Prevention and Control of Pollution) Act, 1981. 2. Environment Protection Act, 1986. 3. Energy Conservation Act, 2001. 4. Coastal Aquaculture Authority Act, 2005.
	IPR Laws	1. Copyright Act, 1957. 2. Patents Act, 1970 (Amendment 1999). 3. Trade Marks Act, 1999. 4. Designs Act, 2000. 5. Semiconductor Integrated Circuits Layout-Design Act, 2000.
	Safety Laws	1. Explosives Act, 1884. 2. Explosive Substances Act, 1908. 3. Inflammable Substances Act, 1952. 4. Dangerous Machines (Regulation) Act, 1983.
	Security Laws	1. Central Industrial Security Force Act, 1968. 2. National Security Act, 1980. 3. Private Security Agencies (Regulation) Act, 2005.
	Laws for Transparency	1. Comptroller and Auditor-General's (Duties, Powers and Conditions of Service) Act, 1971. 2. Central Vigilance Commission Act, 2003. 3. Right to Information Act, 2005.

	Dispute Settlement Laws	1. Indian Penal Code, 1860. 2. Code of Criminal Procedure, 1973. 3. Economic Offences (Inapplicability of Limitation) Act, 1974. 4. Consumer Protection Act, 1986. 5. Arbitration & Conciliation Act, 1996. 6. Competition Act, 2002.
Sixth (Human Resource Development Laws)	Citizenship Laws	1. The Foreigners Act, 1946. 2. The Citizenship Act, 1955.
	Industry-Academia Development Laws	1. Institutes of Technology Act, 1961. 2. Jawaharlal Nehru University Act, 1966. 3. Rajiv Gandhi National Aviation University Act, 2013.
	Labour & Welfare Laws	1. Workmen's Compensation Act, 1923. 2. Industrial Employment (Standing Orders) Act, 1946. 3. Apprentices Act, 1946. 4. Industrial Employment (Standing Orders) Act, 1946. 5. Industrial Disputes Act, 1947. 6. Factories Act, 1948. 7. Employees' State Insurance Act, 1948. 8. Employees' Provident Funds & Miscellaneous Provisions Act, 1952. 9. Payment of Bonus Act, 1965. 10. Payment of Gratuity Act, 1972. 11. Bhopal Gas Leak Disaster (Processing of Claims) Act, 1985.
Seventh (State Acts)	Laws of A.P.	1. Industrial Dispute (Andhra Pradesh Amendment) Act, 1987. 2. Andhra Pradesh Infrastructure Development Corporation Act, 1998. 3. Andhra Pradesh Industrial Workers (Representation) Participation in Management and Relief) Act, 1998. 4. Andhra Pradesh Infrastructure Development Enabling Act, 2001. 5. Andhra Pradesh Industrial Single Window Clearance Act, 2002. 6. A.P. Special Economic Zone Bill, 2005. 7. Jawaharlal Nehru Technological University Act, 2008.

	Laws of Gujarat	1. Gujarat Industrial Relations Act, 1946. 2. Gujarat Co-Operative Societies Act, 1961. 3. Gujarat Land Acquisition (Industrial Areas) Act, 1961. 4. Gujarat Industrial Development Act, 1962. 5. State Tax on Professions, Trades, Callings and Employments Act, Gujarat, 1976. 6. Gujarat Infrastructure Development Act, 1999. 7. Gujarat Special Economic Zone Act, 2004. 8. Industrial Disputes (Gujarat) Amendment Act, 2004. 9. Gujarat Special Investment Region Act 2009. 10. Nirma University of Science and Technology Act, 2003. 11. Dhirubhai Ambani Institute of Information and Communication Technology Act, 2003. 12. Ganpat University Act, 2005. 13. Centre for Environmental Planning and Technology University Act, 2005. 14. Gujarat Technological University Act, 2007.

	Laws of Karnataka	1. Karnataka Co-operative Societies Act, 1959. 2. Karnataka Industrial Areas Development Act, 1966. 3. Karnataka Industries (Facilitation) Act, 2002. 4. Karnataka Policy for SEZ, 2009. 5. Karnataka Information Technology Investment Regions Act, 2010. 6. Vellore Institute of Technology Bangalore Act, 2012. 7. M.S. Ramaiah University of Applied Sciences Act, 2012. 8. KLE Technological University Act, 2012. 9. Rai Technology University, Bangalore Act, 2012. 10. J.S.S. Science and Technology University Act, 2013.
	Laws of Kerala	1. Travancore -Cochin Literary, Scientific and Charitable Societies Registration Act, 1955. 2. Industrial Disputes (Kerala) Amendment Act, 1961. 3. Kerala State Aid to Industries Act, 1963. 4. Kerala Co-operative Society Act, 1969. 5. Cochin University of Science and Technology Act, 1986. 6. Kerala Industrial Infrastructure Development Act, 1993. 7. Kerala Industrial Revitalisation Fund Act, 1999.
	Laws of Maharashtra	1. Maharashtra Industrial Development Act, 1961. 2. BabaSaheb Ambedkar Technological University Act, 1969. 3. Rajiv Gandhi Science & Technology Commission Act, 2004.

	Laws of Orissa	1. Orissa State-Aid to Industries Act, 1978. 2. Orissa Industrial Infrastructure Development Corporation Act, 1980. 3. Biju Patnaik University of Technology Act, 2002. 4. Orissa Industries (Facilitation) Act, 2004.
	Laws of Tamil Nadu	1. Tamil Nadu State Aid to Industries Act, 1922. 2. Anna University Chennai Act, 1978. 3. Tamil Nadu Industrial Establishments (Conferment of Permanent Status to Workmen) Act, 1981. 4. Tamil Nadu Taxation Special Tribunal Act, 1992. 5. Tamil Nadu Acquisition of Land for Industrial Purpose Act, 1997. 6. Tamil Nadu Industrial Township Area Development Authority Act, 1997. 7. Tamil Nadu Special Economic Zones (Special Provisions) Act, 2005.
Eighth (Act of Union Territory)	Laws of Delhi	The Delhi Geo-Spatial Data Infrastructure (Management Control, Administration, Security and Safety) Act, 2011.

Firstly, the Constitution of India holds the umbrella over this classification of legislations. The national space legislations of other countries follow the same path. Besides the Constitution, the Atomic Energy Act, 1962, holds a significant key position because the Department of Atomic Energy (DAE) is the parental body of space activities. Therefore this first category is appeared to be almost all time applicability even in remote future regulatory regime of private actors.

The second category consists of direct laws related with outer space. These are obviously till now telecommunication laws which are already in existence.

The third category deals with Air laws. The reason is that jurisdiction of outer space starts where the same for air ends. It may also be said that outer space is an extension of aerospace. The observations from the history of space regulations (chapter I), private actors in outer space (chapter II) and space regulations outside India (chapter IV) may support the logic behind this extension. Chapter I shows that the objects launched to air first were sent to higher altitude later with the development of technology. Therefore some of the Indian companies in chapter II are treated as private actors in outer space though they are known as aerospace companies. It may further be observed in academic departments or institutions in India that were previously established as department of aeronautical engineering. Now the popular name is department of aerospace engineering. The best example is cited from Indian Institute of Science (IISC) at Bengaluru.[89] The chapter IV also reflects some aerospace laws as enlisted in **Table 20** where the case of Republic of Korea is referred for its Aerospace Industry Promotion Act, 1989.

The fourth category falls in laws on high-end technology like space. Though there are different technological developments, but Acts are in process related with biotechnology and geospatial technology. These upcoming Acts provide deep impetus to develop laws on other high-end technology area like outer space.

The category number five concerns with core legislations for regulation of private actors. This category consists of regulating Acts to finance the private actors. The Central Acts for financing the space projects or to get capital from or outside India for venturing space are legislations for infrastructure development, land, company, banking, insurance, foreign exchange, export-import, revenue, environment, IPR, safety, security, transparency and dispute settlement etc.

A few legislations appears to be for direct financing like banking or insurance whereas the legislations for infrastructure development or land or dispute settlement are basically to attract high profile private actors as investors in space industry. It may be an exciting example from the ongoing problem over spectrum licencing. The foreign telecommunication companies would invest in other countries outside India if the dispute settlement laws are not revisited to balance their business purpose with India's national interest.[90] Therefore overall some legislation is directly connected with financing, or some with safeguarding, or promoting the finance from different angles.

The sixth category of legislation from **Table 28** attracts human resource development laws. It may be connected with the previous fifth category. But the reason for separating it in a different category is that it concerns only with human being and developing their special skills to be used for private actors in outer space. The 11th and 12th Five Year Plan on Department of Space, both have mentioned immensely the role of human resources to develop the national space programme.[91] Even long before these Five-Year-Plans, Bhabha felt that the first step in building institutions was the training and development of people. The reason is that understanding the human factors for the growth of the institution is much behind than progress of science and technology.[92]

However, there are three sides of human resources – one is capacity development of human resources through academia connecting with the industry interface. The academia has a prominent role in undertaking and promoting advanced space research and development of cutting-edge technology.[93] The second one is definitely the excellent recruitment procedure of the applicants who are going to be productive as well as innovative. It is recommended in the 12th FYP.[94] There are legislations related with citizenship, industry-academia development and labour & welfare. The citizenship legislations are the entry point to get into the human resource development laws. The industry-academia legislations are required to form the base of space technology development through skilled manpower and for its subsequent use for developing the private space industry.

These legislations have appeared to play secondary role in regulating the private actors. But these are very crucial in the present context because the foregoing policies direct always to establish India as a competitor in global space industry. So it would require not only excellent space technology but also skilled and innovative manpower. This is maintained from corporate like Godrej and TATA to small start-ups. So it would be wonder to examine below how some University Acts legalise this effort of developing human resources. In this regard, it is repeated that the Basic Space Law, 2008, of Japan in chapter IV has already made such provision in its Article 21. The labour & welfare laws are simply to retain this manpower as a continuous flow in the space industry.

The seventh category relates with some states' legislations like A.P., Gujarat, Karnataka etc. that have maximum probabilities to welcome the private actors in outer space. The reasons are stated below.

The last and eighth category mentions the concerned regulating laws enacted for Union territories. Here it is New Delhi for the time being. The following is the detailed analysis of all categories.

The Constitution of India, 1950, is the first Act in the **Table 28**. In general, the Constitution of India plays the most leading role in framing any legal regulations. It is also observed above from other countries' national legal framework. The Constitution has the top most hierarchy in the domestic legal framework related with anything in India. Articles 51, 73, 77 (3), 246 and 253 are to be analysed for the present study.

Article 51 dealing with fundamental rights provides 'Promotion of International Peace and Security'. It states

> "The State shall endeavour to— (a) promote international peace and security; (b) maintain just and honourable relations between nations; (c) foster respect for international law and treaty obligations in the dealings of organised people with one another; and (d) encourage settlement of international disputes by arbitration."[95]

In comparison of clause (c) with clause (d), the first one is general in nature that means the Constitution states to obey international law within national legal system whereas the later clause would like to resort arbitration in case of international dispute. It is assumed that the clause (d) supports the arbitral provisions of Permanent Court of Arbitration (PCA) for outer space activities named as 'PCA Optional Rules for the Arbitration of Disputes Relating to Outer Space Activities'[96]. It was adopted in 2011[97] much after the constitutional provision under clause (d).

The next is Article 73 is about 'Extent of Executive Power of the Union'.[98] The state is empowered to exercise such rights, authority and jurisdiction as India has ratified all space treaties except Moon Treaty.

There is another Article 77 under the title 'Conduct of business of the Government of India' in same Part of the Constitution. The Article 77 (3) provides

> "The President shall make rules for the more convenient transaction of the business of the Government of India, and for the allocation among Ministers of the said business."[99]

Now as per the constitutional provision for Allocation of Business Rules (AOB), there are two schedules: (i) First Schedule[100] where serial number 45 has mentioned Department of Space and the first item refers Space Commission, as analysed above, and all matters thereto.[101] It implies that this Article has direct nexus with planning of space policy in India. (ii) Second Schedule only distributes the subjects among the departments.[102] There is a review of this AOB Rules in 2010 and it has been proposed in the serial number 13 under the DoS to develop policy, legal and regulatory measures relating to space. The increasing complexity of issues has international consequence for adopting legal measures.[103] In this view, any change in regulatory measures concerned with space has come from Article 77 (3).

The next Article 246 encompasses with legislative relations. The Article 246, 'Subject-matter of laws made by Parliament and by the Legislatures of States' mentions

> "(1) Notwithstanding anything in clauses (2) and (3), Parliament has exclusive power to make laws with respect to any of the matters enumerated in List I in the Seventh Schedule (in this Constitution referred to as the "Union List"). (2) Notwithstanding anything in clause (3), Parliament, and, subject to clause (1), the Legislature of any State also, have power to make laws with respect to any of the matters enumerated in List III in the Seventh Schedule (in this Constitution referred to as the "Concurrent List"). (3) Subject to clauses (1) and (2), the Legislature of any State has exclusive power to make laws for such State or any part thereof with respect to any of the matters enumerated in List II in the Seventh Schedule (in this Constitution referred to as the "State List"'). (4) Parliament has power to make laws with respect to any matter for any part of the territory of India not included in a State notwithstanding that such matter is a matter enumerated in the State List."[104]

Now out of the Union List, also known as Seventh Schedule, the following item numbers are relevant here - item numbers (10) foreign affairs; all matters which bring the Union into relation with any foreign country; (12) United Nations Organisation; (21) piracies and crimes committed on the high seas or in the air; offences against the law of nations committed on land or, the high seas, or, in the air.[105] But the word 'outer space' is not mentioned. It is assumed that there was no such space activity from India or presumption related with space in nearest future when this List was made; so if it is assumed that the item number (21) could be extended to outer space, there would be no extravagance of the list.

The last relevant Article 253 is all about 'Legislation for giving effect to international agreements' and states

> "Notwithstanding anything in the foregoing provisions of this Chapter, Parliament has power to make any law for the whole or any part of the territory of India for implementing any treaty, agreement or convention with any other country or countries or any decision made at any international conference, association or other body."[106]

Hence Indian Parliament has ample power to make any law on ratifying space law treaties. The scope of this Article is so broad that it could even cut across the legislative lists in the Seventh Schedule for implementing 'any decision made at any international conference, association or other body'.[107] In brief the Constitution has already followed the international space law treaties and got ready for any development in space regulation.

Another Act in the first category is the Atomic Energy Act, 1962, that may provide guidelines to the Space Act as proposed in 12th FYP. This Act of 1962 regulates the activities of Department of Atomic Energy (DAE) which was the mentor of space science research in India. Moreover both the sectors are equally strategic and sensitive in nature for India. So, the Atomic Energy Act being a comprehensive one is pioneer in this sense to develop future space legislation. The other near future possibility is deep space exploration like beyond Mars where nuclear or atomic energy is the most reliable one.[108] The private initiative like Mars Foundation[109] adventure for human landing on Mars may require this Act in near future. There is licencing provision through contract with a person according to Section 7.[110] Therefore, the private entities have restrictive permission through licence to work with DAE. It proves that the state maintains sovereignty through licencing. The other provisions like special provisions as to safety (section 17); restriction on disclosure of information (section 18); and prevention of entry into prohibited areas (section 19) are likely to be followed in developing the regulation for private actors in outer space.[111] These provisions attract the issues of safety and national security which are all along the similar line for such actors.

Table 28 guides this research study to telecommunication laws as the second category of laws. While the Constitution lays down the base of legal foundation and Atomic Energy Act bears the mentoring support, it is the telecommunication laws like the Telegraph Act, 1885; Wireless Telegraphy

Act; 1933; Telecom Regulatory Authority of India Act, 1997; the Information Technology Act, 2000; and Telecommunications Convergence Bill, 2001 that include outer space within their framework.

The Indian Telegraph Act, 1885, though made in pre-satellite and pre-internet communication technology era but section 3 (1AA) has explanation that telegraph includes radio waves or Hertizian waves which propagated in space.[112] It interacts with privileges and power of the Central Government that could issue licence according to section 4 and revoke it as well under section 8. So the private actors are regulated by the government. Section 7B provides arbitration in case of disputes.[113] Therefore the sovereignty issue is attracted by licening while dispute settlement is regulated by arbitration. The regulation through Indian Wireless Telegraphy Act, 1933, means to issue licence on constituting the Telegraphic Authority.[114]

The Telecom Regulatory Authority of India (TRAI) Act, 1997, was enactment of National Telecom Policy, 1994. This Act is mainly focussed to regulate the power and function of TRAI, a supervisory and regulatory governmental body that is required to form due to exponential increase of private telecommunication operators. The chapter III provides the settlement of disputes.[115] Similarly, in near future, the Space Regulatory Authority may be required to regulate the private actors in outer space.

The Information Technology Act, 2000, is a part of telecommunication regulations because all the electronic communications are made through on using the information technology in this digital age.[116] The preamble of this Act states that its purpose is to promote electronic commerce. It recognises the UNGA resolution A/RES/51/162 dated January 30, 1997, which adopts the Model Law on Electronic Commerce as adopted by the United Nations Commission on International Trade Law. This resolution recommends that all states would make it possible to follow this Model Law on enacting or revising their laws related with electronic commerce. As mentioned above, the provisions of this Act prescribes digital signature, electronic governance, secure electronic records and secure digital signatures etc.[117] This Act is useful to private actors in outer space to continue their space business on sharing business transactions electronically or it may be said that it supports electronic space commerce.

The Communication Convergence Bill, 2001, is to establish an autonomous Commission to regulate all forms of communication like broadcasting, telecommunication, data-communication, multimedia etc. on converging these under a single umbrella. There would be single regulatory and licencing authority followed by an Appellate Tribunal named as Communications Appellate Tribunal. The provisions of this Bill include regulation of use of spectrum, Communications Commission of India along with its objectives, power, duties and function, frequency spectrum management, licence or registration etc.[118] This Bill is very much effective for space activities by private bodies because it discloses all kinds of communications through space technology. It would give effect the regulatory regime of spectrum management for private actors. The issue of dispute settlement which is much involved with technologies here will be adjudicated by Communications Commission of India.

The Cable Television Networks (Regulation) Act, 1995, does not come directly under telecommunication laws but it is only supportive regulation. Its purpose is to regulate the operation of cable television network in India and the related matters.[119] Some cable channels in television are made available via satellite broadcasting like HBO, MTV, Cartoon Networks etc. This is the link between satellite communications through cable networks.

The third category of laws in **Table 28** is Air Laws. The laws are made for aircraft, airport, air travel and related matters therewith. Its relevancy here is that it may be extended for future space travel through spacecraft and space port in India. The other near future applicability relates with spaceplane for speediest movement from one continent to another.[120]

The Aircraft Act, 1934, is specifically made for the control of manufacture, possession, use, operation, sale, import and export of aircraft.[121] There is still now no full-fledged private effort to manufacture spacecraft in India. There is every possibility to start it because FDI in defence manufacturing is permitted now. So, the aircraft for defence purposes could be manufactured by private actors. FDI in spacecraft manufacturing is still pending due to policy of the government though it is very lucrative business as observed in chapter II. If it is permitted then the same Boeing, Lockheed Martin etc. may start manufacturing in India. Then this Act would be very useful. Section 4A states about the safety oversight functions. The prescribed authority is to look after safety of the place where aircraft is manufactured. Section 5 empowers central government to make rules regulating the manufacturing, possession, use, operation, sale, export and import of the aircraft. Other provisions of this Act deal with different powers of the central government.[122] This Act prescribes the safety issue but government dominance exists. Unlike this

Act the following two Acts are based on safety during air flights as well as in airports.

The Suppression of Unlawful Acts against Safety of Civil Aviation Acts, 1982, is specifically made to check the offence on board aircraft and airport.[123] This Act is assumed to be extended to check the offences in spaceport and on board spacecraft if India had been go away with the upcoming era of commercial spaceflight.

The Anti-Hijacking Act, 1982,[124] is very difficult to imagine and realise in the present context because hijacking which till now only relates with aircraft. It could also be related with spacecraft. Although the possibility may be too remote. But the idea of spaceplane is very close to reality.[125] There is a long wait to see the type and manner of hijacking in future. This Act will be helpful then to regulate anti-hijacking in spaceplane or spacecraft operated by private airlines.

The National Airports Authority Act, 1985, and the Airports Authority of India Act, 1994, are concerned with regulation to develop airport. The first one has established an authority to manage the aerodromes and civil enclaves where domestic air transport is carried on.[126] The second one forms an authority and its management to look after the aerodromes and civil enclaves.[127] Both the Acts may be required if India had planned to establish a spaceport for civilians like spaceport for space tourism in USA.

Unlikely the above two, the Foreign Aircraft (Exemption from Taxes & Duties on Fuel & Lubricants) Act, 2002, is applicable to aircrafts manufactured in foreign countries. The foreign made aircrafts from countries as contracting parties in Chicago Convention, 1944, are exempted from taxes and duties on fuel and lubricants supplied in India.[128] It would help to formulate the legislation for foreign spacecraft in India. There is a sub-sector 'space transport' [11 D] in the services sectoral classification list of World Trade Organisation (WTO) under the sector 'Transport'.[129] The detailed has been mentioned in previous chapter while explaining the regulations of USA. Its future implication is very significant if India will commit to put the space transport under its country specific list of services. Then India has to allow the foreign spacecraft.

The last one in this category is the Airports Economic Regulatory Authority of India Act, 2008, that deals with financing directly.[130] This Act prescribes tariffs for aeronautical services provided at airports. Moreover, the prescribed authority monitors the performance standards of airports as well as to set up appellate tribunal for solving the disputes. Now space tourism or more specifically sub-orbital commercial travel is about to start in foreign countries. The main hurdle is expense to be borne by the concerned passengers. India could lead this opportunity to compare its cheap labour market and excellent cost-effective launch vehicles. But after all it is the policy of government. This Act could be extended then to regulate the tariffs and other charges for services rendered at spaceport.

The fourth category as mentioned above is laws related with high-end technology. There are two laws according to **Table 28**. There are two laws –one on biotechnology and another on geospatial. Unfortunately, the first one is still at Bill stage and later is in draft stage.

The Biotechnology Regulatory Authority of India Bill, 2013, relates with establishment of an authority to regulate the safe use of biotechnology. The preamble and body of the Act do not apparently relate with any space activities.[131] But the microgravity research in space is very much popular and there are lots of biotechnological applications.[132] It includes manufacturing medicines and other health related products in outer space. The big corporate are the actors behind this effort.[133] So there is ample opportunity for private actors to make commercial use of biotechnology in outer space. India is still lacking in this domain. But it is assumed that the application of space biotechnology is not too far away in India and then this Bill (as its present status) shall regulate the commercial activities of private actors in this domain.

The next technology domain is geospatial. The Draft of Vetting of Images and Geospatial Information for Licencing for National Security (VIGIL) Act are in planning stage.[134] It is a joint initiative of the Inter-Ministerial Committee led by Department of Science & Technology with Department of Space to prepare a draft Bill to regulate the dissemination of images like satellite and aerial along with communicating Geo Spatial Information and terrestrial photography through internet as well as in physical form. The regulation for private actors will be implemented through conditions like a transparent licencing and as per existing National Policies. The VIGIL Act will be a strong support to the above mentioned Remote Sensing Data Policy, 2011, and its effective implementation.[135] Another is Draft of National Geospatial Data Authority Bill that is pending since 2009. It mainly covers the regulation of licencing for geospatial data by an authority as prescribed in the Bill.[136]

The Constitution and the Atomic Energy Act ensure that India has already basic legal framework to regulate the cutting-edge technologies like space. Moreover, the telecommunication laws are developed through facilities available from outer space. Air law also guides the upcoming regime regulating the private actors in space. Additionally, the Biotechnology Regulatory Authority of India Bill, 2013, provides a positive impetus to establish law with high-end technology. Now there is requirement for financing the space activities.

Hence fifth category in **Table 28** introduces first the law for regulating basic infrastructure that is needed to build or develop any business entity before financing it. There are seven Acts in **Table 28** like the Indian Contract Act, 1872; the Partnership Act, 1932; the Industries (Development & Regulation) Act, 1951; the Technology Development Board Act, 1995; the Micro, Small and Medium Enterprises Development Act, 2006; the Science and Engineering Research Board Act, 2008; and the Limited Liability Partnership Act, 2008.

Indian Contract Act, 1872,[137] is required for any business contract at the first instance. It covers all the contracts in India. There will be a contract between the government and private actors, or, two or more private actors to pursue any business activity. The contract agreement is preliminary and basic legal instrument between these parties. The importance of this Act is assumed to exist separately even if India had established the Space Act in distant future.

Unlike the above Act, the Partnership Act, 1932,[138] is required to start up a partnership business on space activities like space law firms existing in foreign countries.[139]

The Industries (Development & Regulation) Act, 1951,[140] was enacted to develop and regulate certain industries. The First Schedule of this Act describes a list of industries where some are directly or indirectly related with space activities like industries related with scientific instruments.

The Technology Development Board Act, 1995, connects with financial resources directly. The government has established a Board to develop technology in India. The Technological Development Board (TDB) would initiate to develop technology with the fund as provided under this Act. This Act brings together the R&D and industry. The TDB provides the financial assistance as prescribed under this Act to promote the development of indigenous technology for commercial application.[141]

Therefore it could be applicable to develop space technology by the private actors.

The Micro, Small and Medium Enterprises Development Act, 2006, facilitates 'the promotion and development and enhancing the competitiveness of micro, small and medium enterprises'.[142] Here the enterprises mean industrial undertaking or a business concern or any other establishment, as provided by section 2 (e) of the Act, for manufacturing or producing goods as specified in the First schedule of the above Industries (Development & Regulation) Act.[143] So the enterprises concerning space activities are covered under this Act.

The Science and Engineering Research Board Act, 2008, again directly speaks about financing. The establishment of a Board is required under the Act which will provide financial assistance to persons for pursuing basic research in science and engineering of industrial concerns.[144] For an example, it could be used to develop Indian GIS industry[145] which depends on commercial remote sensing satellite imageries as analysed in chapter II.

The Limited Liability Partnership Act, 2008, remains as tail-ender within this category of Acts. The Act provides for the formation and regulation of limited liability partnerships and the related matters.[146] So this could be useful like the above Partnership Act.

The infrastructure development attracts land laws also in a general way. Currently, these laws are very significant and a matter of serious concern. It is already mentioned during the analysis of land policy. There are three Acts to regulate the area of land if the private actors would like to require. These are the Land Acquisition Act, 1894; the National Highways Act 1956; and the Special Economic Zones Act, 2005 according to **Table 28**.

The first one empowers the government to acquire land for the purposes as prescribed under the Act.[147] The second one National Highways Act, 1956,[148] states that the government has power to declare certain highways as national highways. Section 3A has provision for land acquisition.[149] The Act is attracted here in the context of land acquisition to develop the highways connected with the Special Economic Zone (SEZ) which follows next. The last is Special Economic Zones Act, 2005, that was made for the establishment, management and development for the SEZ; and the matter connected therewith. It could be applied to establish a SEZ for space industry in future. The provisions of this Act are applicable in general to space industries.[150]

The analysis about land laws are dealt subsequently in seventh category where some states like Andhra Pradesh, Karnataka, Tamil Nadu, Kerala, and Orissa would require special attention for suitable land. The major existing ISRO centres[151] and proposed launching site like spaceport at Tuticorin[152] and other ancillary industries are mainly located in these states.

The infrastructure as legally developed above may lead to establish a private space company that is regulated mainly by the company laws. The Companies Act, 1956, is the main Act. It is applicable to any company registered in India. All the provisions of the Act deal with the registration of a company, functioning of a company, dispute settlement and its authority etc.[153]

The Preference Shares (Regulation of Dividends) Act, 1960, is an Act to regulate dividends on preference shares of certain companies.[154] Here it may be considered for regulation of dividends in space companies.

The Securities and Exchange Board of India (SEBI) Act, 1992, was passed to establish a Board to protect the interests of investors in securities as well as to regulate and promote the security market. The investors have securities like shares, debentures etc. of a company.[155] So the investors of a space company may be safeguarded by this Act. The significance of this Act is too much in the present context because a full-fledged space company requires huge investment. Therefore the investors would like to invest a hefty amount in such company. In case of any default by the company regarding securities, the SEBI is required to play a very meaningful and crucial role such that the investors as well as company may survive in the long run.

The last one is the Depositories Act, 1996, that provides regulation for depositories in securities and the matter therewith. The depository means company as prescribed under the Companies Act.[156] It is applicable here for Space Company.

The financial resources or financing the private actors is assumed to be the most challenging one when the above infrastructure development is in process or after that also. In this regard the banking laws in **Table 28** as explained below are very significant for regulating the private actors. The Reserve Bank of India Act, 1934, is an old Act which has established the Reserve Bank of India (RBI). It prescribes government controls and regulations of all other banks.[157] In this sense, this Act has tremendous significance in banking laws of India. The private actors in outer space whether Indian or non-Indian both have to maintain the RBI Act as well as its rules and regulations with guidelines issued from time to time. The main reason is that the space business relates with investment and risks both at extremely high level where RBI is the top most banking body to regulate such huge investment._

The Banking Regulation Act, 1949, brings enactment to regulate the banking sector in general.[158] It deals with the business of banking companies, control over management, prohibition of certain activities in relation to banking companies, suspension of business and winding up of business companies, provisions relating to certain operations of banking companies etc. Moreover, this Act is applicable to certain co-operative societies as prescribed under it. The Act also mentions different type of banks under section 5 like Development Bank (Industrial Development Bank of India, 1964); Exim Bank (Export-Import Bank of India); Reconstruction Bank (The Industrial Reconstruction Bank of India); Small Industries Bank (The Small Industries Development Bank of India) etc. The Reserve Bank of India is at the top.[159]

The private actors in outer space could seek the financial assistance to any above category of bank subject to the rules and regulations prescribed for each category under the Act. In the reverse way, each and every category of bank has responsibility to extend their assistance to the private space companies subject to the other rules and regulations as prescribed. So it will be a two-way communication.

The Export-Import Bank of India Act, 1981, facilitates the private actors that would require export-import system within their space business to be financially sound. It brings the necessity of this Act. It directs to establish a bank for assisting exporters and importers financially or coordinating the institutions related with financing export and import of goods and services for India's international trade.[160] The private actors would be facilitated at the time of import and export during their trade and commerce in space.

The financing of space activities is not only concerned with investment but high risk also. In this view, the insurance laws justify its legal footprint in **Table 28** along with banking laws. It safeguards the investors as well the private actors. The detailed explanation is provided during the analysis of financing issue in earlier chapter. Here it needs two existing laws on insurance – one is Insurance Act, 1938, and another is Insurance Regulatory and Development Authority Act, 1999.

The Insurance Act, 1938, regulates the insurance in space sector though space insurance is comparatively new of its kind especially in India. The interpretation of Section 2 (6B) on 'general insurance business'[161] and then Section 2 (13B) on 'miscellaneous insurance business'[162] provide that space insurance business could be under the ambit of 'miscellaneous insurance business' in the broader category of 'general insurance business'. Hence all the provisions of this Act are assumed to be applicable for insuring the space activities owned or conducted by private actors.

The Insurance Regulatory and Development Authority Act, 1999, is made to establish an authority 'to protect the interests of holders of insurance policies; to regulate, promote and ensure orderly growth of the insurance industry'.[163] Therefore the private actors could entrust an authority to convey and share any problems coming out from their investment to insure their space activities. This is guaranteed by this Act.

Since space is a high investment sector which is agitated times and again here, there would definitely be an essential requirement of other means of resources besides insurance. Thus foreign investment is required for this purpose. Now FDI is only permitted in telecommunication sector.[164] The other space sectors are outside FDI till now though the possibility cannot be ignored in near future. It leads to the analysis of the Foreign-exchange laws in **Table 28**. The Acts are following below.

The Conservation of Foreign Exchange & Prevention of Smuggling Activities Act, 1974 (COFEPOSA ACT), protects the misuse of foreign exchange money on violation of foreign exchange regulation.[165] Then this Act will apply to regulate the private actors as offenders.

The Foreign Exchange Management Act, 1999,[166] is another in this list to regulate the foreign exchange dealt by private actors. The Foreign Contribution (Regulation) Act, 2010, regulates acceptance and utilisation of foreign contribution or foreign hospitality as prescribed under this Act.[167] The reason to attract this Act is same as above.

Investing foreign exchange to finance the sunrise industry like space is not sufficient. So there would be requirement for export and import to invest more in the same business. It necessitates the export-import laws. The Customs Act, 1962, is the main in this category. It deals with foreign going aircrafts for transporting or carrying goods outside India and similarly for bringing back in India.[168] This Act could be applicable for goods related with space activities for private actors which come out or get into India. But in near future, it could be considered for foreign going spaceplane[169] or in distant future it could be applicable for carrying goods through spacecraft also. The hypothetical case may be to deliver goods to private space station by cargo space shuttle from the territory of India.

The Export (Quality Control & Inspection) Act, 1963, has been enforced to maintain the quality of export products and its inspection, and other interconnected matters.[170] It could be applicable to space products made for export.

The Research & Development Cess Act, 1986, interacts with the levy and collection of a cess on all payments which concern with the import of technology. The purpose is to encourage the commercial application of indigenously developed technology as well as to adapt the imported technology for domestic application in a broader way and for matters connected therewith or incidental thereto.[171] This Act is too much applicable for facilitating imported space technology.

The Foreign Trade (Development & Regulation) Act, 1992, facilitates the import into or export from India on developing and regulating the foreign trade.[172] So it could be applied for trade in space activities for import as well as export.

The financing of space activities not only mean how to invest more. Rather how the government would like to impose its revenue slab on this sunrise industry through revenue laws. It is the Income Tax Act where the private actors would expect maximum cooperation from the government.[173] The relevancy of this Act here is whether it will provide tax benefits or holidays for private actors in space and how much this benefit is. There are many special provisions for promoting the new industry under this Act. But there is no provision related with space specifically till now like legislations of Russian Federation or that of Isle of Man as explained in chapter IV.

There are few sections below to get tax relief related with this research study: special provisions for newly established units in SEZ. If there is any new space entrepreneur within SEZ, the advantage will be provided.[174] Also special provisions exist in respect of newly established 100 per cent export oriented undertakings.[175] If some space products are only exported from some newly established undertaking, the provision could be attracted.[176] Investment allowance is applicable for aircraft[177], so it could be extended to spacecraft in future.

There is investment allowance for expenditure on scientific research,[178] expenditure on acquisition of patent rights or copyrights,[179] and expenditure on know-how.[180] A company will take benefit from these provisions for expenditure on space research and related expenditure on acquisition of patent or copyrights as well as know-how. There is provision for expenditure for obtaining licence to operate telecommunication services.[181] It facilitates the telecommunication activities that are one of the space activities. The deductions from total income could be claimed as deduction in respect of certain donations for scientific research under 80GGA.[182] The donations by the companies for space science research, if any, fall under this category.[183]

These provisions are not all conclusive. The significance of this Act would be much felt if the private actors especially the small and medium ones could be encouraged to invest further through more tax benefits in the form of long tax holidays etc. The Central Boards of Revenue Act, 1963,[184] establishes the two apex Boards which control the rules and regulation for revenue for direct taxes (CBDT) and also for excise and customs (CBEC). In the present context, the role of CBDT is concerned more because the above Income Tax Act is framed and amended as per the advices of CBDT.

In the era of environmental degradation, any country including India could not plan any sector which is not environmentally sustainable. Therefore, though the above laws from infrastructure development to revenue, all are equally required for private actors in outer space but financing of space activities first required environmental clearance as well as safeguard. That is why regulation of private actors deserves environmental laws in **Table 28**.

The Air (Prevention and Control of Pollution) Act, 1981,[185] regulates the air pollution specifically. The launching of a spacecraft causes pollution through rocket exhausts by default. Moreover, the burning of solid fuels produces alumina particles. These particles are spread in air causing environmental hazards.[186] On the other hand the cryogenic fuel causes less pollution.[187] India has tried since long back to develop the cryogenic engines indigenously but success has been achieved very recently i.e. January 2014.[188] Hence the space activities attract the provisions of this Act.

The next legislation is Environment Protection Act, 1986, in this category. According to section (2) of this Act, environment 'includes water, air and land and the inter-relationship which exists among and between water, air and land, and human beings, other living creatures, plants, micro-organism and property.'[189] There is no term 'space' or 'outer space' within the definition. Here it is very significant to note that space is only environment that is not legally considered as 'environment'.[190]

However, the provisions of this Act are assumed to link with space activities concerning environments. The reason is that its provisions like general powers of the central government (chapter II)[191] or prevention, control or abetment of environmental pollution (chapter III)[192] could be extended to the space activities which would cause the environmental pollution. Moreover as the boundary between air and outer space is not clearly demarcated, this extension is assumed to be more justified. Therefore being a separate legislation on terrestrial environment, this Act may contribute separately in the upcoming Space Act.

The Energy Conservation Act, 2001, is the era of energy conservation. India has also Act on conservation of energy. It is applicable for every industry including space.[193]

The last one Coastal Aquaculture Authority Act, 2005,[194] provides to set up an authority to maintain coastal aquaculture. The present and future spaceport of India has established and will establish near coastal area.[195] It is quite natural that private space industry will be developed in and around these spaceports. Then the number of launching will be increased more. The changing scenario will produce huge post-launching debris that has maximum probability to fall on the ocean like the present system to fall in the Bay of Bengal.[196] In fact the recent Crew Module Atmospheric Re-entry Module (CARE) made by ISRO was landed over Andaman Sea as a part of ISRO's experiment.[197] So environment of these coastal areas will be affected. Then the authority as prescribed under this Act has to monitor the environmental situation and regulate accordingly.

It is not the case that only environmental safeguard could sustain the private space industry. The technological safeguard through IPR laws would be an urgent demand from the private actors like investors and the customers engaged in high-end technology business like space. It has been analysed in earlier chapter that IPR is more demanding in the private actors' centric space era than state centric space era. This is a brief about the space technologies developed in ISRO centres.[198] ISRO shares some of these technologies to others including private entities.[199] These few technologies developed by ISRO have industrial and commercial applications.[200]

There are few Indian IP Acts that do not refer directly about space sector. ISRO has developed several software for communication, remote sensing and launch vehicle areas[201] and has 45 copyrights for different products[202] developed according to the Copyright Act, 1957.[203] Moreover, there are 240 patents developed by ISRO till now under the provisions of the Patents Act, 1970.[204] ISRO has obtained 10 trademarks followed by the Trade Marks Act, 1999. The trademarks are ISROPOL, ISROSIL, ANTRIX, VIBGYOR etc.[205] The other IP Acts are the Designs Act, 2000,[206] and the Semiconductor Integrated Circuits Layout-Design Act, 2000.[207] The title of these Acts speaks for itself.

The laws related with IPR reflect that these are general IP regulations. ISRO protects its IP with its own TTP along with these IP regulations till now. Moreover, the private entities engaged in space business as mentioned in Chapter II have different capacity level to get into their business like start-ups, licencees for manufacturing and marketing the products developed by technologies offered from ISRO. Sometimes the space technologies developed have non-space applications in domestic market.[208] At the same time there is no hard-core regime of private actors like USA. Therefore, whether there is requirement of a totally separate IP legal regime for private actors in space is a big debate. But there is no doubt about it that many more future technologies will make complexities within itself and its spin-offs. There will be more private actors who are also competitors in future space industry. Then the overall situation will decide the future of IPR regulations for space.

All the above brings safeguard to the financer but the safety is such crucial in space industry whether on earth or in outer space itself that many private actors slow down their targeted projects like SPACE X's further launch.[209] The importance of safety is already analysed in chapter III. The following Acts regulate safety in India.

The Explosives Act, 1884, regulates the manufacture, possession, use, sale, transport and importation of explosives which are defined under section 3 (d) where rocket is one of the items.[210] Hence this Act is very much applicable.

The Explosive Substances Act, 1908, empowers the government to punish any person who endangers or is trying to endanger the life of others with making or possessing explosive substances.[211] The space industry also requires some substances which are explosive in nature. Hence this Act is attracted. Recently, there was an accident in ISRO's space launching centre at Sriharikota which was caused by fire in the solid propellant plant managed by a private company according to lease agreement with ISRO.[212] The solid propellant is one kind of explosive.[213]

The Inflammable Substances Act, 1952,[214] regulates the inflammable substances. The space industry is not devoid of inflammable substances as observed above. These Acts are more required to private actors than state actors because the lacuna in safety may cause the severe damage of the former. It may wind up a space company with heavy monetary compensation.

The Dangerous Machines (Regulation) Act, 1983,[215] relates with producing dangerous machines by any industry and it is a risk to its labourers. This Act is applicable with space activities in general.

The safety within the business follows security of the business from outside as enacted in the following laws. The significance of security especially from national security viewpoint is examined in the earlier chapter. The Central Industrial Security Force Act, 1968,[216] draws attention here because central industrial security force (CISF) is presently in charge of security for all ISRO centres throughout India.[217] The private actors have to interact with them to continue their business with ISRO that is till now the biggest customer of all private actors in India.

The role of National Security Act, 1980, is different. It is mentioned several times in this research study that space is a strategic issue to any country. This strategy covers the national security issue. So if the space activities are totally dominated by private actors, then also state may not lose the full control over the space activities. Hence national security comes into play even for private activities in space. Therefore the National Security Act passed in 1980 is a concern for private actors in space. The Act prescribes preventive detention in certain cases and concerned matters.[218]

The Private Security Agencies (Regulation) Act, 2005, provides the legal norms of private security agencies that safeguard the undertakings established by private actors.[219] Hence on the security issue of space business, this Act is also required.

The laws for transparency are slightly offbeat in respect of the above all laws. But its requirement would provide mobility to the private actors in the long run especially to interact with the government. It follows from the following laws.

The Comptroller and Auditor-General's (Duties, Powers and Conditions of Service) Act, 1971, authorises Comptroller and Auditor

General (CAG) of India to his duties and powers, and other matters connected herewith.[220] The CAG is responsible for auditing Government Company. It was the CAG audit report which revealed the irregularities in ANTRIX-DEVAS agreement.[221] Though CAG is not the authority to audit the private companies but this matter correlates with DEVAS which is a private company. The recent Supreme Court ruling has turned around the concept of government audit only. Rather it has ruled that if the public money or natural resources of the country are misused as in the case of telecom sectors, the CAG has right to audit the non-government sector.[222] Therefore the consideration for this Act for private actors to audit their companies comes under its purview.

The next is Central Vigilance Commission Act, 2003.[223] The chapter II of this research study shows that there are so many private entities who are licencees to make production and marketing of ISRO's technologies. ISRO is a Central Government organisation. So there are continuous interactions between ISRO and these private entities. Thus this Act is very much applicable in the present context. Moreover, the incidence of ANTRIX-DEVAS deal has made it clear how much transparency is required for business related with space activities.[224]

The Right to Information Act, 2005,[225] is a government and public interface to know the information against the queries from the citizen of India made to the public offices. All the necessary information is available unless it is not prohibited as prescribed under the Act. It provides more transparency to the system of government where the common people are major user of the system. ISRO has put separate information webpage as per this Act.[226] The advantage of this information is very much useful to the private actors in outer space to continue their business with ISRO. Also, it is one kind of safeguard to them to know the key personnel of contact in case of any difficulty or problem. Moreover, the citizen's charter webpage provides more transparency from ISRO side to all including the private actors regarding the activities and services rendered by ISRO.[227]

The last in the fifth category related with financing of space activities is obviously dispute settlement laws. These laws are related with any issues concerned with the all Acts cited above.

The Indian Penal Code, 1860, applies as usual for offences as prescribed under this Act.[228] The Code of Criminal Procedure, 1973, applies as usual for offences that are criminal in nature as prescribed under this Act.[229] The

Economic Offences (Inapplicability of Limitation) Act, 1974, covers the economic offences.[230]

The Consumer Protection Act, 1986, is not within the purview of telecommunication laws but the NTP-2012 mentions this Act for disputes related with any telecom services.[231] This Act is a protective measure for any type of person who enjoys the benefit of the service as prescribed under this Act but the service will not be commercial.[232] It is assumed that it could be a very good dispute settlement system for any deficiencies in the service from private actors in outer space. As it is applicable for consumers from any discipline like using other technologies or technological products, so it may be applicable for disputes in space sector.

The Arbitration & Conciliation Act, 1996, has general relevancy in the present context.[233] All the multi-nationals including the domestic start-up companies or entrepreneurs are highly interested to arbitration especially in a big deal where space industry is not an exception. The reasons are so many which are out of context of this research study. So there is a special clause for arbitration within the agreement of these companies with their customers or vice-versa in case of disputes. It shows that any private actors having big commercial motive automatically seeks the provisions of this Act to solve their disputes. Therefore it is assumed that the private actors in outer space are not out of this trend. It is analysed from the preamble of the Act that it is made for domestic as well as international commercial arbitration. The United Nations General Assembly has also recommended an amicable settlement of disputes through these conciliation rules in case of disputes raised between parties within international commercial arbitration.[234] In this view, the recent Vodafone case relating with tax dispute went to international arbitration.[235]

Thus this Act could easily be most suitable for disputes amongst private actors in outer space or with the government or other entities. The main advantage is that the UN itself insists to implement the procedure of dispute settlement through this mode. It was further advanced internationally by Permanent Court of Arbitration through their 'Optional Rules for Arbitration of Disputes Relating to Outer Space Activities' which was effective since December 6, 2011.[236]

The Competition Act, 2002, was passed to regulate the adverse effect of competition in the market.[237] In this way it is applicable in general to the private companies in outer space. There is still no such steep competition amongst such companies. But the effect of booming as well as competitive space industry all over the world attracts Indian counterparts to survive through competition in near future. In this regard, the competition between Space X and Orbital Sciences for commercial orbital transportation services to ISS is very much noteworthy in USA.[238] Therefore this Act is very much applicable to space business.

The sixth category of laws in **Table 28** is human resource development laws. The reason for such laws is mentioned above but these laws are required in compliance with the above laws. Like the above IPR laws already defines the intellectual property which could not be developed without outputs from efficient human resources. Similarly the situation is for environmental laws because the self-conscious private actors in the space industry feel the necessity of environment protection measures. Therefore the analysis of human resource development laws comes in the next sequence.

There are some sub-categories in the sixth category. The first one is citizenship laws. The Foreigners Act, 1946, empowers the Central Government to exercise certain powers in relation with the foreigners' entry into India as well as their presence and departure from this country.[239] It is assumed to be related with working or recruitment of employees in a space company.

The Citizenship Act, 1955, provides acquisition and determination of Indian citizenship.[240] The nationality of the employees in a private space company could be different. The recent controversy of the decision of NASA to keep away the Chinese has made it clear that the space industry deserves highly competitive business market.[241]

This problem may arise in case of India especially in the background success of Chandrayan –I[242] and Mars Orbiter Mission.[243] Moreover, there may be requirement of some scientists and technologists having Indian nationality but their citizenships remain with foreign country to start up the space company at its initial stage or in a later stage of technology upgradation. In this view the domestic branch of a foreign reputed space company, say Airbus Defence & Space[244] will definitely hire some domestic human resources along with their own from foreign countries. Therefore the two laws are contemporary to each other in terms of its applicability.

The next is industry-academia development laws in **Table 28**. The Institutes of Technology Act, 1961, authorises certain institutions of technology of national importance.[245] The Indian Institute of Technologies (IITs) is one of the major academic hubs of developing space technology in

India. Though this Act does not have direct linkage to the space business but it is the Act which governs these institutions that carry on academia-industry relationship. The aerospace engineering departments of four IITs –Bombay, Kanpur, Kharagpur and Chennai are playing prominent role to develop the capacity of human resources.[246] Jugnu was launched in 2011 developed by IIT-Kanpur under the guidance of ISRO.[247]

In case of IIT Bombay, the aerospace engineering department took the credit to fulfill the industrial need through one of the vision and mission statements - 'to provide research and development consultancy which will promote contact with and be of service to industries…'[248] Moreover, this department is keeping its industrial relation steady on undertaking sponsored research, consultancy, and continuing education programs in diverse areas e.g. contribution towards Geosynchronous Satellite Launch Vehicles (GSLV).[249] Another future opportunity lies with their student satellite programme. The first one was 'Pratham' followed by the second 'Advitiya'. Both were joint venture with ISRO.[250] The aerospace giant Boeing India Ltd. was involved with these satellite projects.[251]

The Jawaharlal Nehru University (JNU) Act, 1966, is attracted by the provisions relating with power of the University.[252] The first one provides that JNU could cooperate with private body for promotion of purposes and objects similar to the University.[253] The second one states that JNU is empowered to make research as well as advisory services to other bodies on entering arrangements with them.[254] The other bodies definitely include private bodies.

The interpretation of the two subsections provides that JNU could advise or make research over an arrangement with private body that is engaged with business, say space in the present context. Unlike IITs there is no aerospace engineering department in JNU. But the existing arrangement of University may be utilised as the capacity development of the concerned private body for other infrastructure like space law.[255] Moreover, JNU has granted recognition and accreditation to Raman Research Institute (Bengaluru) as well as Inter University Centre for Astronomy and Astrophysics (IUCAA, Pune). The former has one of its major research areas - astronomy and astrophysics whereas the later has mission 'to promote the nucleation and growth of active groups in astronomy and astrophysics at Indian universities'.[256] Earlier JNU had a project from NASA with School of Life Science on astrobiology.[257] Similarly, it could be done with any private actors in outer space in India and abroad. So the private actors in outer space could get skilled human resources through industry-academia partnership from JNU.

The Rajiv Gandhi National Aviation University Act, 2013, established the university to make study and research of air law with other disciplines related with aeronautics. It is not directly related with space or the word 'space' is not mentioned anywhere in the said Act.[258] Since space is extension of air, this Act could be like extended law. Moreover, one of the objects according to Section 4 (i) prescribes 'connected fields in emerging areas and such areas as may emerge in future'.[259] So it is assumed that the Act could be extended to outer space also; because outer space is very much connected with airspace. The University has power to link up with any industrial association to develop the knowledge on specific programmes on aviation.[260] Therefore like above, the newly formed University could very well supply the skilled manpower to private space industries as well as any other tie-up for promoting the academia-industry relationship.

The last sub-category is labour and welfare laws. Their role is basically supportive in context of other Acts. The Acts are Workmen's Compensation Act, 1923;[261]_Industrial Employment (Standing Orders) Act, 1946;[262] the Apprentices Act, 1946;[263] the Industrial Disputes Act, 1947;[264] the Factories Act, 1948;[265] the Employees' State Insurance Act, 1948;[266] the Employees' Provident Funds & Miscellaneous Provisions Act, 1952;[267] the Payment of Bonus Act, 1965;[268] and the Payment of Gratuity Act, 1972.[269] All these Acts have general applicability to regulate the private actors like such actors in other commercial sector like space.

But the Bhopal Gas Leak Disaster (Processing of Claims) Act, 1985, is placed here because this specific Act covers only the claims and its processing related with the great disaster held at Bhopal as an effect of gas leak.[270] It is very hard to believe how this Act could regulate the private actors in the present context. ISRO is increasing its launch year after another[271] and the possibility of another spaceport besides Sriharikota is under consideration.[272] In addition, the probability of private launches, as mentioned in earlier chapter, could not be set aside in near future. The status of the private launchers may be private outsourcing agents. In this background, it is noted that if the spacecraft misses its trajectory by accident and rush towards a populated place, it is like launching a missile to a country. Still now, the spacecraft will fall in the Bay of Bengal in case of any emergency.[273] This is stated in chapter II that launching a missile and that of spacecraft require same technology and infrastructure. The disaster will be unthinkable as well as immense. Hence it is assumed to consider this Act well in advance to face the similar situation in famous gas leak incident at Bhopal.

The last but one category is State Acts which fall under seventh category as shown in **Table 28**. It is observed from above that 'space' is not mentioned in the 'State List' of the Constitution. In spite of that, certain State Acts are to be followed in persuasion of current domain of national space activities governed by the central government through Space Commission and Department of Space (DoS). Otherwise there could be difference of opinion leading towards disagreement between Centre and State to spread the space commerce through private actors in India.

This research study observes from chapter II as well as **Table 17** that the private companies engaged with space business in India are mainly situated in the states like Andhra Pradesh, Gujarat, Karnataka, Kerala, Maharashtra, New Delhi, Tamil Nadu, U.P. and very few are in other states. It is also further noted that these are based in a particular place of a state like Bengaluru (Karnataka); Hyderabad (A.P.); Ahmedabad and Vadodara (Gujarat); Thiruvananthapuram and Kochi (Kerala); Chennai, Coimbatoor and Madurai (Madras); Mumbai, Nagpur and Pune (Maharashtra). The reason is that ISRO itself remains the prospective and major buyer of the service delivered or products manufactured by these companies. The licencee companies of ISRO have been established for this purpose. According to the companies' names mentioned in chapter II, their maximum concentration is at Bengaluru followed by Hyderabad, Chennai, Mumbai and Ahmedabad. These are the places where more or less ISRO centres exist.

The exception is Chennai, capital of Tamil Nadu. It has most suitable connectivity for Sriharikota, the only spaceport of India till now and not far away from Bengaluru where the head quarter of ISRO is situated. Likely Mumbai, the business capital of India, is another exception in this list. Therefore some of the State Acts where these places are situated get importance with this research study and also significant to analyse the regulatory framework of space activities in India.

The other factors are that each state government has some prioritised sector in its department of science and technology followed by its policy of industrialisation in that sector. Therefore the policy framework in Karnataka differs from Andhra Pradesh whereas Gujarat and other states follow their individual pattern. Only relevant with this research study is how these states are handling or will make an infrastructure plan to develop and promote the aerospace industry. Ultimately, the infrastructure of aerospace industry is prioritised depending on state government's strategy framework. So a very brief account about the policy and development of aerospace industry is a part and parcel of the next phase of analysis. Also some Acts are for financing the space activities from different corners whereas some are for manpower development like the Central Acts above. The sequence of the states is arranged alphabetically.

It starts with Andhra Pradesh where the National Remote Sensing Centre (NRSC)[274] is situated at Hyderabad which is also an aerospace hub.[275] The title of the Acts below speaks for itself along with its relevancy.

The Industrial Dispute (Andhra Pradesh Amendment) Act, 1987;[276] the Andhra Pradesh Infrastructure Development Corporation Act, 1998;[277] the Andhra Pradesh Industrial Workers (Representation) Participation in Management and Relief) Act, 1998,[278] are as usual in the present context.

But the Andhra Pradesh Infrastructure Development Enabling Act, 2001,[279] insists development infrastructure through projects with private sectors' participation. Though 'space' is not enlisted but the last item number (15) of Schedule III refers 'any other projects or sectors as notified by the Government'.[280] This Act is very much required to open up a new sector in the state including 'space'. The state government facilitates the private initiatives to build-up the infrastructure of the state. Therefore the private actors in due course of time will be facilitated to develop their infrastructure in space activities.

The Andhra Pradesh Industrial Single Window Clearance Act, 2002,[281] is the second Act after the above where the state government has taken initiative directly to set-up industrial undertakings through speedy processing on issuing licences, clearances and certificates. Here it is noted that industries for all types of electronic aerospace equipment must require industrial licence.[282] This Act is very much supportive to the space entrepreneurs or start-up companies in space. The foreign investors would also be attracted.

The A.P. Special Economic Zone Bill, 2005, was introduced in the A.P. Legislative Assembly to give effect the SEZ Act passed by the Government of India in 2005.[283] There are two SEZs in A.P. for aerospace and precision engineering industries – one in Ranga Reddy District to be developed by A.P. Industrial Infrastructure Corporation Ltd. (notified status) and other in Ananthapur district by a private developer M/S Lepakshi Knowledge Hub Private Ltd. (formal status).[284] The private companies like Tata Advanced

Systems Ltd., Nova Integrated Systems Ltd. and Samuha Engineering Industries Ltd. are allotted land in Ananthapur district.[285] Samuha is formed on bringing a number of aerospace companies under a single umbrella.[286] Recently, the foundation stone of Samuha Aerospace Park is laid down in Ranga Reddy district. It will be the country's first such park. A proposal came to name the whole area as 'Space City'.[287] This initiative is a kind of example to implement the Space Technology Park according to 12th FYP.[288]

The last is Jawaharlal Nehru Technological University (JNTU) Act, 2008. The University is empowered to provide consultancy services to the industry according to Section 2 (4) (xi) of the Act.[289] So the private space industries could very well approach to the JNTU for consultation.

The next in the order is Gujarat which has special significance with this research study because India's space programme was pioneered by Sarabhai through his personal research interest on cosmic ray in PRL at Ahmedabad.[290] Moreover the department of science and technology,[291] government of Gujarat has been focussed in the area of remote sensing and space application through its nodal agency, Bhaskaracharya Institute for Space Applications & Geoinformatics (BISAG).[292] The use of spatial and geospatial technologies have been used to plan and develop many sectors in the state. With this background, the following state Acts are assumed to be pertinent for this research study.

The Gujarat Industrial Relations Act, 1946,[293] could regulate the relation of employer and employees for easy settlement of disputes in any business including space. The Gujarat Co-Operative Societies Act, 1961,[294] may attract private space companies if they could form a co-operative society to take loan for their business. The titles of Gujarat Land Acquisition (Industrial Areas) Act, 1961,[295] and the Gujarat Industrial Development Act, 1962,[296] speak for itself. The State Tax on Professions, Trades, Callings and Employments Act, Gujarat, 1976;[297] the Gujarat Infrastructure Development Act, 1999;[298] the Gujarat Special Economic Zone Act, 2004;[299] and The Gujarat Special Investment Region Act, 2009,[300] are other few Acts to regulate the private actors as their titles show. In this view, there was a proposal from the state itself during 2011 to establish India's first geospatial park in the state with a view to push research in space technology and surveying activities in various parts of Gujarat.[301] The Bhaskaracharya Institute for Space Applications & Geoinformatics (BISAG) of Gandhinagar has taken the leading role in this regard.[302] All these Acts support the financing whereas the following State

Acts of Gujarat has established the different academic universities including the technical universities for human resource development.

The few are the Nirma University of Science and Technology Act, 2003;[303] the Dhirubhai Ambani Institute of Information and Communication Technology Act, 2003;[304] the Ganpat University Act, 2005;[305] the Centre for Environmental Planning and Technology University Act, 2005;[306] and the Gujarat Technological University Act, 2007.[307]

The next state is Karnataka where the headquarter of the national space agency is situated. Therefore the situation differs from Gujarat. The Karnataka Co-operative Societies Act, 1959;[308] the Karnataka Industrial Areas Development Act, 1966;[309] the Karnataka Industries (Facilitation) Act, 2002;[310] and the Karnataka Information Technology Investment Regions Act, 2010,[311] follow the similarity like other State and Central Acts.

The Karnataka Policy for SEZ, 2009, though basically a policy but it is inseparable from the Acts of the State. According to the follow-up of SEZ Act, 2005, the state government has adopted the policy for SEZ in 2009.[312] A lease agreement to bring the whole process under law will be signed between Karnataka Industrial Areas Development Board (KIAD) as lessor, and a person (lessee).[313] Till now, there exists two SEZ- for aerospace engineering developed by Quest Machining and Manufacturing Pvt. Ltd. at Belgaum and for aerospace industry developed by KIAD at Devanahalli near New International Airport, Bangalore.[314] The KIAD has plan for an Aerospace University and a Technology Innovation Center in collaboration with reputed overseas institutions here.[315] The Vellore Institute of Technology Bangalore Act, 2012;[316] the M.S. Ramaiah University of Applied Sciences Act, 2012;[317] the KLE Technological University Act, 2012;[318] the Rai Technology University, Bangalore Act, 2012;[319] J.S.S. Science and Technology University Act, 2013,[320] are all associated to regulate human resource development in state. These are not all inclusive.

It is also to be mentioned here that Nitte Meenakshi Institute of Technology (NMIT), Bengaluru, an autonomous institution, had very rare status because this institute affiliated under the Visvesvaraya Technological University signed MoU with ISRO for developing student satellite, STUDSAT.[321] It is to be mentioned here that this University is one of the participating members from India in Asia-Pacific Regional Space Agency Forum.[322] STUDSAT-1 was launched in 2010[323] whereas STUDSAT-2 is in process.[324] The institute signed on behalf of other institutes from Karnataka and A.P.[325]

There are two regulations left though they are not Acts. The Karnataka Industrial Policy, 2009-2014, supports the Micro, Small & Medium Enterprises (MSME) Development Act, 2006 (Central Act), facilitating the growth of MSME sector in the Country and so the state has more responsibility to focus on MSME sector. The policy would like to attract the investors and entrepreneurs whatever are the investments. Now one of the policy measures is that '5.3.7 An Aerospace Park in association with Society of Indian Aerospace Technologies and Industries (SIATI) will be developed near Bangalore.'[326] Memorandum of Understanding (MoU) under Karnataka – Israel Program for Industrial R&D (KIRD) was a MoU that was signed in March 2013 between MATIMOP – The Israeli Industry Center for R&D; and the Karnataka Science and Technology Promotion Society (KSTePS); and the Karnataka State Council for Science and Technology (KSCST). The purpose of MoU was to support the joint industrial R&D projects between Israel and Karnataka based companies. One of the areas in which applications were invited was aero and space technology.[327] The text of MoU is not available in public domain but it has soft regulatory impact on private actors in outer space.

Now it is turn for Kerala wherefrom the first Indian rocket was launched. Its geographical location is very close to geomagnetic equator which very few countries have.[328] It was the main attraction to develop rocket launching site. Later the state got two ISRO Centres, VSSC and LPSC.[329] Hence, the state is a major hub of space activities since the beginning of India's space modern era. Some private space entities come up which already mentioned earlier.

The present scenario of aerospace sector in Kerala has been highlighted by the government in the 'Emerging Kerala 2012' global connect.[330] There are two plans as per the following: (i) to renovate the aeronautical material testing laboratory at Steel and Industrial Forgings Ltd. (SIFL)[331]. This is a Kerala Government undertaking company. Such advanced laboratory now exists in Vikram Sarabhai Space Centre (VSSC) for their own purpose and Defence Research Development Corporation (DRDC) also to satisfy their own testing. The upcoming renovated laboratory for advanced testing will attract the aerospace companies like Honeywell, Jaguar, Boeing/Airbus to tie-up their business with SIFL[332] and to establish Aerospace Park at

Kadinalkulam. The reason is that the space capabilities with aviation sector of India have continuous expansion of demand which requires more suppliers.

At present there is a bunch of precision component manufacturers who supply the products to ISRO or Brahmos but the new entrepreneurs are constantly pressing the existing market. Kadinakulam is a proper place because already the manufactures as well as suppliers exist at Veli and Kinfra industrial estates. Moreover, ISRO centre VSSC and Brahmos are very nearby.[333]

The Travancore-Cochin Literary, Scientific and Charitable Societies Registration Act, 1955,[334] was made to improve the legal condition of societies for the purpose mentioned in the preamble itself. The Indian Institute of Space Science and Technology (IIST) was established in 2007, under this Act to promote space science, technology and applications. Such type of initiative was the first step in India to focus only on space science, technology and applications. Later on IIST was designated as 'Deemed University' status under the UGC Act, 1956. Basically it is the newly established educational hub of ISRO. As mentioned earlier, IIST functions as an autonomous body under DoS. Their policy is to recruit the passed out from here in ISRO.[335] So it comes under human resource development laws.

The Industrial Disputes (Kerala) Amendment Act, 1961;[336] the Kerala State Aid to Industries Act, 1963;[337] the Kerala Co-operative Society Act, 1969;[338] the Kerala Industrial Infrastructure Development Act, 1993;[339] and the Kerala Industrial Revitalisation Fund Act, 1999,[340] are other relevant Acts to regulate the private actors. The second Act is a special one because Section 10 of the Act provides government aid to the industries in Kerala.[341] The Cochin University of Science and Technology Act, 1986, have provisions in Sections 2 (iv), 6(xii) and 18 (xxvii) to regulate the capacity development of human resources or the research output which will facilitate the industry. [342] Moreover, one of the representatives in the category of nominated members of the Academic Council is from ISRO as per Section 23 (2).[343]

The next state is Maharashtra. This state has no ISRO centre directly but the city of Mumbai has a great significance. It is business capital of India. It is observed earlier that BARC with TIFR is situated here. So the hub of atomic research is centred at Mumbai. There are many programmes till now where BARC is related with ISRO.[344] The chapter II shows that some of the space companies like Godrej & Boyce Ltd. are situated at Mumbai. With this introduction the following state Acts are assumed to be relevant for this research study. The Acts like the Maharashtra Industrial Development Act, 1961;[345] the Babasaheb Ambedkar Technological University Act, 1969;[346] the Rajiv Gandhi Science & Technology Commission Act, 2004,[347] are relevant in the present context. The title speaks about their area of regulation.

Orisaa comes next. The Indian missiles are test launched from Wheeler Island which belongs to coastal Orissa.[348] Now-a-days the numbers of testing have increased.[349] The ISRO is in a search for second space port besides Sriharikota and one such view that more towards north of Sriharikota, and in between Sriharikota and Wheeler Island.[350] That is why the state of Orissa is important in reference to the future space activities from India. The Acts are the Orissa State-Aid to Industries Act, 1978;[351] the Orissa Industrial Infrastructure Development Corporation Act, 1980;[352] and the Biju Patnaik University of Technology Act, 2002;[353] and the Orissa Industries (Facilitation) Act, 2004.[354] The similar Acts are explained above for other States.

The last state is Tamil Nadu that has full potential to expand the national space programme did not get scope earlier; but now with the proposal of new space port as mentioned above, the whole scenario has been changed. Additionally, the position of the state is in between A.P. and Kerala that both have ISRO centres and well-established space activities as noted above. It leads to develop further the national space strategy in a more advanced way.

The following Acts are concerned here. The Tamil Nadu State Aid to Industries Act, 1922;[355] the Anna University Chennai Act, 1978;[356] the Tamil Nadu Industrial Establishments (Conferment of Permanent Status to Workmen) Act, 1981;[357] the Tamil Nadu Taxation Special Tribunal Act, 1992;[358] the Tamil Nadu Acquisition of Land for Industrial Purpose Act, 1997;[359] the Tamil Nadu Industrial Township Area Development Authority Act, 1997,[360] are few State Acts.

The object of Anna University Act[361] was highly satisfied during the 10th Five Year Plan on developing the microsatellite ANUSAT with technical assistance from ISRO.[362] It was the first satellite built by the Indian University and was launched in 2009.[363] Therefore it is one of the best examples how a private university[364] could build-up a satellite like industry. In this view, this Act is a practical example of human resource development law.

The Tamil Nadu Special Economic Zones (Special Provisions) Act, 2005, is significant one at present. The state government through its nodal agency Tamil Nadu Industrial Development Corporation announced SEZ to establish aerospace park project. The Taneja Aerospace and Aviation Ltd. at Hosur have already possessed some facilities which will be expanded. The other areas are Sriperumbudhur, Perambalur and around Chennai airport.[365] The two Tamil Nadu State Acts have special significance right now - TN Acquisition of Land for Industrial Purposes Act, 1997, and the other is TN SEZ Act, 2005. The reason is proposed spaceport at Tuticorin where there is proposal both from ISRO and the political leaders of TN.[366]

The last of **Table 28** is eighth category that has single Act of National Capital Territory Delhi. The Delhi Geo-Spatial Data Infrastructure (Management Control, Administration, Security and Safety) Act, 2011, regulates the utilisation of geospatial data. Its significance to this research study is that the earth related data captured through remote sensing satellites in outer space are utilised for the different societal plans on earth. The legislation was made by the Government of Delhi to regulate the use of such data for mandatory sharing, accessing and utilisation within public and private bodies.[367]

Institutions

It is mentioned in the introduction of this chapter that institutions come last to regulate private actors in outer space. The mere building of institutional set-up is itself a very soft regulatory instrument. The previous chapter also highlights this issue for different countries. Even there are some countries where they just continuously push their infrastructure to establish an institution through which at least some initiative for regulation will be started. The case of India is not a different cup of tea. Obviously the institutions established at the beginning are not for regulation of private actors. This is valid for every country. The beginning stage belonged to state actors. Then this stage gradually diffused. **Table 29** depicts the number of institutions developed. This is not all inclusive.

Table 29: Institutions for Regulations[368]

Period	Institutions	First Formal Contribution To Regulate	Actors For Regulation
Beginning of Space Programme	International Geophysical Year (IGY) National Committee (1955)	1955	State
	Physical Research Laboratory (PRL) (1954)	1954	As above
	Department of Atomic Energy (Since 1961)	1961	As above
	Planning Commission [Since 4th FYP (1969-1974)]	1969	State & Private
	Indian Committee on Space Research (INCOSPAR)	1962	State
	Thumba Equatorial Launching Station (TERLS)	1963	As above
	Space Science and Technology Centre (SSTC)	1965	State
Current Space Programme (Govt. Side)	Indian Space Research Organisation (ISRO)	1969	State & private
	Space Commission	1972	As above
	Department of Space (DoS)	1972	As above
	Antrix Corporation	1992	As above
Current Space Programme (Non-Govt Side)	Society of Indian Aerospace Technologies & Industries (SIATI)	1991	Private Actors
	Confederation of Indian Industries (CII)	2008	Private Actors
	Federation of Indian Chambers of Commerce & Industry (FICCI)	2008	As above
	Association of Geospatial Industries (AGI)	2009 onwards	As above
	Cellular Operators Association of India (COAI)	1995	As above

It is mentioned in chapter I that India started its space programme with the introduction of International Geosphysical Year (IGY) (1957-58). It is to be noted that space was one of the agenda in IGY. This programme was planned to launch satellites in space to observe and get data of the upper atmosphere. In this view the IGY Indian National Committee was made in 1955.[369] So this was the first institute building process to regulate the national space activities.

IGY follow-up was performed by another institution i.e., Physical Research Laboratory (PRL) at Ahmedabad.[370] Vikram Sarabhai started a modest beginning of cosmic ray research in a small laboratory at his home (Ahmedabad) in 1947.[371] It was funded by government and also supported by the Karmkshetra Educational Foundation and the Ahmedabad Education Society[372]. This was the informal establishment of the later Physical Research Laboratory (PRL) that was officially inaugurated in 1954.[373] There are some observations from the facts that the establishment of PRL is for moving towards the permanent foundation of space programme on establishing a national institute. It was also interesting that there were indirect contribution of two non-government actors on supporting the government institution PRL. So it was rightly said that PRL took the place as the cradle of India's space programme.[374]

Alongside, Sarabhai individually may be treated as an institution. There was some personal contribution besides his interest on cosmic ray research at PRL. This satellite-tracking era of India during IGY was made more social than scientific by Sarabhai. According to the agenda in the international affairs of USA, the Satellite Instructional Television Experiment (SITE) could broadcast into home-receivers provided the host country had some small equipment set-up. It is a commercial benefit for NASA if the large country like India would participate in SITE. But India earlier refused the establishment of broadcasting station of Voice of America. Arnold Frutkin, the then director of NASA's Office of International Programmes, realised that it was not possible from the side of USA government. He persuaded Sarabhai to take the initiative from India's side. Then the rest made the history as the programme became highly responsive from the Indian side.[375]

Afterwards India tried to get the availability of US satellite extended for another year. But US turned down because the contract was valid only for one year.[376] This was the beginning to think self-reliance space programme by Sarabhai, and it is going on till now. Anyway the SITE experiment provided successive impetus after IGY in making India a global partner in science and technology.[377] So the SITE itself was a major gateway of nascent regulatory phase of space programme in India, and, Sarabahi was the brain behind it.

The above institutional development was related with purely research purposes. The Government of India did not have regulatory control of space programmes like other national programmes. Therefore it was ultimately passed over to the Government of India itself under the mentorship of its Department of Atomic Energy (DAE) that was established in 1954 much before IGY programme during 1957-58. Subsequently Atomic Energy Commission (AEC) was formed within DAE. The Prime Minister was in charge of both the establishment. Homi J Bhabha was the first Secretary of DAE as well as Chairman of AEC.[378] The AEC had the resources and freedom to create new scientific programs like space and industrial programs such as satellites. It was previously Sarabhai alone. Now Bhabha was stepped in to develop the national space programme through AEC and DAE. He was also like an institution as observed in the case of Sarabhai.

Here it is required to mention that when India finalised its third five year plan (FYP) having duration 1961-66, there was no provision for space research. The Government of India entrusted the responsibility of looking after space research and peaceful uses of outer space to DAE in August, 1961, with Bhabha as the Secretary.[379] Its effect was observed in fourth FYP. The provision has been made for INSAT-1, the proposed Indian-owned geo-synchronous satellite which will provide a variety of meteorological data.[380] This was for the first time within the Planning Commission (PC) that a major decision was made related with space. In this view, the PC is itself a regulatory institution for national space activities. But it is already mentioned that the 11th FYP onwards there was approach for planning of private actors within national space programme.[381] The 12th FYP clearly acknowledged the complexities in regulation created with the increasing number of private actors in space all over the world.[382] So the PC has currently turned into an institution regulating the private space activities.

The next regulatory institution according to **Table 29** was the Indian Committee on Space Research (INCOSPAR) that took the responsibility for regulating the space programme for the first time in real and practical sense. It would require a little bit history to reflect its analysis in this study. The International Council of Scientific Unions (ICSU), now known as the International Council for Science (ICS) as well as one of the pioneer organisations for IGY programme established a Committee on Space Research (COSPAR) in 1958 as its response to the launching of Sputnik.[383] So Bhabha thought it would be necessary to have similar national Committee of COSPAR. Accordingly, the government created the Indian National Committee on Space Research (INCOSPAR) in February 1962, under the chairmanship of Sarabhai.[384]

INCOSPAR only took the responsibility of space research from DAE but remains within DAE where Bhabha as Director. As a part of the move, the PRL was recognised as appropriate centre for research and development in space sciences. PRL was also funded by DAE. On the other side of this development, Sarabhai was introduced by Bhabha as one of the members of AEC in 1965. INCOSPAR had two purposes: (i) to promote international cooperation in space research and exploration and in the peaceful uses of outer space; and (ii) to cooperate with COSPAR. INCOSPAR generally encourages and supports international activities likely to contribute to the peaceful uses of outer space.[385] Therefore the regulatory role of INCOSPAR was to institutionalise national space activities in India.

The foundation of INCOSPAR follows the establishment of Thumba Equatorial Launching Station (TERLS) that may be treated as pro-institution. The function of TERLS was basically to carry forward the responsibility of INCOSPAR.[386] It was established in 1963, and was funded by the DAE under the leadership of Bhabha. Later UNGA took the decision to sponsor the continuing operations here and so it was dedicated to UN in 1965.[387]

Consequently, the Atomic Energy Commission (AEC) approved the Space Science and Technology Centre (SSTC) in 1965, which was opened at Thiruvananthapuram. The Centre was situated just beside the TERLS. Being Sarabhai's favourite project, the stage was now set for the continuous expansion of 'space' within the 'atomic energy' family of organisations. It was said that, in the eyes of Sarabhai, the DAE was 'the Ministry of Advanced Technologies'.[388] The SSTC was renamed as Vikram Sarabhai Space Centre (VSSC) after his death in 1971.[389]

All institutions developed above are basically for national capacity building of space science and technology. Besides the Planning Commission (later on), all these institutions that started regulating the national space programme did not plan or even think for regulating the private actors in India. This was the scenario at the beginning to develop regulation on making institutions.

The next phase is current stage of regulation as shown in **Table 29**. It started with establishment of Indian Space Research Organisation (ISRO). It was formed under the same parental body DAE on August 15, 1969.[390] After death of Sarabhai, Satish Dhawan transformed ISRO in new shape. The impact was the formation of Space Commission and Department of Space (DoS) in June, 1972. ISRO was brought under DoS in September 1972.[391]

The Annexure III shows the hierarchy of bodies to regulate this current regime. The Prime Minister is at the top of this hierarchy as Minister-in-Charge for Department of Space. There is one Joint Secretary assisted by one director to look after space sector in Prime Minister's Office (PMO).[392]

The Space Commission (SC) is the highest as well as highly empowered body 'to formulate the policies and oversees the implementation of the Indian space programme to promote the development and application of space science and technology for the socio-economic benefit of the country'. The Chairman of ISRO is the Chairman of SC by default. The other members are the Minister of State in PMO; National Security Adviser; Principal Secretary to PM; Cabinet Secretary; Secretary, Department of Expenditure; Secretary to Government of India (GOI) as member-finance; Principal Scientific Advisor to GOI; and two members from academic repute in space science. Additional Secretary of DoS is the secretary of SC.[393]

The highest policy making body concerned with space activities is constituted of ministers, bureaucrats and scientists. The SC has the pioneering role to make any suggestion, formation or addition with respect to domestic space regulation in India. It implies that the government regulates the private actors through the SC since its formation in 1972.[394]

The role of Department of Space (DoS) is simply implementation of the programmes planned by SC through ISRO and other bodies as shown in the chart of Annex III. The Headquarter of DoS is situated at Bengaluru unlike other departmental headquarters situated in New Delhi. This is very meaningful to study the regulatory regime of space in India. It has no official locus standi for the policy making or framing regulation for space activities. The DoS has the role to sanction the budget for space programmes as planned by SC.[395]

The role of ISRO is confined to develop space technology and its application to various national needs.[396] Therefore ISRO is not officially related with the planning and framing the regulatory regime of private actors in outer space. It has only supportive or secondary role in framing regulation being national space agency.

The Antrix Corporation Limited is a wholly owned government company under the administrative control of the DoS. It was incorporated in 1992, as a private limited company owned by Government of India and marketing arm of ISRO like selling space products, technical consultancy services and transfer of technologies developed by ISRO.[397]

Therefore when it comes to regulation, Antrix Corporation plays the supporting role to execute the commercial decision taken by ISRO for business purposes and it has the only authority to communicate on behalf of ISRO to the private actors as business partners like EADS Astrium, Boeing, Mitsubishi Electric, INMARSAT etc.[398]

The current institutional mechanism to regulate space directly or indirectly from the government side is analysed above. But there are some non-governmental bodies or societies that were established to contribute in the development of regulations for private actors in outer space. It is shown in **Table 29**. The first is Society of Indian Aerospace Technologies & Industries (SIATI).[399] Its mission is enhancement of private industry participation in aerospace sector. It also has association for working 'closely with Aero Society, FICCI, CII and such other industry associations for government policy, formulations/modifications for the growth of Aerospace Technology and business.'[400] It is empowered 'to interact with government on offset and other policy and regulations'.[401] Its one of the objectives is 'Organising interactions and deliberations between government bodies, policy makers, regulatory authorities'.[402] Therefore being the largest aerospace society having status of non-profit and non-commercial organisations, SIATI has tremendous role to contribute in placing proposal or pressurising the suitable policy-makers to regulate the private actors in aerospace industry.

The next is Confederation of Indian Industries (CII) having status as a business association.[403] According to the information available, its contribution is still now confined within the major organiser of biggest space expo at Bengaluru since 2008.[404] The CII being mainly an association of private business industries takes the initiative to interact with different private actors over business dialogues in this expo. The exhibitors of 2014 expo are the renowned private actors both from India and abroad as explained in chapter II.[405] This business dialogues since 2008, have some regulatory impact through CII.

The next is Federation of Indian Chambers of Commerce & Industry (FICCI) that has regulatory contribution on geospatial technology. This technology spreads geospatial industry that is already discussed. The FICCI Task Force on Geospatial Technologies is in the charge of sending policy proposals to the Government.[406] Moreover, the FICCI Inputs to 12th

FYP has recommended incentivising R&D in public and private sector. The example is that FICCI has started Lockheed Martin India Innovation growth programme (IIGP) for technology commercialisation.[407] It is further recommended to focus on public-private partnerships models like knowledge parks and incubator programmes to promote the commercialisation, transfer and diffusion of technology. In this view, space is one of the most suitable sectors because India is predominant in space research and development.[408] The FICCI Inputs have also suggested that use of geospatial technology for developing geographical information system (GIS).[409] This business body is one of the pioneering organisations behind the National GI Policy as explained under regulation through policies.[410]

The Association of Geospatial Industries (AGI) is another body to contribute in the policy regulation of geospatial industries. But it is not as old as CII or FICCI.[411]

The Cellular Operators Association of India (COAI) is a non-government society that is engaged for providing best quality modern communication in India. Its membership includes the private telecommunication companies in India. Its mission statement states 'Creating a facilitating ecosystem that provides a nurturing policy, regulatory and legal framework for the industry'.[412] There are some COAI White Papers on different telecommunication services; both present and upcoming ones.[413] There are reports like Industry Submissions and Responses to TRAI since 2003 that are very useful documents to regulate private cellular operators.[414] Recently, COAI has made statements over spectrum swapping issue that has been a long pending contentious issue between the DoT and the Ministry of Defence.[415] It is observed that smart phones serve many purposes for our daily livelihood and the numbers are increasing.[416] So the different facilities are provided by cellular operators. Therefore the regulatory role of COAI for private actors in this domain will be more noteworthy.

There are umpteen numbers of institutions or societies that contribute towards the regulation of private actors. Their roles sometimes may be not only soft but very soft in making the regulations. But it may appear or presume that their key activities related with space science and technology has ample opportunities to contribute towards regulation of private actors. Sometimes these bodies could contribute in real sense and in best way rather than a legal advisory body. Unfortunately, this trend has not been nurtured till now in India.[417]

Conclusion

The regulations in India are arranged thematically by policies, legislations and institutions like each country in previous chapter. The policies are arranged according to the departments of the government. There are prima facie five government departments like Department of Science & Technology (DST), Planning Commission (PC), Department of Space (DoS), Department of Telecommunications (DoT) and Department of Land Resources. Each department is under different Ministries whereas the Planning Commission (PC) itself is an overall plan making body of the government. Each department has different policies.

The Scientific Policy Resolution, 1958 (SPR, 1958), was the backbone of India's modern scientific era. This Resolution was a mixture of Nehru's passion about science and the thoughts of Bhabha. The two masterminds made this document historical. The SPR was followed by other policies in the DST. All these policies especially at the beginning were established with purely nationalistic goal. It strengthens sovereignty of India. Initially, the government has played the leading role for functioning because industrialisation was necessary to improve the national economy according to the founding fathers of modern India. Also, the private bodies had not been competent enough.

Later on the government would expect the private participation along with its functioning. The stages of development through these policies towards regulation were commercialisation, industrialisation, research and development, and finally, innovation. Therefore, though the private actors were dormant at the beginning but they became gradually proactive from SPR 1958 to the latest Science, Technology & Innovation Policy, 2013. This was observed in Science & Technology Policy, 2003, that considered IPR laws for the first time. The indication of IPR laws basically deals the regulation of IP in commercial era that is mainly occupied by the private actors.

These policies were made to develop the foundation of existence of private actors first in national level and then international level in the domain of S&T including space. The draft of National Geospatial Information Policy 2012 was totally a new initiative under DST. It indicated not only the government's desire to implement the geospatial technology through policy regulation but also to regulate the increasing number of private actors using this new technology for commercial purposes. This draft attracts the issues like sovereignty & proprietary rights, national security, IPR, liability and dispute settlement.

Compared to this general science and technology policy development, the existing space policy consists of- (i) SATCOM Policy, 2000, related with telecommunication through satellites, and (ii) the Remote Sensing Data Policy, 2011 (RSDP), for acquiescence and dissemination of remote sensing data. There are other ancillary policies of Department of Space like Industry Participation Policy, Commercialisation Policy, International Co-operation Policy and Human Resource Development Policy. The titles speak for itself.

The SATCOM Policy clearly indicates that building and developing satellite communication infrastructure means strengthening the sovereignty of India. The second part of this policy under the heading 'Norms, Guidelines and Procedure for Implementation' reflects that government does not intend to lose control even in the era of privatisation of global satellite communication systems. It presses to follow international treaties, agreements and regulations to utilise the Indian Satellite (INSAT) capacity for operations outside India.

Moreover, sovereignty of the state is maintained through its functionaries like DoS with the process of authorisation within the text of this policy. In this regard, the security issue is duly considered. The other issue reflected is financing. Also, different national acts are applicable for the operations of the licence holders whereas the DoS is a strict follow-up to the UN treaties, conventions to maintain these procedures. Lastly, it has been proposed in the 12th Five Year Plan (FYP) that the SATCOM Policy, 2000, will be revisited and revised, if required.

The other space policy is Remote Sensing Data Policy, 2011. Here also the government controls like SATCOM Policy but the control is on acquisition or dissemination of data to private parties from Indian Remote Sensing Satellite (IRS). It is assumed that government would like to maintain the monopoly in the name of national security of India. In fact the high resolution data is a threat to any country including India. The licencing procedure exists through the nodal agencies of the government like DoS or ANTRIX. This policy highlights sovereignty and national security. The other ancillary policies of DoS are like Technology Transfer Policy of ISRO that obviously relates with IPR issue. Also ISRO has Intellectual Property Policy.

The Policies under Department of Telecommunication (DoT) are National Telecom Policy, 1994, New Telecom Policy, 1999. The first one attracts the issues of national security and dispute settlement. The second one provides the financing issue. The policies under Department of Land Resources may attract the issue of dispute settlement.

At the outset it is the Planning Commission (PC) of India that is empowered to frame and set the budget for national space programme in each and every Five Year Plan (FYP). The Working Group on Department of Space of the on-going 12th FYP (2012-2017) proposed within its report for some regulatory changes. It followed that the above policies along with some supportive or related legislation regulated the space activities but these were insufficient to bear the obligations from international conventions and treaties as ratified by India. In this regard, India ratified all the international space law treaties and signed Moon Treaty. So the 12th FYP proposed 'Space Act' for domestic space development.

According to the observation made by the PC, the supportive or related legislations exist to regulate space activities in India. Therefore the existing legislations, both Central and State, are attracted or extended for regulating private actors in outer space. However, there is an informal classification of Central Acts assumed to be applicable on private actors like companies associated with business over space activities.

These are based on Acts supporting financing of space activities and for capacity development of human resources; because these are the two areas where India lacks behind even after achieving technological prowess. But before that there are some readymade regulatory instruments in the existing framework. Firstly, the Constitution of India has already reflected the ratification of international treaties including space law treaties amongst its few Articles. Secondly, telecommunication laws have also some direct regulatory influence for using the wireless telecommunication technology especially satellite telecommunication. The Constitution relates with sovereignty whereas the telecommunication laws follow sovereignty and dispute settlement issues.

There are legislations on high-end technology like the Biotechnology law and Geospatial law. The National Geospatial Data Authority Bill for regulating the licencing of geospatial data by an Authority and the Draft of Vetting of Images and Geospatial Information for Licening for National Security (VIGIL) Act to regulate the dissemination of satellite images for geospatial information through internet and physical form. The recent developments have all just started or in the draft stage. Therefore the legal issues are only presumed unlike central and state Acts or policies; but the National Geospatial Data Authority Bill would like to impose licencing of geospatial data by an Authority, and the draft of VIGIL Act is made to keep intact national security. The geospatial law attracts sovereignty and national security.

There are Air Laws which could be extended or amended and may be called as 'aerospace law', for say, if required. Here safety is the main issue followed by financing.

Now in the case of laws for financing directly are banking, insurance, foreign exchange, revenue and export-import laws whereas the indirect legal support comes from laws related with infrastructure development, land, company, environment, IPR, safety, security and dispute settlement. Therefore it is not only the space policies where the legal issues like sovereignty, national security, IPR are reflected but also within the existing legislations.

Next are human resource development laws for capacity development in manpower. The significance of these laws is secondary in nature compared to laws for financing. There are three types of laws like (i) developing industry academia partnerships, (ii) recruiting the efficient manpower, and (iii) keeping and continuing the recruited manpower with labour turnover ratio low. The first type consists of Institute of Technology Act, JNU Act etc. The second type follows Foreigners Act and Citizenship Act. The third type consists of labour and welfare legislations.

The State Acts of A.P., Gujarat, Karnataka, Kerala, Maharashtra, Orissa and Tamil Nadu follow the same pattern.

Finally, there is some Act of National Capital Territory. It is based on geospatial technology which uses satellite remote sensing data. This is Delhi Geo-Spatial Data Infrastructure (Management Control, Administration, Security and Safety) Act, 2011. The national security issue is regulated here.

The regulations of private actors through institutions had not started at the beginning. It was the regulations for institution building for state. It was commenced with the International Geophysical Year (IGY) National Committee. But after the establishment of ISRO, the regulations for private actors through institution have slowly started. Afterwards the societies, private bodies, even business associations like CII, FICCI take the lead to contribute in making regulation for private actors.

Thus space regulations in India carry the same legal issues within its existing policies and legislations. But what are the effects and how much it influences to make regulation for private actors in outer space? It would require comparison of the international scenario of regulations with that of India. Therefore the very reply of this query brings the conclusion of this research study in the next and final chapter.

Notes

1. Data are provided from concerned websites of the government departments.
2. Scientific Policy Resolution, 1958, at http://www.dst.gov.in/stsysindia/spr1958.htm (Accessed August 12, 2013).
3. Ibid.
4. Ibid.
5. Vasantha, A., The Scientific Policy Resolution – A Landmark in Indian Science, 2000, at http://pib.nic.in/feature/feyr2000/fjan2000/f110120002.html (Accessed August 12, 2013).
6. Technology Policy Statement, 1983, at http://www.dst.gov.in/stsysindia/sps1983.htm (Accessed August 12, 2013).
7. Science and Technology Policy, 2003, at http://www.dst.gov.in/stsysindia/stp2003.htm (Accessed August 12, 2013).
8. Science, Technology & Innovation Policy, 2013, at http://www.dst.gov.in/sti-policy-eng.pdf (Accessed August 12, 2013).
9. Ibid.
10. http://www.isro.org/pdf/Outcome%20budget2013-14.pdf, pp. 106-110 (Accessed September 10, 2014).
11. Perspectives for a National GI Policy, at http://nias.res.in/docs/R11-2012-GI-Policy.pdf (Accessed September 30, 2013).
12. Ibid.
13. Remote Sensing Data Policy, 2011, at http://www.isro.gov.in/news/pdf/RSDP-2011.pdf (Accessed September 30, 2013)
14. See n. 11, p. 29.
15. http://agiindia.com/ (Accessed September 30, 2013).
16. See n. 11.
17. http://researchguides.library.yorku.ca/content.php?pid=245987&sid=2176375 (Accessed September 30, 2013)
18. See n. 11.
19. http://www.isro.org/pdf/Outcome%20budget2013-14.pdf, p. 13 (Accessed September 10, 2014)
20. Ibid., p. 10.
21. Satellite Communication Policy, at http://www.isro.gov.in/news/pdf/satcom-policy.pdf (Accessed August 15, 2013).
22. Ibid.
23. Ibid.
24. http://www.isro.gov.in/news/pdf/SATCOM-norms.pdf (Accessed August 15, 2013).
25. Ibid., Article 2.

26. Ibid.
27. Ibid.
28. Ibid.
29. Ibid.
30. Ibid., Article 3.
31. Ibid.
32. Ibid.
33. Ibid.
34. Ibid.
35. http://planningcommission.nic.in/aboutus/committee/wrkgrp12/sandt/wg_dos2905.pdf, p. 97 (Accessed August 12, 2013).
36. See n. 24.
37. Remote Sensing Data Policy, 2011, at http://www.isro.gov.in/news/pdf/RSDP-2011.pdf (Accessed August 15, 2013)
38. Ibid.
39. Ibid.
40. Ibid.
41. Ibid.
42. Ibid.
43. Ibid.
44. Ibid.
45. See n. 35, p. 98.
46. Technology Transfer Policy of ISRO, at http://www.isro.gov.in/ttg/pdfuploads/ISRO%20TT%20policy.pdf (Accessed August 18, 2013)
47. Ibid.
48. Ibid.
49. Ibid.
50. Ibid.
51. Intellectual Property Policy, at http://www.isro.gov.in/ttg/ippolicy.html (Accessed August 18, 2013)
52. Ibid.
53. National Telecom Policy, 1994, at http://www.dot.gov.in/telecom-polices/national-telecom-policy-1994 (Accessed August 20, 2013).
54. Ibid.
55. Ibid.
56. New Telecom Policy 1999, at http://www.dot.gov.in/telecom-polices/new-telecom-policy-1999 (Accessed August 20, 2013).
57. Ibid.
58. Ibid.
59. Ibid.
60. http://www.itu.int/en/ITUR/seminars/rrs/Documents/Tutorial/SM_Fundamentals_Part1.pdf (Accessed August 20, 2013)
61. http://www.dot.gov.in/sites/default/files/NTP-06.06.2012-final.pdf (Accessed August 20, 2013).
62. http://www.thehindu.com/business/Industry/postvodafone-telenor-issues-foreign-telcos-cautious/article5781163.ece (Accessed August 20, 2014).
63. Kalam, APJ A., *Wings of Fire*, 2003 (Hyderabad: Universities Press), p. 22.

64. Second rocket port depends on satellite size, cost-benefit: ISRO, at http://zeenews.india.com/news/space/second-rocket-port-depends-on-satellite-size-cost-benefit-isro_892348.html (Accessed November 26, 2013).
65. See n. 19, p. 12.
66. The National Rehabilitation and Resettlement Policy, 2007, at http://dolr.nic.in/dolr/downloads/pdfs/NRRP2007.pdf (Accessed August 21, 2013).
67. Draft National Land Reforms Policy, 2013, at http://dolr.nic.in/dolr/downloads/PDFs/draft%20National%20Land%20Reforms%20Policy%2024-Jul-2013.pdf (Accessed August 21, 2013).
68. Ibid.
69. http://hcp.co.in/file_manager/publications/Satellite-Imagery-and-GIS-in-Preparation-of-Dev-Plans_Research-Paper.pdf (Accessed August 21, 2013).
70. http://planningcommission.nic.in/aboutus/committee/wrkgrp11/wg11_subspace1.pdf (Accessed August 12, 2013).
71. Ibid.
72. http://planningcommission.nic.in/aboutus/committee/wrkgrp11/wg11_subspace.pdf , pp. 91-92 (Accessed August 12, 2013).
73. Ibid.
74. See n. 35.
75. Ibid.
76. Ibid.
77. http://treaties.un.org/pages/ViewDetailsIII.aspx?&src=TREATY&mtdsg_no=XXIV~1&chapter=24&Temp=mtdsg3&lang=en (Accessed August 15, 2013).
78. United Nations Register of Objects Launched into Outer Space: Notifications from India (Launch Year 1975-present), at http://www.oosa.unvienna.org/oosa/en/Reports/docsind.html (Accessed August 15, 2013).
79. http://www.isro.org/scripts/internationalcooperations.aspx (Accessed October 15, 2013).
80. http://www.isro.org/scripts/citizencharter.aspx (Accessed October 15, 2013).
81. See n. 74, p. 98.
82. See n. 19, p. 12 (Accessed September 10, 2014).
83. See n. 74.
84. http://www.isro.org/satellites/chandrayaan-1.aspx (Accessed September 10, 2014).
85. http://www.isro.org/mars/home.aspx (Accessed September 10, 2014).
86. See n. 70.
87. See n. 19.
88. Data are provided from the texts of these legislations. Details are within the analysis.
89. http://www.aero.iisc.ernet.in/page/history (Accessed November 2, 2014).
90. India's telecom industry is in a mess: Vodafone CEO, at http://www.business-standard.com/article/pti-stories/telecom-industry-in-india-is-a-mess-says-vodafone-india-chief-114091100773_1.html (Accessed November 3, 2014)
91. See n. 72.
92. Chowdhry, Kamla and Sarabhai, Vikram, "Organisation for Developmental Tasks: Atomic Energy Commission of India," *The Indian Journal of Public Administration*, vol. 14, no. 1, 1968, pp. 1-2.
93. Radhakrishnan, K., "Space Technology in India: Challenges Ahead", 10th Convocation Address delivered on 15 September 2012 at National Institute of Technology:

Warangal, 2012, at http://www.isro.org/Ourchairman/Present/_notes/NIT-W10th%20 Convocation%20Address.pdf (Accessed November 15, 2013)

94. See n. 35.
95. Constitution of India.
96. PCA adopts new rules of procedure, at http://pca-cpa.org/shownews.asp?ac=view&pag_ id=1261&nws_id=323 (Accessed August 16, 2013).
97. Ibid.
98. See n. 95.
99. Ibid.
100. http://cabsec.nic.in/allocation_firstschedule.php (Accessed March 10, 2014)
101. http://cabsec.nic.in/showpdf.php?type=allocation_first_shedule_abr43&special (Accessed March 10, 2014).
102. http://cabsec.nic.in/showpdf.php?type=allocation_secondschedule (Accessed March 10,2014)
103. http://cabsec.nic.in/showpdf.php?type=allocation_review (Accessed March 10, 2014).
104. Ibid.
105. Ibid.
106. Ibid.
107. Rao, P. Chandrasekhara, *The Indian Constitution and International Law* (New Delhi: Taxmann, 1993), p. 187.
108. http://www.wired.com/2013/09/plutonium-238-problem/all/ (Accessed March 10, 2014). See also http://www.hq.nasa.gov/office/hqlibrary/pathfinders/nuclear.htm (Accessed March 10, 2014).
109. http://www.marsfoundation.org/ (Accessed March 10, 2014).
110. Atomic Energy Act, 1962. http://dae.nic.in/?q=node/153 (Accessed August 16, 2013).
111. Ibid.
112. The Indian Telegraph Act, 1885, at http://www.dot.gov.in/sites/default/files/the_ indian_telegraph_act_1985_pdf.pdf (Accessed August 20, 2013)
113. Ibid.
114. Indian Wireless Telegraphy Act, 1933, at http://www.dot.gov.in/act-rules/india-wireless-act-1933 (Accessed August 20, 2013).
115. TRAI Act, at http://www.dot.gov.in/act-rules/telecom-regulatory-authority-indiatrai-act-1997 (Accessed August 20, 2013).
116. The Information Technology Act, 2000, http://www.dot.gov.in/sites/default/files/ itbill2000_0.pdf (Accessed August 20, 2013).
117. Ibid.
118. The Communication Convergence Bill, 2001, at http://www.dot.gov.in/sites/default/ files/CCBill_of_pages_41.pdf (Accessed August 20, 2013).
119. The Cable Television Networks (Regulation) Act, 1995, at https://www.google.co.in/ur l?sa=t&rct=j&q=&esrc=s&source=web&cd=1&sqi=2&ved=0CCkQFjAA&url=http% 3A%2F%2Ftdsat.nic.in%2Fbooks%2FTHE%2520CABLE%2520TELEVISION%25 20NETWORKS%2520(Regulation)%2520Act.doc&ei=jR1eUtLTNcz_rAeM0oCICA &usg=AFQjCNEw6ECE8znqp160dxDRHhqjSpA47w&cad=rjt (Accessed August 20, 2013).
120. http://bristolspaceplanes.com/ (Accessed August 31, 2014).
121. The Aircraft Act, 1934, at http://dgca.nic.in/airact/aircraftact.pdf (Accessed August 21, 2013).

122. Ibid.
123. The Suppression of Unlawful Acts against Safety of Civil Aviation Acts, 1982, at http://dgca.nic.in/nat_conv/NatConv_Chap10.pdf (Accessed August 21, 2013).
124. The Anti-hijacking Act, 1982, at http://dgca.nic.in/rules/natleg-ind.htm (Accessed August 21, 2013).
125. See n. 120.
126. The National Airports Authority Act, 1985, at http://dgca.nic.in/rules/natleg-ind.htm (Accessed August 21, 2013).
127. http://dgca.nic.in/rules/natleg-ind.htm (Accessed August 21, 2013).
128. The Foreign Aircraft (Exemption from Taxes & Duties on Fuel & Lubricants) Act, 2002, at http://www.helplinelaw.com/docs/the%20foreign%20aircraft%20(exemption%20from%20taxes%20and%20duties%20on%20fuel%20and%20lubricants)%20act,%202002 (Accessed August 21, 2013).
129. Service Sector Classification List of WTO, at https://www.google.co.in/search?q=space+transport+in+the+wto&oq=space+transport+in+the+wto&aqs=chrome..69i57.11996j0j8&sourceid=chrome&espv=210&es_sm=93&ie=UTF-8 (Accessed August 21, 2013).
130. The Airports Economic Regulatory Authority of India Act, 2008, at http://aera.gov.in/documents/pdf/AERA-Act2008.pdf (Accessed August 21, 2013).
131. The Biotechnology Regulatory Authority of India Bill, 2013, at http://www.prsindia.org/uploads/media/Biotech%20Regulatory/Biotechnology%20Regulatory%20Authority%20of%20India%20Bill.pdf (Accessed August 16, 2013).
132. http://www.novaspacebiotech.ch/company/ (Accessed September 12, 2014).
133. http://www.nasa.gov/centers/marshall/news/background/facts/microgravity.html and http://www.popularmechanics.com/science/health/4320853 (Accessed September 12, 2014).
134. See n. 35, p. 98, Para 5.2.4
135. Ibid.
136. Adhikari, M., *High Resolution Data Dissemination against the Background of National Security in India*, 2012. In Janssen, K. and Crompvoets, J. (Eds.), *Geographic Data and the Law Defining New Challenges* (Leuven: Leuven University Press), p. 133.
137. Indian Contract Act, 1872, at http://chddistrictcourts.gov.in/the%20indian%20contract%20act.pdf (Accessed August 16, 2013).
138. The Partnership Act, 1932, at http://www.mca.gov.in/Ministry/actsbills/pdf/Partnership_Act_1932.pdf (Accessed August 16, 2013).
139. http://shermanhoward.com/services/space/ (Accessed August 16, 2013).
140. The Industries (Development & Regulation) Act, 1951, at http://dipp.nic.in/English/Policies/Industries_act1951.pdf (Accessed August 24, 2013).
141. Technology Development Board Act, 1995, at http://www.tdb.gov.in/writereaddata/html_en_files/pdf/TDB_Act.pdf (Accessed August 21, 2013).
142. The Micro, Small and Medium Enterprises Development Act, 2006, at http://www.msmeodisha.gov.in/PDF/MSMED_Act.pdf (Accessed August 24, 2013).
143. Ibid.
144. The Science & Engineering Research Board Act, 2008, at http://www.egazette.kerala.gov.in/pdf/2010/18/part_01/science_and_engineering.pdf (Accessed August 24, 2013).
145. http://www.gisinindia.com/directory/gis-companies-in-india (Accessed September 11, 2014).

146. The Limited Liability Partnership Act, 2008, at http://www.mca.gov.in/Ministry/actsbills/pdf/LLP_Act_2008_15jan2009.pdf (Accessed August 2013).
147. Land Acquisition Act, 1894, at http://dolr.nic.in/dolr/LandAcquisitionAct1894.asp (Accessed August 21, 2013).
148. The National Highways Act, 1956, at http://www.nhai.org/act1956.htm (Accessed August 21, 2013).
149. Ibid.
150. The Special Economic Zones Act, 2005, at http://commerce.nic.in/aboutus/actspdfs/SEZ%20Act,%202005.pdf (Accessed August 21, 2013).
151. See Annexure I.
152. Devanathan, V. (2014, 1 February) Isro's Mahendragiri centre elevated, gets more powers, *The Hindu,* at http://timesofindia.indiatimes.com/home/science/Isros-Mahendragiri-centre-elevated-gets-more-powers/articleshow/29681520.cms (Accessed September 11, 2014).
153. The Companies Act, 1956, at http://www.mca.gov.in/Ministry/pdf/Companies_Act_1956_13jun2011.pdf (Accessed August 21, 2013).
154. The Preference Shares (Regulation of Dividends) Act, 1960, at http://indiankanoon.org/doc/452163/ (Accessed August 21, 2013).
155. The Securities & Exchange Board of India Act, 1992, at http://www.sebi.gov.in/acts/act15ac.html (Accessed August 21, 2013).
156. The Depositories Act, 1996, at https://nsdl.co.in/downloadables/act.pdf (Accessed August 21, 2013).
157. The Reserve Bank of India Act, 1934, at http://rbidocs.rbi.org.in/rdocs/Publications/PDFs/RBIA1934170510.pdf (Accessed August 23, 2013).
158. The Banking Regulation Act, 1949, at http://www.pnbindia.in/Upload/En/BANK%20REGULATION%20ACT.pdf (Accessed August 23, 2013).
159. Ibid.
160. The Export- Import Bank of India Act, 1981, at http://indiankanoon.org/doc/1084575/ (Accessed August 23, 2013).
161. Insurance Act, 1938, at http://financialservices.gov.in/Insurance/Acts/TheInsuranceAct_1938.pdf (Accessed August 17, 2013).
162. Ibid.
163. Insurance Regulatory and Development Authority Act, 1999, at http://www.irda.gov.in/admincms/cms/frmGeneral_Layout.aspx?page=PageNo108&flag=1&mid=Insurance%20Laws%20etc.%20%3E%3E%20Acts (Accessed August 17, 2013).
164. http://www.dot.gov.in/investment-promotion/fdi-policy-telecom (Accessed September 13, 2014).
165. COFEPOSA ACT, 1974, at http://finmin.nic.in/law/cofeposa.pdf (Accessed August 24, 2013).
166. http://finmin.nic.in/the_ministry/dept_eco_affairs/capital_market_div/FEMA_act_1999.pdf (Accessed August 24, 2013). ~~Customs Act, 1962~~.
167. The Foreign Contribution Regulation Act, 2010, at http://lawmin.nic.in/ld/regionallanguages/THE%20FOREIGN%20CONTRIBUTION%20(REGULATION)%20ACT,2010.%20(42%20OF%202010).pdf (Accessed August 24, 2013).
168. Customs Act, 1962, at http://www.eximguru.com/exim/indian-customs/customs-acts-1962/customs-act-1962-chapter-i-preliminary-short-title-extent-and-commencement-definitions.aspx (Accessed August 16, 2013).

169. See n. 90.
170. The Export (Quality Control & Inspection) Act, 1963, at http://commerce.nic.in/export_quality_control.htm (Accessed August 16, 2013).
171. The Research & Development Cess Act, 1986, at http://rna-cs.com/the-company-secretaries-amendment-bill-2010/ (Accessed August 21, 2013).
172. http://www.cbec.gov.in/customs/cs-act/formatted-htmls/cs-fortrade-regulation.html (Accessed August 16, 2013).
173. Income Tax Act, 1961, http://law.incometaxindia.gov.in/DIT/ (Accessed August 21, 2013).
174. Ibid., Section 10AA.
175. Ibid.
176. Ibid., Section 10B.
177. Ibid., Section 32A.
178. Ibid., Section 35.
179. Ibid., Section 35A.
180. Ibid., Section 35B.
181. Ibid., Section 35ABB.
182. Ibid., Section 80GGA.
183. Ibid.
184. http://www.taxindiaonline.com/RC2/pdfdocs/gazetteindia.pdf (Accessed August 21, 2013).
185. The Air (Prevention & Control of Pollution) Act, 1981, at http://www.envfor.nic.in/legis/air/air1.html (Accessed August 16, 2013).
186. Fawcett, J.E.S., *Outer Space New Challenges to Law and Policy* (Oxford: Clarendon Press, 1984), p. 33.
187. http://space.stackexchange.com/questions/1667/why-are-europe-s-air-space-academy-and-dlr-urging-esa-and-cnes-to-reconsider-t (Accessed September 13, 2014)
188. http://timesofindia.indiatimes.com/india/Isro-successfully-launches-indigenous-cryogenic-engine-powered-GSLV-D5/articleshow/28437867.cms (Accessed September 12, 2014).
189. Environment Protection Act, 1986, at http://envfor.nic.in/legis/env/env1.html (Accessed August 16, 2013).
190. Kellman, B.,Environmental Governance of Space under Law, *2nd Manfred Lachs International Conference on Global Space Governance*, Mcgill University, Quebec, May 30, 2014.
191. See n. 189.
192. Ibid.
193. The Energy Conservation Act, 2001, at http://www.powermin.nic.in/acts_notification/pdf/ecact2001.pdf (Accessed August 24, 2013).
194. The Coastal Aquaculture Authority Act, 2005, at http://previous.wiego.org/informal_economy_law/india/content/fw_coastal_2005.pdf (Accessed August 24, 2013).
195. A spaceport for Tuticorin?, at http://articles.timesofindia.indiatimes.com/2013-08-23/science/41439533_1_gslv-lpsc-tuticorin-district (Accessed August 24, 2013).
196. Madhumathi, D.S., ISRO's 2nd space port to be a 'polar shift'? *The Hindu, September 15, 2013,* at http://www.thehindubusinessline.com/industry-and-economy/isros-2nd-space-port-to-be-a-polar-shift/article2455936.ece (Accessed September 24, 2013).
197. http://www.isro.org/update/18-dec-2014/first-experimental-flight-of-indias-next-

generation-launch-vehicle-gslv-mk-iii (Accessed August 18, 2013)

198. See Annexure I.
199. Technology Offers, at http://www.isro.gov.in/ttg/technologyoffers.html (Accessed August 18, 2013)
200. http://www.isro.gov.in/ttg/pdfuploads/Technologies%20on%20Offer%20for%20 Know%20How%20Transfer.pdf (Accessed August 18, 2013).
201. http://www.isro.gov.in/ttg/copyrights.html (Accessed August 18, 2013)
202. http://www.isro.gov.in/ttg/copyrights_more.html (Accessed August 18, 2013)
203. Indian Copyright Act 1957. http://copyright.gov.in/Documents/CopyrightRules1957. pdf (Accessed August 18, 2013)
204. http://www.isro.gov.in/ttg/patent.html (Accessed August 18, 2013).
205. http://www.isro.gov.in/ttg/trademark.html (Accessed August 18, 2013).
206. The Designs Act, 2000, http://ipindia.nic.in/ipr/design/design_act.PDF (Accessed August 18, 2013).
207. The Semiconductor Integrated Circuits Layout-Design Act, 2000, http://www. krishnaandsaurastri.com/pdfs/ic_act.pdf (Accessed August 24, 2013).
208. See n. 200.
209. http://www.spaceflightnow.com/falcon9/010/140622scrub/#.VBsWFfldUv0 (Accessed September 12, 2014)
210. Explosives Act, 1884, at http://dipp.nic.in/English/acts_rules/Acts/Explosive_ Act_1884.pdf (Accessed August, 2013).
211. The Explosive Substances Act, 1908, at http://dipp.nic.in/English/acts_rules/Acts/ Explosive_Act_1884.pdf (Accessed August, 2013). http://www.mha.nic.in/pdfs/ ExplosiveSubstances%20Act1908.pdf (Accessed August, 2013).
212. Rocket motors destroyed in fire at Sriharikota Space Centre, at http://www.thehindu. com/news/national/andhra-pradesh/rocket-motors-destroyed-in-fire-at-sriharikota-space-centre/article5352423.ece (Accessed November 16, 2013).
213. http://science.howstuffworks.com/rocket3.htm (Accessed November 16, 2013).
214. The Inflammable Substances Act, 1952, at http://www.indiankanoon.org/doc/1565906/ (Accessed August 24, 2013).
215. The Dangerous Machines (Regulation) Act, 1983, at http://agricoop.nic.in/sublegiaim. pdf (Accessed August 24, 2013).
216. The Central Industrial Security Force Act, 1968, at http://www.mha.nic.in/pdfs/ cisfact1968.pdf (Accessed August 23, 2013).
217. http://mha.nic.in/hindi/sites/upload_files/mhahindi/files/pdf/Citi_Chart111208.pdf (Accessed August 23, 2013).
218. The National Security Act, 1980, at http://www.mha.nic.in/pdfs/National_Security_ Act1980.pdf (Accessed August 23, 2013).
219. The Private Security Agencies (Regulation) Act, 2005, at http://www.mha.nic.in/pdfs/ PS_Agencies_Regulation_Act2005.pdf (Accessed August 23, 2013).
220. The Comptroller and Auditor-General (Duties, Power and Conditions of Service Act), 1971, at http://www.cag.gov.in/html/about_legal_dpc.htm (Accessed August 24, 2013).
221. http://www.hindu.com/thehindu/thscrip/print.pl?file=20120309290403100. htm&date=fl2904/&prd=fline& (Accessed August 24, 2013).
222. Anand, Utkarsh, Supreme Court allows CAG to audit private telecom firms, *The Indian Express,* April 17, 2014, at http://indianexpress.com/article/cities/delhi/supreme-court-allows-cag-to-audit-private-telecom-firms/99/

223. The Central Vigilance Commission Act, 2003, at http://cvc.nic.in/cvcact.pdf (Accessed August 24, 2013).
224. Raj, N. Gopal, Norms and procedures flouted in Antrix-Devas deal. *The Hindu,* February 6, 2012, at http://www.thehindu.com/news/national/norms-and-procedures-flouted-in-antrixdevas-deal/article2863453.ece (Accessed August 24, 2013)
225. The Right to Information Act, 2005, at http://www.rtiindia.org/act/ (Accessed August 24, 2013).
226. http://www.isro.org/scripts/righttoinformation.aspx (Accessed August 24, 2013).
227. Ibid., at http://www.isro.org/scripts/citizencharter.aspx (Accessed August 24, 2013).
228. The Indian Penal Code, 1860, at http://www.mha.nic.in/pdfs/IPC1860.pdf (Accessed August 21, 2013).
229. The Code of Criminal Procedure, 1973, at http://www.mha.nic.in/pdfs/ccp1973.pdf (Accessed August 21, 2013).
230. The Economic Offences (Inapplicability of Limitation) Act, 1974, at https://www.google.co.in/search?q=Destruction+of+Records+Act+1917&oq=Destruction+of+Records+Act+1917&aqs=chrome..69i57j0.1473j0j8&sourceid=chrome&espv=210&es_sm=93&ie=UTF-8#es_sm=93&espv=210&q=Economic+Offences+(Inapplicability+of+Limitation)+Act%09%09%09%091974 (Accessed August 21, 2013).
231. See n. 61.
232. Consumer Protection Act, 1986, at http://www.ncdrc.nic.in/1_1.html (Accessed August 21, 2013)
233. Arbitration & Conciliation Act, 1996, at http://keralamediation.gov.in/AC%20Act.pdf (Accessed August 16, 2013).
234. Ibid.
235. http://articles.economictimes.indiatimes.com/2014-07-11/news/51354609_1_india-netherlands-bilateral-investment-treaty-retrospective-tax-amendment-tax-demand (Accessed August 16, 2014).
236. file:///C:/Users/DELL/Downloads/Outer%20Space%20Rules.pdf (Accessed August 24, 2013).
237. The Competition Act, 2002, at http://www.cci.gov.in/images/media/competition_act/act2002.pdf (Accessed August 24, 2013).
238. http://www.ryot.org/competition-for-spacex-orbital-sciences-cargo-ship-rockets-toward-iss/375173 (Accessed September 14, 2014).
239. The Foreigners Act, 1946, at http://mha.nic.in/pdfs/The%20Foreigners%20Act,%201946.pdf (Accessed August 24, 2013).
240. The Citizenship Act, 1955, at http://mha.nic.in/pdfs/ic_act55.pdf (Accessed August 24, 2013).
241. NASA Keeps Chinese Away From Aliens, at http://www.bloomberg.com/news/2013-10-09/nasa-keeps-chinese-away-from-aliens.html (Accessed August 24, 2013). Yanrong, Zhao, China hits at NASA's conference ban, *China Daily,* October 10, 2013, p. 12.
242. See n. 84.
243. See n. 85.
244. http://www.airbus.com/company/worldwide-presence/airbus-in-india/ (Accessed September 14, 2014).
245. The Institutes of Technology Act, 1961, at http://www.iitb.ac.in/legal/IITsAct.pdf (Accessed August 24, 2013).

246. Rao, U.R., *India's Rise as a Space Power* (New Delhi: Foundation Books, 2014), p. 191.
247. http://www.isro.org/satellites/jugnu.aspx (Accessed August 24, 2013).
248. IIT Bombay, at http://www.aero.iitb.ac.in/home/index.php?option=com_content&task=view&id=13&Itemid=21 (Accessed August 24, 2013).
249. Ibid. http://www.aero.iitb.ac.in/home/index.php?option=com_content&task=view&id=36&Itemid=45 (Accessed August 24, 2013).
250. Ibid. http://www.aero.iitb.ac.in/pratham/index.php (Accessed August 24, 2013).
251. Ibid. http://www.aero.iitb.ac.in/pratham/prathamglobal.php; http://www.aero.iitb.ac.in/pratham/Satellite_2_website/team.php (Accessed August 24, 2013).
252. The Jawaharlal Nehru University Act, 1966, Section 5, at http://www.jnu.ac.in/RTI/Act%20&%20Statutes/ACT.pdf (Accessed August 24, 2013).
253. Ibid., Section 5 (14).
254. Ibid., Section 5 (18).
255. http://www.jnu.ac.in/SIS/CILS/ (Accessed August 24, 2013)
256. http://www.jnu.ac.in/AboutJNU/RecognisedInstitutes.asp; See also http://www.rri.res.in/history_overview.html; http://www.iucaa.ernet.in/Mission.html (Accessed August 24, 2013)
257. http://www.jnu.ac.in/Faculty/bctripathy/; Also http://spacescience.arc.nasa.gov/page/post-doctoral-research-space-science-astrobiology-division (Accessed August 24, 2013)
258. The Rajiv Gandhi National Aviation University 2013, at http://indiacode.nic.in/acts-in-pdf/262013.pdf (Accessed August 24, 2013).
259. Ibid., Section 4(i).
260. Ibid., Section 5(1) (v).
261. The Workmen's Compensation Act, 1923, at http://www.coalindia.in/Documents/MineSafety/Workmens_Compensation_Act_1923_28022013.pdf (Accessed August 24, 2013).
262. Industrial Employment (Standing Orders) Act, 1946, at http://pblabour.gov.in/pdf/acts_rules/industrial_employment_standing_orders_act_1946.pdf (Accessed August 24, 2013).
263. Apprentices Act, 1961, at http://mhrd.gov.in/sites/upload_files/mhrd/files/ApprenticeAct1961.pdf (Accessed August 23, 2013).
264. The Industrial Disputes Act, 1947, at http://pblabour.gov.in/pdf/acts_rules/inustrial_disputes_act_1947.pdf (Accessed August 24, 2013).
265. The Factories Act, 1948, at http://labour.nic.in/upload/uploadfiles/files/ActsandRules/Service_and_Employment/The%20Factories%20Act,%201948.pdf (Accessed August 24, 2013)
266. Employees' State Insurance Act, 1948, at http://labour.nic.in/upload/uploadfiles/files/ActsandRules/SocitySecurity/TheEmployeesAct1948.pdf (Accessed August 24, 2013).
267. http://www.epfindia.com/EPFAct1952.pdf (Accessed August 24, 2013).
268. The Payment of Bonus Act, 1965, at http://pblabour.gov.in/pdf/acts_rules/payment_of_bonus_act_1965.pdf (Accessed August 24, 2013).
269. The Payment of Gratuity Act, 1972, at http://labour.nic.in/upload/uploadfiles/files/ActsandRules/SocitySecurity/ThePaymentofGratuityAct1972.pdf (Accessed August 24, 2013).
270. The Bhopal Gas Leak Disaster (Processing of Claims) Act, 1985, at http://chemicals.nic.in/Bhopal_Gas_file1.pdf (Accessed August 23, 2013).

271. http://www.isro.org/rep2014/ISI.html (Accessed September 14, 2014).
272. See n. 64 and 152.
273. See n. 197.
274. See Annexure I.
275. http://www.thehindubusinessline.com/industry-and-economy/logistics/hyderabads-aerospace-hub-bets-on-firstmover-advantage/article3932313.ece (Accessed August 24, 2013).
276. The Industrial Dispute (Andhra Pradesh Amendment) Act, 1987, at http://www.lawsofindia.org/pdf/andhra_pradesh/1987/1987AP32.pdf (Accessed August 24, 2013).
277. The Andhra Pradesh Infrastructure Development Corporation Act, 1998, at http://www.lawsofindia.org/pdf/andhra_pradesh/1998/1998AP37.pdf (Accessed August 24, 2013).
278. The Andhra Pradesh Industrial Workers (Representation) Participation in Management and Relief) Act, 1998, at http://www.lawsofindia.org/pdf/andhra_pradesh/1998/1998AP24.pdf (Accessed August 24, 2013).
279. The Andhra Pradesh Infrastructure Development Enabling Act, 2001, at http://www.lawsofindia.org/pdf/andhra_pradesh/2001/2001AP36.pdf (Accessed August 24, 2013).
280. Ibid.
281. The Andhra Pradesh Industrial Single Window Clearance Act, 2002, at http://www.lawsofindia.org/pdf/andhra_pradesh/2002/2002AP17.pdf (Accessed August 24, 2013).
282. http://www.apindustries.gov.in/FAQs.aspx (Accessed August 24, 2013).
283. The A.P. Special Economic Zone Bill, 2005, at http://tmarch.biz/India/APSEZ%20Bill%20-%202005.pdf (Accessed August 24, 2013).
284. List of formal approvals granted under the SEZ Act, 2005, at http://sezindia.nic.in/writereaddata/pdf/ListofFormalapprovals.pdf (Accessed August 24, 2013).
285. http://www.apindustries.gov.in/Library/SEZ1.pdf (Accessed August 24, 2013).
286. SEZ for aerospace & precision engineering, at http://cm.ap.gov.in/excmysr/15jul08press1.asp (Accessed August 24, 2013)
287. Special Correspondent (2013). "Huge potential for Indian industry in defence sector: DRDO chief", at http://www.thehindu.com/news/national/huge-potential-for-indian-industry-in-defence-sector-drdo-chief/article5315067.ece (Accessed November 6, 2013).
288. See n. 19, p. 12.
289. The Jawaharlal Nehru Technical University Act, 2008, at http://www.jntuk.edu.in/assets/images/JNTUACT.pdf (Accessed November 6, 2013).
290. http://www.prl.res.in/ (Accessed August 2013).
291. Department of Science and Technology, Government of Gujarat, at http://dst.gujarat.gov.in/introduction.htm (Accessed August 24, 2013).
292. Bhaskaracharya Institute for Space Applications and Geo-Informatics, at http://www.bisag.gujarat.gov.in/coll.htm (Accessed August 24, 2013).
293. The Gujarat Industrial Relations Act, 1946, at http://lpd.gujarat.gov.in/allpdfs/XI-1947.pdf (Accessed August 24, 2013)
294. The Gujarat Co-Operative Societies Act, 1961, at http://lpd.gujarat.gov.in/allpdfs/X-1962.pdf (Accessed August 24, 2013).
295. The Gujarat Land Acquisition (Industrial Areas) Act, 1961, at http://www.lawsofindia.org/pdf/gujarat/1961/1961GUJARAT46.pdf (Accessed August 24, 2013).
296. The Gujarat Industrial Development Act, 1962, at http://www.lawsofindia.org/pdf/gujarat/1962/1962GUJARAT23.pdf (Accessed August 24, 2013)

297. The State Tax on Professions, Trades, Callings and Employments Act, Gujarat, 1976, at http://www.rmc.gov.in/PRPFESSION%20TAX%20ACT.pdf (Accessed August 24, 2013).

298. The Gujarat Infrastructure Development Act, 1999, at http://www.lawsofindia.org/pdf/gujarat/1999/1999GUJARAT11.pdf (Accessed August 24, 2013).

299. The Gujarat Special Economic Zone Act, 2004, at http://www.lawsofindia.org/pdf/gujarat/2004/2004GUJARAT11.pdf (Accessed August 24, 2013).

300. Gujarat Special Investment Region Act, 2009, at http://www.gidc.gov.in/pdf/act-and-rules/SIR_ACT_new.pdf (Accessed August 24, 2013).

301. India's first Geospatial Technology Park to be set up in Gujarat, at http://www.narendramodi.in/india%E2%80%99s-first-geospatial-technology-park-to-be-set-up-in-gujarat/ (Accessed August 24, 2013).

302. http://bisag.gujarat.gov.in/ (Accessed August 24, 2013).

303. The NIRMA University of Science & Technology Act, 2003, Section 4 (7), at http://www.lawsofindia.org/pdf/gujarat/2003/2003GUJARAT10.pdf (Accessed August 24, 2013).

304. The Dhirubhai Ambani Institute of Information and Communication Technology Act, 2003, Sections 4 (v) & (vii), at http://www.lawsofindia.org/pdf/gujarat/2003/2003GUJARAT6.pdf (Accessed August 24, 2013).

305. The Ganpat University Act, Section 4 (6), at http://www.ganpatuniversity.ac.in/sites/default/files/arfile/Ganpat%20University%20Act%28Act%20No.%2019%20of%202005%29.pdf (Accessed August 24, 2013)

306. The Centre for Environmental Planning and Technology University Act, 2005, Section 4 (iii), at http://www.lawsofindia.org/pdf/gujarat/2005/2005GUJARAT24.pdf (Accessed August 24, 2013)

307. The Gujarat Technological University Act, 2007, Section 5 (v) and (vii), at http://www.lawsofindia.org/pdf/gujarat/2007/2007GUJARAT20.pdf (Accessed August 24, 2013).

308. The Karnataka Co-operative Societies Act, 1959, at http://www.legalcrystal.com/acts/description/61983 (Accessed August 24, 2013).

309. The Karnataka Industrial Areas Development Act, 1966, at http://www.lawsofindia.org/pdf/karnataka/1966/1966KR18.pdf (Accessed August 24, 2013).

310. The Karnataka Industries (Facilitation) Act, 2002, at http://www.lawsofindia.org/pdf/karnataka/2003/2003KR45.pdf (Accessed August 24, 2013).

311. The Karnataka Information Technology Investment Regions Act, 2010, at http://dpal.kar.nic.in/ao2010/37of2010%20(E).pdf (Accessed August 24, 2013).

312. Karnataka Policy for SEZ 2009, at http://sezindia.nic.in/writereaddata/statePolicies/state%20policy%20of%20sez%2020091.pdf (Accessed August 24, 2013).

313. Lease Agreement Format for Bengaluru Aerospace SEZ, at http://bangaloreaerospacepark.com/downloads/LEASE_AGREEMENT_AEROSPACE_SEZ_format.pdf?TB_iframe=true&height=450&width=850 (Accessed August 24, 2013)

314. List of Formal Approvals granted under the SEZ Act, 2005, at http://sezindia.nic.in/writereaddata/pdf/ListofFormalapprovals.pdf (Accessed August 24, 2013).

315. http://bangaloreaerospacepark.com/facilities/bengaluru-aerospace-park.html (Accessed August 24, 2013).

316. Vellore Institute of Technology Bangalore Act, 2012, Section 7, at http://dpal.kar.nic.in/ao2013/14of2013(E).pdf (Accessed August 24, 2013).

317. M. S. Ramaiah University of Applied Sciences Act, 2012, at http://dpal.kar.nic.in/

ao2013/15of2013(E).pdf (Accessed August 24, 2013).

318. The KLE Technological University 2012, at http://dpal.kar.nic.in/ao2013/22of2013(E).pdf (Accessed August 24, 2013).
319. The Rai Technology University, Bangalore Act, 2012, Section 7 (1) (a) & 7 (iv), at http://dpal.kar.nic.in/ao2013/40of2013(E).pdf (Accessed August 24, 2013).
320. J.S.S. Science and Technology University Act, 2013, Section 7 (v), at http://dpal.kar.nic.in/ao2013/43of2013(E).pdf (Accessed August 24, 2013).
321. Team STUDSAT, at http://www.teamstudsat.com/about1.html and http://www.nmit.ac.in/Centerforsmallsatellite.aspx?LinkId=46 (Accessed August 24, 2013).
322. http://www.aprsaf.org/participants/countries/india.php (Accessed August 24, 2013).
323. http://www.isro.org/satellites/studsat.aspx (Accessed August 24, 2013).
324. Ibid.
325. http://www.nmit.ac.in/Index.aspx (Accessed August 24, 2013).
326. Karnataka Industrial Policy 2009-2014, at http://www.karnatakaindustry.gov.in/documents/Karnataka%20Industrial%20Policy%202009-14%20English.pdf (Accessed August 24, 2013).
327. Karnataka – Israel Program for Industrial R&D (KIRD), at http://kscst.org.in/kird_files/karnataka_israel_program_guidelines.pdf (Accessed August 24, 2013).
328. Lele, A., *Asian Space Race: Rhetoric or Reality*? (New Delhi: Springer, 2013) (India).
329. See Annexure I.
330. Emerging Kerala 2012, at http://www.emergingkerala2012.org/ (Accessed August 24, 2013).
331. SIFL Ltd., at http://www.siflindia.com/ (Accessed August 24, 2013).
332. Aeronautical Material Testing Laboratory at SIFL, at http://www.emergingkerala2012.org/pdf/Airport%20Infra,%20Aerospace%20&%20Helicopter%20services/aeronautical-material-testing-sifl.pdf (Accessed August 24, 2013).
333. Aerospace Park at Kadinamkulam, at http://www.emergingkerala2012.org/pdf/Airport%20Infra,%20Aerospace%20&%20Helicopter%20services/Aerospace%20Park,%20Kadinamkulam.pdf (Accessed August 25, 2013).
334. The Travancore -Cochin Literary, Scientific and Charitable Societies Registration Act, 1955, at http://keralalawsect.org/index.php?option=com_wrapper&view=wrapper&Itemid=135 (Accessed August 24, 2013).
335. Indian Institute of Space Science & Technology, at http://www.iist.ac.in/about-us/about-iist (Accessed August 24, 2013).
336. The Industrial Disputes (Kerala) Amendment Act, 1961, at http://www.keralalawsect.org/images/1961/act%2028%20of%201961.pdf (Accessed August 24, 2013).
337. The Kerala State Aid to Industries Act, 1963, at http://www.lawsofindia.org/pdf/kerala/1963/1963KERALA34.pdf (Accessed August 24, 2013).
338. The Kerala Co-operative Societies Act, 1969, at http://www.keralalawsect.org/images/1969/act%2021.pdf (Accessed August 24, 2013).
339. The Kerala Industrial Infrastructure Development Act, 1993, at http://www.lawsofindia.org/pdf/kerala/1993/1993KERALA3.pdf (Accessed August 25, 2013).
340. The Kerala Industrial Revitalisation Fund Act, 1999, at http://www.lawsofindia.org/pdf/kerala/1999/1999KERALA19.pdf (Accessed August 24, 2013).
341. Ibid.
342. The Cochin University of Science and Technology Act, 1986, at http://www.lawsofindia.org/pdf/kerala/1986/1986KERALA31.pdf (Accessed August 25, 2013).

343. Ibid.
344. Banerjee, Sreekumar, "Founder's Day Speech", Lecture delivered on October 30, 2007 at *Bhabha Atomic Research Centre*, Mumbai, 2007, at http://www.barc.gov.in/presentations/fddir07.html (Accessed August 25, 2013).
345. The Maharashtra Industrial Development Act, 1961, at http://bombayhighcourt.nic.in/libweb/acts/1962.03.pdf(Accessed August 25, 2013).
346. The Babasaheb Ambedkar Technological University Act, 1969, Section 4, at http://bombayhighcourt.nic.in/libweb/acts/1989.22.pdf (Accessed August 25, 2013).
347. The Rajiv Gandhi Science & Technology Commission Act, 2004, Section 6, at http://bombayhighcourt.nic.in/libweb/acts/2004.15.pdf (Accessed August, 2013).
348. http://timesofindia.indiatimes.com/india/Agni-V-missile-successfully-test-launched-from-Wheeler-Island-off-Odisha-coast/articleshow/22594796.cms (Accessed September 24, 2013).
349. http://www.odishareporter.in/top_news/nuclear-capable-agni-iii-ballistic-missile-test-fired-from-wheeler-island (Accessed January 12, 2013).
350. See n. 196.
351. The Orissa State-Aid to Industries Act, 1978, at http://www.lawsofindia.org/pdf/orissa/1978/1978OR32.pdf (Accessed August 25, 2013).
352. The Orissa Industrial Infrastructure Development Corporation Act, 1980, at http://www.lawsofindia.org/pdf/orissa/1981/1981OR1.pdf (Accessed August 25, 2013).
353. The Biju Patnaik University of Technology Act, 2002, Section 4 (5), at http://218.248.11.68/industries/PDF/BPUT_Act_2002.pdf (Accessed August 25, 2013).
354. The Orissa Industries (Facilitation) Act, 2004, at http://www.lawsofindia.org/pdf/orissa/2004/2004OR14.pdf (Accessed August 25, 2013).
355. The Tamil Nadu State Aid to Industries Act, 1922, at http://www.lawsofindia.org/pdf/tamil_nadu/1923/1923TN5.pdf (Accessed August 26, 2013).
356. The Anna University Chennai Act, 1978, Section 4 (iv), at http://www.annauniv.edu/act&statutes.pdf (Accessed August 26, 2013).
357. The Tamil Nadu Industrial Establishments (Conferment of Permanent Status to Workmen) Act, 1981, at http://www.lawsofindia.org/pdf/tamil_nadu/1981/1981TN46.pdf (Accessed August 26, 2013).
358. The Tamil Nadu Taxation Special Tribunal Act, 1992, at http://www.lawsofindia.org/pdf/tamil_nadu/1992/1992TN42.pdf (Accessed August 26, 2013).
359. The Tamil Nadu Acquisition of Land for Industrial Purposes Act, 1997, at http://www.lawsofindia.org/pdf/tamil_nadu/1999/1999TN10.pdf (Accessed August 26, 2013).
360. The Tamil Nadu Industrial Township Area Development Authority Act, 1997, at http://www.lawsofindia.org/pdf/tamil_nadu/1997/1997TN33.pdf (Accessed August 26, 2013).
361. Supra n. 356, Section 4 (iv), at
362. http://planningcommission.nic.in/aboutus/committee/wrkgrp11/wg11_subspace.pdf (Accessed November 15, 2013).
363. http://www.isro.org/satellites/ANUSAT.aspx (Accessed August 26, 2013).
364. https://www.annauniv.edu/aboutus.php (Accessed August 26, 2013).
365. http://tidco.tn.gov.in/upload/writeupontidco.pdf (Accessed August 26, 2013).
366. http://timesofindia.indiatimes.com/home/science/Isros-Mahendragiri-centre-elevated-gets-more-powers/articleshow/29681520.cms and http://www.deccanchronicle.com/131120/news-current-affairs/article/karunanidhi-wants-isros-third-launch-pad-be-

established-tamil (Accessed February 15, 2014).

367. http://planningcommission.nic.in/aboutus/committee/wrkgrp12/sandt/wg_dos2905.pdf (Accessed September 30, 2013)
368. Data are provided from websites of concerned Institutions. Details are within the analysis.
369. Kochar, R., "Science as a Symbol of New Nationhood: India and the International Geophysical Year 1957-58," *Current Science*, vol. 94, no. 6, 2008, pp. 813-816.
370. See n. 290.
371. http://www.prl.res.in/website_english1/about/hist.php (Accessed August 12, 2013).
372. http://www.aes-ahmedabad.ac.in/index.html (Accessed August 12, 2013).
373. See n. 290.
374. Sarabhai, M., *The Voice of the Heart* (New Delhi: Harper Collins, 2004), p. 149.
375. NASA Oral History Transcript (Interview of Arnold W. Frutkin), at http://www.jsc.nasa.gov/history/oral_histories/NASA_HQ/Administrators/FrutkinAW/FrutkinAW_1-11-02.pdf (Accessed August 12, 2013)
376. Ibid.
377. Mitra, A. P., "India in Global Science: Are We Ready for it?" *Journal of the Asiatic Society*, vol. 49, no. 2, 2007, p. 9.
378. Department of Atomic Energy, at http://dae.nic.in/ (Accessed August 14, 2013).
379. Kulkarni, R.P. & Sarma, V., *Homi Bhabha Father of Nuclear Science in India* (Bombay: Popular Prakashan, 1969), p. 33.
380. http://planningcommission.nic.in/plans/planrel/fiveyr/welcome.html (Accessed November 14, 2014).
381. See n. 70.
382. See n. 35.
383. COSPAR, at http://www.icsu.org/what-we-do/interdisciplinary-bodies/cospar (Accessed August 14, 2013).
384. Rao, P.V.M. and Radhakrishnan, P., *A Brief History of Rocketry and ISRO* (Hyderabad: University Press, 2012), p. 5.
385. Ibid.
386. Ibid.
387. Ibid., pp. 23-28.
388. Anderson, Robert S., *Nucleus and Nation: Scientists, International Networks, and Power in India* (Chicago: The University of Chicago Press, 2010), p. 403. See also Shah, A., *Vikram Sarabhai A Life* (New Delhi: Penguin Books India, 2007), pp. 120-142.
389. http://www.vssc.gov.in/internet/compRepository/mediagallery/-1/Test/vssc.htm (Accessed August 14, 2013).
390. ISRO, at http://www.isro.org/scripts/milestones.aspx (Accessed August 14, 2013).
391. Ibid., at http://www.isro.org/pdf/Organisation.pdf (Accessed August 14, 2013).
392. Prime Minister's Office, at http://pmindia.gov.in/rti.php?nodeid=19 (Accessed August 14, 2013).
393. Ibid., at http://www.isro.org/isrocentres/bangalore_spacecommission.aspx (Accessed August 14, 2013).
394. Ibid.
395. http://www.isro.org/pdf/Organisation.pdf (Accessed August 14, 2013). See also at http://www.isro.org/pdf/Outcome%20budget2013-14.pdf, Para 2.2 (Accessed September 10, 2014)

396. Ibid.
397. ANTRIX Ltd., at http://www.antrix.gov.in/aboutus.html (Accessed August 14, 2013).
398. http://www.antrix.gov.in/clients.html (Accessed August 14, 2013).
399. http://www.siati.org/ (Accessed November 13, 2014).
400. http://www.siati.org/about.html (Accessed November 13, 2014).
401. Ibid.
402. http://www.siati.org/objective.html (Accessed November 13, 2014).
403. http://www.cii.in/about_us_History.aspx?enc=ns9fJzmNKJnsoQCyKqUmaQ== (Accessed November 13, 2014).
404. http://www.bsxindia.com/index.asp (Accessed November 13, 2014).
405. http://www.bsxindia.com/pdf/list_of_exhibitors-2014.pdf (Accessed November 13, 2014).
406. http://www.ficci.com/sector-overview.asp?secid=85 (Accessed November 13, 2014).
407. http://www.ficci.com/sector-policy-recommendations.asp?secid=85, p. 49 (Accessed November 13, 2014).
408. Ibid., p. 51.
409. Ibid., pp. 59-65.
410. http://www.ficci.com/sector-government.asp?secid=85 (Accessed November 13, 2014).
411. http://agiindia.com/about-us/objectives/;http://agiindia.com/what-we-do/advisory-initiatives/ (Accessed November 13, 2014).
412. http://www.coai.com/About-Us/About-COAI (Accessed November 13, 2014).
413. http://www.coai.com/Reports-and-Papers/COAI-White-Papers (Accessed November 13, 2014).
414. http://www.coai.com/Reports-and-Papers/COAI-Responses-on-Industry-Issues/To-TRAI (Accessed November 13, 2014).
415. Das Gupta, S. & Mitra, S. (November 19, 2014, Business Standard, p. 4), 'DoT, Defence ministry resolve spectrum swapping issue'.
416. http://www.readersdigest.ca/home-garden/do-it-yourself/10-unbelievably-cool-ways-use-your-smartphone?id=10 (Accessed November 30, 2014).
417. Adhikari, M., "Developing Space Law Education in India: Some Proposals", *Rostrum's Law Review*, vol. I, no. 4, at http://rostrumlegal.com/blog/developing-space-law-education-in-india-some-proposals-by-malay-adhikari/ (Accessed November 13, 2014).

VI. Conclusion

This research study encompasses the historical background starting from astronomy to astronautics, and then technology (astronautics) to regulations. It has helped the countries to carve out their own regulatory responses based on history of outer space.

However, an analysis of history has been done within limited scope of this research study. It has covered different aspects alike astronomy, astronautics, different applications of space technology along with its actors, international space law and space regulations of different countries including India. Thus, it seems, there is no doubt that the history of one country differs from another country. The same is true for private actors e.g. from one company to another.

At the outset, it is clearly mentioned that the technology and its advancement depend on the society, culture of a country as well as that of a company itself. Moreover, the technological prowess could not be compared with one country super developed in space technology with another having low profile in this regard. In case of developing or under developed countries in space technology, the other political and sociological issues decide the momentum of advancement of high-end technology like space.

This research study is an attempt to analyse the regulation of private actors in outer space. But there is not much international regulation till now. It is gradually growing. In such a scenario, the study of India's role becomes important as a rising space power in the 21st century with a good possibility for framing dedicated space regulation.

Chapter I has analysed history from the ancient times. It begins with the early history of astronomy. The findings are that India had very rich heritage in astronomy which was found within its ancient texts written by a large number of scholars from different parts of India. But after sometime, there was fall in scholarship. On the other hand, the Western scholars showed their prowess. For instance, a theoretical study was done to break out gravitational pull of the earth. The pioneers in Western countries like Tislokovosky commenced this work in modern times.

The gun-powder rockets had been discovered before this by the Chinese people and this technology had been transferred from China to the Western world. India had been enjoying this technology with the great fascination from the time of Tipu Sultan. He used it for rockets in his various battles with the British. It is the Western countries who got the opportunity to develop this rocket technology further and applied it for fighting battles but in a more sophisticated way. Therefore if the role of India is considered here for the purpose of this research study, it seems Tipu Sultan unknowingly acted as the early oriental communicator to develop the rocket technology that came to be enriched by the West.

Rockets were invented during World War I. Still it was World War II which showed extensive uses of the modern rocket technology made by the Germans. The whole world was just mesmerised with the attack of vengeance weapons (V-2 rockets). During these World War periods, there were a few scientists who became the visionaries of humanity like Vaun Braun, Oberth, and Goddard. Their tireless efforts enlightened the future of humanity in outer space. The same destructive rockets were dreamt for spaceflights. India was under colonial rule of the British during this period. Therefore, almost a vacuum existed here to develop any scientific progress over the rocketry.

The above dream of great space visionaries was conceptualised first with the programme of International Geophysical Year (1957-58). Here also history played a crucial role. As a basic characteristic, the human beings are very curious to know about the mother earth from the very beginning of human civilisation on earth. This was reflected first in International Polar Year that brought the conception of International Geophysical Year where the scientists were interested to know the information about the upper atmosphere surrounding the earth. They thought about it to make experiment in upper atmosphere, so there was a feeling of outer space within their thoughts. The effect was to make rockets for temporary observations of upper atmosphere and then to make satellites for permanent observations for the same purpose. Thus the same rocket as used for destructive purposes was utilised for scientific purposes in IGY. Finally, the programme of IGY was made capable to launch satellites in outer space by the then USSR. The wave of IGY reached and inspired scientific community in India as analysed in chapter V.

The period of IGY was aftermath of World War II and the cold war prevailed between USA and the, then USSR. Therefore, the United Nations (UN) could not maintain silence over the launching of Sputnik because USA would try to send its satellite to outer space. It became a matter of prestige of every nation. The UN assumed that the international peace would be disturbed over the repetitive launching of satellites by different countries. Therefore, for the first time, need for a law for outer space was felt. It was given effect by the United Nations. It came through the international space law treaties like the Outer Space Treaty, the Registration Convention, the Liability Agreement, the Rescue Agreement and the Moon Treaty. All these treaties had been made over a period of 15 years with the thoughts in the background that the outer space would be used and exploited exclusively for peaceful purposes.

Moreover, it was the states that gave shape and that existed in the texts of these treaties because space technology was highly technical with its high cost. There was no mention of private entities within the text of these treaties. The Article VI of the Outer Space Treaty only mentioned the word 'non-governmental'. But the word was not explained properly. So the ambiguity existed since then whether the word 'private' was also included within the word 'non-governmental'. The international legal norms as well as the respect for the UN Charter were observed within the text of these treaties. These treaties took care of key legal issues of any state like sovereignty, national security of each country. The reason was that the states were the only actors. Therefore, the first hypothesis of this research study that the existing space law provisions are inadequate to regulate private actors in outer space proves to be correct.

The above scenario has gradually changed according to the analytical findings of this research study in chapter II. There are varieties of private actors that mainly comprise companies engaged in space activities. They are start-up companies, space entrepreneurs, big corporate etc. It is shown from analysis in this same chapter that the concentration of these companies is high in the USA and European countries because their space programme had started long before IGY. The IGY programme boosted this momentum. Furthermore, the R&D on space technology brought down the cost of such technology used in different space applications mentioned in chapter II. As a result, these countries especially group I countries in IGY as explained in chapter I, started use of the space technology for industrialisation to develop their national economies.

As a part of this initiative, they insisted strongly on private investment in space business. Therefore, the space activities that were sole domain of the sovereign states gradually found inroads being made by the private actors. This was especially so since the states were sometimes not interested to carry forward the risky, costly and innovative space programmes like commercial space transportation services (COTS), celestial mining etc. They did not wish to risk investment of public money for space activities from national budgets against uncertain returns. It may cause uproar in the country. The countries started to face new legal issues, as examined in chapter III, like IPR, proprietary rights over celestial bodies, environment, financing, ethics etc. that were earlier practically legally non-existing issues in absence of privatisation.

In the wake of current global environmental concerns, it has become a legal challenge from the increasing threats of space debris in outer space. The new commercial space activities like space tourism and celestial mining on Moon or asteroids are going to pollute the outer space environment and pose threats that are still unknown to humankind. The issues that already existed in the texts of space law treaties have become more significant in the regime dominated by the private actors. The example is taken from principle of non-appropriation by states in outer space or celestial bodies. This principle is most debatable now-a-days to decide the ownership of celestial resources e.g. searches for water on the Moon or asteroid mining.

It needs to be noted that the United Nations does not take much initiatives like the post-sputnik period to have serious initiative on developing space law for regulation of activities of the private actors. One of the reasons may be that this development is not in any way still considered a serious threat to international peace and security just like post-sputnik period. In other words whenever the UN thinks that the new development or incident of space activities will cause harm to international peace and security in outer space, it has played some significant role. This international body has played the pioneering role. In the case of outer space activities, this trend has been witnessed from the establishment of the Outer Space Treaty to the International Space Debris Mitigation Guidelines as framed under UNCOPOUS.

But for the increasing number of private space activities, the UN has already acknowledged long back the role of private actors in developing space technologies. It was seen in the course of organising the UNISPACE III in the year 1999. Moreover, the UN has also sought to push all the states to make their respective national space legislation. In this view, the International Law Association made and proposed a uniform structure to be followed by all the countries in drafting national space legislation. However, the United Nations itself has not made any norm till now for drafting of such national space legislation. Instead it has left it to individual nations to make their own regulation for domestic space activities and then to send report to the UN.

The whole scenario brings the countries developed with space technology to think about the regulation of space activities for their domestic purposes. In this way, the concept of domestic space law has evolved beyond the United Nations' framework for international space law. It is for development of national space industry depending mainly on private actors' participation in the country itself. The new rules and regulations have been made along with the already existed one for general purpose. The international space law provisions are strongly followed in making domestic space regulations as the countries have made the required ratification of all or some of the international space law treaties. It varies from country to country as shown in chapter IV.

The Outer Space Treaty, the mother treaty in international space law, has been ratified by most of the countries. Some of the countries have directly mentioned that they implemented the space law treaties in their space regulations. Accordingly, for instance, Article 35 of Basic Space Law of Japan, 2008, prescribes that the legislations have to be made in accordance with international space law. The National Space Policy, 2008, of South Africa insists that any space activities will pursue the international treaties. Similarly, Section 3 of Space Activities Act, 1998, of Australia has set the objective of this Act to implement the obligations as imposed by the UN space treaties.

Moreover, all the countries keep register at the UN to inform and note the details about the launching of space objects into outer space even for launching by the private actors. The private launching indeed is performed on behalf of a state or states according to the existing provision of international space law. It simply indicates that the countries follow the provision of Registration Convention 1972. Therefore, the second hypothesis does not seem to be correct. The heterogeneity between space law treaties and space legislation does not exist because the national space legislation follows the provisions of international space law.

In spite of this, there are some differences between space law treaties and national legislations. It is the specific purpose of a country for which space legislation is made that differs from space treaties. This becomes the foremost difference between the two. Moreover, it appears that regulating space activities depends on the technology achieved by the concerned country. So if a country has opportunity to launch the satellites, then it regulates the satellite launching through combination of all these legal regulatory instruments.

France provides a unique example for establishing a private entity to regulate the launching. Due to excellent performance of the French company Arianespace in the launch sector, the Launch Service Alliance was formed by the company along with US Company Boeing Ltd. and Japanese Company Mitsubishi Ltd. This Alliance institutionalises the launching services. In fact the Space Operation Act, 2008, of France has detailed provisions for space operations including launching for private actors. The other example is cited from National Space Transportation Policy, 2013, of USA. This policy regulation was implemented because of upcoming regime of private commercial space transportation services (COTS). There exist a few companies as shown in chapter II, but the Federal Government could like to privatise the COTS further.

As this research study has sought to place under scanner on developing countries, so some examples for the above difference from the case of Asian countries are discussed in chapter IV. These countries are developing in the sense that their space infrastructure was developed much later than Western countries. But sometimes the countries like China achieved the status of space-faring state. However, China has Interim Measures to administer the permits for civil launch projects. It implies that there are actors within the country capable of civil launching. This is to be mentioned here that China was acceded the Registration Convention before implementing this Interim Measure. Moreover, the China's White Paper on Space Activities 2003, considers the environment of outer space for space debris issue. The environment of outer space was much neglected within the texts of the space law treaties. It is observed in chapter III. Therefore considering the space debris issue within domestic regulation is definitely a new turn but it follows directly or indirectly the provision for environment in Article IX of the Outer Space Treaty and Article VII (1) of the Moon Treaty.

There are examples from other Asian countries. Japan has the Radio Law. The title speaks for the specific purpose. In case of South Korea, the three domestic Acts like Aerospace Industry Promotion Act (1989), Space Development Promotion Act (2005), and Space Damage Compensation Act (2007), indicate the purpose of these Acts. But alike China and Japan, South Korea acceded the Registration Convention long back.

It is also true for developing countries that the national space legislations are made for specific purposes. It varies from country to country. But this is only possible pursuing international space treaties. So there exists no absolute heterogeneity between space law treaties and space regulations in developing countries.

Now, the last hypothesis concerns with India. The programme of IGY has opened the entry of satellite programme in India according to analysis of chapter V. Sarabhai was the key person in this regard. But it could not have been executed without the political support and goodwill of Nehru followed by Bhabha. But there were many persons with or after them whose immense contributions have showed India the path of self-reliance in space technology that was a long-cherished dream of Sarabhai.

All their joint efforts brought the country to achieve from one milestone to another as explained in chapters II and V. Some of prominent examples are establishment of the Thumba Equatorial Rocket Launching Centre, ISRO; developing PSLV (the most cost-effective polar satellite launch vehicle in the world with excellent track record), GSLV, RISAT (satellite having capability to take images of earth during night time or under cloudy atmosphere), SRE facility (Space Capsule Recovery experiment must for human spaceflight), indigenous cryogenic engines (for lifting heavy payloads during human spaceflight), orbiting numerous satellites in single launching etc. The national space missions like Chandrayaan-1, Mangalyan and upcoming Chadrayaan-2 indicate the technological prowess of India in the space sector. The foreign satellites from countries like France (SPOT-7), Germany, UK, Canada etc. have been launched by India through its indigenous workhorse PSLV. The position of India in space technology is well acclaimed internationally. The fact that budgetary sanction has grown for the Department of Space in recent years proves this attainment.

The above technological progress could not have been possible without the successful contribution of national industries in India. They have shared their indigenous technological skill and manpower in all national space missions from Chandrayaan-1 to Mangalyan. The names of some of the companies are mentioned in the chapter II. There are companies established in non-space sectors but now have plans to engage in space activities. Thus contribution of many of the private actors is crucial in the space sector in India. Still some private actors like Walchandnagar Industries Ltd., TATA, Godrej, and L&T have played the pioneering role to privatise India's space activities right from the inception.

In comparison with the widespread national development of space technology in India, the domestic space regulations have not developed to the same extent. The reason behind this slow regulatory process is that all the legislations are adopted through a democratic process through an intense debate in both Houses of the Parliament. It takes a long time. Still this legal vacuum keeps the country away to draw the serious attention of increasing number of private actors. But it is a solid fact that the private actors are very efficient and market based. This fact is proved by the recent success of Mangalyan within a very short period of time. This Mars mission is an initiative by ISRO where a large number of private industry players have contributed.

In view of the above background, the history of policies concerning promotion of science and technology is not weak in India. The Scientific Policy Resolution, 1958, was the first policy document as prepared by Prime Minister Nehru along with Homi Bhabha to develop general science in post-independent India. This Resolution brought the nation under modern scientific era. It is also very interesting that this foundation policy had aimed at rapid industrialisation. It became the earliest provision to attract private actors. Thereafter, the government took initiative to frame and change its scientific policy from time to time depending on national advancement of science and technology, and its societal need during that time. The space policy was framed through SATCOM Policy, 2000, and Remote Sensing Data Policy, 2011. India also has some policies on telecommunication like the latest National Telecom Policy, 2012. But after the spectrum related irregularities, the current scenario indicates that Indian regulations over licencing of telecom spectrum are not sufficiently addressed in the existing regulations.

When legislations are examined, it is mentioned in the beginning that India has not made any comprehensive space legislation. However, India has ratified all international space law treaties besides the Moon

Treaty. Moreover, there is no bar from the Constitutional angle to support implementation of space law. In this situation, India has some telecommunication laws. These could for the time being serve the purpose for regulating the telecommunication industry that is part of growing space industry. There are air related laws. Since air is adjacent to space, so these laws are good resources to develop space law. The rest of the legislations, as shown in chapter V, could only be extended or applicable in general way. The recent legal development related with space sector is significantly noticed in the 12th FYP working paper on Department of Space. It is proposed that 'Space Act' is the need of the hour because of domestic development of space technologies as well as following the global trend of making national space legislation in other foreign countries. But it would require sufficient consultation process with all stake holders in India.

The other regulatory development is in geospatial industry sector where the satellite imageries play a major role. These are the Delhi Geo-Spatial Data Infrastructure Act, 2011; Draft of National GI Policy, 2012; Draft of National Geospatial Data Authority Bill; Draft of Vetting of Images; and Geospatial Information for Licencing for National Security (VIGIL) Act.

India has now its own navigational system comprising of seven satellites called Indian Regional Navigation Satellite System (IRNSS). There is future opportunity for private actors in the navigation business that could be and it will be very lucrative one. The navigation policy is proposed in the 12th Five Year Plan.

The next area of space market in India would be the launch industry. It has already observed in USA as to how the Commercial Space Launch Act, 1984, along with 2004 amendment, serves the regulatory purposes. It is mentioned above that the France Space Operation Act, 2008, is another supportive Act for establishing the launch industry. In the case of India, the domestic workhorse PSLV is most cost effective in the world both for launching foreign and domestic satellites. It is explained in chapter II. Also the geographical location of a part of South India is near geomagnetic equator that scientifically facilitates the space launching with low cost. There was already a search from the ISRO itself for another spaceport. It could be a matter of time before a second one is set up in Tamil Nadu as proposed. The state legislations like the Tamil Nadu Acquisition of Land for Industrial Purpose Act, 1997, and the Tamil Nadu Special Economic Zones (Special Provisions) Act, 2005, would be applicable at the first instance.

The concerned central Acts like the Land Acquisition Act, 1894, and the Special Economic Zones Act, 2005, would also come into play. All these are explained in chapter V. Therefore, it is high time for the government to privatise the launch industry on utilising these scientific, technical and regulatory opportunities.

The next space market would be commercial space transportation services (COTS) from India itself. Alike telecommunication industries, if the foreign companies are allowed to launch their satellites from India, then the foreign companies like Virgin Galactic, Space X, Orbital Science Corporation may launch their space vehicles from Indian soil. Another added advantage for their attraction is that Indian labour market is cheap as compared to the Western countries. It would bring a lot of foreign exchange revenues.

The space transport is one area of services as provided in the list of services under the General Agreement on Trade in Services (GATS) as explained in chapter IV. It is only a matter of time to put this service under schedule of specific commitments of services of any member country of WTO including India. In case India allows space transport in its schedule of specific commitment on services, then it will be compulsory to allow the private company in COTS from other member countries of WTO. It may be conditional market access of space transport in India but there could not be complete denial to such countries. However, India needs this opportunity rather than denial for its own national economic development.

The commercial space transport from India would require the provisions of Insurance Act, 1938, because the technical capability is full of unseen as well as unavoidable risk. It is to be noted here that the accidents occurred during the concerned activities of Space X, Orbital Science Corporation and Virgin Galactic Ltd. The other laws will be required with the development of full-fledged industry in COTS.

In both the cases, commercial space launching and COTS, safety is the prime focus. Therefore, all the safety laws as mentioned in chapter V will be very useful. The same is true for the environment. It is a fact that India developed cryogenic engine that contributes to lesser pollution of the outer space environment. The current trend of increasing number of space launch would cause environmental pollution at the launching site. Therefore, the environmental laws have long standing effect in the era of private actors.

The other business opportunity would be to allow the openings of foreign branches of space companies on Indian soil besides the above companies in launching and COTS. In this regard certain terms and conditions will apply. At the first instance the FDI rules and regulations will be attracted. Moreover the Foreign Exchange Laws, Export-Import Laws will provide good financial support to open such type of branches.

In all these national business prospects related with private actors in outer space, there is no dearth of national human resources to be recruited in such type of companies. The required supply of manpower comes from the academic institutions of national repute like IITs, some Universities. In fact the very Act establishing these academic institutions do make provisions for this.

Lastly the other concerned Central and State Acts will provide good support for any business group or any individual to establish a private company related with any space activities.

So it appears from above that Indian laws and policies are not inadequate for the time being to serve the present national or international commercial need of the private actors. Therefore, the third hypothesis that Indian laws and policies are inadequate to regulate private actors in outer space is not fully untrue. The problem lies elsewhere as explained below.

Every country has passed through a law making regime (soft law period) concerning space activities. As explained in chapter IV, some countries may still be at pre-regulatory period related to space activities alike Singapore and UAE. It results in complex prediction to make any conclusion on the exact position of India in this regard. But certainly it is not under hard core space related regulatory regime like USA, Russian Federation and Australia. At this stage, history has tremendous role to play as it is analysed above. It has been observed that space science and technology is the driving force in this respect.

There is another factor like techno-political angle to form the hard core space related regulatory regime in India. The space portfolio is directly under Prime Minister. So the strategy and policy of each Prime Minister is more relevant. It is also reflection of the ruling government's political mandate while in power. This is another serious concern to decide India's role in legal regulation of private actors in outer space. It does not encourage private actors much. Further the foreign policy of India cannot be ignored to draft any space policies that could play in positioning the country on the global stage.

In this scenario, it is mentioned above that the 12th Five Year Plan has already proposed the 'Space Act' which will be a dedicated legislation like other foreign countries. The technological prowess of the country has been welcomed by its neighbours like China as well as the established space powers such as USA and Russia. The national industries are also highly enthusiastic to participate and invest their business resources in the development of space activities. Their long-pending expectation on national space legislation would be satisfied. Moreover, the Indian companies are capable of opening their foreign branches for space activities. Some initiatives have been already taken in this respect as discussed in chapter II. Thus India could sale its space products all over world making its proposed 'Space Act' more significant and meaningful. In other words, the legal regulation of private actors in outer space would be much developed internationally from the contributions emanating from India.

In view of the above, a few recommendations from this research study would be in order:-

Firstly, India could require at the earliest a business policy for private actors in outer space. This should not be for promoting further commercialisation of ISRO. It would be a business road map to encourage the private actors to invest and increase their capital in a best possible way.

Secondly, a national policy on space launching, like SATCOM, would be need of the hour because of the frequent successful launchings by ISRO. It also seems to be mentioned above that it is the most suitable time now to privatise the space launching sector.

Thirdly, the early framing of navigational policy is recommended though it has been already proposed in 12th Five Year Plan.

Fourthly, it is not only the success in technology that will dominate the international arena but the strategy of a country to implement such a technology is more meaningful. But implementation should first start from each country itself. In this regard, the domestic regulatory regime for outer space is a crucial factor to develop the SAARC satellite as proposed by India at SAARC Summit in Kathmandu (November 2014). Legally speaking, the Indian regulations concerned with satellite data could be more useful to all SAARC countries. Thus, relevant Indian laws could be made that target beyond India. The principle of 'Vasudhaiva Kutumbakam' is applicable to regulatory measures of space activities also. But it should not be uttered only. It could be effectively implemented through making suitable regulations compatible to the private actors of other countries especially those in the neighbouring countries.

Fifthly, India could consider some kind of 'International Code of Conduct for Commercial Space Activities' that will support the development of space regulations of neighbouring countries as well as, other countries in the world. In fact if it could be done and implemented on a priority basis, then the proposed data and other services from SAARC satellite will be more effective.

Lastly, there are several institutions in India that play a very meaningful role in developing regulations for private actors. Some of them are shown in detail in chapter V. They are both governmental and non-governmental institutions. All these institutions have different agendas for regulation because they are established for different purposes. Moreover, there are scientific institutions and non-scientific institutions. Ironically, there is no common platform like annual conference, convention etc. to interact and exchange amongst all these institutions unlike countries outside India. India could take the lesson from Africa such as the African Leadership Conference on Space Science & Technology (ALC). If done in best possible way with the initiative from government or the private actors, then it would contribute much effectively towards the development of legal regulation of private actors in outer space.

Bibliography

PRIMARY SOURCES

A. TREATIES, CONVENTIONS, AGREEMENTS

Treaty on Principles Governing the Activities of States in the Exploration and Use of Outer Space, including the Moon and Other Celestial Bodies (1967), 610 UNTS 205.

Agreement on the Rescue of Astronauts, the Return of Astronauts and the Return of Objects Launched into Outer Space (1968), 672 UNTS 119.

Convention on International Liability for Damage Caused by Space Objects (1972), 961 UNTS 187.

Convention on Registration of Objects Launched into Outer Space (1976), 1023 UNTS 15.

Agreement Governing the Activities of States on the Moon and Other Celestial Bodies (1979), 1363 UNTS 3.

Principles Governing the Use by States of Artificial Earth Satellites for International Direct Television Broadcasting, GA Res. (1982), UN Doc. A/RES/37/92.

Principles Relating to Remote Sensing of the Earth from Outer Space, GA Res. (1986), A/RES/41/65.

Declaration on International Cooperation in the Exploration and Use of Outer Space for the Benefit and in the Interest of All States, Taking into Particular Account the Needs of Developing Countries, GA Res. (1996), UN Doc. A/RES/51/122.

United Nations Charter.

Vienna Convention of the Law of Treaties (1969).

B. STATE POLICY & LEGISLATION

Brazil

Presidential Decree No. 68.009, of January 20, 1971, Creating the Brazilian Commission for Space Activities (Cobae)

Presidential Decree No. 68.532, of April 22, 1971, Creating the National Institute for Space Research (INPE)

Law No. 8.854 of February 10, 1994, Creating the Brazilian Space Agency (AEB)

Presidential Decree No. 1.332, of December 8, 1994, Approving the National Policy for the Development of Space Activities (PNDAE)

Presidential Decree No. 1.953, of July 10, 1996, Creating the National System of Space Activities Development (SINDAE)

Law No. 9.112, of October 10, 1995, Dealing with the Export of Sensitive Goods and Services

The Licensing of Private Enterprises to Prepare Launching Operations from Brazilian Territory, 2001

The Authorization of Private Enterprises to Carry Out Launching Operations on Brazilian Territory, 2002

General Regulation of Space Safety, 2007

Argentina

National Decree No. 995/91, Creation of the National Commission on Space Activities, 1991

National Decree No. 125/95, Establishment of the National Registry of Objects Launched into Outer Space, 1995

Australia

Space Activities Act, 1998.

Canada

Canadian Space Agency Act, 1990

China

China's Space Activities (White Paper), 2003

Chinese Space Activities (White Paper), 2006

Chile

Supreme Decree No. 338 of 2001: Establishment of a Presidential Advisory Committee known as the Chilean Space Agency

European Space Agency

European Space Policy, 2007

European Union

International Code of Conduct of Outer Space Activities

France

French Space Operation Act, 2008

Germany

German Act on Satellite Data Security, 2007

German Space Strategy, 2010

Hong Kong

The Outer Space Act 1986 (Hong Kong) Order, 1990

India

Scientific Policy Resolution, 1958

Technology Policy Statement, 1983

Science and Technology Policy, 2003

Science, Technology and Innovation Policy, 2013

SATCOM Policy

(a) A Policy Framework for Satellite Communication in India (Approved by Government in 1997)

(b) The Norms, Guidelines and Procedures for Implementation of the Policy Frame-Work for Satellite Communications in India (Approved by Government in 2000)
Remote Sensing Data Policy, 2011

CENTRAL ACTS

(1) Constitution of India, 1950

(2) Atomic Energy Act, 1962

(3) Banking Laws

Reserve Bank of India Act, 1934
The Banking Regulation Act, 1949
The Export- Import Bank of India Act, 1981
(4) Insurance Laws
Insurance Act 1938
Insurance Regulatory and Development Authority Act 1999
(5) Laws for Infrastructure Development
Indian Contract Act, 1872
The Partnership Act, 1932
The Industries (Development & Regulation) Act, 1951
Technology Development Board Act, 1995
The Micro, Small and Medium Enterprises Development Act 2006
The Science and Engineering Research Board Act, 2008
The Limited Liability Partnership Act 2008
(6) Company Related Laws
Companies Act 1956
The Companies (Donations to National Funds) Act, 1951
The Depositories Act, 1996
The Securities and Exchange Board of India Act, 1992
The Preference Shares (Regulation of Dividends) Act, 1960
(7) Environmental Laws
Environment Protection Act, 1986
The Air (Prevention and Control of Pollution) Act, 1981
The Energy Conservation Act, 2001
Coastal Aquaculture Authority Act, 2005
(8) IPR Laws
Intellectual Property Policy
Copyright Act 1957
Patents Act 1970 (Amendment 1999)
Trade Marks Act 1999
The Designs Act, 2000
The Semiconductor Integrated Circuits Layout-Design Act, 2000
(9) Revenue Laws
Sale of Goods Act, 1930
Income Tax Act 1961
Central Boards of Revenue Act 1963
(10) AIR Laws
Aircraft Act, 1934
The National Airports Authority Act, 1985
The Airports Authority of India Act, 1994
The Suppression of Unlawful Acts against Safety of Civil Aviation Acts, 1982
The Anti-Hijacking Act, 1982
The Foreign Aircraft (Exemption from Taxes & Duties on Fuel & Lubricants) Act, 2002
The Airports Economic Regulatory Authority of India Act 2008
(11) Dispute Resolution Laws
The Indian Penal Code, 1860
The Code of Criminal Procedure, 1973

The Economic Offences (Inapplicability of Limitation) Act, 1974
Consumer Protection Act, 1986
Arbitration & Conciliation Act, 1996
The Competition Act, 2002

(12) Human Resource Development Laws
The Foreigners Act, 1946
The Citizenship Act, 1955
The Institutes of Technology Act, 1961
The Jawaharlal Nehru University Act, 1966
National Institute of Technology Act, 2007
The Rajiv Gandhi National Aviation University Act, 2013

(13) Land Laws
The National Highways Act, 1956
The Special Economic Zones Act, 2005

(14) Safety Laws
Explosives Act, 1884
The Explosive Substances Act, 1908
The Inflammable Substances Act, 1952
The Dangerous Machines (Regulation) Act, 1983

(15) Security Laws
The Central Industrial Security Force Act, 1968
National Security Act 1980
The Private Security Agencies (Regulation) Act, 2005

(16) Telecommunication Laws
The Indian Telegraph Act, 1885
The Indian Wireless Telegraphy Act, 1933
National Telecom Policy, 1994
Telecom Regulatory Authority of India (TRAI) Act, 1997
New Telecom Policy, 1999
The Information Technology Act, 2000
The Communication Convergence Bill, 2001
National Telecom Policy 2012 (NTP-2012)
The Cable Television Networks (Regulation) Act, 1995

(17) Export-Import Laws
Customs Act, 1962
The Export (Quality Control & Inspection) Act, 1963
The Research & Development Cess Act, 1986
The Foreign Trade (Development & Regulation) Act, 1992

(18) Foreign Exchange Laws
The Conservation of Foreign Exchange & Prevention of Smuggling Activities Act, 1974 (COFEPOSA ACT)
The Foreign Exchange Management Act, 1999
The Foreign Contribution (Regulation) Act, 2010

(19) Labour & Welfare Laws
Workmen's Compensation Act, 1923
Apprentices Act, 1946
Industrial Employment (Standing Orders) Act, 1946

The Industrial Disputes Act, 1947
The Factories Act, 1948
Employees' State Insurance Act, 1948
Employees' Provident Funds & Miscellaneous Provisions Act 1952
The Payment of Bonus Act, 1965
The Payment of Gratuity Act, 1972
The Bhopal Gas Leak Disaster (Processing of Claims) Act, 1985

(20) Laws for Transparency
The Comptroller and Auditor-General's (Duties, Powers and Conditions of Service) Act, 1971
The Central Vigilance Commission Act, 2003
The Right to Information Act, 2005

(21) Laws on Other High-End Technology
The Biotechnology Regulatory Authority of India Bill, 2013

Italy
Reorganization of the Italian Space Agency Act, 2007

Japan
Basic Space Law, 2008
Law Concerning the National Space Development Agency of Japan (JAXA)
Japan's Basic Plan for Space Policy, 2013

Malaysia
Malaysian Communications and Multimedia Act, 1998

Mexico
Act establishing the Mexican Space Agency, 2010

Nigeria
National Space Policy, 2001
Nigerian Insurance Act, 2003
The Communications Act, 2003
National Geoinformation Policy, 2003
National Space Research and Development Agency Act, 2010

Norway
Act on Launching Objects from Norwegian Territory etc. into Outer Space, 1969

Philippine
Bill on Philippine Space Act, 2012

Republic of Kazakhstan
Law of the Republic of Kazakhstan on Space Activities, 2012

Republic of Korea
Aerospace Industry Promotion Act, 1989
Space Development Promotion Act, 2005
Space Damage Compensation Act, 2007

Russian Federation
Law of the Russian Federation on Space Activity, 1993

South Africa
Space Affairs Act, 1993
Space Affairs Amendment Act of South Africa, 1995
South African National Space Agency Act, 2008
National Space Policy, 2008

Spain
Royal Decree Establishing the Registry of Objects Launched into Outer Space, 1995

Sweden
Act on Space Activities (1982:963)
The Swedish National Space Board's Long-term Strategy focused on 2011-2015

Thailand
Space Master Plan, 2005

The Netherlands
Law Incorporating Rules Concerning Space Activities and Establishment of a Registry of Space Objects, 2007

Ukraine
The Law on Ukrainian Space Activities, 1996

United Kingdom
Outer Space Act, 1986
United Kingdom Space Agency Civil Space Strategy 2012-2016

United States of America
Commercial Space Launch Act, 1984
Land Remote Sensing Policy Act, 1992
Commercial Space Act, 1998
National Space Policy, 2010
National Space Transportation Policy, 2013

Venezuela
Agency Law Bolivarian for Space Activities

SECONDARY SOURCES

BOOKS

Adhikari, M. (2012). High Resolution Data Dissemination against the Background of National Security in India. In Janssen, K. and Crompvoets, J. (Eds.) *Geographic Data and the Law Defining New Challenges*. Leuven (Belgium): Leuven University Press.

Agarwal, D.P. (2009). *Harappan Technology and Its Legacy*, New Delhi: Rupa & Co.

Alam, Ishrat (2011). Technology and Economic Progress in Medieval India. In Prabhat Patnaik (Ed.), *Excursus in History Essays on Some Ideas of Irfan Habib*, New Delhi: Tulika Books.

Alvi, M.A. and Rahman, A. (1968). *Jahangir – The Naturalist*. New Delhi: National Institute of Sciences in India.

Anderson, Robert S. (1975). *Building Scientific Institutions in India: Saha and Bhabha.* Montreal: Centre for Developing-Area Studies (McGill University).

-------------------------- (2010). *Nucleus and Nation: Scientists, International Networks, and Power in India.* Chicago: The University of Chicago Press.

Angelo, Joseph A. (2009). *Space Technology.* New Delhi: Pentagon Press.

Ansari, S.M. Razaullah (2009). Reception of Indian Astronomical Treaties and Handbooks in Sanskrit by Muslim Scholars of Medieval India. In J.V. Narlikar (Ed.), *Science in India,* New Delhi: Viva Books.

Beresford, S.M. (1960). The Future of National Sovereignty. In A.G. Haley and W.H. Hanover (Ed.), *Second Colloquium on the Law of Outer Space London 1959 Proceedings.* Vienna: Springer-Verleg.

Braun, W.V. and Ordway, F. I. (1975), *Space Travel,* New York: Thomas Y. Crowell Company.

Brno, C. and Edith, W. (2008), *National Space Law Development in Europe Challenges for Small Countries,* Vienna: Bohlau Verlag.

Brooks, Peter W. (1958). Aeronautics. In Charles Singer et al. (Eds.) *A History of Technology,* Vol. V. Oxford: Clarendon Press.

Chapman, S. (1959). *IGY: Year of Discovery the Story of the International Geophysical Year,* Michigan: The University of Michigan Press.

Chatterjee, P. and Finger, M. (1994). *The Earth Brokers: power, politics and world development.* London: Routledge.

Cho, G. (2005). *Geographical Information Science- Mastering the Legal Issues.* Chichester (England): John Willy & Sons Ltd.

Chowdhury, I. and Dasgupta, A. (2010). *A Masterful Spirit Homi J. Bhabha 1909-1966.* New Delhi: Penguin Books.

Cheng, Bin (1998). *Studies in International Space Law.* Oxford: Clarendon Press.

Delupis, I. (1974). *International Law and the Independent State.* Essex (Great Britain): Gower Press Ltd.

Desai, B. H. (2004). *Institutionalizing International Environmental Law.* New York: Transnational Publishers.

Dikshitar, V.R. Ramachandra (1944). *War in Ancient India.* Madras: Macmillan & Co. Ltd.

Doyle, Stephen E. (2002). *The Origins of Space Law and the International Institute of Space Law of the International Astronautical Federation,* San Diego (California): Univelt.

__________________ (Ed.) (2012). *The International Geophysical Year Initiating International Scientific Space Co-operation.* Paris: International Astronautical Federation.

Dornberger, Walter S. (1964). The German V-2. In Eugene M. Emme (Ed.) *The History of Rocket Technology.* Detroit: Wayne State University Press.

Dunk, F. G. Von Der (2002). Space for Dispute Settlement Mechanisms-Dispute Resolution Mechanisms for Space? A Few Legal Considerations. In Corinne M. Contant Jorgenson (Ed.) *Proceedings of the 44th Colloquium on the Law of Outer Space,* Washington: American Institute of Aeronautics and Astronautics.

_________________ (2010). Regulation of Space Activities in the Netherlands from Hugo Grotius to the High Ground of Outer Space. In Ram S. Jakhu (Ed.) *National Regulation of Space Activities.* New York: Springer.

Eisenhower, Dwight D. (1963). *The White House Years Mandate for Change 1953-1956.* London: Heinemann.

Emme, Eugene M. (1964). *History of Rocket Technology.* Detroit: Wayne State University Press.

Falk, Richard A. (1962). Space Espionage and World Order: A Consideration of Samos-Midas Program. In Ronald J. Stranger (Ed.) *Essays on Espionage and International Law*. Ohio: Ohio State University Press.

Filho, J.M. (2003). A Remote Sensing Convention for the Advancement of Space Law. In Corinne M. Contant Jorgenson (ed.), *Proceedings of the 46th Colloquium on the Law of Outer Space*. Washington: American Institute of Aeronautics & Astronautics.

_____________ (2010). Regulation of Space Activities in Brazil. In Ram S. Jakhu (Ed.) *National Regulation of Space Activities*. New York: Springer.

Finch, E.R. and Moore, A.L. (1985). *Astrbusiness A Guide to the Commerce and Law of Outer Space*. New York: Praeger.

Galloway, Eilene (1959). The Community of Law and Science. In Andrew G. Halley and W.H. Hanover (Eds.) *First Colloquium on the Law of Outer Space The Hague 1958 Proceedings*. Vienna: Springer-Verlag.

Goddard, Robert H. (1948). *Development Liquid-Fuel Rocket Research 1929-1941* In Esther C. Goddard and G. Edward Pendray (Eds.), New York: Prentice Hall Inc.

Gode, P.K. (1953). *History of Fireworks in India: between A.D. 1400 and 1900*, Bangalore: Indian Institute of Culture.

Goh, G.M. (2007). *Dispute Settlement in International Space Law: A Multi-Door Courthouse for Outer Space*. Leiden: M.N. Publishers.

Goldman, N. C. (1985). *Space Commerce Free Enterprise on the High Frontier*. Massachusetts: Ballinger Publishing Company.

Greenberg, Joel S. (2003). *Economic Principles Applied to Space Industry Decisions*. Virginia: American Institute of Aeronautics and Astronautics.

Griffiths, J. (1990). Spaceflight. In Ian McNeil (Ed.) *An Encyclopedia of the History of Technology*, London: Routledge.

Gorove, S. (1983). International Space Law in Perspective – Some Major Issues, Trends and Alternatives. In *Recueil Des Cours 1983 Vol. III*. The Hague: Martinus Nijhoff Publishers.

Gupta, Mohan (2007). Astronomical Observations in the Vedas. In G.C. Pande (Ed.) *A Golden Chain of Civilizations: Indic, Iranic, Semitic and Hellenic up to c. 600 BC*. New Delhi: Centre for Studies in Civilizations.

Habib, Irfan (2008). *Technology in Medieval India c 650-1750*. New Delhi: Tulika Books.

Haley, Andrew G. (1963). *Space Law and Government*. New York: Appleton-Century-Crofts.

Hall, A. R. (1956). A Note on Military Pyrotechnics. In Charles Singer et al. (Eds.) *A History of Technology*, Vol. II, Oxford: Clarendon Press.

Hardin, Garrett (1972). *Exploring New Ethics for Survival the Voyage of the Spaceship Beagle*. New York: The Viking Press.

Hermida, Julian (2004). *Legal Basis for a National Space Legislation*. Kluwer Academic Publishers: Dordrecht.

--------------------- (2010). Regulation of Space Activities in Argentina. In Ram S. Jakhu (Ed.) *National Regulation of Space Activities*. New York: Springer.

Hingorani, R.C. (Ed.) (1972). *International Law through United Nations*. Bombay: N.M. Tripathy Pvt. Ltd.

Hobe, S. (2011). Vladimir Mandl and Alex Meyer: Two Pioneers of Space Law. In Corinne M. Contant Jorgenson (Ed.) *Proceedings of the 53rd Colloquium on the Law of Outer Space*, Washington: American Institute of Aeronautics and Astronautics.

Hobe, S. et al. (Eds.) (2009), *Cologne Commentary on Space Law*, Vol 1, Cologne: Carl Heymanns Verlag.

Jakhu, R.S. et al., (2011). *The Need for an Integrated Regulatory Regime for Aviation and Space ICAO for Space?*, New York: Springer.

-------------------- (2010), Regulation of Space Activities in Canada. In Ram S. Jakhu (Ed.) *National Regulation of Space Activities*. New York: Springer.

Jenks, C. Wilfred (1965). *Space Law*. London: Stevens & Sons.

Kalam, APJ A. (2003). *Wings of Fire*. Hyderabad: Universities Press.

Kaul, Ranjana (2012), International Space Law: Future Outlook. In Arvind Gupta et al. (eds.) *Space Security Need for Global Convergence*, New Delhi: Pentagon Security International.

Kay, G.R. (1981). *Hindu Astronomy Ancient Science of the Hindus*. New Delhi: Cosmo Publications.

------------- (1973), The Astronomical Observatories of Jai Singh. Varanasi: Indological Book House.

Khanolkar, G.D. (1969). *Walchand Hirachand Man, His Times and Achievements*. Bombay: Walchand Hirachand Company Ltd.

Kelsen, H. (1952). *Principles of International Law*. New York: Rinehart.

Kochhar, R. and Narlikar, J. (1993). *Astronomy in India Past, Present and Future*. Pune: Inter-University Centre for Astronomy & Astrophysics and Bangalore: Indian Institute of Astrophysics.

Kochhar, R. and Narlikar, J. (1995), *Astronomy in India a Perspective*, New Delhi: Indian National Science Academy.

Kopal, V. (2011). The Life and Work of Professor Vladimir Mandl—A Pioneer of Space Law. In Corinne M. Contant Jorgenson (Ed.) *Proceedings of the 53rd Colloquium on the Law of Outer Space*, Washington: American Institute of Aeronautics and Astronautics.

Kulkarni, R.P. & Sarma, V. (1969). *Homi Bhabha Father of Nuclear Science in India*. Bombay: Popular Prakashan.

Lachs, M. (1964). The International Law of Outer Space. In *Recueil Des Cours 1964 Vol. III.* The Hague: Martinus Nijhoff Publishers.

Ley, W. (1969). *Rocket, Missiles and Men in Space*, New York: The New American Library.

Lewis, John S. (1996). *Mining the Sky Untold Riches from the Asteroids, Comets and Planets*. New York: Basic Books.

Lyall, F. and Larsen, Paul B. (2009). *Space Law: A Treatise*, Surrey (England): Ashgate.

Malkov, Sergey P. and Doldirina, C. (2010). Regulation of Space Activities in Russian Federation. In Ram S. Jakhu (Ed.) *National Regulation of Space Activities*. New York: Springer.

Marshack, Alexander (1958). *The World of Space the Story of the International Geophysical Year*, New York: Dell Publishing Co. Inc.

Matte, N.M. (1969). *Aerospace Law*, London: Sweet & Maxwell.

McDougall, Walter A. (1985). *The Heavens and the Earth: A Political History of the Space Age*. New York: Basic Books Inc.

Michaelis, Anthony R. (1978). Space Technology. In Trevor I. Williams (Ed.) *A History of Technology*, Vol. VII, Part II. Oxford: Clarendon Press.

Mitra, A.P. (1985). *Indian IGY Programme – Achievements*. New Delhi: Indian National Science Academy.

Narlikar, Jayant V. and Kochhar, Rajesh K. (2009). Post-Independence Indian Achievements in Astronomy. In J.V. Narlikar (Ed.), *Science in India*, New Delhi: Viva Books.

Needham, Joseph (1954). *The Grand Titration Science & Society in East and West*,London: George Allen & Unwin Ltd.

Nehru, Jawaharlal (1934). *Glimpses of World History*. Allahabad: Kitabistan.

Ohashi, Yukio (2009). The Mathematical and Observational Astronomy in Traditional India. In J.V. Narlikar (Ed.), *Science in India*, New Delhi: Viva Books.

Pagkratis, Spyros (2011). European Space Activities in the Global Context. In Kai-U-Schrogwl et al (Eds.) *Yearbook on Space Policy 2009/2010*. New York: Springer Wien.

Pelton, Joseph N. (2010). The International Challenges of Regulation of Commercial Space Flight, In Joseph N. Pelton and Ram S. Jakhu (Eds.), *Space Safety Regulations and Standards*, Oxford: Elsevier.

Pendray, G. E. (1948), The Man Who Ushered in the Space Age, In Esther C. Goddard and G. Edward Pendray (Eds.), *Rocket Development Liquid-Fuel Rocket Research 1929-1941*, New York: Prentice Hall Inc.

Piramal, G. and Herdeck, M. (1985). *India's Industrialists*, Vol. I, Washington D.C.: Three Continents Press Inc.

Pop, V. (2009). *Who Owns the Moon? Extraterrestrial Aspects of Land and Mineral Resources Ownership*. Bucharest (Romania): Springer.

Pratt, T. et al (2003). *Satellite Communications*. New York: John Wiley & Sons.

Ptolemy (1952). *The Almagest*, Vol. I-V, Translated by R. Catesby Taliaferro et al., Chicago: Encyclopedia Britannica Inc.

Raghavan,V.(1952). *Yantras or Mechanical Contrivances in Ancient India*.Bangalore: The Indian Institute of Culture.

Rao, P.V.M. and Radhakrishnan, P. (2012). *A Brief History of Rocketry and ISRO*. Hyderabad: University Press.

Reijnen, G.C.M. (1981). *Utilization of Outer Space and International Law*. Amsterdam: Elsevier.

Sarabhai, M. (2004). *The Voice of the Heart*. New Delhi: Harper Collins.

Sarma, Nataraja (2009). India – A Hub of Ancient Astronomy. In J.V. Narlikar (Ed.), *Science in India*, New Delhi: Viva Books.

Sen, S.N. (1971). A Survey of Source Materials. In D.M. Bose et al (Eds.), *A Concise History of Science in India*, New Delhi: Indian National Science Academy.

Sekhar, J. Chandra and Prasad, Gangadhar M. (Eds.) (2008), *Eternally Talented India 108 Facts*, Vivekananda Life Skills Academy: Hyderabad

Shah, A. (2007). *Vikram Sarabhai A Life*, New Delhi: Penguin Books India.

Smith, Bradford L. (2001). New Initiatives in Intellectual Property Law for Space Activities. In Corinne M. Contant Jorgenson (Ed.) *Proceedings of the 43rd Colloquium on the Law of Outer Space*, Washington: American Institute of Aeronautics and Astronautics.

Spangenburg, R. and Moser, Diane K. (1999). *Wernher von Braun: Space Visionary and Rocket Engineer*. Hyderabad: University Press.

Sriram, M.S. and Ramasubramanian, K. (2009). Contributions of Nilakantha Somayaji to the Kerala School of Astronomy. In J.V. Narlikar (Ed.), *Science in India*, New Delhi: Viva Books.

Sterns, P. and Tennen, L.I. (2011). Should There Be An Environmental "Code of Conduct" for Activities in Outer Space? In Corinne M. Contant Jorgenson (Ed.) *Proceedings of the 53rd Colloquium on the Law of Outer Space*, Washington: American Institute of Aeronautics and Astronautics.

Temple, William F. (1954). *The True Book about Space-Travel*. London: Frederick Muller Ltd.

Thapar, Romila (1999). History of Science and the Oikoumene. In S. Irfan Habib and Dhruv Raina (Eds.) Situating the History of Science- Dialogues with Joseph Needham. New

Delhi: Oxford University Publication.

Traa-Engelman, H.V. (2010).The Need for A Uniform Law System Protecting Intellectual Property Rights in Outer Space. In Corinne M. Contant Jorgenson (Ed.) *Proceedings of the 51st Colloquium on the Law of Outer Space*, Washington: American Institute of Aeronautics and Astronautics.

Tronchetti, F. (2013). *Fundamentals of Space Law and Policy*. New York: Springer.

Vereshchetin, V. S. et al. (1981), *Outer Space: Politics and Law*, Moscow: Progressive Publishers.

Williams, Sylvia M. (1997). Dispute Settlement and Space Activities: A New Framework Required? In Corinne M. Contant Jorgenson (Ed.) Proceedings of the 39th Colloquium on the Law of Outer Space, Washington: American Institute of Aeronautics and Astronautics.

Wilson, J. Tuzo (1961), *IGY the Year of the New Moons*, Michael Joseph Ltd: London.

Zhao, Yun (2009). *Space Commercialization and the Development of Space Law from a Chinese Legal Perspective*, New York: Nova Science Publishers.

ARTICLES

Adhikari, M. (2014). Developing Space Law Education in India: Some Proposals, Rostrum's Law Review, I(IV).

[http://rostrumlegal.com/blog/articles/rostrum-law-review/page/2/]

Aoki, S. (2009). Current Status and Recent Developments in Japan's National Space Law and its Relevance to Pacific RIM Space Law and Activities, *Journal of Space Law*, 35 (2): 363- 438.

Arenales-Vergara, Oscar A. (2004). Colombia: reasons to create a national space agency, *Advances in Space Research*, 34 (10): 2209-2214.

Bockstiegel, K.H. (1985). Proposed Draft Convention on the Settlement of Space Law Disputes, *Journal of Space Law*, 12 (2):136-162.

Brearley, A. (2006). Mining the Moon: Owning the Night Sky? *Astropolitics*, 4(1): 43-67.

Cheng, Bin (1998), "Article VI of the 1967 Space Treaty Revisited: 'International Responsibility', 'National Activities' and 'The Appropriate State' ", *Journal of Space Law*, 26 (1): 7-30.

Cooper, J. C. (1957). The Russian Satellite- Legal and Political Problems, *The Journal of Air Law and Commerce*, 24(4): 379-383.

Cuijpers, C. (2009). The Legal Angle of Geo-info. *GIS Development*. 13(8):38.

Deem, Charles L. (1984).Liability of Private Space Transportation Companies to Their Customers. *Insurance Counsel Journal*, 51 (3): 340-361.

Diederiks-Verschoor, I.E. H. (1998). The Settlements of Disputes in Space: New Developments. *Journal of Space Law*, Vol. 26 (1): 41-49.

Doyle, Stephen E. (1998). Using the Extraterrestrial Resources under the Moon Agreement of 1979. *Journal of Space Law*, 26(2): 111-128.

Gal, Gyula (1998). Elements of Space Law in the Hungarian Legal System. *Journal of Space Law*, 26(1): 61-65.

Ghosh, A. (2007). Tipu Sultan: A Pre-British Engagement with Modern Technology. *Journal of the Asiatic Society*, 49 (4), 1-17.

Halim, D. and Medeni, T. (2012). A Comparative Strategic Analysis of Space Technologies: Developing a Road Map for Turkey. *International Journal of eBusiness and eGovernment Studies*, 4(2): 1-10.

Hingorani, R. C. (1957). An Attempt to Determine Sovereignty in Upper Space. *Kansas City Law Review*, 26(1): 5-12.

Husby, E. (1991). Sovereignty & Property Rights in Outer Space. *Journal of International Law & Practice*, 3(1): 359-372.

Hwang, Chin Young (2006). Space activities in Korea—History, current programs and future plans. *Space Policy*, 22(3): 194-199.

Gorove, S. (1979). The Geostationary Orbit: Issues of Law & Policy. *The American Journal of International Law*, 73(3): 444-461.

Kochhar, R. (2008). Science as a Symbol of New Nationhood: India and the International Geophysical Year 1957-58. *Current Science*, 94(6): 813-816.

Larsen, Paul B. (2002). Future Protocol on Security Interests in Space Assets. *Journal of Air Law & Commerce*, 67(2): 1072-1106.

Lee, J.J. and Chung, S. (2011). Space policy for late comer countries: A case study of South Korea. *Space Policy*, 27(4): 227-233.

Lee, Ricky J. (2000). Reconciling International Space Law with the Commercial Realities of the Twenty-first Century. *Singapore Journal of International and Comparative Law*, 4 (1): 194-251.

Lee, Yoon (2007). A Review of the Space Development Promotion Act of the Republic of Korea. *Journal of Space Law*, 33(1): 125-190.

Martinez, P. (2012). The African Leadership Conference on Space Science and Technology for Sustainable Development. *Space Policy*, 28(1): 33-37.

Morring, F. (2013). Selling Space Ukranian Officials travel world to capitalize on Soviet-era capability. *Aviation Week & Space Technology*, 175(38): 28-29.

Murthi, KRS. (2001). Commercial Availability of High Quality Remote Sensing Imageries: Legal Issues. *Singapore Journal of International and Comparative Law*, 5 (1): 149-155.

Ortiz, Jairo A. Becerra (2008). Asurvey of Colombia's new outer space policy: Reforms in Colombian law. *Acta Astronautica*, Vol. 63, Issue 1-4: 560-563.

Ozalp, T. (2009). Space as a strategic vision for Turkey and its people. *Space Policy*, 25(4): 224-235.

Rao, M. and Murthi, KRS. (2006). Keeping up with remote sensing and GI advances—Policy and legal perspectives. *Space Policy*, 22(4): 262-273.

Reijnen, G.C.M. (1979). Outer Space Law and Private Enterprise in Outer Space: An International Perspective. *Houston Journal of International Law*, 2(1): 65-76.

Rhee, Sang-Myon (2009). Current Status and Recent Developments in Korea's National Space Laws. *Journal of Space Law*, 35(2):523-537.

Sachdeva, G.S. (2011), Commercial Order of Outer Space: Quest for Ethical Values, *Indian Journal of International Law*, 51(1): 21-41.

Tarikhi, P. (2009). Iran's space programme: Riding high for peace and pride. *Space Policy*, 25(3): 160-173.

Zhao, Y. (2007). National Space Legislation in Mainland China. *Journal of Space Law*, 33(2): 427-436.

NEWSPAPER ARTICLE

Laxman, S. (2013, 20 September). 2nd Private Firm Rockets Cargo to ISS. *The Times of India*, pp. 21.

Vijay, T. (2013, 8 May). Drawing the line on Google. *The Hindu*, pp. 11.

INTERNET RESOURCES

Boroffice, R.A. (2008). The Nigerian Space Programme: An Update. *African Skies*. 12: 40-45.

http://www.saao.ac.za/~wgssa/archive/as12/boroffice.pdf (Accessed on 10 July, 2013)

Coppinger, Rob (2008, 07 October). Swedish Spaceport awaits government go-ahead.

http://www.flightglobal.com/news/articles/swedish-spaceport-awaits-government-go-ahead-316843/ (Accessed on 17 April, 2013).

Clarke, Arthur C. (1945). Extra-Terrestrial Relays Can Rocket Stations Give World-wide Radio Coverage? *Wireless World*, October, 305-308.

http://www.tnmoc.org/sites/default/files/Extra-Terrestrial%20Relays2.pdf (Accessed on 20 January, 2013)

Livingston, David M. (1999), The Ethical Commercialization of Outer Space.

http://www.spacefuture.com/archive/the_ethical_commercialization_of_outer_space.shtml (Accessed on 30 July, 2014).

Raj, N. Gopal (2012, 06 February). Norms and procedures flouted in Antrix-Devas deal. *The Hindu*. http://www.thehindu.com/news/national/norms-and-procedures-flouted-in-antrixdevas-deal/article2863453.ece (Accessed on 24 August, 2013).

Martinez, P. (2008). "The 2nd African Leadership Conference on Space Science and Technology for Sustainable Development".

http://www.saao.ac.za/~wgssa/archive/as12/PMartinez2.pdf (Accessed 15 November, 2013)

Sagar, D. (1999). The Privatization of INMARSAT- Special Problems, in *International Organisations and Space Law* (ESA SP- 442), 127-146.

http://adsabs.harvard.edu/full/1999ESASP.442..127S (Accessed 25 April, 2013)

Selding, Peter B. de (2013). "Thales Alenia Space Asks France to Ease Imagery Sale Restrictions",

http://www.spacenews.com/article/military-space/37148thales-alenia-space-asks-france-to-ease-imagery-sale-restrictions (Accessed 30 September 2013)

Sundahl, M. (2013), The Space Assets Protocol One Year Later: An Update and Reassessment, http://www.americanbar.org/content/dam/aba/publications/air_space_lawyer/ASL_V26N1_sundahl.authcheckdam.pdf (Accessed on 25 July, 2013).

ANNEXURE

ANNEXURE I

ISRO Centres & Activities

1. Vikram Sarabhai Space Centre (VSSC) is responsible for the development of satellite launch vehicles and associated technologies. ISRO Satellite Centre (ISAC) is with developing satellite technology and implementation of satellite systems for scientific, technological and application missions.
2. Satish Dhawan Space Centre (SDSC), Sriharikota has developed the facilities for solid propellant processing, static testing of solid motors, launch vehicle integration and launch operations, range operations comprising telemetry, tracking and command network and mission control centre.
3. Liquid Propulsion System Centre (LPSC) is assigned to develop the liquid and cryogenic propulsion for launch vehicles and satellites. Space Application Centre (SAC) is assigned with the development of payloads for communication, meteorological and remote sensing satellites.
4. Master Control Facility (MCF) is responsible for carrying out operations after launching of satellites like initial orbit raising of satellites, in-orbit payload testing, and on-orbit operations throughout the life of these satellites.
5. ISRO Inertial System Unit (IISU) is with research and development in inertial sensors and systems and allied satellite elements.
6. The Laboratory for Electro-Opto System (LEOS) is responsible for research and development in the field of electro-optic sensors and cameras required for satellites and launch vehicles.
7. National Remote Sensing Centre (NRSC) is responsible for remote sensing satellite data acquisition and processing, data dissemination, aerial remote sensing and decision support for disaster management.
8. Semi-Conductor Laboratory (SCL) works with design and development of Very Large Integration (VLSI) devices and development of systems for telecommunication and space sectors.

ANNEXURE II

Technologies Innovated by ISRO & Applications

1. MMIC Phase Shifter for RF and microwave industries,
2. Safety Ohm Meter used in automobile, aerospace and other industries,
3. Optical Imaging System –technology used here for know how transfer to industries,
4. Surface Treatment Technology for know how offer to industries,
5. New technologies on offer for Know How Transfer to industries. Technologies in Chemical, Electronics, Mechanical and Materials, Sensors, Antenna, Application and Software domains,
6. Fibre Optic Liquid Level Detector for industrial and commercial applications,
7. Elastic Raman LIDAR for remote sensing the atmospheric water vapour and aerosols in the boundary layer,
8. Phantom Connectivity patented as 'Phantom Network Toggling Technique' for secured data communication between organisational network and third party network without connecting to them,
9. S3D Software for to perform feasibility analysis for a satellite mission on various parameters like orbit, attitude, camera detectors size, look-angles, focal length etc before launching the satellite; Silica Granules used as filler materials for paints, polymer/metal and ceramic matrices to reduce density and improve thermal properties,
10. Silica Fibres for high-temperature insulation upto 1500 C; Medium Density Ablative (MDA) for lightweight thermo-structural material for thermal protection and insulation used in providing effective thermal protection top a re-entering space capsule,
11. CAS Resin used as adhesive for providing strong bonds between metals and various substances,
12. Coating Compound EPY1061 for industrial applications such as bonding, sealing, coating, potting, laminating, molding etc; Ultra Wide Band Filter having wide commercial and special application,
13. PSC- NC- 020, a glue, having wide range of applications in aerospace area; Thermal Control Coating- the black paint having wide commercial and special application,
14. Fleet Monitoring Systems used in the organizations and industries engaged with surface transportation for monitoring position and speed

of vehicles and ships in the Indian region including the territorial waters of India; Light Emitting Diodes having wide commercial and other applications,

15. Satellite based Interactive IP Network (SIIP) which is developed for EDUSAT programme is low cost and most suitable for small size broadcasting network requirements.

ANNEXURE III

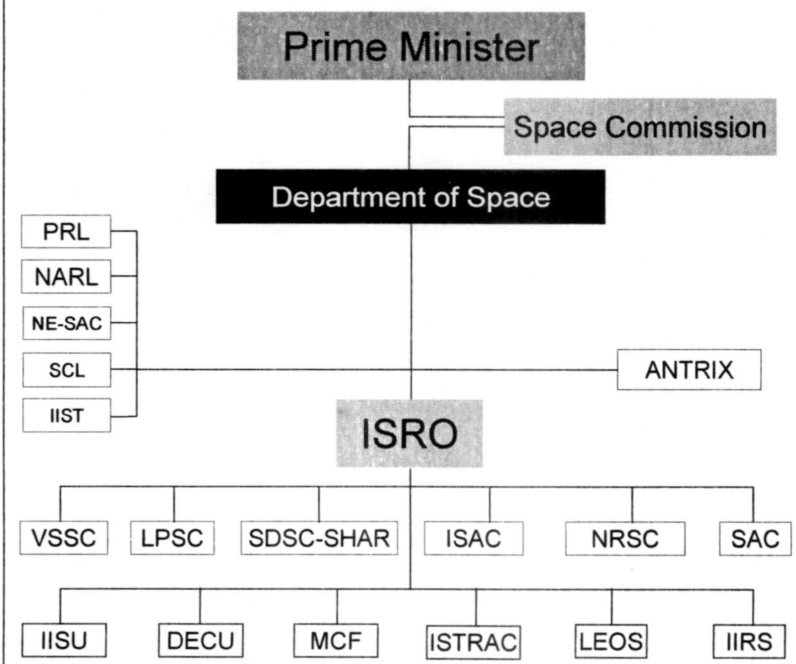

NRSC: National Remote Sensing Centre **PRL:** Physical Research Laboratory **NARL:** National Atmospheric Research Laboratory **NE-SAC:** North Eastern Space Applications Centre **SCL**: Semi-Conductor Laboratory **ISRO:** Indian Space Research Organisation **Antrix:** Antrix Corporation Limited **VSSC:** Vikram Sarabhai Space Centre **LPSC:** Liquid Propulsion Systems Centre **SDSC:** Satish Dhawan Space Centre **ISAC:** ISRO Satellite Centre **SAC:** Space Applications Centre **IISU:** ISRO Inertial Systems Unit **DECU:** Development and Educational Communication Unit **MCF:** Master Control Facility **ISTRAC:** ISRO Telemetry, Tracking and Command Network **LEOS:** Laboratory for Electro-optic Systems **IIST:** Indian Institute of Space Science and Technology **IIRS:** Indian Institute of Remote Sensing.